# Antique Trader™

# Lamps

# & *Lighting*

## PRICE GUIDE

### Edited by
### Kyle Husfloen

Published by
Antique Trader Books, A Division of

krause
publications

700 E. State Street • Iola, WI 54990-0001
Telephone: 715/445-2214

Please call or write for our free catalog of publications.
Our toll-free number to place an order or obtain a free catalog is 800-258-0929 or please
use our regular business telephone, 715-445-2214.

Library of Congress Catalog Number: 2001099542
ISBN: 0-87349-416-4

Printed in the United States of America

# TABLE OF CONTENTS

## *Chapter 1: Early Non-Electric Lamps & Lighting*

## *Chapter 2: Electric Lamps & Lighting*

## *Chapter 3: Other Lighting Devices*

## *Chapter 4: Lighting Gallery*

# INTRODUCTION

It is hard to imagine a time when a source of light wasn't readily available at the flip of a switch, but there are those who can remember a time when most Americans still had to light their nighttimes with kerosene lamps. Right through the Depression years of the 1930s many in rural areas of this country had no electrical hookups, and cooking and lighting relied on a ready supply of wood or kerosene.

Since the dawn of time, man has searched for ways to make his survival during nighttime hours more safe and comfortable. Fire, of course, was that miraculous source for the ancients, providing heat, security, light and the common means of cooking food. Today we consider a fireplace an attractive option in a new home, mainly for show and ambiance, but for centuries it was the center of home life around the world. Well into the 18th century in Europe and America, the average working class family often had only a fireplace for nighttime lighting, heat and cooking. A few crude iron grease lamps might have been available to burn animal fat, but better quality candles were considered a luxury. By the very late 18th century, a few scientists had experimented with more refined burning fluids, and wealthy individuals, such as George Washington, might be lucky enough to afford one of the new Argand lamps. Through the mid-19th century, however, many families still relied only on candlelight to augment the light of the fireplace. Some cities had begun building gas production plants to supply some wealthy homes, and high quality but expensive whale oil became more widely available. Even a nasty, volatile liquid fuel called camphene became popular by the 1840s. However, it was quite liable to explode during use or even while a lamp was being filled, so it had serious drawbacks. At last, not long before the start of the American Civil War, oil drilling became big business in Pennsylvania and, shortly after that, the most popular petroleum derivative, kerosene, hit the market. Safer, cleaner and brighter than early fuels, within a few years it was the standard in nearly every American home, with gaslight still pretty much restricted to use in big cities. For the next seventy-five years kerosene lamps were necessities in average American homes. Of course, the next major jump in technology was provided through the genius of Thomas Edison, who finally developed an efficient and relatively safe way to produce and distribute electric power. Remember, however, that it took decades before a skeptical public felt secure enough to rely solely on electric power. Right through World War I many finer ceiling fixtures were designed to use both natural gas and electricity, and kerosene table lamps were often kept in reserve, even in urban areas.

The history of man's use of light and its gradual evolution from fireside to neon billboard is endlessly fascinating. What makes the long story even more exciting is that collectors today have such a huge variety of lighting devices to collect. Ancient Roman oil lamps can be found on the market selling for a fraction of even an average example of a 20th century Tiffany lamp. There is, clearly, something to suit every collecting interest and budget. This book is designed to provide a comprehensive guide to the types of lighting devices most popular on the collecting marketplace today. From candlesticks and early kerosene lighting you can follow the evolution of household lighting right into the mid-20th century.

We are pleased to have had a number of authorities in specialized areas of lighting provide us with detailed listings and great photos, and we have also drawn from numerous auctions and sales around the country. You will find pieces listed here that have sold for many thousands of dollars, but also fascinating and historical objects that can still be found for under $100.

It is our hope that this guide will prove "enlightening" and educational, lighting the way to an even greater understanding and appreciation of how lighting devices have served our ancestors and continue to fascinate us today.

Our nearly 1,400 individual detailed listings are highlighted by nearly 700 black-and-white photographs. In addition we provide a 16-page full-color supplement showing many dazzling examples of antique and collectible lighting. To round out our text we are providing a Glossary of Lamp & Lighting Terms, a Bibliography of important references and an Appendix listing a number of specialty collecting clubs.

As with each of our price guides, we remind the reader to use it only as a guide. The condition, rarity and local market can make a great difference on what a lamp may sell for. Even some of the rarest of 20th century lamps, such as Handels and Pairpoints, featuring the same design, can sell for quite different amounts due to variations in the quality and detail of the painting and the style and finish of the lamp base.

Whatever type of lighting you may collect, it is important to learn all you can about how to judge quality and rarity of pieces.

The editor and staff have taken great care to edit and review all of our listings for accuracy and clarity. We have arranged the listings by chapters, beginning with the lighting of the 19th century and ending with the most popular types of electric lighting of the first half of the 20th century. Within the main chapters subcategories focus on particular lamp varieties and makers for easier research.

We must acknowledge our debt of gratitude to our Special Contributors, as well as a large number of dealers and auction houses who generously shared information and photographs from their sales held in recent years. An alphabetical listing of them follows here:

Albrect Auction Service, Vassar, Michigan; Alderfers, Hatfield, Pennsylvania; Christie's, New York, New York; Collectors Sales & Services, Pomfret Center, Connecticut; Copake Country Auction, Copake, New York; DeFina Auctions, Austenburg, Ohio; William Doyle Galleries, New York, New York; DuMouchelles, Detroit, Michigan; John Fontaine Gallery, Pittsfield, Massachusetts; Garth's Auctions, Delaware, Ohio; Green Valley Auctions, Mt. Crawford, Virginia; Jackson's Auctioneers & Appraisers, Cedar Falls, Iowa; Robert G. Jason-Ickes, Olympia, Washington; Parker-Braden Auctions, Carlsbad, New Mexico; Dave Rago Arts & Crafts, Lambertville, New Jersey; Skinner, Inc., Bolton, Massachusetts; Slawinski Auction Company, Felton, California; Sotheby's, New York, New York; Temple's Antiques, Eden Prairie, Minnesota; and Treadway Gallery, Cincinnati, Ohio.

We hope that every user of *Antique Trader Lamps & Lighting Price Guide* will find it interesting and informative. We welcome all letters from readers, especially those of constructive critique, and we make every effort to respond personally.

## Kyle Husfloen, Editor

*Please note: Though listings have been double-checked and every effort has been made to ensure accuracy, neither the compilers, editors nor publisher can assume responsibility for any losses that might be incurred as a result of consulting this guide, or of errors, typographical or otherwise.*

**ON THE COVER:** Left - A Victorian kerosene peg lamp with a shaded pink satin mother-of-pearl Swirl pattern glass font and matching crimped and ruffled shade, complete with original brass burner, low columnar brass candlestick base and chimney, overall 12 5/8" h., $695. Courtesy of Temple's Antiques, Eden Prairie, Minnesota; Center - one of a pair of sapphire blue pressed flint glass fluid lamps with Arch patterned fonts attached by wafers to the hexagonal tiered cascade base, Pittsburgh, circa 1840-50, the pair, $7,425. Courtesy of Collector's Sales & Service, Promfret Center, Connecticut. Right - a large Victorian hanging kerosene parlor lamp with a blue Cut Velvet glass shade and matching font in a jeweled brass frame, shade 14" d., $1,760. Courtesy of Gene Harris Antique Auction Center, Marshalltown, Iowa.

# SPECIAL CONTRIBUTORS

**Aladdin Lamps:**

**Thomas Small**
**201 Hemlock Lane**
**Meyersdale, PA 15552**
**e-mail: koko@shol.com**

**Fairy Lamps:**

**Jim Sapp**
**Fairy Lamp Club & Newsletter**
**Ph: (703) 971-3229**
**e-mail: sapp@erols.com**
**Web site: www.fairylampclub.com**

**Kerosene Lamps & Lighting:**

**Catherine M.V. Thuro**
**Toronto, Ontario, Canada**

**Dennis Hearn**
**Radio City Station**
**P.O. Box 1555**
**New York, NY 10101-1555**
**Web site: www.Oillamp.com**

**Miniature Lamps:**

**The Miniature Lamp Collectors Club**
*Night Light,* **newsletter**
**Bob Culver**
**38619 Wakefield Ct.**
**Northville, MI 48167-9060**
**Ph: (248) 473-8575**
**e-mail: rculver107@aol.com**

# COLLECTING GUIDELINES FOR EARLY ELECTRIC LAMPS & LIGHTING

### by Stephen Ristagno

Thomas Edison is given credit for inventing the first light bulb on October 21, 1879, and along with Harvey Hubbell's invention of the pull switch socket, these two men would change the way homes were illuminated during the first quarter of the 20th century. While the first light bulb was thought of as a novelty and not taken seriously for several years, it wasn't long before Louis Comfort Tiffany and his counterparts at The Phillip Handel Company and The Pairpoint Lamp Company were producing table lamps and light fixtures to satisfy the needs of the early 20th century consumer.

## Tiffany

Louis Comfort Tiffany, son of the famous New York City jeweler, began his career as a painter and interior designer, but soon made his mark producing glass and eventually stained and leaded glass table lamps. The process of producing a leaded glass table lamp was labor intensive and required many hours to accomplish.

First a pattern was made, then a mold was needed to form the size and shape of the shade. Individual pieces of colored glass were cut into shapes and then joined together with lead and solder to make the shade. The earliest Tiffany shades were geometric patterns, but soon the shades became very complex floral patterns. Tiffany lamps were extremely expensive in their day, and many other companies started to produce electric lamps in that very competitive market. Among the companies that competed in the leaded table lamp market were: The Duffner and Kimberly Company, Bigelow and Kennard, The Mosaic Lamp Company of Chicago, Suess Ornamental Lamps Company, Bradley and Hubbard, and Handel & Company.

*Certainly among the "best" of Tiffany's leaded lamps is the one shown above, with a 21" d. "Laburnum" pattern shade on a reticulated Tiffany bronze base. It reached an astounding $129,000 at auction.*

Courtesy of Skinner, Inc., Bolton, Massachusetts.

*A "good" Tiffany lamp is represented by the piece at left with a 20" w. leaded glass "Harvard" pattern shade on a signed base. It sold a few years ago for $11,500.*

Courtesy of William Doyle Galleries, New York, New York.

*In the field of Tiffany leaded lamps, the example at far left is among the "better" ones. It features a 20" d. "Autumn Poppy" pattern shade on a marked Tiffany base. The auction price was $81,200.*

Courtesy of Fontaine's Auction Gallery, Pittsfield, Massachusetts.

## Duffner and Kimberly

The Duffner and Kimberly Company produced magnificent leaded glass table lamps, although very little is known about this firm. It is known that it was in business from 1906 until 1926 and manufactured leaded glass table lamps from 1906 until 1911. At their best, Duffner and Kimberly lamps matched the quality of some of Tiffany's finest pieces. When the firm was established in 1906, its output was small and frequently unsigned. Fortunately for collectors, Duffner and Kimberly advertised quite extensively, and these ads provide positive identification for sixteen lamps and chandeliers. Duffner's shortcoming was that it didn't make its own glass, so the lamps didn't have the same depth and color that Tiffany lamps possessed. In the last few years, Duffner and Kimberly lamps have become a hot commodity in the lamp market. Some outstanding examples have commanded prices that begin to approach those for Tiffany's.

*Duffner and Kimberly is another company whose lamps are increasing in demand. This example with a 21-1/2" d. leaded shade in the Louis XV pattern, sold for $26,450.*

Courtesy of Skinner, Inc., Bolton, Massachusetts.

*Bigelow and Kennard leaded glass lamps are also bringing some remarkable prices. This floor lamp with a 24" d. ornately leaded shade sold for $32,200.*

Courtesy of Sotheby's, New York, New York.

## Bigelow and Kennard

Bigelow and Kennard was located in Massachusetts and produced fine leaded lamps that were similar in design to Tiffany lamps. Bigelow and Kennard even signed its lamps along the inner edge of the leading just as Tiffany lamps were signed. Its lamps don't come on the market very often and, as a result, they tend to command high prices. Bases for the lamps were of the highest quality and were most often made of bronze.

## Mosaic Lamp Company of Chicago

The Mosaic Lamp Company—Chicago, often mistakenly referred to as "The Chicago Mosaic Lamp Company," made leaded lamps around the same time as Tiffany and Duffner and Kimberly. Its shades tended to be of a much simpler design and often featured a floral pattern. The shades and bases are rarely signed. Chicago Mosaic lamps are highly collectible and are still affordable to the average collector. As with any good lamp, however, the prices are starting to climb.

*The Mosaic Lamp Company of Chicago made lamps which are also growing in demand today. With an 18" d. leaded glass floral shade, the lamp above sold for $3,360.*

Courtesy of Fontaine's Auction Gallery, Pittsfield, Massachusetts.

*Suess lamps with leaded glass shades are also developing a strong market. The table lamp at right, with a 24-1/4" d. blossom-decorated shade, brought an auction price of $9,775.*

Courtesy of Skinner, Inc.,
Bolton, Massachusetts.

## Suess Ornamental Glass Company

The Suess Ornamental Glass Company of Chicago, Illinois is just now starting to be recognized as makers of quality leaded lamps. Although there is a catalog dating from 1907 that documents many of the Suess patterns, it has only been in the last couple of years that Suess lamps have started to command the prices they deserve. Suess made very large diameter table lamp shades with some as large a 30" wide and supported on equally large solid bronze bases. These shades and bases are rarely signed.

## Bradley and Hubbard

Bradley and Hubbard is well know for its metalwork and better quality lamps. In addition to leaded lamps, it also made bent-panel table lamps and painted lamps that appealed to middle class buyers of that day. Bradley and Hubbard's bent-panel lamps are among the best selling lamps today. Bent-panel lamps are just what the name implies: lamps whose shades are composed of curved or bent panels of slag glass. To produce the shade, panels of glass were heated in a kiln and bent around a mold and then, after annealing, assembled in the metal framework of the shade. Most shades were composed of multiple panels, six to eight being most common, but a simple shade may have had as few as three panels. The glass panels can be plain or painted, and the metal frame can be quite intricate with floral or scenic

*This Bradley and Hubbard table lamp with a bent-glass paneled shade on a gilt-metal Aladdin lamp-shaped base sold for $2,800 in 2000.*

Courtesy of Fontaine's Auction Gallery,
Pittsfield, Massachusetts.

filigree designs over each panel. Many Bradley and Hubbard shades are signed along the lower edge, while their bases have a signature at the very top, just below the light sockets.

## Phillip Handel Company

The Phillip Handel Company of Meriden, Connecticut began making leaded glass lamps in the late 1890s, with many of its designs being similar to those by Tiffany. It is the reverse-painted shades, however, which have become most associated with this firm. Handel produced lamps with domed glass shades that were handpainted on the interior with elaborate landscape scenes, florals or birds. Together with The Pairpoint Manufacturing Corporation, Handel established itself as a premier manufacturer of reverse-painted table lamps and fixtures. Its shades are some of the most sought after on today's market.

Handel lamp shades were generally textured on the exterior surface by coating them with fish glue. Once the glue had hardened, the shade was fired in a kiln. The heat caused the glue to contract and fall away, removing tiny flecks of glass. This left a somewhat frosted effect, sometimes referred to as "chipped ice." Another finishing technique involved the application of fine glass granules which, when fired, left a soft frosted and textured effect. The shade was then reverse-painted on the interior and sometimes artist-signed. Most Handel bases are also signed, although many have just a felt pad on the bottom with a silk tag that reads "Handel Lamps." The prices for Handels have been escalating sharply in the last few years, and many new auction records have been established. A Handel 18" diameter scenic "Riverbed" table lamp sold for an unbelievable $81,400; an 18" diameter Handel floral "Poppy" sold for nearly $69,000 and a rare 18" diameter Handel "Peacock" acid-textured shade on signed base reached a record $56,000.

*This Handel lamp features a 16" d. six-panel bent glass shade with metal overlay on a signed Handel base. It sold for $5,320.*

Courtesy of Fontaine's Auction Gallery, Pittsfield, Massachusetts.

*A fine quality Handel table lamp with an 18" d. reverse-painted shade in the "Exotic Bird" pattern. The shade is artist-signed by Bedigie, a top Handel artist, and the base carries the Handel mark. The sale price on this lamp was $17,360.*

Courtesy of Fontaine's Auction Gallery, Pittsfield, Massachusetts.

## Pairpoint Manufacturing Corporation

The other notable manufacturer of reverse-painted table lamps was The Pairpoint Manufacturing Corporation. This firm, located in New Bedford, Massachusetts, was unique in its approach to lamp shade production. Pairpoint made shades that were "blown-out" or "puffed" (i.e. "puffy"), with the design in high relief. After the glass was blown into a mold and annealed, it then had the mold marks or seams polished off, thus leaving a frosted, smooth surface. The shade was then reverse-painted, which brought life to the elaborate molded designs, which often featured colorful floral bouquets complete with butterflies and bees. Most Pairpoint "Puffy" shades are signed, but their distinct shape makes them instantly recognizable. All Pairpoint bases are signed with their trademark, a capital letter "P" inside a diamond.

As with Handel, Pairpoint lamps have become extremely collectible. A few have recently set new auction records. Among these were a 14" "Puffy" Lilac pattern shade on a signed base that sold for a record $145,600; an Apple Tree "Puffy" that sold for over $65,500 and a 16" diameter "Puffy" Begonia shade and base that set a record of $67,200.

Each year more collectors discover these lamps and add them to their collections, leaving fewer great examples in the marketplace.

As prices for Handel and Pairpoint lamps soar, the lamps of most of the lesser known makers are also commanding stronger prices. Even the lamps of little known early makers such as Classique and Moe Bridges Company (both of Milwaukee, Wisconsin), Phoenix, Jefferson, Riviere, Pittsburgh, Jeanette Lamp Company (of Pennsylvania), Wilkinson, and Williamson & Company are now being sought out and making their mark among collectors.

More and more collectors are entering the market each year, and today it is

*In addition to its famous "Puffy" shades, Pairpoint also produced simpler, smooth-sided shades such as this Landsdowne pattern shade reverse-painted with a cottage landscape scene. This type lamp shade generally commands much less than the "Puffy" types. Sale price: $3,360.*

Courtesy of Fontaine's Auction Gallery, Pittsfield, Massachusetts.

*One of the real stars among Pairpoint "Puffies," this lamp with a 16" d. Begonia pattern shade sold for $67,200 in 2000.*

Courtesy of Fontaine's Auction Gallery, Pittsfield, Massachusetts.

stronger than ever. These lamps are not only attractive to look at, they are useful and, of course, can make great investments. Twenty years ago only select lamps from the major manufacturers were commanding strong interest on the market. Today a diverse range of decorative and well-made lamps are selling to a much wider spectrum of appreciative buyers.

## HELPFUL REFERENCES

*Handel Lamps, Painted Shades & Glassware*, Robert DeFalco, Robert and Carole Goldman Hibel (1986)

*The Handel Lamps Book*, Carole Goldman Hibel, John Hibel and John Fontaine (1999)

*The Painted Lamps of Handel*, Joanne C. Grant (1978)

*Pairpoint Lamps, A Collectors Guide*, Louis O. St. Aubin, Jr. (1974)

*Pairpoint Lamps*, Edward and Sheila Malakoff (1990)

*The Lamps of Tiffany*, Dr. Egon Neustadt (1970)

*Louis C. Tiffany's Glass - Bronzes - Lamps - A Complete Collector's Guide*, Robert Koch (1971)

*Not a name widely recognized, the Wilkinson firm also produced some fine leaded glass lamp shades. The piece on the left, with a 20" d. shade decorated with colorful water lilies, sold for $7,840 in 2000.*

*Moe Bridges of Milwaukee made some fine quality reverse-painted shades for its lamps. The center lamp has an 18" d. shade with a landscape scene. Both the shade and base are signed. The sale price was $4,480.*

*Another lamp company that made nice reverse-painted shades was Pittsburgh. The lamp on the right, with a 16" d. shade decorated with a seascape, brought $3,416 at auction.*

All courtesy of Fontaine's Auction Gallery, Pittsfield, Massachusetts.

# Collecting Tips

♦ Remember when looking at even the finest reverse-painted shades that the quality of the painting, detail of the design and depth of color can greatly effect the retail value. For instance, two Handel shades in the same pattern can have a value range of thousands of dollars because of differences in the overall quality.

♦ Artist-signed reverse-painted shades often bring premium prices, but keep in mind that even the most noted of these artists could have an "off" day. A fabulous unsigned shade may be a better investment than an average quality "artist-signed" shade. Also, an unsigned shade can have a forged signature added to increase the "value."

♦ Always try to purchase a lamp with a shade and base produced by the same company. You can still have a nice lamp with a shade by one firm and a base by another, but generally collectors prefer that the two parts are from the same maker. This is especially true for Handel, Pairpoint and Tiffany lamps.

♦ When examining the metal base of a lamp, make sure the original patina is in top condition. Some quality bronze or bronze-patinated bases were "over-polished" in the past, removing their aged look. This greatly reduces their value. Although a new patina can be applied, it is an expensive procedure and cannot completely restore the full value of the base.

♦ Be aware that there are firms copying and reproducing the classic leaded and reverse-painted shades today. If you buy such a lamp for what it is—a decorative accent piece—that's fine. Just make sure you don't pay a premium price for a newer piece. As they say, know your lamps or know your seller.

♦ Always try to buy the best lamps that you can comfortably afford. Lower end lamps tend not to appreciate in value as quickly as more high-end examples. This is a strong case for quality over quantity.

♦ Buying at auction can pose special problems. Lamps should always be carefully inspected prior to purchase. You should be particularly careful since sometimes other people's "mistakes" end up being offered and resold to an unsuspecting newcomer.

♦ Never buy a lamp that is severely damaged or one that has had extensive repairs if your goal is investment quality lamps. A damaged or repaired lamp is usually worth only about 10 percent of its pristine counterpart.

# CHAPTER 1

# Early Non-Electric Lamps & Lighting

## Aladdin® Mantle Lamps

The Mantle Lamp Company of America, creator of the world famous Aladdin Lamp, was founded in Chicago in 1908. Like several of its competitors, the Aladdin coupled the round wick technology with a mantle to produce a bright incandescent light comparable to the illumination provided by a 60 to 75 watt bulb. Through aggressive national advertising and an intensive dealer network, the Aladdin Lamp quickly overcame its competitors to become the standard lighting fixture in the rural American home.

From the company's origin until 1926, Aladdin Lamps were produced in table, hanging, and wall bracket styles made mostly of brass and finished in either satin brass or nickel plate. With the purchase of an Indiana glass plant in the mid-1920s, the Mantle Lamp Company began to make its own glass shades and chimneys, in addition to the manufacture of glass lamp bases. Glass shades, both plain and decorated with reverse painting, were made in a variety of styles. Later, colorful parchment shades were produced in a myriad of colors and with decorations ranging from large, gaudy flowers in the early 1930s to delicate florals and intricate geometrics, sometimes with flocking, from the mid-1930s through the post-war years.

Aladdin kerosene lamps are probably best known for the colorful glass bases made from the late 1920s to the early 1950s. The earliest glass lamps were vase lamps that consisted of a glass vase finished in different colors that had a drop-in brass kerosene font. Later, seventeen different glass patterns were produced and most patterns were offered in a variety of different glass colors. Crystal glass lamp bases commonly came in clear, green, or amber colors, but for a few years crystal bases were produced in ruby red and cobalt blue. The latter two colors are especially prized by collectors. A translucent to opaque glass called moonstone was produced during the 1930s and was available in white, green, rose, and for one pattern in the late 1930s, yellow. A few styles had white moonstone fonts attached to a black stem and foot. Other lamps had a moonstone font mounted on a metallic base.

An ivory to white glass called Alacite is unique to the Aladdin Lamp. The late 1930s glass formula contained uranium oxide, and the ivory to marble-like appearance sometimes leads to its confusion with the Crown Tuscan glass of Cambridge. With the commencement of the Manhattan Project, this compound was placed on the restricted list and, as a consequence, the glass formula was changed. Early Alacite lamp bases will glow under a black-light, whereas later ones will not. The later Alacite lamps also tend toward a white color rather than ivory.

Aladdin kerosene lamps are still being made today. The Mantle Lamp Company left Chicago in 1948 and was absorbed into Aladdin Industries, Inc. In April 1999, the Aladdin Mantle Lamp Company was formed in Clarksville, Tenn. The new limited partnership produces kerosene lighting for domestic and foreign markets and supplies/accessories for older lamps.

Aladdin kerosene lamps and their related accessories have been avidly collected over the last thirty years. As a consequence, prices have risen steadily even for the common lamps. Expectedly, condition of the lamp or shade is a very important consideration in determination of value. Glass damage, electrification, or missing parts can seriously depreciate value. By comparison, lamps in mint, unused condition and in the original carton fetch premium prices.

—Thomas W. Small

*Aladdin Hanging Lamp*

**Hanging lamp,** decorated w/hand painted roses on ball shade, Model No. 6 (ILLUS.) ............................................ **$4,000-5,000**

*Aladdin Student Lamp*

**Student lamp,** original w/functional tank,
unelectrified, Model No. 4
(ILLUS.) ............................................. **7,500-8,500**

*Aladdin Table Lamp, Model No. 1*

**Table lamp,** nickel plated w/embossed
foot, 1/2 qt. font, Model No. 1
(ILLUS.) .................................................. **600-700**
**Vase lamp,** blue variegated, gold foot edge,
three feet, 10 1/4" h. ................................. **600-700**
**Vase lamp,** green w/dark green foot edge,
model No. 12, six feet, 10 1/4" h. ........... **250-300**
**Vase lamp,** variegated green, gold foot
edge, three feet, 10 1/4" h. ...................... **300-350**

*Aladdin Table Lamp, Model No. 8*

**Table lamp,** brass finish, No. 8 flame
spreader & No. 401 shade, Model No. 8
(ILLUS.) .................................................. **450-550**
**Table lamp,** nickel finish, No. 10 flame
spreader, Model No. 10 .......................... **450-550**
**Table lamp,** nickel plated, No. 6 flame
spreader, Model No. 6 ............................ **80-100**

*Aladdin Vase Lamp*

Vase lamp, variegated peach, gold foot
edge, three feet, 10 1/4" h. (ILLUS.)...... **300-350**
*The following pattern glass names are from J.W.*
*Courter reference books on Aladdin Lamps.*

Table lamp, Beehive patt., clear,
Model B ...................................................... **100-125**
Table lamp, Beehive patt., green or amber
crystal ...................................................... **125-175**
Table lamp, Cathedral patt., green or am-
ber crystal .............................................. **150-200**
Table lamp, Cathedral patt., rose moon-
stone ....................................................... **450-500**
Table lamp, Cathedral patt., white moon-
stone ....................................................... **400-500**
Table lamp, Corinthian patt., amber or
green crystal ............................................ **125-150**
Table lamp, Corinthian patt., clear .............. **80-100**
Table lamp, Corinthian patt., white moon-
stone font w/green, rose or black foot ... **350-450**
Table lamp, Diamond Quilted patt., green
moonstone ............................................... **350-400**
Table lamp, Lincoln Drape patt., short, am-
ber or ruby crystal w/metal collar at font
top .......................................................... **100-125**
Table lamp, Lincoln Drape patt., short, ruby
crystal, raised glass collar at font
top .......................................................... **900-1,000**
Table lamp, Lincoln Drape patt., tall, cobalt
blue, foot top w/circular ring ............. **1,300-1,500**
Table lamp, Lincoln Drape patt., tall, cobalt
blue, scalloped ring on foot top ....... **1,900-2,100**
Table lamp, Lincoln Drape patt., tall, ruby
crystal, lower value for light ruby, higher
for dark .................................................... **850-1,100**
Table lamp, Lincoln Drape patt., tall, slightly
tapered stem, Alacite .............................. **150-200**

*Aladdin Table Lamp, Orientale Pattern*

Table lamp, Orientale patt., ivory, green, or
bronze enamel, metallic finish
(ILLUS.)..................................................... **150-175**
Table lamp, Queen patt., green, white, or
rose moonstone on metallic foot ........... **250-350**
Table lamp, Simplicity patt., Alacite, green
or white enamel....................................... **150-175**
Table lamp, Simplicity patt., rose
enamel...................................................... **175-200**
Table lamp, Solitaire patt., white moon-
stone......................................................... **2,800-3,000**
Table lamp, Venetian patt., clear, fused
stem-foot/bowl, Model A......................... **350-400**
Table lamp, Venetian patt., green or peach
enamel...................................................... **125-150**
Table lamp, Venetian patt., white
enamel...................................................... **100-125**
Table lamp, Vertique patt., green moon-
stone......................................................... **350-400**
Table lamp, Vertique patt., yellow moon-
stone......................................................... **500-600**
Table lamp, Victoria patt., ceramic w/floral
decoration & gold bands......................... **600-650**
Table lamp, Washington Drape patt., clear
crystal, plain stem, w/or without oil
fill .............................................................. **75-100**
Table lamp, Washington Drape patt., clear,
green, or amber w/open, thick round
stem .......................................................... **100-150**
Table lamp, Washington Drape patt., green
or amber crystal, plain stem................... **100-150**

## Miscellaneous

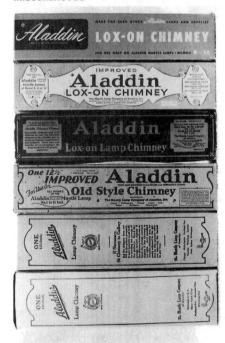

*Aladdin Lamp Chimneys*

Chimneys, boxed, each (ILLUS.).............. **100-125**
Mantles, boxed, each (ILLUS. top next
page)........................................................... **5-15**

*Aladdin Mantles*

**Mantles,** boxed, each (ILLUS. left).............. **75-100**
**Mantles,** boxed, each (ILLUS. right) .............. **40-50**

*Aladdin Matchholder*

**Matchholder,** copper w/accessories & in-
 struction booklet (ILLUS.)...................... **100-150**
**Other matchholders,** each .............................. **25-40**
**Shades,** floral, No. 601F roses .................. **600-700**
**Shades,** green cased, No. 202 artichoke,
 No. 204 eight panel, each ................... **900-1,100**
**Shades,** plain, No. 201, No. 301, No. 401,
 No. 501 (for Model No. 11), No. 601,
 each .......................................................... **100-125**
**Shades,** plain, opal No. 205 w/fire polished
 bottom rim............................................... **400-500**
**Shades,** reverse painted, No. 601 Log Cab-
 in, No. 616 Gristmill, No. 620 Windmill,
 each ......................................................... **350-400**
**Shades,** reverse painted, No. 616F pop-
 pies, No. 620F roses, each ................ **800-1,000**
**Shades,** Whip-O-Lite parchment, floral,
 geometric, or scenic, 14" h., each......... **150-200**

*Aladdin Wicks*

**Wicks,** boxed, mounted, each (ILLUS. left
 stack) ............................................................ **40-50**
**Wicks,** boxed, No. 11 & No. 12, each
 (ILLUS. right center & right) ....................... **10-15**
**Wicks,** boxed, No. 6, mounted, each
 (ILLUS. left center) ...................................... **20-25**

# Candlesticks & Candleholders

*French Second Empire Candelabra*

**Candelabra,** gilt-bronze & cut crystal, four-light, a slender reeded central top shaft supporting a cupped socket surrounded by three scroll leaf-trimmed upturned candlearms w/sockets all connected to a scroll-cast mount above the tall facet-cut crystal shaft fitted into an acanthus leaf-case socket raised on three animal legs resting on a tripartite flat base, Second Empire era, France, mid-19th c., 16" h., pr. (ILLUS.) ....................................... **$2,000**

**Candelabra,** sterling silver, three-light, Colonial Revival paneled baluster-form standard, three convertible sockets, early 20th c., Tiffany & Co., 17 5/8" h., pr. ......... **3,738**

**Candelabra,** brass & crystal, six-light, a pyramid prism finial supporting a crystal beadwork stem, decorated w/scrolling arms, prism garlands & beads, brass base supporting six scrolling arms ending w/candleholders, 19th c., 13" d., 29" h., pr. (some decoration missing)........... **728**

**Candleholder,** brass, Arts & Crafts style, three-light w/a tiered design, three square candle sockets w/square rims raised on a C-form squared upright & spaced along an angled flat bar w/an angular curled tall upper foot & a squared small curl at the lower end, impressed "Hand Wrought L.C. Shellbarger," early 20th c., 12" l., 6" h. ......................................... **330**

**Candleholder,** wrought iron, a tall cylindrical shaft w/a candle ejector knob & angled rim handle, set on a disk drip pan base raised on three short legs w/penny feet, early, 9 1/2" h. ...................................... **495**

**Candleholder,** wrought iron, table model, an arched low tripod base w/penny feet supporting a very slender upright pointed rod fitted w/an adjustable flat cross-arm w/square brackets & fitted at each tip w/a candle socket w/drip tray, 22 1/4" h.............. **770**

**Candleholder,** wrought iron trammel-style, a thin bar w/a slender sawtooth trammel bar ending w/a short arm supporting a small oval pan w/two cylindrical candle sockets & a rush light holder, sockets w/push-ups, 27" l. ............................................ **495**

**Candleholder,** wrought iron w/domed wooden base & handle w/old red paint, 5" h. .................................................................... **275**

**Candleholders,** brass, ship's gimbal spring-loaded holders, traces of original nickel finish, 19th c., 11" h., pr...................... **316**

**Candlestand,** cast iron & brass, floor model, a two-armed stand w/two brass candle cups & drip pans fitted to a horizontal sliding carrier & ending w/a tripod base, brass finial & standard decoration, 18th c., 48 1/4" h. (wear) ..................................... **3,105**

**Candlestand,** wrought iron, a rounded arch tripod base w/penny feet centering a tall tapering turned & pointed bar mounted w/an adjustable double arm w/a candle socket at each end, squared iron brackets w/hooks below the arms, 19th c., 23 1/4" h............................................................ **1,815**

**Candlestick,** Bennington pottery, tall ringed columnar shaft on a flaring round foot,

mottled brown Flint Enamel glaze w/some dark green, mid-19th c., 8" h. ......... **825**

*Rare Early Blown Glass Candlestick*

**Candlestick,** blown glass, clear, tall cupped socket w/original pewter insert & bulbed bottom attached w/a wafer to the tall hollow standard w/applied rings applied to a heavy disk foot, probably Pittsburgh, ca. 1820-30, 9 1/8" h. (ILLUS.) .......................... **2,475**

**Candlestick,** brass, a dished saucer base centering a short spiral-twist standard supporting a cylindrical socket, polished, early, 6 1/4" h. (minor dents, old solder on threads of base) ......................................... **220**

**Candlestick,** brass, a flaring paneled & stepped base below the slender trumpet-form standard w/base & top rings below the cylindrical ringed socket, copper-colored patina w/traces of silver plating, 19th c., 9 1/2" h.............................................. **220**

**Candlestick,** brass, a round dished base centered by a domed support for the columnar shaft w/flared rim & side push-up knob, England, late 18th - early 19th c., 6 3/4" h. ............................................................ **385**

**Candlestick,** brass, a round ringed & domed foot below the solid knob- and ring-turned shaft w/a wide center drip pan, tall cylindrical socket, late 18th - early 19th c., 7 3/8" h. (minor dents) ............... **1,100**

**Candlestick,** brass, a square platform base raised on small peg feet, a conical lower shaft tapering to a flaring ring-turned upper shaft supporting the tall ring-turned candle socket, single-piece shaft, early, 9" h.................................................................. **248**

*English Candlestick with Bell*

**Candlestick,** brass, a wide flat-bottomed dished base w/low upright sides centering a tall slender ring-turned shaft w/an open yoke suspending a bell below the tall knobbed cylindrical socket w/flared rim, England, 12 1/2" h. (ILLUS.) .................. 495

**Candlestick,** brass, capstan-form, a wide flared cylindrical base supporting a wide flat disk centered by the turned & shaped cylindrical socket w/pick hole at the side, probably 18th c., 5 1/4" h. (repair to top flange)................................................. 495

**Candlestick,** brass, domed base & baluster stem w/mid-drip pan, early Dutch, 12 3/8" h. .................................................. 3,520

**Candlestick,** brass, hand-hammered, a flared rim on an egg-shaped candlecup, slender shaft ending in a bulbed cone on a disk base, incised mark of Jarvie, Chicago, early 20th c., 11" h. (spotting) ............. 431

**Candlestick,** brass, Queen Anne style, scalloped domed foot below the knob-turned slender shaft below a tapering flange & the tall cylindrical socket w/scalloped socket rim, England, 18th c., 7 7/8" h. (minor casting flaws) ...................... 660

**Candlestick,** brass, Queen Anne-style, a round slightly domed scalloped foot centering a very slender shaft topped by a compressed knob below the cylindrical socket w/flared rim, w/push-up, England, 18th c., 9 3/8" h. (repair to rim)...................... 275

**Candlestick,** brass, ring-turned & stepped domed base w/a ring-turned & tapering columnar shaft below the tall cylindrical socket, polished, 19th c., 8 1/2" h. ................ 248

**Candlestick,** brass, round domed base w/flat top centered by a baluster-turned stem & tall cylindrical socket, Spain, probably 18th c., 8 3/4" h. ............................. 550

**Candlestick,** brass, round flat-topped domed foot centered by a rod- and ring-turned shaft w/a ring-turned tall cylindrical socket, shaft screws into base, early, 7 1/2" h. ....................................................... 440

**Candlestick,** brass, wide round shallow dished base centered by a shaft w/an urn-form section below a spiraled section below the ringed cylindrical candle socket, standard screws into the base, early, 6 3/4" h. .................................................. 303

**Candlestick,** bronze, figural, two-light, cast in full-relief at the top w/the form of a female bearing a child on her shoulders w/outstretched arms supporting baskets, cast by Gorham, by Willard Paddock, inscribed "1912 by W.D. Paddock," 29 1/2" h. .................................................. 1,610

**Candlestick,** pressed flint glass, a paneled tulip-form socket on a tapering octagonal shaft w/faceted rings on a narrow octagonal base, New England Glass Co., fiery opalescent, first half 19th c., 9 3/8" h. (small chips) ..................................................... 743

**Candlestick,** pressed flint glass, hexagonal, scalloped rim socket, opaque medium blue, Pittsburgh, 9 5/8" h. (pewter socket missing, small edge chips) ............... 220

**Candlestick,** pressed flint glass, hexagonal w/flaring base & wafer, canary, 7 1/2" h. (broken blister inside socket) ........................ 138

**Candlestick,** pressed flint glass, Petal & Loop patt., the petal-form socket attached by a wafer to the loop design base, attributed to the Boston & Sandwich Glass Co., deep cobalt blue, 7" h. (few tiny flakes on foot edge)..................... 1,760

**Candlestick,** pressed flint glass, round base, hexagonal knopped stem, opalescent tulip-shaped socket, canary, Pittsburgh, ca. 1860, 9 1/4" h. (pewter insert missing, chips & crack in socket) .......... 110

**Candlestick,** pressed flint glass, vase-shaped w/flared rim socket, cobalt blue, 15 3/4" h. ................................................. 176

**Candlestick,** taper jack-type, a small round reticulated base w/three hearts, cast handle on base, slender shaft wrapped w/an old wax taper below the top cross-bar & urn finial, England, late 18th - early 19th c., 5" h. ...................................... 770

**Candlesticks,** Battersea enamel, tall cylindrical socket w/flaring flattened rim above a tall slender ringed standard & domed paneled foot, decorated w/dark blue enameling & white enamel panels all hightlighted w/gilt & colored florals, England, 18th c., 9" h., pr. (chips on bobeches & small flake on one stick)........ 2,530

*Early Dutch Brass Candlesticks*

**Candlesticks,** brass, a domed, stepped round base below the ring- and knob-turned standard centered by a wide disk-form drip tray, tall ring-turned cylindrical shaft, Holland, 18th - 19th c., minor battering, 7 1/2" h., pr. (ILLUS.) ........................ **385**

*Early English Brass Candlesticks*

**Candlesticks,** brass, a flaring petal-form rounded base supporting a ringed graduated shaft w/a side candle ejector knob & a tall cylindrical socket w/flared rim, one ejector knob missing, minor dents, England, mid-18th c., 8 1/4" h., pr. (ILLUS.) ...................... **1,380**

**Candlesticks,** brass, a stepped domed round foot below a small double-knop stem supporting a tall cylindrical shaft bulbed at the bottom & w/a flared rim, w/push-ups, 19th c., 8" h., pr. ...................... **220**

**Candlesticks,** brass, a tall open double spiral-twist standard w/a tall slender ringed socket w/flattened rim, on a wide round dished foot w/flared sides, Europe, late 19th c., 18 1/4" h., pr. ...................... **460**

**Candlesticks,** brass, flaring domed & stepped octagonal base below the tapering knob-turned standard & waisted cylindrical socket, early, 9" h., pr ...................... **660**

**Candlesticks,** brass, "King of Diamonds" patt., a squared foot w/beveled corners supporting a tall knob- and ring-turned shaft w/a bulbous diamond pattern central knob, tall cylindrical socket w/flat-

tened rim, w/push-ups, England, late 19th c., 12 1/2" h., pr. ...................... **495**

**Candlesticks,** brass, Neo-classical w/push-ups, 5 1/2" h., pr. ...................... **105**

**Candlesticks,** brass, octagonal base w/turned standard, w/push-ups, Victorian, 12" h., pr. ...................... **121**

*Early Pricket Candlestick*

**Candlesticks,** brass, pricket-type, a dished top centered by a tall tapering candle spike above a baluster-, ring- and knob-turned stem above a lower disk on a flaring cylindrical base raised on ball feet, ecclesiastical markings, early, 15" h., pr. (ILLUS. of one) ...................... **3,300**

*Brass Pricket-type Candlestick*

**Candlesticks,** brass, pricket-type spike above ring & turned column over wide drip pan above ring & turned baluster stem on domed circular ringed foot, Europe, late 17th to early 18th c., dents & repairs, 15" h., pr. (ILLUS. of one) ............... **805**

**Candlesticks,** brass, "Prince of Diamonds" patt., a squared domed foot below the tall shaft w/ringed sections above & below the central bulbous diamond patterned section, a tall cylindrical socket w/flared rim, w/push-ups, marked "The Diamond Prince," England, 19th c., 11 7/8" h., pr. ....... **448**

**Candlesticks,** brass, "Princess of Diamonds" patt., a squared domed foot below the tall shaft w/ringed sections above & below the central bulbous diamond patterned section, a tall cylindrical socket w/flared rim, w/push-ups, marked "The Diamond Princess," England, 19th c., pr. ..... **448**

**Candlesticks,** brass, Queen Anne-style, a round scalloped base below the slender ring-turned shaft w/a tall cylindrical socket w/flattened rim, England, 18th c., 7 1/2" h., pr. ...................................................... **1,870**

**Candlesticks,** brass, Queen Anne-style, scalloped base & baluster stem w/seam, 6 3/4" h., pr. (one has old repair) .................. **990**

**Candlesticks,** brass, Queen Anne-style, square base w/invected corners, detailed stem w/scalloped lip, 8" h., pr. .................... **1,045**

**Candlesticks,** brass, "Queen of Diamonds" patt., a squared domed foot below the tall shaft w/ringed sections above & below the central bulbous diamond patterned section, a tall cylindrical socket w/flared rim, w/push-ups, marked "The Queen of Diamonds," England, 19th c., 11 1/4" h., pr. .................................................................. **644**

**Candlesticks,** brass, round tapering foot below a baluster- and ring-turned shaft w/a tall cylindrical socket w/flattened rim, original push-ups, 19th c., 12" h., pr. ............ **275**

**Candlesticks,** brass, rounded stepped & domed foot w/scalloped edge tapering to a tall slender paneled & ring-turned shaft below the tall ring socket w/a removable scalloped bobêche, France, late 19th - early 18th c., 9 5/8" h., pr. ...................... **1,650**

**Candlesticks,** brass, square base, knob-turned column w/flaring socket, late 19th to early 20th c., 10 1/2" h., pr. ...................... **110**

**Candlesticks,** brass, square bobêche over baluster-shaped stem & square base, ca. 1800, 9 1/2" h., pr. .......................................... **280**

**Candlesticks,** brass, tapering baluster-form fluted shaft, domed paneled square base w/dentil borders, 19th c., 9 5/8" h., pr. (small base loss, wear) ............................. **403**

*Early Brass Candlesticks*

**Candlesticks,** brass, trumpet-form base tapering to wide drip pan below cylindrical sausage-turned column, England, late 17th c., 7 9/16" h., pr. (ILLUS.) ................. **13,800**

**Candlesticks,** brass, Victorian w/push-ups, diamond & beehive detail, 10 3/4" h., pr. ...... **110**

**Candlesticks,** brass w/push-ups, baluster-shaped stem resting on chamfered base, early 19th c., 10 1/2" h., pr. ........................... **308**

**Candlesticks,** brass, wide domed base w/turned baluster stem, mid-drip plate, not seamed, one w/casting holes filled w/solder, 11 1/4" h., pr. .................................. **495**

**Candlesticks,** bronze, a cylindrical socket on a slender upper shaft above a figural seahorse shaft, on a round disk foot w/concentric ridges, green patina, one signed & dated by E.T. Hurley, 1916, Kentucky, 10 3/4" h., pr. ............................. **2,530**

**Candlesticks,** bronze, a flared bobeche inserted into an urn-form socket held in a three-prong bulbed standard over a swirled round foot, dark brown patina, impressed mark of Tiffany Studios, No. 1213, 16 3/4" h., pr. (minor wear) .............. **1,955**

**Candlesticks,** gilt-metal, Art Nouveau design w/floral & foliate decoration, ca. 1900, 8" h., pr. (minor scratches).................. **345**

**Candlesticks,** hand-hammered copper, Arts & Crafts style, each w/a cylindrical stem surmounted by a bowl-form drip pan centered by a cylindrical candle cup, all on a domed foot, applied trefoil mounts at joints, dark brown patina, ca. 1900, 11 3/8" h., pr........................................... **575**

**Candlesticks,** pewter, capstan bases, knopped standard, 4 3/4" h., pr. (somewhat battered w/repair)................................. **715**

**Candlesticks,** pressed flint glass, a petal socket above a figural dolphin standard on a double-step square base, canary yellow, Boston & Sandwich Glass Co., mid-19th c., 10" h., pr. (one w/tiny chip on tip of dolphin tail, & tiny spall on corner of base)................................................................ **1,430**

**Candlesticks,** pressed flint glass, a wide flaring hexagonal tulip-form socket w/scalloped rim on a ringed tapering hexagonal shaft on a round foot, pewter socket inserts, opaque blue, Pittsburgh, mid-19th c., 9 3/4" h., pr. (small flakes) ........ **495**

**Candlesticks,** pressed flint glass base & blown hollow socket w/baluster stem, clear, 8 1/8" h., pr. (checks in base in the making, no inserts) ....................................... **358**

**Candlesticks,** pressed flint glass, hexagonal tulip-form socket on a ringed stem & hexagonal base, canary yellow, Boston & Sandwich Glass Co., mid-19th c., 7 1/4" h., pr. (normal mold roughness)......... **330**

**Candlesticks,** pressed flint glass, jade green petal socket attached w/a wafer to a reeded columnar milk white shaft w/square foot, mid-19th c., some mold roughness, 9" h., pr................................. **2,090**

**Candlesticks,** pressed flint glass, petal socket attached w/a wafer to a ribbed columnar standard w/a stepped square base, canary yellow, attributed to Boston

& Sandwich Glass Co., ca. 1840-60, 9 1/2" h., pr. ................................................. **770**

**Candlesticks,** silver on copper, telescoping design, Sheffield, England, 7 3/4" h., pr. (silver worn) ..................................................... **220**

*Russian Silver Candlesticks*

**Candlesticks,** silver, on shaped square base w/scrolling stylized dolphins to corners, stem w/flat leaf motifs, bell-shaped flat leaf sockets, Russian, 13 3/4" h., pr. (ILLUS.) ............................................................. **805**

**Candlesticks,** silver-plated, each w/stepped square base w/canted corners & conforming baluster-form stem terminating in a spool-form candle cup, George II-Style, 20th c., 7 3/4" h., pr. ........... **172**

**Candlesticks,** sterling silver, each in the form of a Doric column w/a chased, reeded stem, the shoulder beaded w/embossed rosette band, on a square stepped base, Gorham Mfg. Co., Providence, Rhode Island, 1908, 8 3/4" h., set of 4 ................................................................. **1,725**

**Candlesticks,** sterling silver, Rococo style w/a slightly domed, stepped & scalloped round foot below the tall slender shaft w/a ringed knob below a slender urn-form section connected to the tall ringed cylindrical candle socket w/wide flattened & scalloped rim, each engraved on side of base "The Gift of Eliz. Sauvaire to her grandson Thos. De Jersey 1759," William Cafe, London, England, 1758-59, 8 1/2" h., pr. ...................................... **5,940**

**Candlesticks,** sterling silver, square base w/gadrooned borders, the stem, socket & detachable bobêche also gadrooned, monogrammed to base, Robert Makepeace & Richard Carter makers, George III period, England, 9 1/2" h., pr. ................. **4,888**

**Candlesticks,** wrought iron, wedding ring hogscraper-type, round base & cylindrical shaft w/brass ring, mid-19th c., 13 1/4" h., pr. (corrosion) ............................ **4,025**

**Chamberstick,** brass, a shallow round dished base w/upright finger loop handle at the side, a cylindrical shaft w/candle ejector knob & a flared flattened socket rim, 19th c., 4 3/4" h. ....................................... **275**

**Chamberstick,** silver plate, round w/an embossed scalloped rim w/repoussé roses & foliate designs, a C-scroll edge handle, Tiffany & Co., New York, late 19th - early 20th c., 2 1/4" h. ..................................... **86**

**Chamberstick,** sterling silver, circular dished form w/C-scroll handle, cylindrical turned stem, flared socket rim, London hallmarks for 1755-56, 4 1/4" h. (old repair, snuffer not marked) .............................. **633**

**Chamberstick,** sterling silver, maker's mark "AK," ribbed borders, monogrammed, London, 1804, 2 1/8" h. (extinguisher missing) .......................................... **173**

**Chambersticks,** tin w/riveted handles, old worn black paint, 6 5/8" h., pr. ....................... **138**

*Bronze Girandoliers*

**Girandoliers,** gilt bronze & crystal, relief-molded figure of a woman forms base beneath the three candle sockets, each w/a flower form bobêche & ten cut crystal prism pendants, 15" h., 19th c., pr. (ILLUS.) ...................................................... **173**

**Girandandoles,** cast brass & marble, a stepped white marble base w/brass trim supporting a cast figure of a standing Victorian lady in an exotic bloomer outfit, a slender shaft at the back topped w/down-scrolled leaves centering a candle socket, each leaftip hung w/a long triangular glass prism, good patina w/areas of original gilding, mid-19th c., 15" h., pr. ................ **220**

**Wall sconce,** tin, round reflector pan w/radiating small mirrored segments, cylindrical socket w/fluted edge bobêche, American, second quarter 19th c., 10" d., 11" h. (wear, corrosion, minor imperfections) ............................................................. **2,185**

**Wall sconces,** tin, the extended back plate w/a fluted round top, single candle socket in the half-round tray base, 19th c., 3 1/4" w., 9 1/2" h., pr. (minor corrosion) ...... **978**

# Fairy Lamps

*Amber Embossed Fairy Lamp*

**Amber embossed shade,** fairy-size, embossed overall w/crosses surrounded by diamonds, rests on the smooth shoulder of a matching swirl-molded lamp cup w/two rows of applied & tooled petals around the rim, cup marked "Rd 176239," 4 3/4" d., 4 1/4" h. (ILLUS.) .......................... **$250**

*Amber Ribbed Fairy Lamp*

**Amber ribbed shade,** fairy-size, on the smooth shoulder of a matching handled cylindrical base w/a flared, ribbed rim & foot, 4 1/4" w., 5" h. (ILLUS.) ......................... **150**

*Amethyst Diamonds Fairy Lamp*

**Amethyst Four-in-One Diamonds patt. shade,** pyramid-size, in a clear Clarke Fairy Pyramid swirl design lamp cup, 2 3/4" d., 3 5/8" h. (ILLUS.) ............................ **200**

*Amethyst & White Swirl Fairy Lamp*

**Amethyst & white swirl shade,** fairy-size, vertically ribbed & resting in a smooth-shouldered matching lamp cup, 3 5/8" d., 4 5/8" h. (ILLUS.) ............................................. **250**

*Baccarat-signed Blue Fairy Lamp*

**Baccarat blue Pinwheel patt. shade,** fairy-size, in a matching scalloped upwardly flared base marked "Baccarat Déposé," 5 1/2" d., 4" h. (ILLUS.) .................................... **350**

*Clear Baccarat Pinwheel Fairy Lamp*

**Baccarat clear Pinwheel patt. shade,** fairy-size, in a matching scalloped upwardly flaring base marked "Baccarat Déposé," 5 1/2" d., 4" h. (ILLUS.) .................. **250**

*Baccarat "Rose Tiente" Fairy Lamp*

**Baccarat "Rose Tiente" Pinwheel patt. shade** & matching base, marked "Baccarat," France, early 20th c., 5 3/4" d., 4 1/2" h. (ILLUS.) ............................................ **350**

*Blue Cased & Embossed Fairy Lamp*

**Blue cased in white shade,** overall embossed reverse drape patt. in a clear Clarke lamp cup base, 4" d., 4 1/2" h. (ILLUS.) .............................................. **200**

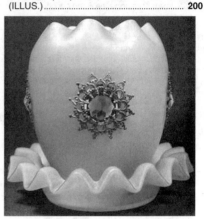

*Blue Satin Jeweled Fairy Lamp*

**Blue cased white satin shade,** w/an inwardly pinched top rim, decorated around the sides w/four ormolu frames each holding a colored jewel, on a matching saucer base w/flared, ruffled rim, 5 5/8" d., 5 1/4" h. (ILLUS.) .................... **250**

*Blue Craquelle Shade & Aladdin Lamp*

**Blue craquelle design shade,** fairy-size, resting in the integral lamp cup of a white porcelain Aladdin lamp-shaped base trimmed in gold, candle depression marked "S. Clarke Patent Trade Mark Fairy," base marked "Rd No. 93321," 9 1/2" l., 5 1/2" h. (ILLUS.) ............................. **500**

*Decorated Blue Fairy Lamp*

**Blue decorated shade,** fairy-size, blue ground decorated w/pink flower & green leaves, resting on the smooth shoulder of the matching lamp cup, 3 1/3" d., 4 1/2" h. (ILLUS.) ............................................ **250**

*Fairy Lamp with Decorated Blue Shade*

**Blue decorated shade,** pyramid-size w/three air vents, decorated w/white enameled flowers, resting in a clear ribbed lamp cup w/crenellated rim, 3 3/4" d., 4 5/8" h. (ILLUS.) ............................. **150**

*Blue Diamond Point Fairy Lamp*

**Blue Diamond Point patt. shade,** pyramid-size, w/a polished top rim, in a matching Clarke Fairy Pyramid lamp cup, 2 3/4" d., 3 5/8" h. (ILLUS.) ............................................ **150**

*Embossed Shade in Ceramic Base*

**Blue embossed shade,** pyramid-size, overall embossed leaf design, on a signed Taylor, Tunnicliffe & Co. creamware flower bowl base decorated w/blue flowers, an integral lamp cup w/a ribbed shoulder, marked "S. Clarke's Patent Trade Mark Fairy" inside candle depression, 5 7/8" d., 5" h. (ILLUS.) ......................... **750**

*Striped & Ribbed Fairy Lamp*

**Blue & frosted clear stripe ribbed shade,** conical w/a flared crimped top, in a matching low footed bowl base w/flared crimped rim, 6" d., 4 3/4" h. (ILLUS.) ............. **250**

*Frosted Blue Petal-form Fairy Lamp*

**Blue frosted satin shade,** an inward-crimped shade w/five applied clear frosted petals around the sides, on a matching pedestal base w/five applied frosted clear leaf-form feet & three upturned leaves, 9 1/2" h. (ILLUS.) ................................ **500**

*Blue Hobnail Fairy Lamp*

**Blue Hobnail patt. shade,** pyramid-size, in a clear Clarke lamp cup, 3" d., 4" h. (ILLUS.) ............................................................. **150**

*Blue Mother-of-Pearl & Swirl Lamp*

**Blue mother-of-pearl satin shade,** fairy-size, Diamond Quilted patt. cased in white & w/an overall embossed reverse swirl mold design, matching smooth-shouldered lamp cup, 3 3/4" d., 5" h. (ILLUS.) ............................................................. **250**

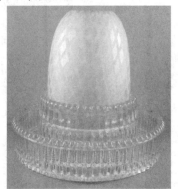

*Blue Satin Shade in Flower Bowl Base*

**Blue mother-of-pearl satin shade,** fairy-size, Diamond Quilted patt., in a clear Clarke Trade Mark Fairy Pyramid flower bowl base w/integral lamp cup, 7 1/4" d., 6 1/2" h. (ILLUS.) ............................................. **300**

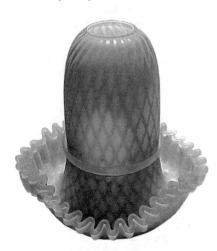

*Blue Mother-of-Pearl Satin Fairy Lamp*

**Blue mother-of-pearl satin shade,** fairy-size, Diamond Quilted patt., in a clear frosted lamp cup w/a diamond patt., raised on a matching mother-of-pearl Diamond Quilted squared base w/upright crimped rim & cased in white on the exterior, 6 1/4" w., 6 1/4" h. (ILLUS.) ................... **750**

*Blue & Green Satin Fairy Lamp*

**Blue mother-of-pearl satin shade,** fairy-size, Stripe patt., cased in white & tapering to a puckered, scalloped top, resting in a tricorner green mother-of-pearl satin Swirl patt. pond lily-style base w/recessed center, 5 1/2" w., 4 3/4" h. (ILLUS.) ............................................................. **750**

*Blue Stripe Satin & White-based Lamp*

**Blue mother-of-pearl satin shade,** fairy-size, Stripe patt., tapering to a puckered top w/scalloped rim & scalloped & flared bottom rim, in a clear pressed glass Clarke lamp cup raised on the central column of a reversible glossy white base w/upright petticoat rim, 7" d., 6" h. (ILLUS.) .......................................................... **750**

*Mother-of-Pearl Shade on Plateau*

**Blue mother-of-pearl satin shade,** pyra-mid-size, Diamond Quilted patt., cased in white, in a Clarke glazed creamware lamp cup w/gold trim marked by Taylor, Tunnicliffe & Co. on the bottom, cup fits in the ring of an ormolu stand attached to a beveled mirror plateau, 4 1/2" d., 5 1/2" h. (ILLUS.) ........................................... **450**

*Blue Diamond Quilted Satin Lamp*

**Blue mother-of-pearl satin shade,** pyra-mid-size, Diamond Quilted patt. cased in white, in a clear Clarke Fairy Pyramid lamp cup (ILLUS.)............................................. **200**

*Blue Opaque Building Fairy Lamp*

**Blue opaque figural shade,** modeled as a tall six-sided building w/embossed win-dows, doors & shingle roof, on a con-forming base w/stone block design & containing an integral candle cup, 4" w., 6" h. (ILLUS.)..................................................... **150**

*Blue Paneled & Threaded Fairy Lamp*

**Blue paneled & threaded shade,** pyramid-size, on a clear Clarke lamp cup, 3" d., 3 5/8" h. (ILLUS.).......................................... **200**

*Davidson "Pearline" Fairy Lamp*

**Blue "Pearline" shade,** deeply ribbed blue shade w/opalescent white vertical stripes, by George Davidson in the Brideshead patt., embossed "Rd 130643," in a clear Clarke Fairy Pyramid lamp cup, 2 3/4" d., 3 3/4" h. (ILLUS.)........... **150**

*Decorated Blue Satin Shade & Stand*

**Blue satin decorated shade,** pyramid-size, the blue ground enameled w/white flowers, leaves & a decorative ring around the top opening, on a clear Clarke lamp cup, cup fits into an ormolu stand w/openwork trim attached to a blue plush mirror plateau base, 4 7/8" d., 8 7/8" h. (ILLUS.)............................................................. **600**

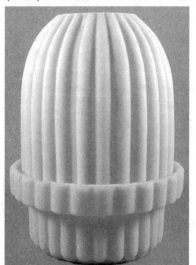

*Blue Satin Ribbed Fairy Lamp*

**Blue satin ribbed shade,** fairy-size, narrow vertical ribbing, in a smooth-shouldered

matching lamp cup, 3 5/8" d., 4 5/8" h. (ILLUS.)......................................................... **250**

*Blue Satin Star-design Fairy Lamp*

**Blue satin shaded to white shade,** fairy-size, impressed overall w/six-point stars, cased in white, in a clear Clarke lamp cup resting on the central low column of the matching blue satin cased reversible base w/fluted rim, 6 1/2" d., 4 5/8" h. (ILLUS.)................................................. **750**

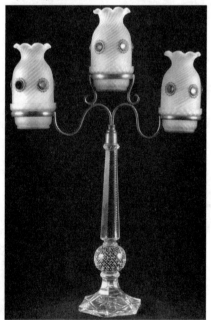

*Blue Shades on Crystal Standard*

**Blue satin shades,** epergne-style, three pale blue shades w/molded swirl design & flared top rim, each w/five colored jewels set in brass frames around the sides, each resting in a matching quilted satin lamp cup in supporting brass rings, raised on a slender cut crystal standard w/a controlled bubble ball, 22" h. (ILLUS.)....................................................... **1,500**

*Blue Mother-of-Pearl Satin Lamp*

**Blue shaded mother-of-pearl satin shade,** blue shaded to white, Diamond Quilted patt., on a clear Clarke lamp cup resting on the internal shoulder of a matching bulbous white base w/ruffled outwardly flared blue rim, 5 1/4" d., 7 1/2" h. (ILLUS.) ........................................... **500**

*Shaded Blue Satin Fairy Lamp*

**Blue shaded satin shade,** fairy-size, blue shaded to white cased in creamy white, w/a crimped upper rim, in a clear Clarke Fairy lamp cup resting on six rounded scallops on the upright rim of the matching bowl-shaped base, 5 1/8" d., 5 5/8" h. (ILLUS.) ............................................................. **500**

*Satin Glass Fairy Lamp-Vase Epergne*

**Blue shaded satin shade,** epergne-style, blue shaded to white, a fairy-size central shade cased in creamy white in a clear Clarke lamp cup, the cup resting on the inward-turned crimped rim of the matching bowl, bowl rests in an ormolu frame attached to a round mirror plateau w/beveled & notched edge, each frame arm supporting a matching bulbous satin glass bud vase w/flared & scalloped rim & applied opaque berry prunt, 10 1/4" d., 6 1/2" h. (ILLUS.) ........................................... **2,000**

*Blue Satin Decorated Fairy Lamp*

**Blue shaded to white decorated satin shade,** fairy-size, blueberry blue decorated in enamel w/an English robin in flight & stylized foliage, on a short pedestal-style creamware lamp cup marked "S. Clarke's Patent Trade Mark Fairy," on an integral flower bowl base decorated in a swirled tapestry design & w/an inwardly curved rim, base marked "Patent Taylor, Tunnicliffe & Co. - 1443," 8 1/4" d., 6 1/4" h. (ILLUS.) ........................................... **1,000**

### Shaded Blue Satin Decorated Lamp

**Blue shaded to white decorated satin shade,** pyramid-side, cased in white & decorated in dark green w/a wild rose design, in a clear Clarke Fairy Pyramid lamp cup, 2 3/4" d., 3 5/8" h. (ILLUS.).......... **250**

### Jeweled Shaded Blue Fairy Lamp

**Blue shading to light blue shade,** chimney-style w/fluted top rim & the sides mounted w/four colored jewels set in brass filigree frames mounted in holes cut in the sides, on a matching blue bulbous base w/six hand-tooled clear applied leaf-form feet, 4" d., 10" h. (ILLUS.)..... **350**

### Blue Shaded Decorated Satin Lamp

**Blue shaded to white decorated satin shade,** pyramid-size, cased in white & enamel-decorated w/a floral lace design, on a clear pressed glass Clarke lamp cup, 3" d., 3 1/2" h. (ILLUS.) .......................... **200**

### Figural Birdcage Fairy Lamp

**Blue shading to white figural shade,** a ribbed satin finish figural birdcage trimmed w/gold bands & protruding feeders, brass fitting w/finger ring at top opening, 4 1/4" w., 6" h. (ILLUS.) .......................... **250**

*Blue & White Candy Stripe Fairy Lamp*

**Blue & white candy stripe shade,** fairy-size, shade embossed w/reverse swirl design, in a clear Clarke lamp cup, 4" d., 4 1/2" h. (ILLUS.) ............................................. **300**

*Frosted Blue & White Swirl Lamp*

**Blue, white & clear frosted Cleveland Swirl patt. shade,** fairy-size, in a match-ing lamp cup w/crimped rim & raised on a matching base w/upturned fluted rim, 6 1/2" d., 6 1/4" h. (ILLUS.) ............................ **750**

*Blue & White Cleveland Swirl Lamp*

**Blue & white Cleveland Swirl shade,** fairy-size, vertical ribbing, on a Taylor, Tunni-cliffe & Co. glazed creamware base w/gold trim marked "S. Clarke Patent Trade Mark Fairy" in black, 4 1/4" d., 5" h. (ILLUS.) .................................................... **400**

*Blue Nailsea-style Shade & Base*

**Blue & white Nailsea-style shade,** fairy-size, blue w/overall white loopings, in a clear Clarke lamp cup resting on three in-wardly curved sections of the upturned fluted & ruffled rim of the matching Nailsea-style bowl base, 7" w., 6 1/2" h. (ILLUS.) ............................................................ **750**

*Lamps in Stands with Nailsea Shades*

**Blue & white Nailsea-style shade,** fairy-size, blue w/white loopings, on a clear Clarke lamp cup resting in a three-legged brass stand decorated w/glass green grape leaves & frosted green grapes, 10" h., pr. (ILLUS.) ........................................ **1,500**

*Blue & White Nailsea Fairy Lamp*

**Blue & white Nailsea-style shade,** fairy-size, light blue w/overall white loopings, in a clear Clarke lamp cup resting on the top shoulder of a matching base w/a downturned ruffled rim & applied clear frosted foot, original Clarke paper label, 7 3/4" d., 5 3/4" h. (ILLUS.) ............................ **900**

*Unusual Nailsea-style Fairy Lamp*

**Blue & white Nailsea-style shade,** tall shade, between fairy & pyramid size, in transparent blue w/wide white loopings, in a clear lamp cup marked "Arcadian Light" w/flat vertical ribbing & a horizontal unevenly scalloped rim, 3 3/4" d., 4 1/4" h. (ILLUS.) ............................................ **500**

*Nailsea & Crystal Fairy Lamp Epergne*

**Blue & white Nailsea-style shades,** epergne-style, fairy-size, blue w/overall white loopings, in clear Clarke lamp cups held in rings of an ormolu frame raised on a cut crystal pedestal standard w/a repair, 14" w., 18" h. (ILLUS.)............................ **750**

*Blue Nailsea & Creamware Lamp*

**Blue & white Nailsea-type shade,** fairy-size, blue ground w/delicate overall blue loopings, resting on the ribbed shoulder of a creamware lamp cup trimmed in blue & gold & marked "S. Clarke's Patent Trade Mark Fairy" raised on the integral post of a Tapestry Ware flower bowl base w/incurved ruffled rim marked "Taylor, Tunnicliffe & Co.," 8 1/8" d., 7 1/2" h. (ILLUS.)............................................................. **750**

*Blue & White Spatter Pyramid Lamp*

**Blue & white spatter shade,** pyramid-size, blue ground w/white swirled spatter in the arabesque design, in a clear Clarke Fairy Pyramid lamp cup, 3" d., 3 1/2" h. (ILLUS.)............................................................. **200**

*Blue & White Swirl Embossed Shade*

**Blue & white swirl shade,** fairy-size, embossed reverse swirl design, in a clear Clarke lamp cup (ILLUS.) ............................... **300**

*Blue & White Verre Moiré Fairy Lamp*

**Blue & white Verre Moiré Nailsea-type shade,** pyramid-size, blue ground w/overall white loopings, resting in Clarke Fairy Pyramid lamp cup, on a matching blue & white Verre Moiré base w/upturned crimped rim, 5 3/4" d., 4 1/4" h. (ILLUS.) ............................................. **500**

*Brass Jeweled Filigree Fairy Lamp*

**Brass jeweled filigree shade,** fairy-size, the dome set w/eight large colored jewels in individual filigree framed alternating w/eight smaller jewels, on a four-footed brass base w/integral candle cup, 3 1/2" d., 4 1/4" h. (ILLUS.) ............................ **250**

*Jeweled Brass Fairy Lamp*

**Brass jeweled shade,** rounded pierced cast shade mounted overall w/colored jewels of varied sizes, w/an integral side finger handle, on a three-footed matching base, 4" d., 4 1/4" h. (ILLUS.) ........................ **250**

*Rare Decorated Burmese Fairy Lamp*

**Burmese decorated shade,** fairy-size, satin finish decorated in a prunus design, in a satin finish Burmese lamp cup marked "S. Clarke Patent Trade Mark Fairy" containing a clear ribbed Clarke candleholder & a Burglar's Horror candle, the cup resting on top of a matching Burmese petticoat base w/unrefired foot, 5" d., 5 3/4" h. (ILLUS.) ......................................... **2,000**

*Decorated Burmese & Ceramic Lamp*

**Burmese decorated shade,** fairy-size, satin finish, decorated in the woodbine design, on a creamware flower bowl base decorated w/polychrome flowers & signed "Taylor, Tunnicliffe & Co.," the shade atop an integral lamp cup w/ribbed shoulder marked "S. Clarke's Patent Trade Mark Fairy" inside candle depression, 7 1/2" d., 6" h. (ILLUS.) ...................... **1,000**

### Decorated Burmese Shade & Base

**Burmese decorated shade,** fairy-size, satin finish, decorated w/red forget-me-not-like flowers & green leaves, in a clear Clarke lamp cup marked "S. Clarke Trade Mark Fairy" on a matching Burmese quatrefoil base w/unrefired Burmese foot, 5 3/4" w., 5 3/4" h. (ILLUS.)...... **2,500**

rim & an unrefired Burmese foot, 4 1/4" d., 6 3/4" h. (ILLUS.)........................ **2,500**

### Ivy-decorated Burmese Fairy Lamp

**Burmese decorated shade,** fairy-size, satin finish enamel-decorated in the ivy design, in a clear Clarke lamp cup resting on a matching decorated Burmese reversible base w/a downturned petticoat rim, 6 3/4" d., 5 3/8" h. (ILLUS.) .................. **1,500**

### Burmese Lamp with Red Flowers

**Burmese decorated shade,** fairy-size, satin finish, decorated w/small red forget-me-not-like flowers & green leaves, in a clear Clarke lamp cup marked "S. Clarke Patent Trade mark Fairy," in a matching Burmese deep base w/upright crimped

### Webb Burmese Decorated Fairy Lamp

**Burmese decorated shade,** fairy-size, satin finish, Webb shade decorated in prunus design, in a satin finish Burmese lamp cup marked "S. Clarke Patent Trade Mark Fairy" containing a ribbed Clarke candleholder & a Burglar's Horror candle, cup rests atop the petticoat rim of a matching Burmese base w/unrefired foot, 5" d., 5 3/4" h. (ILLUS.)....................... **2,000**

*Prunus-decorated Burmese Lamp*

**Burmese decorated shade,** pyramid-size, satin finish decorated in a prunus design, in a clear Clark Fairy Pyramid lamp cup, 2 3/4" d., 3 3/4" h. (ILLUS.) ........................... **400**

*Burmese Base & Decorated Shade*

**Burmese decorated shade,** pyramid-size, satin finish shade decorated in the prunus design, on a clear Clarke lamp cup resting on an undecorated satin finish Burmese tri-fold base w/unrefired Burmese applied feet, 3 1/2" w., 5 1/2" h. (ILLUS.) ......................................................... **800**

*Rare Decorated Burmese Epergne*

**Burmese decorated shades,** epergne-style, fairy-size, three satin finish shades decorated in a prunus design, on clear Clarke lamp cups in matching Burmese bowls on crystal supporting arms w/three crystal fronds w/applied tooled leaves, a central elevated satin finish decorated Burmese bowl w/crystal support arm w/applied leaves, all on a mirrored plateau base, 12" d., 11" h. (ILLUS.) .............. **6,500**

*Tall Marked Burmese Epergne-Lamp*

**Burmese decorated shades,** epergne-style, pyramid-size, satin finish, four shades decorated in the woodbine design in clear Clarke lamp cups, the center lamp elevated, alternating w/three undecorated satin finish Burmese bud vases w/fluted, flared rims w/rings & berry prunts fitted into the metal rings of a seven-armed ormolu frame rising above a miniature Burmese rose bowl all supported by an ormolu fitting on a tubular trumpet-form center pedestal of unrefired Burmese, the frame marked "Clarke's Trade Mark Cricklite," 8 1/2" d., 12" h. (ILLUS.) ......................................................... **3,000**

*Ornate Burmese Fairy Lamp Epergne*

**Burmese decorated shades,** epergne-style, two satin finished Burmese fairy-size shades & three satin finished Burmese posey vases & a satin finished Burmese central column, all decorated in color w/a prunus design, includes two Clarke lamps, two Clarke candle cups & two Clarke candles, metal washer at top of central post embossed "Clarke's Patent Fairy Lamp," 9" w., 10" h. (ILLUS.) ............. **2,500**

*Burmese & Creamware Epergne*

**Burmese shade,** epergne-style, pyramid-size, a satin finish undecorated shade on the ribbed shoulder of a Taylor, Tunnicliffe & Co. creamware lamp cup w/a ribbed design petticoat rim, the integral candle cup marked "S. Clarke's Patent Trade Mark Fairy Pyramid," in an ormolu frame also supporting three Tapestry Ware ceramic bud vases w/gilt knobs, 5 3/4" d., 4 3/4" h. (ILLUS.) ............................ **650**

*Burmese Lamp-Epergne in Frame*

**Burmese shade,** epergne-style, pyramid-size, satin finish undecorated shade in a Clarke Burmese lamp cup, in a cast brass frame w/four downward turned legs & four upward turned vase holders fitted w/undecorated Burmese bud vases w/fluted rims, unrefired Burmese collars & berry prunts, 7 1/2" w., 4 1/4" h. (ILLUS.) .......................................................... **1,000**

*Burmese Shade & Reversible Base*

**Burmese shade,** fairy-size, satin finish decorated in a forget-me-not design, in a Clarke Burmese lamp cup resting in a center post of an undecorated Burmese reversible base w/an angled petticoat rim, 6 3/4" d., 5 1/2" h. (ILLUS.) .......................... **1,000**

*Burmese Shade on Ceramic Base*

**Burmese shade,** fairy-size, satin finish decorated in the prunus design, resting in a signed Taylor, Tunnicluffe & Co. Tapestry Ware flower bowl w/integral lamp cup marked "S. Clarke's Trade Mark Fairy Pyramid," 6" d., 5" h. (ILLUS.) ........................ **750**

*Burmese Lamp with Woodbine Design*

**Burmese shade,** fairy-size, satin finish decorated in the woodbine design, in a Clarke Burmese lamp cup resting on the rim of a matching quatrefoil base w/an unrefired Burmese foot, 5 1/2" w., 5 1/2" h. (ILLUS.) .. **2,000**

*Burmese Shade in Doulton Base*

**Burmese shade,** fairy-size, satin finish decorated w/a forget-me-not design, resting on a signed Doulton Burslem Tapestry Ware handled base marked "S. Clarke's Patent Trade Mark Fairy" inside candle depression, 6 x 8 1/4", 6" h. (ILLUS.) ......... **1,000**

*Decorated Fairy Size Burmese Lamp*

**Burmese shade,** fairy-size, satin finish decorated w/green ivy leaves, in a Burmese lamp cup on a matching quatrefoil satin finish decorated base w/applied unfired foot, 5 3/4" w., 5 3/4" h. (ILLUS.) ................. **2,000**

*Marked Webb Burmese Fairy Lamp*

**Burmese shade,** fairy-size, satin finish, in a clear ribbed Clarke lamp cup marked "Fairy Lamp Patent Nov 9, 1886 - 352296 American Patent," resting on a Webb Burmese reversible base w/upturned ruffled rim marked "Thomas Webb & Sons - Queen's Burmese Ware Patented" & "S. Clarke's Patent Trade Mark Fairy," 7 1/4" d., 5 1/2" h. (ILLUS.) ............................ **500**

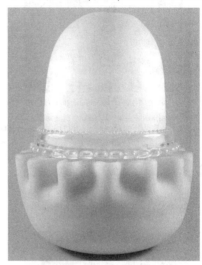

*Webb Burmese Shade & Base*

**Burmese shade,** fairy-size, satin finish, in a clear ribbed lamp cup resting on a matching satin-finish Burmese base w/a deep rounded bottom & upright fluted rim, base acid-stamped "Thomas Webb & Sons," 5" d., 6" h. (ILLUS.) ............................. **750**

*Webb Burmese Marked Fairy Lamp*

**Burmese shade,** fairy-size, undecorated satin finish shade resting in a Clarke pressed glass lamp cup, fitted in a reversible matching Burmese base w/fluted downturned rim marked "Thomas Webb & Sons - Queen's Burmese Ware - Patented" & "S. Clarke's Patent Trade Mark Fairy," 7 1/4" d., 6" h. (ILLUS.) ...................... **500**

*Undecorated Burmese Fairy Lamp*

**Burmese shade,** plain satin finish shade on a Clarke Burmese lamp cup (ILLUS.)............ **350**

*Glossy Burmese & Creamware Lamp*

**Burmese shade,** pyramid-size, glossy finish plain shade resting in a rose- and foliage-decorated creamware base signed "Taylor, Tunnicliffe & Co. - 1513" on bottom & "S. Clarke's Trade Mark Fairy Pyramid" in blue in the candle recess, 4" d., 4" h. (ILLUS.)................................................. **750**

*Burmese Fairy Lamp-Menu Holder*

**Burmese shade,** pyramid-size, satin finish, in a clear Clarke lamp cup resting on a matching Burmese satin finish base w/crimped piecrust rim & applied unrefired Burmese tooled leaf to support a menu card, 4 1/4" w., 5 1/2" h. (ILLUS.) ....... **500**

*Burmese Shade on Ormolu Base*

**Burmese shade,** pyramid-size, satin finish, in a clear Clarke swirl design lamp cup resting atop the forked ormolu stand cast w/three grape leaves & two sheaves of grain above a round foot, 5 1/4" w., 9 3/4" h. (ILLUS.)........................................... **350**

*Burmese & Creamware Fairy Lamp*

**Burmese shade,** pyramid-size, satin finish, on a glazed creamware base w/gold trim marked "S. Clarke Patent Trade Mark Fairy" & "Fairy Pyramid" in black & "Taylor, Tunnicliffe & Co." on the bottom, 3 1/8" d., 3 3/4" h. (ILLUS.)............................ **350**

*Burmese Fairy Lamp Epergne*

**Burmese shades,** epergne-style, fairy- and pyramid-size, four satin finish undecorated Burmese shades, one fairy-size & three pyramid-size, each in clear Clarke lamp cups & each supported in a brass ring attached to a beveled & scalloped mirrored plateau, 10" d., 7 1/2" h. (ILLUS.) ...................................................... **1,250**

*Rare Burmese Fairy Lamp Epergne*

**Burmese shades,** epergne-style, fairy-size, seven satin finish undecorated shades in clear Clarke lamp cups on matching Burmese bases w/crimped & fluted rims, each lamp base attached to a central frog w/clear crystal arms, on a scalloped & beveled mirrored plateau, 14 1/2" d., 13 1/2" h. (ILLUS.) ...................................... **8,000**

*Burmese Fairy Lamp-Vase Epergne*

**Burmese shades,** epergne-style, fairy-size, three satin finish undecorated shades each in a clear Clarke lamp cup & alternating w/three Burmese bud vases w/fluted flaring rims & unrefired Burmese collars, all supported in rings on a six-arm ormolu frame arising from a miniature Burmese rose bowl raised on an ormolu fitting atop a tubular Burmese center post issuing from a large Burmese flower bowl base w/upturned piecrust rim, on four unrefired Burmese ball feet, 11 1/4" d., 13" h. (ILLUS.) ............................................. **3,000**

*Burmese Epergne of Lamps & Vases*

**Burmese shades,** epergne-style, fairy-size, three undecorated satin finish shades in Clarke Burmese lamp cups, resting in a footed ormolu frame also supporting three Burmese bud vases w/fluted & flared rims & unrefired Burmese collars & berry prunts, a raised center support holds a larger, taller matching decorated Burmese bud vase w/petticoat rim, 7" w., 8 1/4" h. (ILLUS.) ......................................... **2,000**

*Two-Light Burmese Vase Epergne*

**Burmese shades,** epergne-style, pyramid-size, two undecorated satin finish shades in clear Clarke lamp cups resting in a brass stand w/a central post supporting a Burmese posey vase w/crimped & fluted rim, 7" w., 7" h. (ILLUS.) .............................. **1,000**

ed & flared rims, unrefired Burmese collars & berry prunts, raised center support holds larger matching decorated Burmese vase w/petticoat rim, 6 3/4" w., 8" h. (ILLUS.) .................................................. **2,500**

### Wonderful Burmese Epergne-Lamp

**Burmese shades,** epergne-style, three satin finish Burmese fairy-size shades decorated in the ivy design in Clarke clear lamp cups marked "Clarke Patent Trade Mark Fairy," resting in a footed ormolu frame also supporting three matching decorated Burmese bud vases w/fluted & flared rims & unrefired Burmese collars & berry prunts, raised center support holds larger matching decorated Burmese vase w/petticoat rim, the ormolu frame marked "Clarke's Trade Mark Cricklite," 15" w., 11" h. (ILLUS.) .................................. **5,000**

### Two-lamp Burmese Epergne

**Burmese shades,** epergne-style, two satin finish fairy-size shades decorated in the prunus design, in Clarke Burmese lamp cups resting in petticoat-rimmed matching bowls, a matching elevated bud vase w/petticoat rim inserted into a decorated miniature rose bowl on a trumpet-form Burmese base, 13" w., 10 3/4" h. (ILLUS.) ......................................................... **5,500**

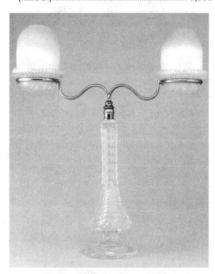

### Burmese & Cut Glass Fairy Lamp

**Burmese shades,** fairy-size, two satin finish plain shades in clear Clarke lamp cups marked "S. Clarke Patent Trade Mark Fairy" on rings of a two-arm ormolu frame marked "Clarke's Trade Mark Cricklite," supported atop an English brilliant cut glass standard & foot, 17 1/2" w., 15" h. (ILLUS.) ............................................... **1,000**

### Decorated Burmese Epergne-Lamp

**Burmese shades,** epergne-style, three satin finish Burmese pyramid-size shades decorated in the prunus design in Clarke clear lamp cups resting in a footed ormolu frame also supporting three matching decorated Burmese bud vases w/flut-

*Burmese Hops-decorated Fairy Lamp*

**Burmese unrefired & decorated shade,** pyramid-size, decorated w/hops in color, in a clear Clarke lamp cup, 3" d., 4" h. (ILLUS.) .......................................................... **500**

*Satin Fairy Lamp on Mirrored Plaque*

**Butterscotch mother-of-pearl satin shade,** fairy-size, Diamond Quilted patt., in a clear Clarke lamp cup resting on a similarly-colored satin bowl shading to opaque w/a crimped top edge & opaque finial on the bottom, in a brass supporting ring attached to an oval mirrored wall plaque, 9" w., 13" h. (ILLUS.) ........................ **800**

*Cameo Shade on Creamware Base*

**Cameo glass shade,** fairy-size, three-color cameo in pink cut to white cut to a frosted yellow ground w/a design of a flowering cherry branch, resting on the ribbed shoulder of a creamware lamp cup marked "S. Clarke's Patent Trade Mark Fairy," in a Tapestry Ware flower bowl base marked by Taylor, Tunnicliffe & Co., 7 1/2" d., 6" h. (ILLUS.) ................................ **2,000**

*Fairy Lamp with Red Cameo Shade*

**Cameo two-color shade,** fairy-size, red satin ground overlaid in white & cut w/a floral design, resting on the horizontal scalloped rim of an opaque white lamp cup w/interior raised ring & embossed swirl design, 4" d., 5 1/4" h. (ILLUS.).......... **1,500**

**Caramel-shaded satin shade,** deep peach color shading to creamy white in a crimp-topped Clarke clear lamp cup resting on a matching squatty bowl w/inward-fluted rim, 4 1/2" d., 5 1/2" h. (ILLUS. top of next page) ....................................................... **500**

*Caramel-colored Satin Fairy Lamp*

*Citron Verre Moiré Nailsea-style Lamp*

**Citron green & white Verre Moiré Nailsea-type shade,** pyramid-size, citron ground w/overall white loopings, in a Clarke Fairy Pyramid lamp cup, set in a matching upright curved bowl w/six outward drawn loops, 4 1/2" d., 5 1/2" h. (ILLUS.) .............................................. **500**

*Citron Nailsea-style Shade & Base*

**Citron Nailsea-style shade,** fairy-size, dark citron ground w/overall broad white loopings, resting on the shoulder of the matching Nailsea-style base w/crimped rim, 4" d., 4" h. (ILLUS.) .................................... **600**

*Nailsea Verre Moiré Citron Fairy Lamp*

**Citron Verre Moiré Nailsea-type shade,** fairy-size, citron ground w/overall white loopings, in a Clarke Patent Trade Mark Fairy lamp cup recessed in a matching bowl base w/upright sides & crimped rim, 5 1/2" d., 4 1/2" h. (ILLUS.) ............................ **750**

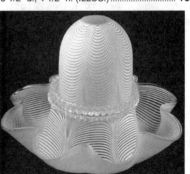

*Citron Nailsea Fairy Lamp*

**Citron & white Nailsea-style shade,** fairy-size, a citron ground w/overall white loopings, in a Clarke lamp cup resting on the center post of a matching dished base w/flaring, ruffled sides, 8 1/4" d., 5 3/4" h. (ILLUS.) ............................................... **500**

*Citron Nailsea Shade & Crimped Base*

**Citron & white Nailsea-style shade,** fairy-size, citron ground w/overall white loopings, in a clear Clarke lamp cup resting on a deep citron base w/inward tightly crimped rim, 6" d., 5 1/4" h. (ILLUS.)............. **500**

*Clear Cricklite & Crystal Epergne*

**Clear Clarke Cricklite shade,** epergne-style, in a brass ring embossed "Clarke Cricklite" in a clear Clarke Cricklite lamp cup w/original hand-stitched silk bead-trimmed shade, raised on a cut crystal standard above two cut crystal bud vases on a brass frame w/a footed base, 9" w., 19" h. (ILLUS.).............................................. **1,500**

*Clarke Fairy Lamps on Silver Column*

**Clear Clarke Cricklite shades,** epergne-style, five shades in clear Clarke lamp cups on the arms of an ormolu frame attached to a tall weighted silver plated classic Corinthian column base, each glass shade w/the original yellowish gold fabric & blue wooden-beaded shade, 17" w., 31" h. (ILLUS.) ................................ **2,000**

*Two-light Clarke Fairy Lamp & Shades*

**Clear Clarke Cricklite shades,** two shades in brass rings marked "Clarke Cricklite" in clear Clarke Cricklite lamp cups on the rings of an ormolu frame raised on a cut crystal standard, each glass shade covered w/the original pink silk Clarke shades, 16" w., 17" h. (ILLUS.) .................. **1,250**

*Clarke Fairy Lamps on Column Base*

**Clear Clarke Cricklite shades,** two shades in clear Clarke lamp cups w/porcelain dishes & Clarke advertising raised on an ormolu two-arm frame attached to a weighted brass classic Corinthian column base, 13 1/2" w., 18" h. (ILLUS.)........... **500**

*Clear Glass & Brass Fairy Lamp*

**Clear plain shade,** fairy-size, in a Clarke spun brass handled lamp cup & porcelain candle cup, lamp holder & candle cup printed & embossed w/Clarke advertising, 4 1/2" w., 3 1/3" h. (ILLUS.) .................... **200**

**Clear ribbed shade,** fairy-size, in a Clarke spun brass handled lamp cup w/porcelain candle cup, holder & candle cup printed & embossed w/Clarke advertising, 4" d., 3 1/2" h., each (ILLUS. of two bottom of page) ................................................. **200**

*Cranberry & Clear Wee Fairy Lamp*

**Cranberry & clear shade,** a wee-size shade w/three rows of applied clear tooled petals, in a Clarke clear swirl design lamp cup embossed "Clarke's Patent Wee Fairy," 2 1/2" d., 3" h. (ILLUS.) ............................................................. **600**

*Two Embossed Shades on Bases*

**Cranberry or green waffle-embossed shade,** pyramid-size, each w/an applied brass ring around the top opening, each fitted into a brass lamp cup w/slotted openwork design & depression for candle, 4 3/4" d., 3 3/4" h., each (ILLUS. of two) ................................................................. **200**

*Cranberry Spangled Shade on Base*

**Cranberry silver-spangled shade,** pyramid-size, threaded on the exterior in green glass, on a signed Taylor, Tunnicliffe & Co. creamware flower bowl base decorated w/polychrome flowers, an integral lamp cup w/ribbed shoulder marked "S. Clarke's Patent Trade Mark Fairy" inside candle depression, 5 7/8" d., 5" h. (ILLUS.) ............................................................. **750**

*Clear Ribbed Glass & Brass Lamps*

*Dark Blue Drapery Fairy Lamp*

**Dark blue cased Drapery patt. shade,** fairy-size, cased in white, in a clear Clarke lamp cup resting on the rim of the matching quatrefoil base w/an opaque foot, 5 1/2" w., 6" h. (ILLUS.) ...................... **1,000**

*Bisque Dog Head Fairy Lamp*

**Figural bisque shade,** model of a brown-painted Pekinese dog head w/brown transparent eyes & a black collar around the neck, 3 1/2" w., 3 7/8" h. (ILLUS.) .......... **350**

*Figural Bisque Castle Fairy Lamp*

**Figural bisque lamp,** modeled as a tall castle w/a red-painted shingled roof, white walls & a green base w/a covered arch gate, 4 3/4" w., 8 1/4" h. (ILLUS.) .................. **500**

*Figural Bisque Cat Wee Fairy Lamp*

**Figural bisque shade,** model of a grey & black-painted wee-size cat head w/green transparent eyes, 1 1/4 x 2 1/4", 2 1/2" h. (ILLUS.) ............................................................. **500**

*Bisque Monkey Figural Fairy Lamp*

**Figural bisque shade,** pyramid-size, molded & hand-colored full-relief figure of a monkey in clothing playing a mandolin while seated on a crescent Man-in-the-Moon w/pierced star openings, impressed fleur-de-lis design on the unpainted back, 3 1/2" w., 3 1/2" h. (ILLUS.) ..... **350**

*Bisque Terrier Head Fairy Lamp*

**Figural bisque shade,** model of a brown Terrier head w/transparent amber eyes & a blue rope around the front of the neck, rear impressed w/a stylized fleur-de-lis design, 4" w., 4 1/4" h. (ILLUS.) ..................... **350**

*Bisque Castle-form Fairy Lamp*

**Figural bisque shade,** two-piece, model of a castle w/an open chimney & windows on an earthtone matching base, marked "Oliver K. Whiting & Co., Regent St. W. 1," 4 3/4" d., 5 3/4" h. (ILLUS.) ..................... **500**

*Castle-form China Fairy Lamp*

**Figural china shade,** a model of a castle w/a painted scene depicting a lady seated in a room, three air vents in the upper walls as windows, the top resting on a matching hillside foot which allows access to the candle cup, 4 1/4" d., 6" h. (ILLUS., two views) ..................................... **1,000**

*Blue Crown-form Fairy Lamp*

**Figural crown glass shade,** pyramid-size, blue ground w/clear overshot coating, commemorating Queen Victoria's Golden Jubilee, in a clear Clarke lamp cup, 3 2/8" d., 4 1/2" h. (ILLUS.) ............................... **350**

*Three Crown-shaped Fairy Lamps*

**Figural crown glass shades,** in cranberry, opaque white & cobalt blue w/overshot exterior trim, each in a clear Clarke lamp cup, commemorating Queen Victoria's Golden Jubilee, 3 5/8" d., 4 3/8" h., each (ILLUS. of three) ............................................ **350**

*Figural Green Owl Head Fairy Lamp*

**Figural frosted green glass shade,** modeled as a two-faced owl head w/red-painted eyes, in a clear Clarke pyramid lamp cup, 4" d., 4 1/2" h. (ILLUS.) ................ **200**

*Royal Worcester Figural Fairy Lamp*

**Figural porcelain fairy lamp,** a Royal Worcester porcelain figural Water Carrier, Model No. 125, trimmed in orange & gold & date coded for 1903, supporting a single pegged clear Clarke lamp cup & stamped "Trade Mark Cricklite," the clear Clarke shade w/a replacement beaded shade, figure 10 1/2" h., overall 19" h. (ILLUS.) ...... **3,500**

*Royal Worcester Figural Fairy Lamp*

**Figural porcelain fairy lamp,** epergne-style, a Royal Worcester porcelain figural of a Grecian Water Carrier trimmed in green & gold, supporting a three-arm ormolu frame w/three rings stamped "Clarke's Patent Cricklite" & each holding a clear Clarke Cricklite shade in a clear Clarke lamp cup, w/replacement bead-trimmed shades, Royal Worcester Model No. 125 base w/date code for 1903 & marked "Trade Mark Cricklite," figural base 16" h., overall 25" h. (ILLUS.) ...... **3,000**

*Royal Worcester Epergne Fairy Lamp*

**Figural porcelain fairy lamp,** epergne-style, a Royal Worcester porcelain figural Water Carrier base, Model No. 125, decorated in green & gold, date coded for 1903 & stamped "Trade Mark Cricklite," supporting seven rings stamped "Clarke's Patent Cricklite" & holding clear Clarke Cricklite shades in clear Clarke lamp cups, each w/replacement beaded shades, figure 22" h., overall 35" h. (ILLUS.) ...... **5,000**

*Royal Worcester Bather Fairy Lamp*

**Figural porcelain fairy lamp,** the figural base by Royal Worcester in the form of the Surprised Bather decorated in pale blue & lilac, Model No. 486, date-marked for 1905 & stamped "Trade Mark Cricklite," supporting a single Clarke Cricklite clear shade in a clear Clarke lamp cup held in a brass ring embossed "Clarke Cricklite," w/a pale mauve replacement bead-trimmed shade, base 11" h., overall 19" h. (ILLUS.) ...... **4,000**

*Porcelain Castle-form Fairy Lamp*

**Figural porcelain shade,** model of a castle trimmed in gold w/open arched windows & doors, on a base w/majolica-like applied yellow flowers, green leaves & gold trim, signed w/maker's mark of a curved line w/four leaves & a tassel, 5 1/4 x 5 3/4", 4" h. (ILLUS.) .......................... **350**

*Porcelain Lion Head Fairy Lamp*

**Figural porcelain shade,** model of a lion head, translucent & painted in shades of brown & tan, number "4" incised in base, 4 5/8" w., 3 1/2" h. (ILLUS.) ............................ **250**

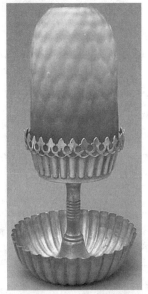

*Clear to Cranberry Shade on a Base*

**Frosted clear shading to cranberry shade,** fairy-size, embossed w/a honeycomb design, resting in a punched brass cup atop a center column of pressed brass attached to an upturned fluted base, base marked "Samuel Clarke Trade Mark Fairy - US Pat. Appl'd For," 4 1/4" d., 8 1/2" h. (ILLUS.) ............................ **600**

*Frosted Yellow, Clear & White Lamp*

**Frosted yellow, clear & white Cleveland Swirl patt. shade,** fairy-size, resting in a matching lamp cup w/a crimped rim & in a matching saucer base w/upturned flaring & crimped rim acid-marked "Clarke Patent Fairy," 6 1/2" d., 6 1/4" h. (ILLUS.) ..... **750**

*Gold Satin Swirl Pattern Fairy Lamp*

**Gold mother-of-pearl satin shade,** fairy-size, Swirl patt., cased in creamy white w/an inwardly crimped top rim, in a clear Clarke Trade Mark Fairy lamp cup, 4" d., 4 1/3" h. (ILLUS.) ............................................. **250**

*Gold Mother-of-Pearl Satin Fairy Lamp*

**Gold mother-of-pearl satin shade,** pyramid-size, Diamond Quilted patt., cased in white, in a clear Clarke Fairy Pyramid lamp cup, 2 3/4" d., 3 3/4" h. (ILLUS.).......... **200**

*Lighthouse-shaped Fairy Lamp*

**Gold shading to white figural shade,** model of a lighthouse w/a brass finger ring at top opening, cased in white, 3 1/2" d., 8 1/4" h. (ILLUS.) ............................ **250**

*Green Satin Swirl Pattern Fairy Lamp*

**Green satin embossed Swirl patt. shade,** pyramid-size, in a clear Clarke Fairy Pyramid lamp cup, 3" d., 3 1/2" h. (ILLUS.)........ **150**

*Green Spangled Fairy Lamp*

**Green silver-spangled & threaded shade,** pyramid-size, molded in a swirled rib design & threaded around the sides in green, in a clear Clarke Fairy Pyramid lamp cup, 3" d., 3 1/2" h. (ILLUS.) ................ **250**

*Hexagonal Honeycomb Fairy Lamps*

**Hexagonal honeycomb colored shades,** pyramid-size, each w/the embossed honeycomb design & in various colors overshot w/clear, in a clear Clarke lamp cup, includes red, citron & white, each (ILLUS. of group)............................................................ **150**

*Light Blue Iridized Petal-form Lamp*

**Light blue iridized floral-shaped shade,** fairy-size, blue ground w/three rows of applied clear frosted & iridized petals w/a yellowish color, on a matching waisted & bulbous base shading from light blue to clear w/four applied frosted & iridized petal-form feet, 5" d., 7" h. (ILLUS.) ............. **350**

*Frosted Lime Green Fairy Lamp*

**Lime green frosted shade,** pyramid-size, an embossed leaf & diamond design, on a matching ribbed lamp cup sitting atop a frosted green shading to clear slender pedestal w/six applied leaves forming the feet, 2 3/4" d., 9 5/8" h. (ILLUS.) .................. **350**

**Peach Blow shade,** fairy-size, pink shading to near white cased in creamy white, in a clear Clarke lamp cup resting on an in-ward-turned & crimped matching bowl, 4 1/4" d., 5 1/2" h. (ILLUS.) ........................... **750**

*Pairpoint Puffy Pansy Fairy Lamp*

**Pairpoint "Puffy" Pansy shade,** tapering form molded w/blossoms & reverse-painted w/naturalistic colors, raised on a turned walnut standard, 4 1/4" d., 7 5/8" h. (ILLUS.) ......................................... **1,500**

*Pink-cased Flower-form Fairy Lamp*

**Pink cased in clear flower-form shade,** pyramid-size, scalloped top rim & three rows of applied hand-tooled clear petals, on a pressed & stamped pewter-like met-al stand, 3 3/4" d., 6" h. (ILLUS.) .................. **350**

*Pink Cased & Ribbed Fairy Lamp*

**Pink cased & ribbed shade,** fairy-size, cased in white, in a clear Clarke lamp cup resting on the center post of a matching pink cased base w/a fluted rim, shade acid-marked "Rd 50725" & "Trade Mark Fairy," 6 2/3" d., 4 3/4" h. (ILLUS.)................. **500**

*Peach Blow Fairy Lamp*

*Pink Reverse Drape Fairy Lamp*

**Pink cased satin Reverse Drape patt. shade,** fairy-size, cased in white, embossed drape design, in a clear Clarke lamp cup, 4" d., 4 1/2" h. (ILLUS.) ............... **250**

*Pink Cross-decorated Fairy Lamp*

**Pink mica-textured shade,** fairy-size, decorated w/four crosses each in a different color of jewels, a jeweled ring near top, in a low matching saucer base w/integral candleholder, 3 3/4" d., 4" h. (ILLUS.).......... **200**

*Pink Diamond Quilted Satin Lamp*

**Pink mother-of-pearl satin shade,** pyramid-size, Diamond Quilted patt., cased in white, in a clear Clarke Fairy Pyramid lamp cup, 2 3/4" d., 3 2/3" h. (ILLUS.).......... **200**

*Pink Satin & Flower Bowl Fairy Lamp*

**Pink mother-of-pearl satin shade,** pyramid-size, Diamond Quilted patt., in a clear Clarke Patent Trade Mark flower bowl base w/integral two-shoulder lamp cup, 6" d., 3 5/8" h. (ILLUS.)........................... **250**

*Pink Opalescent Fairy Lamp*

**Pink opalescent shade,** pyramid-size, a tapering light pink blossom form w/opalescent upper half, w/six upturned applied petals, on a matching base w/six downturned applied petals & an integral candle cup, 3 1/2" d., 3 3/4" h. (ILLUS.).............. **350**

*Pink & Red Swirl Fairy Lamp*

**Pink & red swirl shade,** pyramid-size, pink ground w/red peppermint swirls & embossed vertical ribbing, in a matching lamp cup, 2 3/4" d., 3 1/2" h. (ILLUS.).......... **250**

*Pink Satin Drape Design Fairy Lamp*

**Pink satin cased embossed shade,** fairy-size, deeply embossed reverse drape design, cased in white, resting in a ribbed pink lamp cup fitted onto the central column of a matching pink satin cased bowl w/fluted rim, 6 1/2" d., 7 1/2" h. (ILLUS.)...... **850**

*Pink Satin Jeweled Fairy Lamp*

**Pink satin glass shade,** cased in white, ovoid form w/the sides mounted w/four colored glass jewels, in a matching low saucer base w/flared crimped rim, 7" d., 5 1/4" h. (ILLUS.) ............................................. **250**

*Pink Satin Petal-embossed Lamp*

**Pink satin petal-embossed shade,** pyramid-size, on a ribbed pink Clarke lamp cup, 3" d., 3 1/2" h. (ILLUS.) .......................... **200**

*Pink Satin & Green Glass Fairy Lamp*

**Pink satin shade,** pyramid-size, vertically ribbed, resting in a matching lamp cup which rests in a clear green goblet-form bowl attached to a clear pink leaf-shaped base w/one end forming a handle, on five tooled leaf feet, 5 1/4" l., 7 1/2" h. (ILLUS.)..... **300**

*Pink Satin Swirl Fairy Lamp*

**Pink satin swirl-embossed shade,** pyramid-size, in a clear Clarke lamp cup, 3" d., 3 1/2" h. (ILLUS.).................................. **150**

*Pink Shaded Chimney-style Lamp*

**Pink shading to white frosted shade,** chimney-style, ovoid form w/widely rolled & ruffled top opening & embossed w/opposing diagonal ribs, rests on a matching deeply fluted & ruffled low base, 7 1/2" d., 5 3/4" h. (ILLUS.) ............................ **500**

*Swirled Pink & White Spatter Lamp*

**Pink & white spatter Reverse Swirl patt. shade,** fairy-size, stripes of white & pink in a matching base w/a row of applied clear icicles around the lamp cup rim & another row on the bottom forming feet, 3 1/4" d., 4" h. (ILLUS.) .................................... **250**

*Tall Pink & White Spatter Fairy Lamp*

**Pink & white spatter shade,** pyramid-size, shade cased in clear & w/an embossed petal design, in a matching ribbed lamp cup resting in a matching pedestal base w/a downturned row of six applied clear leaves at the top & six applied leaves

forming the feet, 4 1/2" d., 8 1/2" h. (ILLUS.) ............................................................ **300**

*Pink & White Fairy Lamps & Vases*

**Pink & white striped shades,** epergne-style, three alternating opaque pink & white striped fairy-size shades in the Cleveland patt. embossed w/ribs, each dome acid-marked "Rd 50725 - Trade Mark - Fairy," w/Clarke Trade Mark Fairy straight-sided lamp cups supported in brass cup rings on an ormolu frame w/smaller rings for three matching bud vases w/horizontal piecrust rims, frosted glass retaining rings & pontil knobs, on a matching ball-shaped center bowl w/up-turned ruffled rim, 10" d., 7 3/4" h. (ILLUS.) ........................................................ **3,500**

*Pink & White Swirl Ribbed Fairy Lamp*

**Pink & white swirl-embossed shade,** pyramid-size, cased in white, in a matching lamp cup & raised on the eight-point star rim base w/four applied clear tooled feet, 4" d., 5 2/3" h. (ILLUS.) .................................... **350**

*Spatter Glass Shades on Clear Bases*

**Pink, yellow & white spatter glass shade,**
fairy-size, embossed w/vertical ribbing &
cased in white, on a clear Clarke lamp
cup resting in the bowl of a clear glass
standard by Thomas Webb & Sons which
consists of three clear reeded free-form
arms rising from a clear foot, 5" d., 11" h.,
each (ILLUS. of two) ........................................ **400**

*Lithophane Paneled Fairy Lamp*

**Porcelain lithophane shade,** domed
shade w/two lithophane panels known as
"Little Miss Muffet," one panel depicting a
girl scared by a frog in her dish, the other
showing a child in the woods w/a rabbit,
four notched air vents on the bottom rim,
in a low matching saucer base w/integral
candleholder, 4" d., 4 1/4" h. (ILLUS.)........... **600**

*Porcelain Lithophane Fairy Lamp*

**Porcelain lithophane shade,** the shade
molded w/grapevines & grapes on all
sides & fitted w/a removable lithophane
panel depicting a female figure, w/a porcelain candle cup, 4 x 5 1/8", 6 1/4" h.
(ILLUS.)........................................................ **1,000**

*Rainbow Mother-of-Pearl Satin Lamp*

**Rainbow mother-of-pearl satin shade,**
fairy-size, Diamond Quilted patt., cased
in white & w/a crimped upper rim, resting
on a clear Clarke lamp cup atop the star-
form center post of the matching shallow
base w/a flaring crimped rim, 7 3/4" d.,
7 1/2" h. (ILLUS.)......................................... **5,000**

*Red Satin Ribbon Shade on Base*

**Red satin mother-of-pearl shade,** fairy-size, red cased in white w/a Ribbon patt., crimped rim & scalloped & flared base rim, resting in a tricorner green-striped pond lily base w/recessed center, 5 1/2" w., 4 3/4" h. (ILLUS.)............................. **750**

*Red & White 'Cracked Ice' Fairy Lamp*

**Red & white 'cracked ice' shade,** fairy-size, a red ground w/an overall mottled white casing, in a matching smooth-shouldered lamp cup w/applied tooled clear feet, 6" d., 5 1/4" h. (ILLUS.) ................. **350**

*Red Nailsea-style Fairy Lamp*

**Red & white Nailsea-style shade,** fairy-size, deep red ground w/overall white loopings in a clear Clarke lamp cup rest-ing on the center post of a deep red bowl base lined in white & w/a flaring ruffled rim, 9 1/2" d., 5 1/4" h. (ILLUS.) .................... **650**

*Deep Red Nailsea-style Fairy Lamp*

**Red & white Nailsea-style shade,** fairy-size, deep red w/overall white loopings, in a clear Clarke lamp cup resting on the center post of a matching ruffled & flared cased reddish pink bowl base, 8 1/4" d., 5 3/4" h. (ILLUS.)............................. **500**

*Red Nailsea-style Shade & Base*

**Red & white Nailsea-style shade,** fairy-size, red ground w/delicate white loop-ings, in a clear Clarke lamp cup resting on the top edge of a ruffled & crimped tri-corner matching base, 7" w., 6 1/2" h. (ILLUS.)............................................. **750**

*Hanging Nailsea-style Fairy Lamp*

**Red & white Nailsea-style shade,** hang-ing-type, the shade in red w/overall white loopings, in a clear Clarke lamp cup rest-ing inside the rim of a matching hanging base w/a ribbon petticoat rim, bottom ball & clear frosted prunt, suspended on three chains, lamp itself 7 1/2" d., 7 1/2" h. (ILLUS.)............................................. **850**

**Red & white Nailsea-style shades,** fairy-size, red ground w/delicate overall white loopings, each in clear Clarke lamp cups on rings of a two-arm ormolu frame marked "Clarke's Trade Mark Cricklite" attached atop a blown crystal standard w/a brass connector ring & flared glass foot, 14" w., 18 1/2" h. (ILLUS. top of next page)......................................... **750**

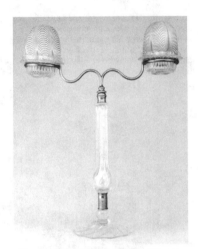

*Two-arm Lamp with Nailsea Shades*

**Red & white spatter glass shade,** pyramid-size, red & white cased spatter shade w/embossed vertical ribbing, in a matching lamp cup resting in a stamped & molded brass stand w/two gargoyle handles, 2 3/4" w., 4 1/2" h. (ILLUS.) ............ **350**

*Finely Looped Nailsea-type Fairy Lamp*

**Red & white Verre Moiré Nailsea-type shade,** fairy-size, a red ground w/fine overall white loopings, in a clear ribbed Clarke Patent Fairy lamp cup, 4" d., 4 1/2" h. (ILLUS.) ........................................... **250**

*Wee Fairy Red Nailsea Lamp*

**Red & white Nailsea-type shade,** wee-size, the red shade w/bold white overall loopings, in a clear Swirl & Diamond Point clear cup marked "Clarke's Patent Wee Fairy," 2" d., 3" h. (ILLUS.) .................... **900**

*Red & White Nailsea Fairy Lamp*

**Red & white Verre Moiré Nailsea-type shade,** pyramid-size, red ground w/overall white loopings, in a clear Clarke Fairy Pyramid lamp cup, 3" d., 3 1/2" h. (ILLUS.) ........................................................ **200**

*Spatter Glass & Brass Fairy Lamp*

*Reddish Pink Pyramid Fairy Lamp*

**Reddish pink satin shade,** pyramid-size, shade w/scalloped bottom rim & crimped top opening, in a clear diamond design lamp cup marked "Eden Light," 2 3/4" d., 4 3/4" h. (ILLUS.) ............................................ **150**

*Flower-decorated Rose Fairy Lamp*

**Rose amethyst decorated shade,** pyramid-size, h.p. w/large white & blue blossoms w/yellow centers & shaded green leaves, in a clear Clarke Fairy Pyramid lamp cup, 2 3/4" d., 3 1/4" h. (ILLUS.) .......... **150**

*Rose Red Berry-form Fairy Lamp*

**Rose red berry-form shade,** pyramid-size, bumpy surface overshot in clear, in clear Clarke Fairy Pyramid lamp cup, 2 3/4" d., 3 3/4" h. (ILLUS.) ............................................ **150**

*Three Rose Red Shaded Fairy Lamps*

**Rose red shaded to creamy white shade,** fairy-size, enamel-decorated in green in

the Wild Rose patt., on a clear Clarke lamp cup, 4" d., 5" h., each (ILLUS. back left & right) ................................................. **250-300**

**Rose red shaded to creamy white shade,** pyramid-size, enamel-decorated in green in the Wild Rose patt., on a clear Clarke lamp cup, 3" d., 3 1/2" h. (ILLUS. front with two matching fairy-size lamps) ....... **200-300**

*Ruby Opalescent Striped Fairy Lamp*

**Ruby opalescent striped shade,** cone-shaped w/crimped & flared top, resting in a matching low base w/flaring crimped rim, 6" d., 4 3/4" h. (ILLUS.) ............................ **250**

*Ruby Red Diamond Quilt Fairy Lamp*

**Ruby red Diamond Quilted shade,** fairy-size, on a clear Clarke lamp cup (ILLUS.) ..... **150**

*Ruby Red Swirl Fairy Lamp*

**Ruby red embossed Swirl shade,** pyramid-size, in a clear Clarke Fairy lamp cup, 3" d., 3 5/8" h. (ILLUS.) ............................ **150**

*Flame-shaped Ruby Red Fairy Lamp*

**Ruby red flame-molded shade,** pyramid-size, on a clear Clarke Fairy Pyramid lamp cup, 2 3/4" d., 3 3/4" h. (ILLUS.)........... **150**

*Ruby Red & Bisque Fairy Lamps*

**Rudy red Diamond Quilted shades,** pyramid-size, each resting on a clear pressed glass lamp ring atop tall footed standard behind figural bisque cherubs holding garlands of flowers, bases marked "DRGM registered Germany," each 4" w., 10 1/2" h., pr. (ILLUS.) ......................... **350**

*Silver-spangled Blue-threaded Lamp*

**Silver-spangled blue-threaded shade,** pyramid-size, silver spangled ground w/random blue threading & a molded swirl design, in a clear Clarke Fairy Pyramid lamp cup, 3" d., 3 1/2" h. (ILLUS.)......... **250**

*Green Threaded Spangled Fairy Lamp*

**Spangled glass shade,** pyramid-size, green w/silver mica spangles & threaded around the sides in green glass, resting in a clear Clarke lamp cup, 3" d., 3 1/2" h. (ILLUS.)............................................................. **250**

*Red & Yellow Spatter Fairy Lamp*

**Spatter glass shade,** fairy-size, mottled brown & white w/white casing & cased on the exterior w/a clear reverse swirl design, in a matching smooth-shouldered lamp cup, 3 3/4" d., 4 1/2" h. (ILLUS.)........... **300**

*Spatter Reverse Swirl Fairy Lamp*

**Spatter glass shade,** fairy-size, mottled brown, yellow & pink w/embossed reverse swirl design cased in white, resting in a matching lamp cup, 3 3/4" d., 4 1/2" h. (ILLUS.) ............................................. **300**

*Red & White Spatter Fairy Lamp*

**Spatter shade,** fairy-size, deep pinkish red ground w/overall fine white spattering, vertical ribbing, in a clear ribbed Clarke Patent Fairy lamp cup, 4" d., 4 1/2" h. (ILLUS.) .......... **250**

*Tan Satin Decorated Fairy Lamp*

**Tan satin decorated shade,** fairy-size, light tan enameled in white w/flowers, buds & leaves, the top opening outlined w/three enameled rings, on a smooth-shouldered base lightly flashed in amethyst w/gold iridescence, 4 1/2" h. (ILLUS.) ......................... **250**

*Teal Diamond Point & Swirl Lamp*

**Teal blue Diamond Point & Plain Swirl shade,** wee-size, in a matching ribbed clear Clarke lamp cup, 2 1/4" d., 3 1/8" h. (ILLUS.) ............................................................. **400**

*Chimney-style Ruffled Fairy Lamp*

**Transparent yellow w/pink rim shade,** open-topped chimney-style, a tapering six-sided shape w/a mold-blown diamond optic design, ruffled rim on shade & matching base, 6" d., 6 1/2" h. (ILLUS.) ..... **350**

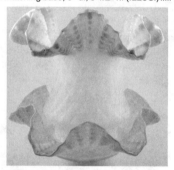

*Shaded Turquoise Blue Fairy Lamp*

**Turquoise blue shading to frosted clear shade,** chimney-style, the shade w/an embossed diamond quilted design shades from a deeply ruffled & crimped rim to frosted sides, in a matching saucer base w/matching fluted rim, 6 1/2" d., 5 1/2" h. (ILLUS.) ............................................. **350**

*Blue & White Nailsea-style Lamp*

**White & blue Nailsea-style shade,** fairy-size, white ground w/delicate overall royal blue loopings, on a clear Clarke lamp cup marked "U.S. Patent Nov 9, 1886 - #352296 - S. Clarke Patent Trade Mark

Fairy," cup resting on the raised column of a reversible glossy white base w/upright petticoat rim, 7" d., 5 1/2" h. (ILLUS.) .............. **750**

*Christmas Tree-decorated Lamp*

**White decorated shade,** fairy-size, decorated w/two Christmas trees trimmed w/transparent jeweled ornaments, resting on a Clarke glazed creamware base w/gold trim, base marked "Taylor, Tunnicliffe & Co.," 4 1/4" d., 5" h. (ILLUS.) ............. **350**

*Opaque Nailsea-style Fairy Lamp*

**White opaque & frosted clear Nailsea-style shade,** fairy-size, frosted clear w/overall white loopings, in a clear Clarke lamp cup resting on the rim of the center post of the matching dished base w/an upturned ruffled rim, 9 1/4" d., 6" h. (ILLUS.) ............................................................ **750**

*White Bristol Glass Decorated Lamp*

**White satin Bristol glass shade,** fairy-size, decorated w/flowers & leaves, broad decorative ring of brown & gilt tortoiseshell design around the top & on the rim of the matching lamp cup, 3 1/2" d., 4 1/2" h. (ILLUS.) ............................................. **350**

*White Satin Cased Fairy Lamp*

**White satin cased in butterscotch shade,** an ovoid form tapering to a flared & fluted top opening, sits on the shoulder of a matching cased base w/a downturned piecrust rim, 5" d., 5 1/2" h. (ILLUS.) ............. **350**

*Yellow Appliqued Glass Fairy Lamp*

**Yellow appliqued shade,** fairy-size, the yellow ground decorated w/five rows of clear tooled applied leaves, resting on the ribbed inner shoulder of the integral lamp cup of the pressed clear Clarke base in the diamond & star design, 7" d., 5" h. (ILLUS.) .................................................. **500**

*Yellow Cased Petal-embossed Lamp*

**Yellow cased in clear shade,** pyramid-size, w/an overall molded petal design, on a clear Clarke lamp cup, 3" d., 3 1/2" h. (ILLUS.) ............................................. **150**

*Bird-decorated Yellow Satin Lamp*

**Yellow cased in satin shade,** pyramid-sized, enamel-decorated w/a large colorful English robin in flight among colorful foliage, in a clear pressed Clarke lamp cup, 3" d., 3 1/2" h. (ILLUS.) .......................... **300**

*Yellow Satin & Lace Design Lamp*

**Yellow cased in white satin shade,** fairy-size, decorated w/a delicate lacy design, on a pegged clear Clarke lamp cup fitted to a short square brass candlestick, 4 1/4" w., 8" h. (ILLUS.) .................................. **300**

**Yellow cased in white satin shade,** fairy-size, enamel-decorated w/an English robin & colorful foliage, in a clear frosted

*Decorated Yellow Satin Fairy Lamp*

Clarke lamp cup resting on the rim of a matching quatrafoil base marked "S. Clarke Pat. Trademark Fairy," w/an applied frosted foot, 5 1/4" w., 6" h. (ILLUS.) ............................................................. **700**

*Yellow Satin Fairy Lamp Epergne*

**Yellow satin shade,** epergne-style, fairy-size, a single cased satin shade in a clear Clarke fairy lamp cup resting on the up-right ribbon rim of a matching yellow satin base w/four frosted, applied feet, the base straddles an ormolu frame which attaches to a scalloped, beveled & notched mirror plateau & also supports six rings each holding a matching bulbous satin bud vase w/a flared, scalloped rim & applied opaque berry prunts, 10 1/4" w., 6 3/4" h. (ILLUS.) ......................................................... **2,000**

*Yellow Satin Air-Trap Pattern Lamp*

**Yellow satin shade,** fairy-size, produced w/an air-trapped ribbon swirl design, resting on the smooth shoulder of a matching lamp cup, 3" d., 5" h. (ILLUS.)....... **250**

*Yellow Satin Thorn-design Shade*

**Yellow satin w/pulled thorn design shade,** pyramid-size, cased in white, ruffled top rim & a scalloped lower rim, in a Clarke Fairy Pyramid lamp cup, 2 3/4" d., 3 3/4" h. (ILLUS.) ............................................ **200**

*Yellow, White & Frosted Swirl Shade*

**Yellow, white & frosted clear Cleveland Swirl patt. shade,** fairy-size, in a Clarke Trade Mark Cricklite lamp cup, in a matching deep flaring basket base w/rolled & ruffled rim & four pulled-up corners, 7 3/4" w., 4 3/4" h. (ILLUS.).................. **500**

*Yellowish Vaseline Quilted Fairy Lamp*

**Yellowish vaseline Diamond Quilted shade,** pyramid-size, the shade trimmed in yellow opalescence, rests on the smooth shoulder of a matching lamp cup w/two applied rows of opposing tooled petals at the rim, cup marked "Rd 176239," 3 7/8" d., 3 2/3" h. (ILLUS.) ........... **250**

*Yellowish Vaseline Appliqued Lamp*

**Yellowish vaseline shade,** fairy-size, applied w/three tooled matching clear applied leaves, on a matching base w/seven upturned tooled leaves & an integral candle cup, 3 1/2" d., 3" h. (ILLUS.) ............. **300**

# Miniature Lamps

*Our listings are generally arranged numerically according to the numbers assigned to the various miniature lamps pictured in Frank R. & Ruth E. Smith's book* Miniature Lamps, *now referred to as* Smith's Book I, *and Ruth Smith's sequel,* Miniature Lamps II. *All references are to* Smith's Book I *unless otherwise noted. Lamps are glass unless otherwise noted.*

**Banquet lamp,** white opaque font, stem & ball shade, all w/blue transfer & white enamel floral decoration, brass connector, square brass foot, overall 17" h. (missing burner, connector rod replaced)... **$330**

**Milk glass,** base & ball-shaped shade w/embossed scroll & floral design, maroon flowers w/yellow centers, leaves & scrolls in dark green, light green band at bottom of shade & below collar of base, overall 7 7/8" h. (normal roughness on bottom of shade)............................................... **523**

**Clear,** "Little Beauty" finger-type, applied handle, embossed name on side, clear glass chimney, Nutmeg burner, 6 1/4" h., No. 16 (slight chip on chimney base) ............. **95**

**Clear,** "Nutmeg" lamp, embossed "Nutmeg" on font, clear chimney, narrow brass band forms removable handle, Nutmeg burner, 2 3/4" h., No. 29 ..................... **77**

**Cobalt blue,** "Nutmeg" lamp, embossed "Nutmeg" on font, clear chimney, narrow brass band forms removable handle, Nutmeg burner, 2 3/4" h., No. 29 .................... **61**

**Green,** "Nutmeg" lamp, embossed "Nutmeg" on font, clear chimney, narrow brass band forms removable handle, Nutmeg burner, 2 3/4" h., No. 29 .................. **228**

**Cranberry,** glow lamp, embossed ribs, flowers & vines, glass wick holder, 5" h., Book II, No. 29 ............................................... **165**

**Amethyst,** "Little Buttercup" finger-type, applied handle, embossed name on side, clear chimney, Hornet burner, 6 7/8" h., No. 36 ................................................................... **97**

**Blue,** "Little Buttercup" finger-type, applied handle, embossed name on side, clear chimney, Hornet burner, 6 7/8" h., No. 36 ..... **111**

**Clear,** "Little Buttercup" finger-type, applied handle, embossed name on side, clear chimney, Hornet burner, 6 7/8" h., No. 36 ....... **52**

**Milk glass,** short cylindrical waisted font, painted floral decoration, Nutmeg burner, 3" h., No. 39 ...... **38**

**Clear,** "Little Jewel," name embossed on side of font, paneled foot & side finger loop handle, w/burner, 3 1/8" h., No. 44 ......... **80**

**Blue,** paneled w/mold-blown font & pressed base & handle, finger hold closed, Nutmeg burner, 3 1/2" h., No. 47 ......... **127**

**Amber,** "Log Cabin" or "School house" lamp, applied handle, Hornet burner, 3 3/4" h., No. 50 ...... **187**

**Amber,** Shoe lamp, applied handle pressed into place, Hornet burner, 3 1/2" h., No. 51 ...... **899**

**Amber,** ribbed low cylindrical font w/an attached cylindrical basketweave pattern match holder w/ring handle to the side, ribbed conical matching shade, clear chimney, Hornet burner, 8" h., No. 52 ......... **252**

**Embossed blue milk glass,** w/brass hanger & nickel reflector, Nutmeg burner, 3" h. to top of collar, No. 56 ...... **100**

*Beaded Heart & Cosmos Lamps*

**Green,** Beaded Heart patt., hearts around font raised on pedestal w/round domed foot, collar w/split & piece missing, no chimney or shade, 5" h., No. 109 (ILLUS. left) ...... **850**

**Clear,** Beaded Heart patt., Acorn burner, 5 1/2" h., No. 109 ...... **80**

**Green,** Beaded Heart patt., Acorn burner, 5 1/2" h., No. 109 ...... **206**

**Amber,** Daisy with Large Bull's-eye patt., octagonal stem, no chimney or shade, 4 3/4" h., No. 112 (ILLUS. top next column) ...... **160**

**Amber,** Fish-scale patt., Nutmeg burner, 5" h., No. 116 ...... **50**

**Blue,** Fish-scale patt., Nutmeg burner, 5" h., No. 116 ...... **202**

**Clear,** Fish-scale patt., Nutmeg burner, 5" h., No. 116 ...... **87**

**Green,** Fish-scale patt., Nutmeg burner, 5" h., No. 116 ...... **80**

**Vaseline,** Fish-scale patt., Nutmeg burner, 5" h., No. 116 ...... **175**

**Clear,** "waffle" bulbous tapering font, raised on a slender brass pedestal base w/a flaring foot, cranberry chimney, Acorn burner, 8 1/4" h., No. 117 ...... **90**

*Amber Daisy with Bull's-eye Lamp*

**Milk glass,** font & shade w/ribbed pattern, pewter pedestal base, Acorn burner, 7 3/4" h., No. 128 (heavy paint on base) ...... **53**

**Clear,** pressed bell-shaped base, Acorn burner, clear glass chimney, original brass burner, matching shade, Westmoreland patt., ca. 1889, Gillinder & Sons, 7 1/2" h., No. 144 ...... **325**

**Blue,** font w/raised diamonds, brass saucer base, 4 3/8" h., Book II, No. 156 ...... **77**

**Milk glass painted blue,** embossed scrolling & flowers gilded, Hornet burner, 8 3/4" h., No. 157 ...... **143**

**Clear,** Greek Key patt., round font w/band of design raised on round pedestal base, w/matching chimney, 8 1/4" h., No.166 ...... **190**

**Milk glass,** finger lamp, short waisted cylindrical form w/applied handle, orange band around top w/black & orange rings & an orange ring at lower edge, band of h.p. flowers around middle, 3" h., Book II, No. 166 ...... **180**

**Clear,** Greek Key patt., paneled rounded font w/band of design on a paneled stem & square foot w/further design, w/insert collar, no chimney, 3 1/2" h., No. 167 ...... **110**

**Clear,** stem lamp w/swirl pattern, brass insert in glass collar, top of collar marked "Patented Sep. 19 & Nov. 14, 1911," Acorn burner, 4 7/8" to top of font, 5 1/8" to top of collar, Book II, No. 179 ...... **41**

**Milk glass,** plain & embossed beaded panels on base & globe-chimney, Hornet burner, 8 1/2" h., No. 184 ...... **72**

**Milk glass,** w/wide embossed ribs, painted blue shading to white, Nutmeg burner, 7" h., No. 189 ...... **89**

**Milk glass,** base & ball-shaped shade w/embossed flowers & beading, Apple Blossom patt., Nutmeg burner, 7" h., No. 193 (chips on bottom of shade hidden by burner gallery, flake on top of shade) ...... **88**

**Milk glass,** base & umbrella shade w/embossed flowers & beading, Apple Blossom patt., Nutmeg burner, 7 1/4" h., No. 194 (chip on rim at base of shade) ................ **99**

**Milk glass,** paneled bulbous base & domical shade "Sunflower" lamp, multicolored decorations, Nutmeg burner, 8" h., No. 206 ................ **352**

**Milk glass,** w/embossed Maltese Cross, blue paint, Hornet burner, Eagle Glass & Mfg. Co., Wellsburg, W.Va., ca. 1894, 9 1/2" h., No. 214 ................ **60**

**Blue opaque,** w/swirl-ribbed band on base & globe-chimney, Hornet burner, 7 3/4" h., No. 215 ................ **400**

*Painted "Nellie Bly" Miniature Lamp*

**Milk glass,** called the "Nellie Bly" lamp, milk glass base & clear shade w/upper part of shade painted white to resemble frosting, upper part of both base & shade w/orange ground, floral sprays in white, yellow & green, Hornet burner, 9" h., No. 219 (ILLUS.) ................ **53**

**Milk glass,** base & ball-shaped shade embossed w/fleur-de-lis & other designs, Acorn burner, clear glass chimney, 7" h., No. 228 (normal roughness on top & bottom edges of shade) ................ **66**

**Milk glass,** Acanthus patt., ball shade & base w/embossed swirled ground & upright leaves painted green, chip on rim of shade & chips & roughness on bottom edge of shade, 8 1/2" h., No. 230 (ILLUS. top of next column) ................ **100**

*Acanthus Pattern Miniature Lamp*

**Milk glass,** bell-shaped base w/globe-chimney shade w/embossed scroll leaf design, trimmed in blue w/blue flowers, Nutmeg burner, 8 3/4" h., No. 240 ................ **272**

**Milk glass,** square base w/embossed overlapping leaves design & square ribbed shade w/draped swag border highlighted in gold, clear glass chimney, Nutmeg burner, 8" h., No. 255 ................ **220**

*Amethyst Opalescent Miniature Lamp*

**Amethyst opalescent,** embossed overlapping leaves pattern w/gold trim, Hornet burner, 9" h., No. 257 (ILLUS.) ................ **231**

**Cobalt blue,** embossed overlapping leaves pattern w/gold trim, Hornet burner, 9" h., No. 257 ................ **350**

**Milk glass,** w/embossed lion's heads in gilt & globe-chimney shade w/h.p. florals, clear chimney, Nutmeg burner, 8 1/2" h., No. 268 ................ **249**

**Milk glass,** w/embossed beads & scrolling, fired-on painted flowers in red & green & green beads, Nutmeg burner, 8 1/4" h., No. 283 ................ **400**

**Cased pink,** Cosmos patt., domed shade w/embossed flowers & matching rounded base, no color trim, burner cover & shade spider missing, normal mold roughness, overall 6 1/4" h., No. 286 (ILLUS. right on previous page with Beaded Heart lamp) ................ **160**

**Cased pink,** Cosmos patt., base & umbrella shade w/pink-stained band & colored florals, Nutmeg burner, 7" h., No. 286 (replaced burner top & spider, non-disfiguring flat chip on outside edge of shade crown)................................................................ **358**

**Cased yellow,** Cosmos patt., base & umbrella shade w/pink-stained band & colored florals, Nutmeg burner, 7 1/2" h., No. 286 ............................................................. **417**

*Sylvan Pattern Miniature Lamp*

**Milk glass,** Sylvan patt., ribbed shade & paneled, rounded font on foot, undecorated, Westmoreland Specialty Company, 8 1/4" h., No. 296 (ILLUS.) ......................... **60**

**Milk glass,** ribbed panel pattern, green decoration, Nutmeg burner, 8" h., No. 311 ......... **253**

**Milk glass,** orange ground fading to yellow, blue flowers & green leaves in fired-on paint, Nutmeg burner, 8 3/4" h., No. 314 ...... **284**

*Floral-decorated Milk Glass Lamp*

**Milk glass,** painted blue around top of shade & base, blue & green floral decorations, Nutmeg burner, 8 1/4" h., No. 315 (ILLUS.)..................................... **189**

**Cased pink,** melon-ribbed, glossy finish, Nutmeg burner, 7" h., No. 390...................... **407**

**Yellow satin,** footed bulbous shouldered base & globe-chimney shade w/embossed pansy pattern, Nutmeg burner, 8 3/4" h., No. 398............................ **670**

**Banquet lamp,** white metal w/brass finish, filigree font holder, solid textured stem & ornate foot, ring attached to hold cranberry Hobbs Optic shade, overall 16 1/2" h., Book II, No. 422 (electrified through font, wear to brass finish, shade ring loose, hard-to-see chip on interior rim of shade) .......................................... **143**

**Ceramic base,** "stein" lamp, cylindrical base w/applied handle, round milk glass shade, horse head decoration, drop-in brass font flashed black w/copper highlights, Hornet burner, Handel Ware, 11" h., Book II, No. 444 ............... **2,310**

*Hobnail Mini Lamp and Shade*

**Blue,** Hobnail patt., open tapering cylindrical shade on matching base w/stem base, normal edge roughness on shade, no shade ring, overall 6 3/4" h., No. 477 (ILLUS.)................................................................ **80**

**Vaseline,** "Cathedral lamp," pedestal lamp w/embossed base & shade, Nutmeg burner, 8 3/4" h., No. 480 ............................... **775**

**Amber,** pedestal base w/flaring tulip-form shade w/Stars & Bars embossed design, clear chimney, Nutmeg burner, L.G. Wright Glass Company, 8" h., No. 482 ........ **135**

**Amberina,** pedestal base w/flaring tulip-form shade w/Stars & Bars embossed design, clear chimney, Nutmeg burner, L.G. Wright Glass Company, 8" h., No. 482 .......... **155**

**White bisque,** figural Skeleton bust lamp, blue & orchid trim, green glass eyes, foreign burner, possibly German, No. 490 ..... **4,400**

**Clear,** w/purplish opal swirl, Nutmeg burner, 6 1/2" h., No. 512............................................. **760**

**Greenish gold,** Tiffany lamp, twist design base w/flaring foot & cupped top, matching chimney, flaring ruffled shade marked "The Twilight," Nutmeg burner, base & shade signed "L.C.T.," 12 3/4" h., No. 586 .. **2,750**

**Red satin,** Artichoke patt., base only w/burner & chimney, 3 1/4" h., Book I, Fig. III................................................................ **2,200**

**Blue satin,** Artichoke patt., Nutmeg burner,
8" h., Book I, Figure III ..................................... **935**
**Milk glass,** Artichoke patt., w/green & yellow paint, Nutmeg burner, 8" h., Book I,
Figure III .......................................................... **275**

# Kerosene Lamps & Related Lighting

Kerosene lamps were used from about 1860 until replaced by electric lighting when it became available. In cities and towns this was generally from about 1900 until 1920. Rural electrification occurred in the 1930s or later.

Today, kerosene lamps are sought after for their appearance and function. Some owners light them occasionally, while a few enjoy them every night. Certainly experimenting with the lamps can add another dimension to collecting. Try placing lamps strategically—not just to illuminate a room but to create dramatic shadows.

If a hanging lamp is the only source of illumination in a room, patterns of light and shadow and perhaps colors will be splayed out on the ceilings and walls. The flickering of an open flame will create shadows in motion which can give a favorite piece of folk art or furnishings, such as a clock or collectible, a different nighttime look. Natural wood finishes which can look flat under incandescent light will glow with a warm sheen to create the mood of a century ago. Most examples shown here are ones that would have been relatively inexpensive when they were made and are compatible with country furnishings. There was tremendous competition and production in the kerosene lamp business. This led to the creation of an astounding variety of lamps and accessories. Because electric lighting was not perfect, kerosene lamps were preserved for emergencies. Thus Americans are blessed with a good supply and an appreciation that will ensure a continuing demand.

—Catherine Thuro

Photographs by Catherine M.V. Thuro.

Note: Lamps do not include burner & chimney, unless otherwise noted. Pricing information provided by Dennis Hearn and Antique Trader Price Guide editors.

*Evaluating Early Lighting:* Here are some important factors to consider when evaluating early glass lamps. First, look for mold marks. Three mold marks indicate production before 1880. Next, check the metal collar of the lamp: a grey petrified-looking cement is a good indication of age. Then check the bottom of the base—it should show dull, uneven wear. Finally, any markings, such as patent dates, can provide a good indication of age and add to the value.

Collectors should also take note of lamp patterns currently being reproduced. These include: Sweetheart, Bullseye Fine Detail, Princess Feather, Daisy, Shield & Star, Prince Edward, Coolidge Drape and Heart & Star.

Finally, remember that prices vary greatly depending on geographic region and marketplace. Expect to pay less at flea markets and auctions and more in reputable shops and shows. With the advent of the Internet and auction sites, prices can vary greatly. Excellent buys can be found when posted by inexperienced sellers but be sure to ask questions before bidding. Expect to pay a premium from reputable and experienced sellers as they attract more buyers and will guarantee the quality and authenticity of pieces they sell.

—Dennis Hearn

## Pre-Kerosene Lamps

**Hand lamp,** pressed waffle design, flared font w/applied handle, burning fluid burner, ca. 1850 (ILLUS. right)............ **$300-325**
**Table lamp,** free-blown squatty round font above a flared columnar standard, w/whale oil burner, ca. 1850 (ILLUS. left) ............................................. **250 -275**

*Various Pre-Kerosene Lamps*

**Table lamp,** pressed Star-and-Punty patt, slightly flared font w/smooth domed top, w/burning fluid burner, ca. 1850 (ILLUS. center bottom of previous page) ........... **325-350**

# Kerosene Lamps

**Hand lamp,** blue opalescent blown glass, Sheldon Swirl patt., footed ...................... **550-650**
**Hand lamp,** blue blown glass, Whirlpool patt., footed............................................... **250-300**
**Hand lamp,** clear blown glass, Bull's-eye patt. .............................................................. **125-150**

*Polka Dot Pattern Kerosene Hand Lamp*

**Hand lamp,** opalescent blown Polka Dot patt. w/cranberry or ruby dots, clear pressed handle & round patterned base, unusual crimped chimney (ILLUS.)... **900 and up**

*Various Quartered Block Table Lamps*

**Hand lamp,** flat base, clear pressed glass, Quartered Block patt., w/handle, flat bottom, kerosene slip or prong burner & "pie crust" chimney, ca. 1890 (ILLUS. center)........................................ **125-150**
**Hand lamp,** footed, clear pressed glass, Quartered Block patt., one-piece, kerosene slip or prong burner & "pie crust" chimney, ca. 1880s (ILLUS. right) ........ **125-175**

*Ribbed Pattern Kerosene Hand & Table Lamps*

**Hand lamp,** clear blown glass rounded ribbed font tapering into flared foot, ca. 1860s (ILLUS. center front with other ribbed lamps)............................................. **100-125**

**Hand lamp,** clear blown glass rounded ribbed font w/applied handle, ca. 1860s (ILLUS. right front with other ribbed lamps)....................................................... **150-175**

**Hand lamp,** clear blown glass rounded, ribbed font w/applied handle, ca.1860s (ILLUS. left front with other ribbed lamps)....................................................... **100-125**

*Atterbury & Co. Kerosene Hand Lamp*

**Hand lamp,** footed, clear blown glass ribbed Atterbury Filley patt. font w/patent-dated pressed handle & base, ca. late 1860s-1870s (ILLUS.)............................... **75-100**

*Adams & Co. Kerosene Hand Lamp*

**Hand lamp,** footed, pressed opaque white glass, flared foot below tapered font w/drip-trough & clear shoulder, Collins burner & milk glass Sun chimney, rare combination, Adams & Company, 1870s (ILLUS.)............................................... **1,200-1,500**

*Kerosene Lamps*

**Hand lamp,** tin & glass, painted tin w/handle & removable glass font, w/Columbia burner & chimney combination, font & holder marked "Bradley's Security Factory Lamp" (ILLUS. left)............................... **250-300**

*Adjustable Hanging Kerosene Lamp*

**Hanging lamp,** elaborate cast-iron adjustable arms, delicate open design & original finish, the arms support fonts w/a frosted Star design & Vienna shades, ca. 1870s-80s (ILLUS.)........................... **1,500-2,000**

**Mechanical lamp,** Wanzer Mechanical lamp, metal base w/forced draft for operation even without a chimney, complete w/key, combination 5" d. shade holder & opalescent Hobnail shade (ILLUS. far right on previous page with hand lamp), lamp base only .......................................... **550-650**
**Mechanical lamp shade,** 5" d. opalescent Hobnail patt. ...................................... **150 and up**
**Mechanical lamp shade holder,** for Wanzer Mechanical lamp, 5" d. ............................... **50**

*Kerosene Parlor Lamp*

**Parlor lamp,** milk glass, low rounded shade tapering to slightly flaring rim above squatty pear-shaped base, both decorated w/raised & painted flowers, ca. 1880s-1890s (ILLUS.) ................................... **325 and up**

*Parlor Vase Lamp*

**Parlor vase lamp,** white glass ball shade w/original hand-painted roses & leaves, matching red-painted vase holder & gold-plated metal parts (ILLUS.) .............. **375 and up**

*Student Lamp*

**Student lamp,** all-original Leader student lamp w/rectangular burner & chimney & milk glass Vienna shade, nickel-plated brass, ca. 1880 (ILLUS.) .................. **750 and up**
**Student lamp,** brass & glass, Manhattan Brass Co., original nickel-plate base & cased green glass shade (ILLUS. center back w/hand lamp on previous page)................................................... **450 and up**

*Corn Table Lamp*

**Table lamp,** clear blown, Corn design patented by Daniel Ashworth, base marked w/1873 patent date, La Belle Glass Company, Bridgeport, Ohio (ILLUS.) ....... **250 and up**

**Table lamp,** clear blown glass, Corn-in-Shield patt., Oval Band patt. base ... **250 and up**

*Eyewinker Table Lamp*

**Table lamp,** clear blown glass, Eyewinker patt. round font w/Bubble Base, Dalzell, Gilmore & Leighton Company (ILLUS.) ..................................................... **125-150**

*Ewing Patent Table Lamp*

**Table lamp,** clear blown glass font above Ewing patent drip catcher above clear glass plain stem on round base, ca. 1870s (ILLUS.) ......................................... **150-225**

*Gaiety Table Lamp*

**Table lamp,** clear blown glass, Gaiety patt., ribbed font decorated w/opalescent feathered design, rounded pressed base, slip burner w/special crimped top (ILLUS.) ..................................................... **425-500**

**Table lamp,** clear blown glass, McKee Tulip patt. ..................................................... **300 and up**

*Blown Glass Table Lamps*

**Table lamp,** clear blown glass, plain design, rounded font w/brass stem & square marble base, ca. 1860s (ILLUS. of three w/chimneys & burners), lamp only, each .............................................................. **90-150**

**Table lamp,** clear blown glass, plain design, w/appropriate burner & chimney combinations, add to the lamp value (as illustrated) ...................................................... **250-375**

**Table lamp,** clear blown glass, rounded ribbed font, columnar standard w/flared ribbed base, ca. 1850s-1870s (ILLUS. on p.65 back left with other ribbed lamps) ...................................................... **125-150**

**Table lamp,** clear blown glass, rounded ribbed font on a free-form, knopped round base, ca. 1860s-1880s (ILLUS. on p.65 back right with other ribbed lamps) ...................................................... **125-175**

**Table lamp,** clear blown glass, Wild Rose patt., Riverside patented collar .............. **250-300**

*Bull's-eye & Fleur-de-Lis Table Lamp*

**Table lamp,** clear pressed glass, Bull's-eye & Fleur-de-lis patt. font tapering to a panelled stem & scalloped base, 1860s (ILLUS.) ...................................................... **150-200**

**Table lamp,** clear pressed glass, Chadwick patt., w/milk glass base ........................... **225-325**

**Table lamp,** clear pressed glass, Daisy and Button patt. font, plain shoulder & pressed six-sided base, ca. 1890s (ILLUS. top of next column) ................... **125-150**

**Table lamp,** clear pressed glass, Moon and Crescents patt. ......................................... **350-450**

*Daisy & Button Table Lamp*

**Table lamp,** clear pressed glass, Quartered Block patt., w/handle, footed, kerosene burner & "pie crust" chimney, ca. 1880s (ILLUS. on p.65 left with other Quartered Block lamps) ............................................. **150-200**

*Sawtooth Table Lamp*

**Table lamp,** clear pressed glass, Sawtooth patt., large round font, brass connector & pressed opaque white glass Baroque base, lip burner & tall chimney (ILLUS.) ...................................................... **300-350**

*Veronica Table lamp*

**Table lamp,** clear pressed glass, Veronica patt. (on inside of font), rounded font tapering to brass stem on a marble base, Hobbs, Brockunier & Company, ca. mid-1860s - mid-1870s (ILLUS.) ................... **150-200**

*Snowflake Pattern Table Lamp*

**Table lamp,** cranberry or ruby blown opalescent glass Snowflake patt., square font, metal screw connector w/glass

sleeve, clear pressed base, Hobbs, Brockunier & Company (ILLUS.) ...... **750 and up**

*Cut-overlay Table Lamp*

**Table lamp,** cut-overlay, inverted pear font in white cut to green, tapering brass connector, green alabaster Baroque base (ILLUS.) ........................................... **1,800 and up**

*Figural Table Lamp*

**Table lamp,** figural, angular frosted & clear glass font w/star- and cross-like designs, above spelter fisherwoman holding spear w/a basket full of fish at her feet, all on tiered square metal base, Bradley & Hubbard Mfg., ca. 1888 (ILLUS.) .................. **250-300**

**Table lamp,** figural, clear blown glass font & spelter figure of Mary & her Lamb......... **125-225**

*Empress Eugenie Table Lamp*

**Table lamp,** figural, clear frosted glass font w/Greek Key design above spelter bust of Empress Eugenie (wife of Napoleon III), soapstone base, ca. 1870s (ILLUS.).................................................... **175-225**

**Table lamp,** green blown glass, Vera patt............................................................. **175-225**

**Table lamp,** marigold Carnival blown glass, Zipper Loop patt.................................... **750-850**

**Table lamp,** Ripley Wedding Lamp, two matching blue Ripley patented fonts flanking toothpick holder on an alabaster glass base........................................ **1,800 and up**

# Other Kerosene Lamps

**Angle kerosene ceiling lamp,** three-light, ovoid stamped brass central font suspended from a high arched wire handle, font issuing three short arms w/angled burners fitted w/clear ball globes & conical milk glass shades, wick adjuster marked "Angle Manufacturing Company, Providence," early 20th c., w/old glass .................................................... **1,000-1,200**

**Banquet lamp,** a domed open-topped blue opaque shade w/a brass crown resting in a deep pierced brass ring suspending prisms & raised on a burner above an Acanthus Leaf patt. onion-form font on a brass ring connection to a tall baluster-form Acanthus Leaf patt. standard set on a domed pierced brass footed base, w/chimney, Consolidated Lamp & Glass Co., late 19th c., overall 26 1/2" h. (ILLUS. center below) .................................... **495**

**Banquet lamp,** a dusty rose satin ball shade embossed w/cherub faces & acanthus leaf scrolls raised on a burner above a collar on a bulbous ornately embossed font & connector to a white alabaster columnar stem above the ornate pierced & scrolled gilt cast-iron foot, late 19th c., overall 28" h. .................................... **297**

*Banquet & Gone-with-the Wind Lamps*

**Banquet lamp,** a glass ball shade decorated w/h.p. flowers on a kerosene burner raised above a pierced gilt-metal urn-form font raised on a pedestal composed of brass knobs & a white onyx rod above the domed & pierced metal foot base, late 19th c., electrified, overall 29 1/4" h. ..... **193**

*Consolidated Pink Banquet Lamp*

**Banquet lamp,** a large cased pink glass ball shade above a squared squatty cased pink font w/molded scrolls above a connector ring & a tall slender baluster-shaped matching pedestal on a domed

pierced brass footed base, Consolidated Lamp & Glass Company, ca. 1900, overall 25" h. (ILLUS.) ........................................... **606**

*Porcelain & Glass Banquet Lamps*

**Banquet lamp,** a white milk glass ball shade decorated in blue w/a Dutch Delft-style landscape, raised on a brass foreign burner above the porcelain base w/an onion-form font ornately molded w/scrolls & applied flowers above a slender matching scroll-molded shaft & domed scroll-molded three-footed base, base marked "Germany - RW - Rudolstadt," early 20th c., overall 21 1/2" h. (ILLUS. left) ...................................................... **358**

*Large & Small Banquet Lamps*

**Banquet lamp,** cast- and wrought-iron tripod base w/scrolled trim & pierced knop supporting a bulbous brass font & burner, a ball-shaped pink cased glass shade, Plumb & Atwood Victor burner, overall 18 1/2" h. (ILLUS. right bottom previous page)................................................................ **220**

**Banquet lamp,** figural, a h.p. white ball shade decorated w/scrolls framing a transfer-printed color scene of cupids, clear glass chimney, brass shade ring & burner on a brass collar above the bulbous bronzed metal ornately scroll-embossed font tapering to a lower knop held aloft by a large full-figure cupid above an ornately embossed metal flaring & stepped base w/four scroll feet, late 19th c., 30" h. ....................................... **385**

**Banquet lamp,** Louis XVI-style, gilt-bronze & marble, the bulbous dark marble font set in a bronze openwork laurel leaf band fitted w/three large rams' head masks at the top of three tall slender curved supports centered by a slender standard & raised on a tripartite marble base w/metal bun feet, the tall kerosene burner fitted w/an open-topped ball shade acid-etched overall w/delicate florals & a frosted glass chimney, electrified, Europe, late 19th c., 24" h. ........................................ **2,070**

**Banquet lamp,** milk glass ball shade w/colored transfer decal of cherubs, brass burner & embossed collar above the compressed onion-form font w/cherub decoration over small connector to the tall baluster-form milk glass pedestal w/further cherubs, on a gilded cast-iron domed & scroll-cast four-footed base, late 19th c., electrified, overall 30" h. .......... **330**

*Consolidated Monarch Banquet Lamp*

**Banquet lamp,** Monarch model, a cased yellow glass ball shade on a tall burner & brass shoulder over a bulbous matching glass font on a pierced metal cupped connector on the tall baluster-form matching glass pedestal base raised on a pierced cast metal domed foot, Consolidated Lamp & Glass Co., ca. 1890, overall 37 1/2" h. (ILLUS.)..................................... **770**

**Banquet lamp,** pressed clear glass, a brass Duplex double wick burner on the half-round font w/an overall diamond design above a tall slender diamond design standard w/brass screw connectors above the deep round diamond design foot, late 19th - early 20th c., overall 24" h. (ILLUS. on previous page right with Delft-style banquet lamp) ...................... **413**

*Fostoria Colony Pattern Banquet Lamp*

**Banquet lamp,** pressed clear glass, Fostoria's Cascade or Colony patt., the domed swirled ribbed foot supporting a tall swirled rib baluster-form standard below a ball connector & a half-round swirled font, two-section w/screw connectors, Stern Bro's New York double wick burner, overall 20 1/2" h. (ILLUS.) ....................... **550**

**Banquet lamp,** white metal, brass & onyx, a heavy ornately cast squared footed base below sections of white onyx & brass connectors forming the standard supporting the squatty bulbous brass font w/applied scroll trim & a flared shoulder band below the burner, the red cased ball shade decorated on the exterior w/five panels of acid-etched floral & butterfly design, the shade interior frosted, overall 33" h. (ILLUS. on previous page center with small banquet lamp)................................ **248**

**Banquet lamp,** white metal w/bronze finish, the ornate tall base w/a domed cast four-legged bottom supporting a figural cherub standard holding a bulbous font w/pierced scrolling decoration below the burner, a pink cased glass ball shade w/bright gilt scrolling dragons, brass drop-in font, overall 31" h. (ILLUS. on p.72 left with small banquet lamp) ................ **990**

*Banquet lamp*

**Banquet lamp,** glass ball shade in deep red decorated w/gilt & enameled florals, above a rounded brass font raised on a serpentine scroll-trimmed iron base w/claw-form feet, Reform-Kosmos-Brenner Patent burner, late 19th c., overall 17" h. (ILLUS.) ................................................. **275**

*Banquet lamp*

**Banquet lamp,** composite-type, black round stepped ceramic foot w/a brass domed top & slender brass standard supporting a squatty rounded clear glass font cut w/thumbprints, brass Hink's Duplex Patent burner, rounded open-topped clear glass shade cut w/strawberry diamonds & fans, clear chimney, base stamped "Veritas Lamp Works," late 19th c., overall 22 1/2" h. ......................................... **209**

*Cranberry Glass Bracket Lamp*

**Bracket lamps,** a squatty bulbous cranberry glass font decorated w/scrolling gilt designs & fitted w/a brass collar, burner & clear chimney, supported on an ornate scrolling brass swing arm attached to a cast-brass scrolling wall bracket mount, pr. (ILLUS.) ....................................................... **495**

*Early Bradley and Hubbard Lamp*

**Bradley & Hubbard table lamp,** 10" d. domical open-topped milk glass shade h.p. w/delicate roses, violets & forget-me-nots, w/a three-arm spider support over silvered-metal baluster-form reservoir & circular domed base w/gadrooned border, raised "B & H" on reservoir screw cap, late 19th c., 20 1/4" h. (ILLUS.) ............................................................ **863**

**Cranberry glass & nickeled-iron table lamp,** a square stepped raised iron foot

*Large Group of Cut-Overlay Lamps*

supporting a ring-turned pedestal below the bulbous onion-form optic Herringbone patt. font, brass collar & burner supporting a tall tulip-form frosted Rubina shade w/a deeply ruffled flaring rim, acid-etched overall w/a design of delicate flowers & butterflies, clear chimney, 6 3/4" d., overall 14 1/4" h. ............................ **395**

**Cranberry glass table lamp,** a mold-blown ringed baluster-form pedestal base w/round cushion foot tapers to a stepped ringed font below a brass collar & burner supporting a Rubina Inverted Thumbprint patt. ribbed tulip-form shade w/a flaring crimped & ruffled rim, enameled white flowers on the pedestal, 6 1/2" d., overall 17" h. ................................................................ **595**

*Cut-Overlay Lamp on Ornate Base*

**Cut-overlay table lamp,** amethyst cut to clear cylindrical font tapering slightly to the collar, on an applied glass collar above an elaborate cast-brass base w/curled leaves above a ribbed urn stan-

dard & foot on a stepped black marble base w/brass trim, New England, ca. 1850-60, 13 3/4" h. (ILLUS.) ....................... **2,475**

**Cut-overlay table lamp,** inverted bell-form font, cobalt blue cut to white cut to clear, cut w/slash, punty & oval designs, a brass connector to the tall waisted matching cut standard on a square stepped marble base w/gilt-metal trim, minor imperfections, possibly Boston & Sandwich Glass Co., ca. 1860-80, 16 1/4" h. (ILLUS. above front row, far left with the large group) ............................. **9,775**

**Cut-overlay table lamp,** inverted bell-form glass font, cobalt blue cut to white cut to clear, cut w/oval designs, on a brass connector to the tall slender waisted matching cut standard on a stepped marble base w/gilt-metal trim, minor imperfections, possibly Boston & Sandwich Glass Co., ca. 1860-80, 16 1/2" h. (ILLUS. above front row, far right with the large group) ......................................................... **12,650**

**Cut-overlay table lamp,** inverted bell-form glass font, transparent teal blue cut to clear, cut w/slashes, punties & ovals, on a brass connector raised on a similar cut overlay tall waisted standard on a square stepped marble base w/gilt-metal trim, minor wear, possibly New England, ca. 1860-80, 16 1/8" h. (ILLUS. back row, far left with large group, above) ...................... **4,025**

**Cut-overlay table lamp,** inverted pear-shaped font, transparent amethyst glass cut to clear w/quatrefoil, oval & punty designs, raised on a flared fluted columnar brass standard & square stepped marble base w/brass trim, minor wear, possibly Boston & Sandwich Glass Co., ca. 1860-80, 10 5/8" h. (ILLUS. center, front row with large grouping, above)........................ **2,530**

**Cut-overlay table lamp,** inverted pear-shaped glass font, cranberry cut to white cut to clear, cut ovals & punty designs, raised on a flared fluted brass columnar standard & a square stepped marble base w/brass trim, imperfections, possibly New England, ca. 1860-80, 13 1/2" h. (ILLUS. back row, second from right with large group, above) ..................................... **1,955**

**Cut-overlay table lamp,** inverted pear-shaped glass font, cranberry cut to white cut to clear, w/quatrefoils, stars & ovals, raised on a flared brass fluted columnar standard on a square stepped marble base w/brass trim, very minor wear, possibly Boston & Sandwich Glass Co., ca. 1860-80, 12 1/2" h. (ILLUS. back row, second from left with large group, above on previous page) ............................ **2,070**

**Cut-overlay table lamp,** squatty inverted pear-shaped glass font, white cut to transparent green w/gilt outlines on font, cut w/punty & oval designs, on a brass connector w/suspended leaves over a similar tall waisted overlay standard on a square stepped marble base w/gilt-metal trim, minor imperfections, possibly Boston & Sandwich Glass Co., ca. 1860-80, 16 1/4" h. (ILLUS. back row, far right with large group, above on previous page) ....... **6,900**

**Cut-overlay table lamp,** the bulbous inverted pear-shaped font in pink cut to white cut to clear above a metal connector to a lime green opaque columnar glass shaft on a flaring ribbed connector to the stepped square white marble base w/gilt-metal trim, gilt trim on the font, ca. 1860-70, 13 3/4" h. (ILLUS. left, below) .............. **1,045**

*Two Fine Cut-Overlay Lamps*

**Cut-overlay table lamp,** the bulbous inverted pear-shaped font in white cut to cranberry w/ovals, stars & quatrefoils, w/a brass collar & raised on a reeded brass columnar standard on a stepped painted white marble square base w/an embossed brass band, mid-19th c., 15" h. (minor chips on base) .................... **920**

**Cut-overlay table lamp,** the bulbous inverted pear-shaped font in white cut to opaque blue above a metal connector to the opaque blue glass columnar stem above a flaring ribbed connector on the stepped square white marble base w/gilt-metal trim, ca. 1860-70, 14" h. (ILLUS. right, above) .................................. **1,760**

**Cut-overlay table lamp,** the inverted bell-form font & slender waisted standard in cranberry cut to white cut to clear w/ovals, loops, quatrefoils & circles, a brass collar & connector between the font & standard & a flaring ringed brass foot raised on a painted black marble stepped square base w/embossed sheet brass band, mid-19th c., 17" h. (chips to base) ...................... **4,600**

**Cut-overlay table lamp,** the inverted pear-shaped glass font cut from cobalt blue to white to clear, brass collar w/burner supporting a tall white cut to clear tulip-shaped shade, the font raised on a brass connector to the black opaque glass pedestal stem on a stepped square foot, ca. 1860, chips & edge grinding on shade, overall 21 1/4" h. .......................... **1,650**

**Cut-overlay table lamps,** tall ovoid font, cobalt blue cut to white cut to clear, cut w/slash, punty & oval designs, raised on a flared fluted columnar brass standard & square stepped marble base w/brass trim, minor imperfections, possibly Boston & Sandwich Glass Co., ca. 1860-80, 11 3/4" h., pr. (ILLUS. on previous page front row, second from left & right with the large group) ...................... **4,025**

**Finger lamp,** pressed glass cranberry opalescent Coin Spot patt., footed bulbous font w/clear applied side handle, w/old burner, ca. 1900, 3 1/2" h. ...................... **715**

**Finger lamp,** pressed glass Emma patt., squatty bell-shaped font in a clear opalescent Coin Spot patt., applied clear side handle, w/burner, ca. 1900, 3 1/4" h.............. **275**

**Finger lamp,** pressed squared blue opalescent Hobb's Snowflake patt. font, applied blue loop handle, w/burner & ribbed edge chimney, Hobbs, Brockunier & Co., ca. 1890, font 3" h., overall 9 1/2" h. ...................... **770**

**Finger lamp,** pressed squared cranberry opalescent Hobb's Snowflake patt. font, applied clear loop handle, w/burner & ribbed edge chimney, Hobbs, Brockunier & Co., ca. 1890, font 3" h., overall 9 1/2" h. ................................................. **990**

**Gone-with-the-Wind table lamp,** a frosted clear glass ball shade ornately embossed overall w/leafy scrolls & roses, joined by the burner fitting & gilt brass flared & scalloped shoulder collar to the bulbous ovoid matching glass base raised on a scroll-pierced squared metal foot, electrified, ca. 1900, 23 1/2" h. ...................... **275**

**Gone-with-the-Wind table lamp,** a large ball shade molded in relief w/a band of large elephant heads w/the trunks hanging down & painted in shades of dark brown & mottled yellow & orange, a wide scrolled metal collar to the waisted bulbous font molded w/matching elephant heads & similar paint, on a domed pierced cast-metal footed base, Bradley & Hubbard, ca. 1900, 26" h. ............................ **4,200**

**Gone-with-the-Wind table lamp,** a large milk glass ball shade decorated w/oversized wild rose blossoms in pink & red w/green leaves against a shaded pink &

red background, above a scalloped flaring brass collar & a squatty bulbous matching font, raised on a pierced brass domed & footed base, no chimney, electrified, ca. 1900, 22" h. (ILLUS. left below)...................... **413**

*Two Gone-with-the-Wind Floral Lamps*

**Gone-with-the-Wind table lamp,** a large milk white ball shade decorated w/large pink & white rose blossoms & green leaves against a shaded dark to light green ground, above a wide scalloped brass collar & bulbous tapering ovoid matching font, raised on a pierced & domed cast-brass footed base, ca. 1900, overall 23" h. (ILLUS. right with two other Gone-with-the-Wind lamps, next page) ........ **231**

*Baccarat Gone-with-the-Wind Lamp*

**Gone-with-the-Wind table lamp,** a milk glass ball globe shade painted w/a scene of dogs playing in a garden w/tall green trees & blue skies w/white clouds in the background, a brass burner & collar on the oblong milk glass lower globe deco-

rated w/a full color lakeside landscape, on a domed brass base w/thick curved corner feet, both shade & base signed "Baccarat," France, late 19th c., 18" h. (ILLUS.)........................................................... **1,848**

*Gone-with-the-Wind Table Lamp*

**Gone-with-the-Wind table lamp,** a milk glass ball shade enameled in yellow & painted w/a large stylized leafy flower, stamped brass collar above the matching ovoid glass base raised on a pierced cast-brass scrolly footed base, electrified w/font drilled, late 19th c., 23 1/4" h. (ILLUS.)............................................................. **303**

**Gone-with-the-Wind table lamp,** a milk white ball shade decorated w/large pink & red roses w/green leaves against a shaded pink to white ground, above a wide brass collar w/burner above the bulbous matching font, raised on a pierced brass domed & footed base, overall 23" h. (ILLUS. left, top next page)..... **248**

**Gone-with-the-Wind table lamp,** a milk white globe shade w/molded poppy blossoms & leaves alternating w/smooth panels hand-decorated w/stylized four-petal blossoms, overall purple & pink background shading, above a wide scrolled brass collar above the matching tapering ovoid glass font on a pierced, high four-footed metal base, electrified, no chimney, ca. 1900, overall 22" h. (ILLUS. right, in previous column) ............................... **413**

**Gone-with-the-Wind table lamp,** Artichoke patt., mold-blown frosted clear ball shade on a shade ring w/burner above the matching inverted pear-shaped font on a squared pierced metal base w/chimney, overall 16" h. (ILLUS. on pg. 71 left with banquet lamp) ................................................... **264**

**Gone-with-the-Wind table lamp,** Artichoke patt., mold-blown frosted ruby ball shade on a shade ring w/burner above the matching inverted pear-shaped font on a square pierced metal base w/chimney, overall 16" h. (ILLUS. right with banquet lamp, page 71) ....................................... **495**

**Gone-with-the-Wind table lamp,** large frosted clear molded Grape patt. ball shade above a wide scrolled brass collar above the matching bulbous, tapering matching font, on a scroll-pierced domed & footed brass foot, w/chimney, overall

*Three Gone-with-the-Wind Lamps*

24" h. (ILLUS. center with rose-decorated lamps) .......................................... **468**

**Gone-with-the-Wind table lamp,** spherical milk glass globe painted w/red florals on a shaded green ground, brass burner & shoulder fittings above the matching inverted pear-shaped base raised on a gilt-metal scroll-footed base, original burner marked "Fostoria," late 19th c., 20 1/2" h. ..... **325**

to the ceiling plate, ca. 1890, shade 7" h. (ILLUS.) ............................................. **264**

**Hall hanging lamp,** a bulbous tapering molded blown pink opalescent shade in the Lattice patt., in a brass frame w/chains & ceiling plate, original font, ca. 1890, shade 7" h. (ILLUS. right with ruby hall lamp below) ............................................... **242**

*Blue Hobnail Hall Hanging Lamp*

**Hall hanging lamp,** a bulbous blown glass blue Hobnail patt. shade, fitted in a brass frame w/base & crown & four long chains

*Two Victorian Hanging Hall Lamps*

**Hall hanging lamp,** an ovoid egg-shaped deep ruby glass optic ribbed shade fitted in a brass frame w/bottom pull ring, flared crown & four hanging chains to ceiling plate, chip on base of shade hidden by frame, ca. 1890, shade 8 3/4" h. (ILLUS. left) ...................................................... **209**

*Lithophane & Ruby-Flashed Hall Lamp*

**Hall hanging lamp,** lithophane & ruby-flashed glass, an upright square form w/beveled corners, each side panel set w/a white porcelain lithophane plaque above a narrow leaf- and flower-engraved ruby-flashed panel all framed in brass, narrow ruby-flashed engraved panels also at each corner, late 19th - early 20th c., 9 1/2" h. (ILLUS.) .................. **1,495**

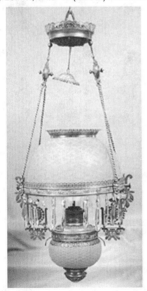

*Rare Cut Velvet Hanging Lamp*

**Hanging parlor lamp,** 14" d. domical blue Cut Velvet glass shade mounted in a pierced brass & button-stamped ring & topped w/a pierced brass crown, the ring suspending facet-cut prisms, pierced leafy scrollwork side brackets w/large reddish jewels joining shade to brass font frame w/squatty bulbous blue Cut Velvet font w/brass drop, suspended on forked brass chains adjusting below pierced ceiling cap & smoke bell, ca. 1890 (ILLUS.) ........................................................ **1,760**

**Hanging parlor lamp,** a 14" d. domed, open-topped cranberry Hobnail patt. shade fitted in a pierced brass ring frame hung w/faceted prisms & fitted w/a brass crown, hung from forked brass chains joined to an upper brass ring, fitted w/a simple bulbous brass font marked "Rayo" & flanked by long thin brass S-scrolls, finger ring at bottom of font, late 19th c., electrified, 33" h. ............................................. **825**

**Hanging parlor lamp,** a 14" d. domical open-topped rubina Hobnail patt. glass shade fitted w/a brass crown & jeweled ring suspending prisms & hung from two forked chains joined above to a pierced brass fitting hung from additional chains below the ceiling cap, the lower brass scrolling frame supporting a clear Hobnail & Diamond patt. glass font, late 19th c., overall 40" h. ............................................. **1,760**

*Fine Victorian Hanging Lamp*

**Hanging parlor lamp,** a 17" d. domical open-topped cranberry Hobnail patt. shade w/a brass crown, chains & ring suspending faceted prisms above the pierced leafy nickel-plated support arms & trim around the bulbous brass font, w/original burner, late 19th c. (ILLUS.) ...... **1,650**

**Hanging parlor lamp,** a 20" d. open-top domed cranberry Hobnail patt. shade fitted w/a serrated brass crown & fitted into an embossed brass shade ring w/pierced upper rim & hung w/facet-cut prisms, ornate stamped brass framework of pierced leafy scrolling grapevines centering a brass cup holding a clear bulbous oil font, w/clear glass chimney & four delicate brass suspension chains, electrified, ca. 1890 ..................................... **1,150**

*Jeweled Lamp with Pink Shade*

**Hanging parlor lamp,** a domed frosted pink 14" d. open-topped shade w/a brass crown & set in a pierced brass shade ring suspended by four chains from a metal cross below the pierced & scalloped ceiling cap, a squatty clear pattern glass font set in a brass cup support suspended between ornately scrolling brass arms joined to the shade ring & fitted w/colored glass 'jewels,' clear & colored prisms incomplete, ca. 1890s, 28 1/2" h. (ILLUS.) ............................................................ **715**

*Cranberry Opalescent Parlor Lamp*

**Hanging parlor lamp,** a domed open-topped cranberry opalescent Hobnail patt. shade, fitted in a pierced brass shade ring hung w/prisms above a large bulbous brass font w/a scrolled brass frame, suspended on chains above an upper ring w/prisms & the ceiling plate w/smoke bell (ILLUS. previous column) ......................................... **3,250**

**Hanging parlor lamp,** a high domed open-topped milk glass shade decorated w/a colorful transfer-printed scene of Kate Greenaway-style Victorian children relaxing on the grass under a large leafy tree, a squatty bulbous milk glass font w/matching decoration, ornate stamped brass cap ring & support ring for the shade w/brass suspension chains, stamped brass fittings around the font w/delicate scrolling brasswork connecting the shade ring & font & continuing into a scrolling base drop, the shade ring hung w/numerous faceted prisms, ca. 1890, overall 32" h. ......................................... **770**

*Rare Victorian Parlor Hanging Lamp*

**Hanging parlor lamp,** a wide open-topped domical blue satin glass shade w/a diamond lattice design fitted w/a pierced brass flared crown & resting in a pierced brass shade ring suspended from four chains & hung w/facet-cut prisms, two pierced leafy scroll brass brackets set w/large round red jewels suspend the burner & brass collar on the compressed spherical matching blue satin glass font w/a brass drop ring, ca. 1890s (ILLUS.) ......................................................... **4,480**

**Hanging parlor lamp,** domical 13 1/2" d. blue opaque glass shade in a wide brass shade ring & a brass crown, above a bulbous embossed brass font & scrolling brass frame, suspended by four chains joined to an upper ring suspended w/glass prisms, further prisms around shade ring, ca. 1890 (ILLUS. left. below)...... **825**

*Two Kerosene Hanging Parlor Lamps*

**Hanging parlor lamp,** domical 13 1/2" d. deep cranberry Hobnail patt. shade, in a stamped brass shade ring & w/a brass crown above a bulbous brass font w/scrolling brass frame, suspended on chains below an upper ring & ceiling plate, clear prisms around the shade ring, w/brass smoke bell, ca. 1890 (ILLUS. right with blue opaque shaded lamp).................................................................. **770**

*Victorian Hanging Parlor Lamp*

**Hanging parlor lamp,** original embossed brass frame supporting a green & red floral-decorated milk glass domed shade & matching bulbous font, ornate scrolling brass lower frame, cut crystal prisms, original smoke bell & match holder, removable electric socket, chain mechanism complete, Miller Co., ca. 1890s, 15" d. (ILLUS.)................................................. **784**

**Iron table lamp,** Renaissance-style urn-form base w/an ornate stepped domed

foot & pedestal w/scrolls & gadrooning supporting the tall font embossed w/a wide band of frolicking cherubs & a gadrooned rim band flanked by long C-scroll handles w/griffin-head terminals, brass burner supporting a bulbous amber glass tulip-form shade w/a diamond quilted design & a deeply ruffled flaring rim, 7 1/2" d., 16 1/4" h.............................................. **395**

*Victorian Organ Lamp*

**Organ floor lamp,** a large red globe shade w/worn gilt rampant lion, raised on a burner collar & brass bulbous font fitted in a pierced wrought-iron holder on a tall slender scrolling leaf-trimmed standard surrounded at the base w/a long coiled salamander & flanked by three tall scrolling snake legs w/leafy scroll decoration, marked "R. Hollings & Co. Boston," damage, salamander's feet need repair, late 19th c., 60 1/2" h. (ILLUS.).............................. **715**

*Late Victorian Organ Lamp*

**Organ floor lamp,** a milk glass ball shade painted w/large deep red & white blossoms & green leaves against a shaded dark green to yellow ground, on a burner above an ornately pierced bulbous brass font holder raised on a slender brass standard which continues down through the center of three rounded brass shelves flanked by four slender legs ending in pad feet, ca. 1890, overall 64" h. (ILLUS.) .............................................................. **575**

*Satin Peg Lamp on Figural Base*

**Peg lamp,** a squatty bulbous cased pink satin glass font in the Prism & Diamond patt., attached to a socket held aloft by a white metal figure of a young man in Napoleonic dress standing on a high, round socle base, base w/a plaque reading "Depart Pour La Promenade - Par Rancoulet," w/a pink shading to clear shade reverse acid-etched w/lilies, base w/old, dull brass colored repaint, overall 20" h. (ILLUS. without shade) .................................... **385**

**Peg lamp,** a squatty bulbous optic-ribbed shaded dark to light cranberry font decorated w/colorful enameled blossoms, fitted in a period brass beehive design candlestick, the burner fitted w/a tulip-form cranberry shade w/a deeply crimped & ruffled rim w/tiny enameled floral beading around the top, late 19th c., overall 16 3/4" h. .......................................................... **413**

**Peg lamp,** cased shaded pink satin glass mother-of-pearl Swirl patt. shade & font, the inverted tulip-form shade w/a wide flaring & crimped rim fitted on a kerosene burner w/clear chimney above the squatty bulbous matching font fitted on a reeded columnar gilt-metal base, shade 5 3/4" d., overall 12 5/8" h. ............................ **695**

**Peg lamp,** cranberry optic-ribbed onion-form font enameled w/dainty white flowers & a dotted gold center band, original brass fittings & burner, 3 3/8" d., 5 5/8" h. ....... **95**

**Peg lamp,** dark cranberry glass shade & font, the tall optic-ribbed inverted tulip shade w/a flaring & crimped rim resting on a kerosene burner w/clear chimney above the squatty bulbous tapering optic-

patterned matching font trimmed w/gilt scrolls, raised on a tall ornate reeded columnar brass candlestick base w/scrolled capital & stepped embossed foot, shade 5" d., overall 16 1/4" h. .................................. **450**

**Peg lamp,** frosted lime green glass shade & font, the tall slender inverted tulip-form shade w/a flaring ruffled rim decorated w/a gilt rim band & gilt mistletoe sprigs w/white berries, on a kerosene burner w/clear glass chimney above the squatty bulbous optic ribbed matching font raised on an ornate brass reeded columnar candlestick w/scrolled capital & stepped square embossed base, shade 4 1/2" d., overall 15 3/4" h. ...................................... **395**

**Peg lamp,** satin glass font, shaded yellow mother-of-pearl Swirl patt., original brass fittings & burner, 3 3/8" d., 6" h. ................... **165**

**Peg lamp,** squatty bulbous cranberry cut to clear glass font w/two rows of thumbprints, attached to a period brass beehive-design candlestick, w/a tulip-form cranberry glass shade w/applied white threading around the flaring ruffled rim, overall 16 1/2" h. ............................................. **198**

**Peg lamp,** squatty bulbous green iridescent optic ribbed glass font w/a brass collar & kerosene burner w/clear glass burner, fitted into a brass candlestick base w/cylindrical shaft w/ejector & low round dished foot, late 19th c., overall 9 3/4" h. .................. **110**

*Decorated Cranberry Peg Lamps*

**Peg lamps,** a bulbous squatty cranberry glass font w/a satin finish, decorated w/bright gilt tulip-like flowers & leaves, fitted on slightly differing period brass candlesticks, w/matching burners, late 19th c., overall 14 1/2" & 15" h., pr. (ILLUS.) ........ **358**

**Peg lamps,** a squatty bulbous amber iridescent Loetz-type font w/applied random threading, fitted on a period brass ring-turned candlestick, fitted w/a creamy iridescent tulip-form shade w/a random crackled finish & a flat, flaring rim, late 19th c., overall 15" h., pr. ............................. **275**

**Student lamp,** a domed open-topped green-cased glass shade above a burner & acorn-form brass font issuing from the mouth of a scrolling griffin-form cross-arm w/a longer acorn-form font w/raised torch design at opposite end of the adjustable arm, on a tall slender standard w/a scrolled loop top & centered on a squared base w/notched corners & embossed bands on four paw feet, by Edward Miller, late 19th c. .............................. **9,250**

**Student lamp,** brass cylindrical font connected to a curved arm w/a single burner & ring supporting a pyramidal milk glass shade, adjusting on a slender rod standard w/a ring loop at the top & centered on a low domed round foot, late 19th c., electrified, 20 1/4" h. (needs rewiring, chip on base rim of shade)........................................ **248**

*Post & Company Student Lamp*

**Student lamp,** brass, double burner, a rounded domed foot supporting a slender standard w/large cylindrical font & arched loop upright handle, the font issuing straight arms ending in slender cylindrical burner supports & shade rings, original domed open-topped milk glass shades w/clear chimneys, stamped mark "Post & Co.'s American Student Lamp, Cincinnati," about 24" h. (ILLUS.) .............. **2,090**

**Student lamp,** brass, single-light, a round domed foot centered by a tall slender rod w/top ring, an adjustable cross arm w/an upright cylindrical font opposite a slender cylindrical burner support fitted w/a slender clear glass chimney & a milk glass ball shade, ring beneath burner marked "Cleveland Safety Library Lamp," never electrified, last quarter 19th c., 20 7/8" h. ..... **440**

**Student lamp,** kerosene-type, a round domed foot supporting a tall slender shaft w/top ring handle, adjustable cross-arm w/a cylindrical oil tank opposite a short arm & cylindrical base supporting a bulbous font w/burner fitted w/a brass shade ring holding a domed, open-topped ribbed green-cased shade, burner marked "Manhattan Brass Co.," late 19th - early 20th c., electrified, 20 1/2" h. (some damage) ........................................ **330**

**Student lamp,** single-arm, brass, a domical open-topped green-cased shade in a ring above a cylindrical column at the end of

a curved arm opposite the cylindrical font adjusting on a slender metal standard w/a ring top & flaring round foot, late 19th - early 20th c., minor chip on top shade flange, dent in base, electrified, 21 1/4" h. ........................................ **330**

*Fine Viennese Parlor Lamp*

**Table lamp,** 10" d. domed & melon-ribbed open-topped shade in satiny yellow overlaid on white & decorated w/scrolling tan foliage & blue blossoms, brass ring, burner & stamped collar above the matching lobed ovoid glass font on a bronzed metal scrolled foot, Vienna, Austria maker's name on burner & under font, late 19th c., 21" h. (ILLUS.)............................................ **2,000**

**Table lamp,** 7 1/2" d. domical open-topped porcelain lithophane shade w/four panels showing different ladies in garden settings, colorful tinted interior, raised on a Meissen porcelain base w/a bulbous basketweave font w/applied gilt-trimmed floral sprigs supported by three standing cupids w/delicate coloring all on a round mottled brown base, blue Crossed Swords mark, late 19th c., overall 13 1/2" h. ..................... **2,585**

**Table lamp,** blown glass Hobb's Snowflake patt., the squatty squared blue opalescent font raised on a clear stem w/round scalloped foot, Hobbs, Brockunier & Co., ca. 1890, two holes in metal connector, w/burner, 9 1/2" h. ................................... **440**

**Table lamp,** blown glass Hobb's Snowflake patt., the squatty squared cranberry opalescent font raised on a clear glass connector sleeve on the clear stem w/round scalloped foot, Hobbs, Brockunier & Co., ca. 1890, crack in connector sleeve, w/burner, 9" h.................................................. **523**

**Table lamp,** blown glass squared cranberry opalescent Seaweed patt. font, raised on a clear ringed glass pedestal on a square foot, w/old burner, ca. 1890, 9" h. .............. **1,430**

**Table lamp,** Burmese glass, 10" d. domical shade & base handpainted & enameled w/Egyptian decoration of five ibis birds in flight in sunrise sky w/pyramids & palm

*Parlor Lamp with Scene of Lions*

tree oasis scene, original Burmese glass chimney, gilt metal mounts, not electrified, Mount Washington, late 1890s, 20" h........ **10,350**

**Table lamp,** clear opalescent glass squatty bulbous Coin Spot font raised on a clear glass pressed Inverted Thumbprint & Fan pedestal base, 8 1/2" h. ........................... **220**

**Table lamp,** clear pressed flint glass, Bellflower patt., the bulbous font in ribbed single vine Bellflower patt. tapering to a glass connector to a flaring paneled glass pedestal base w/round scalloped rim, ca. 1860, 7 1/4" h. (flakes on base) ....... **220**

**Table lamp,** domical open-topped milk glass shade decorated in deep red w/a scene of a lion & lioness on a faux mosaic tile ground resting on a three-arm ring suspending facet-cut prisms, brass collar on the tall ovoid glass base w/matching decoration, on a round antiqued brass footed base, unmarked, probably Bradley & Hubbard, turn-of-the-century factory conversion to electric, 29" h. (ILLUS. above)............................................................. **2,070**

**Table lamp,** pressed blue glass 'match holder' base lamp, squatty bulbous ringed font raised on a tapering cylindrical standard above the squared foot w/a pair of shallow indentations on the top to hold matches, ca. 1890, 7 1/2" h. (minor roughness on base corners, minor flakes under base) ....................................................... **275**

**Table lamp,** pressed glass, a kerosene burner & brass collar on the squatty ringed onion-form blue opaline glass font above a turned brass connector & flaring ringed pedestal on a square white marble foot, ca. 1860, 9" h. .......................................... **61**

**Table lamp,** pressed glass Coolidge Drape patt., scalloped pedestal base, cobalt blue, flat chip & flake under base, ca. 1900, 9" h. (ILLUS. left below)....................... **198**

**Table lamp,** pressed glass Eason patt., a bulbous cranberry opalescent Coin Dot patt. font above a clear ribbed standard & ribbed domed foot, w/burner, 9 1/2" h. (ILLUS. right with Coolidge Drape lamp) ...... **385**

*Coolidge Drape & Eason Lamps*

*Two Riverside Glass Table Lamps*

**Table lamp,** pressed glass Fern patt., the squatty bulbous green patterned font w/shell-form leaf clusters raised on a tall slender clear glass pedestal w/round foot w/embossed beading underneath, Riverside Glass Co., ca. 1900, 10" h. (ILLUS. left, bottom previous page)........................... **138**

**Table lamp,** pressed glass Panel patt., a short wide cylindrical green font raised on a tall slender clear glass pedestal w/round foot, Riverside Glass Co., ca. 1900, 7 1/2" h. (ILLUS. right with Fern lamp, bottom previous page) ........................ **138**

**Table lamp,** pressed glass, the spherical blue font w/a raised berry design, a brass connector to the clambroth glass pressed pedestal squared base w/rounded corners, ca. 1870, 9" h............................... **275**

**Table lamp,** pressed Triple Swag & Diamond clear pear-shaped font w/brass collar & connector to the milk white pedestal on a stepped square base, 12 1/4" h. ......................................................... **77**

*Ripley "Marriage" Lamp*

**Table lamp,** Ripley Marriage lamp, double bulbous blue fonts w/burner rings flank a clambroth match holder & harp-form support joined by a brass collar to the milk glass pedestal base w/stepped squared & scrolled foot, marked w/1870 patent date, D.C. Ripley and Company, very minor base chips, 12 3/4" h. (ILLUS.)............. **1,265**

**Table lamp,** Ripley Marriage lamp, pressed glass w/stepped squared milk glass base w/brass connnector to a white clambroth upper section w/top center well flanked by blue clambroth fonts w/brass collars, marked "D.C. Ripley, Pat. Pending," ca. 1880s, 12 1/8" h. (minor roughness on base)............................................................ **770**

**Table lamp,** "Ripley Marriage lamp," two bulbous translucent blue fonts flanking a central match holder & joined on a tapering flange to a threaded brass connector on an opaque milk glass stepped, square pedestal foot, connector dated "1868,"

lamp marked "D.C. Ripley, Patent Pending," brass font collars w/kerosene burners, 11 1/2" h. .................................................. **880**

*Fine Cut Velvet Kerosene Table Lamp*

**Table lamp,** spherical opalescent glass ball shade on a burner & wide brass collar fitted on a large ovoid melon lobed Cut Velvet Diamond Quilted patt. base in deep pink shaded to white, on a high brass foot cast w/an acanthus leaf band & blocked feet w/classical details, w/chimney, late 19th c., 17" h. (ILLUS.) .................................. **495**

*Tall Green Glass Kerosene Lamp*

**Table lamp,** wide squatty mushroom-shaped shade tapering to a flared cylindrical top opening, in deep green glass w/a frosted interior & decorated w/dainty enameled flowers & gilt trim, raised on a shade ring above a burner & brass shoulder w/a drop-in font, a tall baluster-form matching base resting on a round brass foot, w/a Success burner, ca. 1890, shade 10" d., overall 22" h. (ILLUS.)............................................................ **303**

*Table Lamp*

**Table lamp,** paneled flaring cast-iron pedestal base supporting a frosted clear glass paneled font, fitted w/a five-panel shade w/a brass frame enclosing lithophane panes w/various scenes, four panes marked "PPM," panes 5 x 5 1/4", overall 16 1/2" h. (ILLUS.) ................................ **319**

**Treen kerosene table lamp,** a bulbous ring-turned hardwood font w/a brass collar & tinned interior raised on a slender ring- and knob-turned wood pedestal & square, stepped wood base, 19th c., 8 3/8" h. .................................................................... **248**

*Wall-Mounted Kerosene Lamp*

**Wall-mounted kerosene lamp,** a cranberry Coin Dot patt. ball shade on a brass burner above the large ovoid brass font fitted into an open brass pierced cup support supported on a cast-brass arm w/pierced scroll bracket & swinging on a cast-brass wall mount hanger, marked "1889 Imperial (Im'pd) Climax," late 19th c., some repair on burner, 14" h. (ILLUS.) ...................... **795**

*Victorian Kerosene Wall Sconces*

**Wall sconces,** a cast-brass Neoclassical design w/an ornate cartouche-form wall plate supporting a scrolled griffin-mounted swing arm w/a tall oblong font supporting a burner & ring fitted w/a white opalescent Hobnail patt., flaring & ruffled crown-style shade, overall 15" h., pr. (ILLUS.) ............................................................. **385**

*Unusual Wedgwood Jasper Lamp*

**Wedgwood Jasper Ware table lamp,** the classical urn-form light blue jasper ware base decorated w/white relief classical figures & mounted w/a brass foot, connector ring, collar & scroll handles, the top brass cap supporting a clear half-round glass font fitted w/a kerosene burner & spider supporting a domical open-topped milk glass shade & clear glass chimney, England, ca. 1871, impressed mark, vase base 17 1/2" h. (ILLUS.) ............................................................. **920**

# Lamps, Miscellaneous

*Early American Argand Lamp*

**Argand lamp,** brass, two-arm model, the acanthus leaf finial above a fluted reservoir flanked by foliate & scroll buttresses, overhanging prisms above a fluted stem flanked by two arms terminating in electrified candle sockets w/added plaques w/"B. Gardiner - N. York," & frosted & etched tulip-shaped shades, over outscrolling leaves w/hanging pendent prisms above a foliate & turned shaft on a square metal base, first half 19th c., 24 1/2" h. (ILLUS.) ...................................... **$2,115**

*Early English Argand Lamp*

**Argand lamps,** bronze & glass, double-arm, a central upright lobed urn-form font above turned cross arms ending in burners supporting frosted & etched tulip-form glass shades, raised on a squared, stepped pedestal & square foot, labeled "Messenger & Sons," England, manufactured for Alfred Welles, Boston, early 19th c., surface wear, soiling, 20" h., pr. (ILLUS. of one) ........................................... **2,185**

**Argand lamps,** bronze & glass, each w/a caryatid-form standard supporting an urn-form oil font w/a classical head & drape border continuing to a scroll arm w/socket surmounted by a ball & trumpet-form floral-etched glass shade & a glass scalloped bobêche hung w/long triangular prisms, the whole raised on a square stepped base, J. & I. Cox, New York City, ca. 1840, electrified, 22 3/4" h., pr. (bobéches possibly later, one repaired) ..... **4,830**

**Astral lamp,** a large spherical open-topped frosted & etched glass shade w/a Gothic panel design, fitted on a wide brass ring suspending long triangular prisms above the gilt-bronze pedestal base w/a baluster-form stem above four cast dolphins above the domed & squared rococo-style footed base, electrified, mid-19th c., 23" h. ............................................................. **1,840**

**Astral lamp,** brass base w/inverted pear-shaped font supporting a round collar hung w/long triangular prisms above a floriform capped fluted column standard raised on a molded spreading base on a square marble foot, the spherical frosted, molded & etched glass shade w/Gothic arch windows alternating w/arching columns, mid-19th c., electrified, 24" h. (one prism missing, one incomplete) .................... **431**

*Fine Cut-Overlay Astral Lamp*

**Astral lamp,** cut-overlay glass & gilt brass, a clear frosted wheel-cut & acid-etched tulip-form shade w/Gothic arches & roundels resting on a font ring suspending long triangular prisms above the cut-overlay standard in red cut to white w/gilt & polychrome foliate & scroll designs, on a scrolling gilt-brass base, attributed to the Boston & Sandwich Glass Co., mid-19th c., electrified, one prism missing, gilt wear, minor shade chips, 33" h. (ILLUS.) ........................................................ **3,450**

**Astral lamp,** gilt-brass, a square C-scroll & foliate-cast foot below the reeded columnar standard w/a scrolled capital below the flaring rounded burner supporting a tall tulip-form shade w/ruffled rim in clear frosted glass engraved w/swags & grape clusters, Cornelius & Co., Philadelphia label, patent-dated April 1, 1843, 26" h. (no burner, minor gilt wear)......................... **1,035**

### Fine Glass & Brass Astral Lamp

**Astral lamp,** gilt-brass, glass & marble, the tall slender ribbed standard of opalescent & blue glass w/gilt trim supported by a foliate & scroll gilt-brass base on a square white marble foot, the brass font suspending long triangular prisms & supporting a bulbous vase-form clear & frosted glass shade wheel-cut w/shields, lyres & foliate designs, mid-19th c., 30" h. (ILLUS.)....................................................... **3,450**

**Betty lamp,** brass, tapering flattened oblong font w/unusual double burner w/two wick supports & brass pick suspended from the curved upright handle & straight iron hanger bar w/hooked end, 19th c., 5" h. plus hanger.............................................. **193**

**Betty lamp,** wrought iron, flat-topped oblong oil font w/silhouetted chicken finial, upright end handle w/wire hanging hook & wick pick, pitted, 7 1/4" h. plus hanger & pick.............................................................. **660**

**Betty lamp,** wrought iron, low tapering oblong font w/top opening & upright end handle w/chain & pick, 19th c., 4 3/4" h. ....... **220**

**Betty lamp on stand,** tin, a round saucer base centered by a slender cylindrical stem supporting the deep pointed oblong tin font w/rim spout & strap handle from top to the center of the stem, Portsmouth, New Hampshire, 19th c., worn layers of silver paint, 6" h. .............................................. **165**

**Fluid burning lamp,** blown glass, 'sparking' lamp, a waisted cylindrical font w/applied loop handle, cobalt blue, w/original brass collar & camphene burner, mid-19th c., 3 3/4" h. ......................................................... **1,760**

**Fluid burning lamp,** blown & pressed glass, a cobalt blue blown font w/sixteen ribs swirled to the right, a rolled mouth & angled wide shoulder above tapering cylindrical sides, attached w/a wafer to a lacy glass cup plate foot No. R-54, Boston & Sandwich Glass Co., ca. 1828-35, slight refracting half-inch line on rim of font, 7" h. (ILLUS. top of next column) ..... **11,000**

**Fluid burning lamp,** blown & pressed glass, a spherical blown font attached

### Unique Blown & Pressed Early Lamp

w/wafers to a tall pressed square scrolled standard & paw foot lion head base, possibly Boston & Sandwich Glass Co., late 1820s, 8 1/4" h. ............................................. **1,100**

**Fluid burning lamp,** pewter, a domed reeded round base w/a short shaft supporting a cylindrical font w/a squatty bulbous bottom, the tapering shoulder fitted w/a camphene burner, a strap handle from base of font to base, 19th c., 6" h. plus burner ................................................................. **413**

### Rare Paneled Pressed Glass Lamp

**Fluid burning lamp,** pressed flint glass, a slightly tapering octagonal font on a baluster- and knob-form paneled standard & square base, bright teal bluish green, attributed to Boston & Sandwich Glass Co., ca. 1840-60, 10 1/2" h. (ILLUS.) ........ **6,600**

**Fluid burning lamp,** pressed flint glass, Acanthus Leaf patt. font, blue leaf-molded font on a clambroth vasiform standard

*Large Group of Glass Fluid Lamps*

w/four leaves above the tiered beaded square base, sand finish, New England Glass Co. or Boston & Sandwich Glass Co., mid-19th c., imperfections, 10 1/4" h. (ILLUS. far right with large group above) .................................... **1,150**

**Fluid burning lamp,** pressed flint glass, Bigler patt. font on an octagonal concave paneled standard & square base, deep amethyst, possibly Boston & Sandwich Glass Co., ca. 1840-60, imperfections, w/whale oil burner, 9 1/2" h. (ILLUS. fourth from left with large group above) ..... **2,185**

**Fluid burning lamp,** pressed flint glass, Bigler patt. font on an octagonal concave paneled standard & square base, amethyst, possibly Boston & Sandwich Glass Co., ca. 1840-60, minor imperfections, 9 1/2" h. (ILLUS. fifth from left with large group above) .................................................. **2,185**

*Powder Blue 'Onion' Table Lamp*

**Fluid burning lamp,** pressed flint glass, 'Onion' lamp, a squatty bulbous finely ribbed font w/collar raised on a ringed metal connector to the tall slender ribbed standard & widely flaring ribbed foot, powder blue, complete w/12" d. frosted clear floral-engraved shade, original double brass burner, mid-19th c., overall 21 1/2" h. (ILLUS. of base) .......................... **2,090**

**Fluid burning lamp,** pressed flint glass, the arched faceted font on a hexagonal tiered standard & hexagonal base, cobalt blue, probably New England, mid-19th c., minor imperfections, 9 1/4" h. (ILLUS. fourth from right with Acanthus Leaf lamp group above) ............................................. **3,105**

**Fluid burning lamp,** pressed flint glass, Three-Printie Block patt. font, on a knop above a paneled hexagonal base, canary yellow, probably New England, mid-19th c., minor imperfections, 8" h. (ILLUS. third from left with Acanthus Leaf lamp group above) .................................................. **374**

**Fluid burning lamp,** pressed flint glass, Three-Printie Block patt., waisted paneled standard & square foot, original pewter whale oil burner, sapphire blue, Boston & Sandwich Glass Co., 9 3/4" h. ... **3,300**

**Fluid burning lamp,** pressed flint glass, Waisted Loop patt. font, on a pressed octagonal base, canary yellow, possibly Boston & Sandwich Glass Co., ca. 1840-60, 10 1/2" h. ................................... **1,980**

**Fluid burning lamp,** pressed flint glass, Waisted Loop patt. font, on a pressed square monument base, canary yellow, possibly Boston & Sandwich Glass Co., ca. 1840-60, minor chips on base, 10 1/2" h. (ILLUS. fifth from right with Acanthus Leaf lamp group above) ............. **2,990**

**Fluid burning lamps,** pressed flint glass, Bigler patt. font on an octagonal concave paneled standard & square base, sapphire blue, possibly Boston & Sandwich Glass Co., ca. 1840-60, 9 3/4" h., pr. (ILLUS. far left with Acanthus Leaf lamp group above) ................................................ **4,600**

**Fluid burning lamps,** pressed flint glass, Loop patt. font, on a hexagonal standard & tiered hexagonal base, canary yellow, probably New England, mid-19th c., minor imperfections, 8" & 8 1/2" h., 2 pcs. (ILLUS. second from right with Acanthus Leaf lamp group above) .................................. **805**

**Fluid burning lamps,** pressed flint glass, tapering Loop patt. font raised on a waisted paneled standard on a round foot, dark sapphire blue, original pewter collar & camphene burner, 9" h., pr. (usual mold roughness, small open bubble on base of one) .................................................. **7,150**

**Grease lamp,** wrought iron, hanging-type, a shallow square pan w/one corner partitioned, suspended from a twisted slender post swinging below an adjustable tall racket trammel, early, adjusts from 28 1/4" h. ......................................................... **303**

**Lard lamp,** cast iron & tin, a low cylindrical font w/small angled wick spout & upright curved handle ending in wire picks, the font raised on a slender cylindrical stem w/a ring strap handle resting in a dished base, brass label marked w/finial, "S.N. & H.C. Ufford, 113 Court St, Boston, Kinnear's Patent, Feb. 4, 1851" .......................... **165**

**Lard lamp,** painted tin & cast iron, trunnion type, the tin lozenge-shaped font w/two wick tubes suspended from a cast-iron foliate frame & base, gilt, green & red decoration on a yellow ground, brass stamped label "S.N. & H.C. Ufford 117 court St. Boston Kinnear Patent Feb. 4, 1851," Boston, mid-19th c., 9 x 12" (minor paint loss) ................................................ **489**

**Lard lamp,** tin, a short wide cylindrical font w/two short wick openings raised on a slender cylindrical shaft on a round low domed foot, a C-scroll strap handle from base of font to side of shaft, weighted base, 19th c., 6 3/8" h. ..................................... **165**

*Tower-shaped Glass Night Light*

inserted in a rounded wooden block base, early, 11" h. ............................................ **385**

*Fine Victorian Sinumbra Lamp*

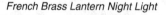

*French Brass Lantern Night Light*

**Night light,** brass, glass & cast white metal, a tall twisted brass upright w/arched top suspending on chains a squared brass filigree lantern w/a ruby jewel set in the front & holding a ruby glass candle cup, the ornate scroll-cast footed base in white metal, France, late 19th c., overall 12 1/4" h. (ILLUS.) .......................................... **275**

**Night light,** pressed blue opaque glass, modeled as a cylindrical block tower w/arched opening at one side below the conical fish scale-design roof w/vent holes & a metal vent cap, marked on base "Déposé - Pantin," w/numbers, France, early 20th c., 3 1/2" d., 7 1/2" h. (ILLUS. top next column) ................................. **195**

**Pan lamp,** wrought iron, an arched tripod base w/scalloped collar fitted above the legs centering a tall slender iron rod w/a small round open fluid pan on adjustable bracket, ring finial at the top, old dark pitted finish, 24 3/4" h. .......................................... **605**

**Rush lamp,** wrought iron & wood, a wrought-iron upright w/rush holder top, a short side upturned arm w/candle socket,

**Sinumbra table lamp,** gilt-brass & glass, a slender columnar standard raised on a petal-molded square base, the squatty wide clear frosted & engraved shade w/a tall flaring central opening decorated w/flowers & baskets, the shade ring hung w/cut prisms, mid-19th c., 31" h. (ILLUS.) .. **2,875**

**Whale oil lamp,** tin & glass, a clear cylindrical glass font w/brass collar & two-wick whale burner flanked by upright tin round frames enclosing bull's-eye focusing lenses, all on a slender cylindrical tin shaft & round disk weighted base, old worn black finish, first half 19th c., 8 1/2" h. (old repairs, one lens chipped) ....... **248**

**Whale oil table lamps,** pressed sapphire blue flint glass, the tapering ovoid fonts w/the Arch patt. fitted w/original pewter collar & double burner, fonts joined w/a wafer to an ornate flaring tiered octagonal pedestal base, Pittsburgh, ca. 1830-50, 10 3/8" h., pr. ......................................... **7,425**

# CHAPTER 2

# Electric Lamps & Lighting

## Handel Lamps

*The Handel Company of Meriden, Connecticut (1885-1936) began as a glass and lamp shade decorating company. It became a major producer of decorative electric lamps which have become very collectible today.*

*Handel Lily-form Boudoir Lamp*

**Boudoir lamp,** a bronzed metal lily pad-form rounded base w/turned up edges centering two naturalistic upright stems, the taller stem ending in a large floriform slag glass shade w/overlapping green & white slag petals, the shorter stem ending in a green slag bud, base w/brown patina, raised mark on base illegible, ca. 1903, 13" h. (ILLUS.) ..................................... **$460**

**Boudoir lamp,** a small pyramidal green slag glass shade in a brass frame, raised on a squared gilt brass base w/a stepped flaring foot, shade & base signed, worn gilding, early 20th c., 16 1/4" h. ..................... **880**

**Boudoir lamp,** small domical hexagonal reverse-painted shade w/a slightly scalloped base rim, decorated w/a tropical sunset scene w/palm trees & reflections in water in shades of green, blue, orange & yellow, signed "Handel 6313 W.R.," on a slender copper base w/molded braiding above a quatrefoil foot, cloth label under base, ca. 1916, 14 1/2" h. (rim chips on shade) ............................................... **2,587**

**Boudoir lamp,** 6" w. bell-shaped bent-glass six-paneled shade w/a flat drop rim, the upper panels in striated yellow & deep red slag glass overlaid w/filigree of palm trees, the pale yellow border panels w/a looping metal filigree, on a slender paneled Handel base w/a hexagonal foot ....... **2,464**

*Handel Boudoir Lamp with Landscape*

**Boudoir lamp,** 6 3/4" d. conical reverse-painted shade decorated w/a landscape in shades of green, brown & blue, signed "Handel 6363" w/an "R" within a diamond, on a vase-form patinated copper base w/a round foot & applied Handel label, repaired rim chip on shade, ca. 1910, overall 13 3/4" h. (ILLUS.) ................ **4,312**

**Boudoir lamp,** 7" d. domical reverse- and obverse-painted shade, decorated w/a winter landscape of a group of four tall bare trees above snowy ground w/a cluster of shrubbery beyond, against a pale yellow sky, in shades of dark brown, black & white, on a signed Handel tree trunk base, shade signed "Handel 5624 R.D." ............................................. **3,640**

**Boudoir lamp,** 7" d. domical reverse-painted shade, a clear frosted ground decorated w/an unusual design of stalks of bamboo in shades of green, on a slender bronzed metal base w/oblong panels in the standard, shade & base signed, 15" h. ............................................. **1,840**

**Boudoir lamp,** 7" d. domical reverse-painted shade decorated in the Arts & Crafts style w/thin blue & green alternating stripes radiating from the top center to a border of yellow, blue & red scrolls & small red rose blossoms w/green leaves all on a frosted ground, on a slender ribbed & scroll-cast gilt-metal Handel base, shade signed "Handel 7063 A.G.".... **1,344**

*Handel Boudoir with Winter Scene*

*Handel Boudoir with Autumnal Scene*

**Boudoir lamp,** 7" d. domical reverse-painted shade decorated w/a continuous sunset landscape w/tall slender trees w/bushy tops in meadows beside a small pond, in shades of dark green, brown, umber, tan & golden yellow, raised on a slender bronzed metal Handel ribbed shade w/flaring paneled foot, shade signed (ILLUS.) ........................................... **3,360**

**Boudoir lamp,** 7" d. domical reverse-painted shade decorated w/a desert scene of silhouetted camel riders & walkers against a pale yellow & gold background w/pyramids & mountains, artist-signed, No. 6557, on a slender simple bronzed metal Handel base w/gently lobed foot ...... **3,304**

**Boudoir lamp,** 7" d. domical reverse-painted shade decorated w/a snowy winter landscape w/a cluster of leafless trees in the foreground & further trees in the distance, in brown, rust, green, white & pale orange, raised on a signed tree trunk base, shade ring signed "Handel 5624" (ILLUS. top next column) ............................. **3,360**

**Boudoir lamp,** 7" d. domical reverse-painted shade decorated w/scattered clusters of pink blossoms & green leaves on a frosted paneled ground, No. 6834, on a painted white slender reeded Handel metal base ................................................. **2,800**

**Boudoir lamp,** 7" w. molded domical squared reverse-painted shade w/a lightly scalloped rim, decorated w/a wide band of rust & yellow roses & green & grey leaves around the lower border, creamy frosted white upper section, raised on a slender ribbed standard w/an Oriental-style pierced round Handel base in grey, shade No. 6698, artist-signed ....... **2,800**

**Boudoir lamp,** 7 3/8" d. tapering hexagonal shade w/flattened bottom rim reverse-painted w/an overall leafy jungle scene w/green & yellow leaves & pink berries & a blue parrot, signed "Handel.7010.AG," raised on a fluted columnar base w/a scroll-pierced round foot, molded Handel mark, ca. 1910, overall 13" h. ...................... **3,450**

*Handel Landscape Boudoir Lamp*

**Boudoir lamp,** 7 1/2" w. paneled conical reverse-painted shade w/a blue background & green & sunset pink, the exterior w/a landscape of leafy trees & water, signed inside "Handel 6232," raised on a slender six-sided metal base flaring at the bottom & w/a greyish green patina, impressed "Handel," cap indented, 14" h. (ILLUS.) ...................................................... **2,185**

**Boudoir lamp,** 8" d. domed reverse-painted shade w/a scalloped edge, painted w/a small basket of colorful flowers against a pale yellow ground w/a scalloped orange border band painted to resemble basketweave, raised on a slender painted metal base also resembling a wide basketweave design, shade signed "Handel 7969," base w/felt tag ................... **1,792**

**Boudoir lamp,** 8" d. domical hexagonal reverse-painted shade, decorated w/overall scattered pink & yellow roses on leafy stems w/small butterflies scattered between on a frosted ground, on a simple frosted glass pedestal Handel base w/round foot & metal banding.................... **2,576**

**Boudoir lamp,** 8" d. domical reverse-painted shade decorated w/a continuous band of large & small pink rose blossoms & leaves around the lower border against a shaded grey to white front & lightly ribbed ground, on a metal Handel slender ribbed pedestal on a round Chinese-style pierced round foot, shade No. 6918, artist-signed.................................................. **2,744**

**Boudoir lamp,** 8" d. domical reverse-painted shade decorated w/deep rose blossoms w/yellow centers & green leaves against a shaded blue, yellow & green ground w/three multi-colored butterflies, raised on a slender bronzed metal pedestal base w/round foot, shade signed & numbered, base w/original patina & impressed signature, overall 14" h.................. **2,970**

**Boudoir lamp,** 8" d. domical sand-finished reverse-painted shade w/a tree-lined waterfront scene w/a windmill, signed "Handel 6497" on rim, raised on a brown patinated metal flared & ribbed base, overall 15 1/2" h...................................................... **1,380**

*Handel Boudoir Lamp with Roses*

**Boudoir lamp,** 8" w. domed hexagonal vertically ribbed reverse-painted shade decorated w/scattered orangish red rose blossoms & leafy stems & small butterflies on a frosted ground, raised on a slender bronzed metal wicker-design standard w/a round foot, shade signed "Handel 6242 M.P." (ILLUS.) ...................... **1,960**

**Boudoir lamp,** 7" d., domical reverse-painted shade decorated w/a scene of pond lilies & cattails against a blue ground, marked "Handel 6554," raised on a slender baluster-form metal base w/dished rounded foot, 13 1/2" h. (two rim chips on shade, corroded base finish, finial missing) ................................................................. **1,840**

*Handel Boudoir Lamp with Meadow*

**Boudoir lamp,** 7" d. bell-form reverse-painted shade decorated w/a meadow landscape in a natural palette, rim signed "Handel 6231," raised on a slender bronzed-metal standard w/a ribbed, flaring round foot impressed "Handel," 14" h. (ILLUS.).............................................. **2,645**

**Boudoir lamp,** 7" d. domical arched panel-molded reverse-painted shade signed "Handel #6562A," decorated w/a black foreground Mt. Fuji landscape w/trees, lakeside pagoda & the distant grey mountain against a bluish grey sky, raised on a slender bronzed metal reeded standard & round stepped foot embossed "Handel," overall 14" h. ............................................... **3,300**

**Boudoir lamp,** 8" d. domical ribbed textured reverse-painted shade, decorated w/a watercolor palette featuring a harbor scene w/sailing vessels, brown tones against blue water & sky at sunset, signed "6356 Handel Co.," raised on a single-socket slender reeded cylindrical standard on a round patinated metal base, impressed "Handel," wear to patina, ca. 1916, 14 1/2" h. (ILLUS. top of next page).............................................................. **2,300**

**Boudoir lamp,** 7" d. domical reverse-painted shade molded w/four sets of four ver-

*Handel Harbor Scene Boudoir Lamp*

tical ribs, the interior painted w/tall sailing ships in port w/windmills on the far shore, pastel sea & sky ground, signed "Handel 6356" on edge, raised on a slender ribbed cast-metal base w/round foot also labeled "Handel," 14 1/2" h. ........................ **2,415**

**Desk lamp,** a bell-form hexagonal shade w/flat rim band composed of a pierced metal overlay in a tropical palm tree design over panels of sunset-colored slag glass, the lower curvilinear border over green & white slag glass, raised on a scroll-trimmed tall C-form arm above the circular bronze base, shade marked, early 20th c., 14 1/2" h. (cracked shade border segments) .............................................. **2,300**

*Handel Desk Lamp*

**Desk lamp,** long cylindrical open-bottomed shade in acid-etched Mosserine glass, supported on a long bronze bracket raised on a tall curved upright arm above

the scalloped oblong base, shade & base marked, shade 10 1/2" l., overall 15 1/2" h. (ILLUS.).................................... **1,540**

**Desk lamp,** a 5 1/2 x 8" domed leaded glass shell-form shade composed of a geometric design of alternating narrow & wide segments of mottled white, amber & pale blue glass, raised on a bronzed metal base w/a curved ribbed standard above a round domed foot, original patina, 4 1/2" h., base 7" d. .............................. **1,430**

*Handel Desk Lamp*

**Desk lamp,** a patinated bronze base w/a naturalistic oblong foot surmounted by an adjustable arched neck mounted w/a scroll & terminating in a green half-round glass shade molded overall w/pine needles, the base w/a Handel fabric label, the shade printed "Handel - Mosserine - 6132 1/2," damage at end of neck, ca. 1910, 11 1/2" h. (ILLUS.).............................. **546**

**Desk lamp,** an open-bottomed 8" d. cylindrical adjustable shade of moss green chipped ice-design glass fitted in a forked bracket & raised on a high curved bronzed metal standard adjusting on an oblong foot, shade numbered, base signed, overall 12" h....................................... **880**

**Desk lamp,** the half-round tubular reverse-painted shade w/an acid-textured exterior & the interior painted w/an autumnal landscape, swiveling on a reeded patinated bronze arm & an adjustable curved standard w/scroll decoration on a scallop-cast oval foot, dark brown patina, unsigned, ca. 1915, 12" h. ........................ **1,495**

**Desk lamp,** a cylindrical horizontal shade w/flat oblong opening, decorated w/green on the textured exterior & cased in white, marked "Mosserine Handel 6010," mounted between curved brackets joined at the top of a tall curved adjustable shaft above an oblong weighted base w/a threaded "Handel" label on the felt liner, 8" l., 15" h. ..................................... **1,380**

**Desk lamp,** 7" d. domical reverse-painted shade decorated w/a peachy pink sky, dark leafy trees along a waterway & distant red rooftops hidden behind a bluish grey meadow, suspended in a bronze bell-form harp joining a slender standard on a widely flaring lobed foot, adjustable, shade signed "Handel #6578A," base incised "Handel," overall 19" h. ...................... **3,575**

**Desk lamp,** 7 1/2" d. curved conical six-panel leaded glass shade composed of amber slag glass panels w/six green decorative glass diamonds around the rim, the shade suspended & swiveling from an adjustable bronzed metal harp joined to a slender four-ribbed pedestal on a flaring four-lobed foot, 19" h. ...................... **1,495**

**Floor lamp,** 9 7/8" d. domical reverse-painted shade w/a 'chipped ice' exterior finish, painted w/a stylized grape & vine border in purple, black, spring & moss green, against a speckled turquoise blue & rose ground, signed "Handel 734-6849," suspended from a wide bronze harp above a slender bronze standard w/a round dished foot w/knob-cast border band, overall 56 1/2" h. ......................................... **6,815**

**Floor lamp,** 10" d. domical reverse-painted shade decorated in the 'Oriental Pheasant' patt., a long-tailed exotic bird flying among dark purple foliage & large bluish purple & yellow blossoms all against a deep reddish orange ground, shade suspended from a high looped harp on a tall slender standard w/three outswept feet, shade signed "Handel 7009"...................... **12,320**

**Floor lamp,** 10" d. domical reverse-painted shade, decorated w/an autumnal landscape w/meadows in the foreground & a small pond flanked by large trees w/green, yellow, orange & maroon leaves w/further fall trees in the distance & a sunset sky in yellow, orange & dark grey, shade signed "Handel 6268R," shade suspended in a looped harp above a tall slender standard w/a round dished foot, base signed w/felt tab .......................... **5,600**

**Floor lamp,** 10" d. domical reverse-painted shade in the 'Jungle Bird' patt., pairs of large dark red & dark blue parrots perched on large arched brown branches w/scattered dark green & brown leaves against a shaded golden yellow background, shade signed "Handel 6852," suspended in an arched harp above the tall slender standard w/a round dished base w/small knob feet ............................... **8,960**

**Floor lamp,** 10" d. domical shade w/brown chipped-ice exterior suspended in a shaped bell frame above the tall slender lamp base w/a round, domed foot, bronzed-metal base w/recent patina, shade & base signed, 57" h. ........................ **2,530**

**Floor lamp,** 16" d. domical reverse-painted shade in the 'Hydrangea' patt., decorated w/large clusters of deep rose, pink & lavender blossoms among light yellow & brown leaves against a mottled yellow ground, shade signed "Handel 6739," on a tall slender Handel standard on a tripod base w/cabriole legs ending in scroll feet (ILLUS. of the shade top next column)..... **17,920**

*Handel Hydrangea Floor Lamp Shade*

**Floor lamp,** 22" w. eight-panel bent caramel slag glass shade, each tapering panel overlaid w/a metal graduated block-style filigree above a dark gold slag border band w/further lattice filigree & small painted green diamonds, signed, on a tall bronzed metal standard w/a domed four-buttress foot................................................. **6,720**

**Floor lamp,** 24" d. conical shade w/lobed rim, decorated w/panels of intricate metal filigree in a palm tree design over panels of mottled orange, yellow & red slag glass representing a sunset skyline, on a tall bronzed metal Handel base w/a slender reeded shaft & a waisted & lobed heavy foot ........................................................ **11,200**

**Floor lamp,** 25" w. octagonal pyramidal shade composed of graduated blocks of striated green slag glass above a flat drop body of green slag overlaid w/metal filigree bands w/delicate bare trees, raised on a tall Handel bronzed metal standard w/four figural griffins perched around the round foot................................. **17,360**

*Handel Leaded Floor Lamp Shade*

**Floor lamp,** 28" d. domical leaded glass shade composed of radiating squares of dark green slag glass w/a wide border band w/a deep red Greek key design, on a tall slender bronzed metal standard w/a round foot (ILLUS. of shade) .................... **10,640**

**Floor lamp,** the domical six-paneled slag glass shade w/pierced metal overlay of water lilies & cattails over red, orange, green & yellow striated glass panels, raised on an adjustable curved arm & a reeded gilt-metal standard, the base realistically cast w/water lilies & cattails, on four petal feet, base w/fabric label reading "Handel Lamps," ca. 1910, overall 51" h............................................................ **3,795**

**Floor lamp,** torchere-style, inverted flaring trumpet-form shade acid-etched & enameled w/a shield & coat of arms, on a tall slender ring-turned metal standard w/a round, domed foot, 67" h. (three significant shade rim chips)...................................... **403**

*Hall Light Decorated with Parrot*

**Hall light,** 6" d. spherical shade w/textured amber exterior painted on the exterior w/a green & blue parrot & leafy grape-vines, a round stepped bronze-patinated ceiling plaque w/a gadrooned rim above a chain & shade mount, tassel base drop, shade signed "Handel 7006 RA" on rim, minor rim nicks, overall 28" h. (ILLUS.)...... **2,530**

*Handel Spherical Hall Light*

**Hall light,** 9 5/8" d. spherical shade w/chipped ice finish, the exterior painted w/a highly stylized floral & geometric design in yellow, green & salmon, the patinated metal mount terminating w/a faux tassel drop, overall 29" h. (ILLUS.)............... **764**

*Handel Hall Fixture*

**Hall light,** 10" d. spherical painted glass shade, grey textured glass internally mottled w/orange & amber & painted on the exterior w/a forest scene w/birds in shades of charcoal, green, yellow, orange & brown, brown patina, swag tassel, Model 6885, probably painted by Henri Bedigie, ca. 1923, 24" h. (ILLUS.).. **11,500**

*Handel Spherical Peacock Hall Light*

**Hall light,** 10" d. spherical painted shade decorated w/a colorful stylized design of a peacock perched on brown branches w/red & yellow blossoms & green leaves, against a textured tan ground, a pierced scrolled hanger & bell-shaped cap at the top & metal drop & tassel at the bottom, shade signed "Handel 7257" (ILLUS.)........ **6,664**

*Unique Handel Night Light*

**Night light,** 7" h. pointed upright egg-shaped reverse-painted shade decorated w/stylized red exotic birds perched on branches of purple & red blossoms & green leaves, all against a deep yellow ground, on a round Oriental-style pierced bronzed metal base, shade signed "7095 F.C. Handel" (ILLUS.) ................................... **1,792**

*Handel Slag Glass Piano Lamp*

**Piano lamp,** 6 1/8" w. tapering square slag glass shade w/four mottled green & amber panels w/striated yellow border within a metal diamond design overlay, on a single-socket base w/slender arched reeded arms attached to a round domed weighted base, impressed mark on base, metal tag on shade, cracks, 7 1/2" h. (ILLUS.) ........................................................... **1,380**

*Handel Slag Glass Lamp with Overlay*

**Table lamp,** 19 1/2" d. domical paneled leaded glass shade, composed of geometric tile & grapevine border metal filigree overlay over eight striated green slag glass bent panels & a drop apron, marked w/Handel tag, on a two-socket ribbed baluster-form bronze metal tagged Handel base, one cracked apron panel, joinery, 22 3/4" h. (ILLUS.).............. **1,955**

*Fine Handel Leaded Glass Lamp*

**Table lamp,** 22" d. domed leaved glass shade composed of pink & yellow striated glass flower segments arranged on an entwined green leafy vine, graduating geometric amber & white striated tile background segments, impressed "1993 - I - 25 - Handel" on top of shade opening, on a five-socket slender bronzed metal marked Handel base w/raised foliate designs & a dark brown & green patina, 28" h. (ILLUS.) ............................................. **8,050**

*Water Lily Handel Table Lamp*

**Table lamp,** bronze & leaded glass, the floriform piece composed of three water lily-form blossoms w/the petals in white & striated green slag glass above two bronze buds & the bronze stemmed base rising from the center of lily pad leaves, raised Handel mark, one loose petal, early 20th c., 10 1/4" h. (ILLUS.) ...................... **3,220**

**Table lamp,** 10 1/2" d., domical shade w/'chipped ice' finish painted w/stylized Arts & Crafts blossom clusters alternating w/leaf clusters around the rim w/slender lines radiating down from the top center, a yellow ground w/orange & red flowers & green leaves, raised on a slender bronzed-metal reeded standard on a domed & pierced base w/four scrolled feet, shade & base both marked, overall 19" h. (two flat chips to shade edge, hidden by shade ring)........................................... **880**

*Handel Lamp with Two-color Shade*

**Table lamp,** 12" d. domical mushroom-shaped painted shade w/the upper portion in pale pink above a wide scalloped border band in light green, the section separated w/delicate white enameled leafy scrolls w/small pink blossoms w/jeweled centers, raised on a bronzed metal slender base w/four pierced & scroll-cast openings above the flaring, round scroll-cast foot, shade signed "Handel Co. 2583" (ILLUS.) ........................ **1,288**

**Table lamp,** 12" d. domical open-topped 'Tam-o'-Shanter' form shade reverse-painted w/a green scrolling stylized leaf design, sanded exterior, signed on the rim "Handel Co. 2642," mounted on a three-arm spider w/pierced swastika border above a paneled flaring cast-metal base, converted from a fluid lamp, corrosion, socket repair, 19" h. ............... **546**

**Table lamp,** 12 1/2" d. reverse-painted scenic lamp, flared 'Tam o' Shanter' glass shade w/tall leafy & evergreen trees against pale yellow & sunset pink textured background, rim signed "Handel 2967," raised on spider ring above brass & white columnar base, overall 22 1/2" h. (minor nicks on rim)..................................... **1,150**

**Table lamp,** 14" d. domed textured Teroma-style clear shade reverse-painted w/six red roses on thorny leafy green stems, marked in red "Handel 1521" & "A.C." in the design, mounted on a bronzed metal slender squared two-socket standard on a flaring square foot impressed "Handel," overall 21" h. (re-wired, replaced fitter cap) ............. **2,300**

**Table lamp,** 14" d. domical reverse-painted shade, decorated w/a border band of pink & rose-colored dogwood blossoms & green leaves against a solid light peach background, shade signed "Handel 6980," on a slender bronzed metal standard on a round flattened foot w/lappet rim band, base signed w/felt tab.......... **3,080**

**Table lamp,** 14" d. domical reverse-painted shade decorated w/geraniums in green & reddish orange on a yellow ground, chipped ice exterior finish, on a baluster-turned patinated metal base, shade signed "Handel GC 6588," 20" h. (flake on shade rim) .............................................. **1,980**

**Table lamp,** 14" d. domical tannish brown textured glass shade w/light reflective opal white interior, a molded basketweave border design w/four drop-ring "buckles" to simulate Mission furniture pulls, mounted on a slender baluster-form copper-finished metal standard w/domed round Handel base, overall 21" h. (base finish worn).............................. **2,300**

**Table lamp,** 14" d. mushroom-shaped open-topped bent-panel slag glass shade, the wide rolled sides tapering to a flared & serrated top opening, composed of large & small panels of streaked deep maroon, green & white slag glass w/a band of red diamond-shaped inserts around the lower border, on a slender gilt bronzed metal lappet-embossed Handel shade ........................................................ **2,184**

**Table lamp,** 14" d. scenic landscape domed shade of Teroma-style textured glass reverse-painted as mountainous scenic view w/leafy trees in foreground, "Handel 7147," raised on copper colored two-socket base w/"Handel" label of felt, 20 1/2" h. (some wear to metal patina, needs rewiring) ........................................ **4,025**

**Table lamp,** 15" d. conical shade decorated on the exterior w/a continuous heavily wooded landscape w/a stream in the foreground, on a slender bronzed metal Handel base w/round paneled foot, No. 5942 ............................................................. **5,600**

**Table lamp,** 15" d. conical shade decorated on the exterior w/overall delicate vines w/clusters of long green leaves, painted on the interior w/tall slender trees along a hillside, on a slender flaring ribbed bronze metal Handel base, No. 6411 ........ **6,720**

*Scarce Handel Wisteria Table Lamp*

**Table lamp,** 15" d. domical reverse- and obverse-painted shade, decorated on the exterior w/dark & light green leaves suspended from the upper rim, the interior painted w/large clusters of deep purple & deep red wisteria blooms, all above a mottled frosted white & pale yellow ground, on a slender Handel bronzed metal paneled standard w/a wide round paneled foot, signed on shade ring (ILLUS.) ...................................................... **6,720**

**Table lamp,** 15" d. domical mushroom-shaped reverse- and obverse-painted shade, the clear frosted ground painted on the exterior w/green acanthus leafage trim & gilt & on the interior w/large crimson spider mums, raised on a plain slender metal standard w/a round base & original green & brown mottled patina, original sockets & chains, shade signed

*Table Lamp with Handel Shade*

"Handel Co. 2558," the base marked by Bradley & Hubbard, 18 1/2" h. (ILLUS. ).... **2,530**

**Table lamp,** 15" d. domical reverse- and obverse-painted shade, decorated w/a scattered stand of tall leafless trees in a snowy landscape w/a forest of trees in the background under a yellow sky, in shades of dark & light brown, white, black & grey, shade signed "Handel 5994," slender bronzed metal base w/round scalloped foot & felt Handel label ................ **6,160**

**Table lamp,** 15" d. domical reverse-painted 'Basketweave' shade, molded w/vertical ribs & horizontal ridges, painted w/a profusion of pastel rose blossoms in shades of pink, rose & yellow w/green leaves interspersed, impressed "Handel" on top rim, mounted on a slender cast metal squared shaft w/a flaring squared foot, base w/"Handel" threaded label, small interior shade rim chip, 22" h. ........................ **2,185**

*Handel Lamp with Dutch Landscape*

**Table lamp,** 15" d. domical reverse-painted shade, 'chipped ice' exterior finish, interior painted w/silhouetted Dutch landscape in brown w/light pink & green, patinated metal base w/slender ribbed standard on a flaring ribbed foot, signed three times, 22 1/2" h. (ILLUS.) .................. **3,300**

**Table lamp,** 15" d. domical reverse-painted shade, decorated w/a winter landscape, a pair of tall bare trees beside a curving lakeside bank covered in snow, a thick forest of trees in the background under the pale yellow sky w/small tan clouds, on bronzed metal slender ribbed Handel base w/a round ribbed foot, shade signed "Handel 5624 R.C." ..................................... **4,032**

**Table lamp,** 15" d. domical reverse-painted shade, "Tropical Sunset" patt., a continuous scene of a tropical inlet framed by grasses & tall palm trees w/a sailboat in the distance under a full moon, in shades of dark & lighter brown, dark blue, peach w/a pale cream moon & stars, signed "Handel 6971A," on a slender ribbed bronzed metal standard w/a flaring ribbed round foot............................................. **5,600**

**Table lamp,** 15" d. mushroom-shaped leaded glass shade composed of radiating blocks of green slag glass extending to the rounded drop apron w/a white slag Greek key border band, raised on a tall very slender signed Handel base w/a wide spade leaf design foot ........................ **4,032**

**Table lamp,** 15 1/2" d. domical leaded glass shade, composed of small rectangular green slag pieces in a radiating design, border band of stylized ivory blossoms, raised on a slender patinated bronze pedestal w/a flaring disk foot, unmarked, 22 1/2" h. ........................................ **1,980**

**Table lamp,** 16" d. domical leaded glass shade, composed of overall scattered small dark pink cherry blossoms among dense light & dark green leaves, the top center of the shade w/a pierced design of entwined branches, raised on a slender tree trunk base ........................................... **21,280**

*Rare Handel Leafy Vine Table Lamp*

**Table lamp,** 16" d. domical reverse-painted shade, decorated w/a rare design of large leafy vines in shades of orange, brown & blue w/clusters of white & pale yellow blossoms against a light green ground, shade signed "Handel 7131," on a slender Handel bronzed-metal ring-turned base (ILLUS.)................................... **7,840**

**Table lamp,** 16" d. domical reverse-painted shade decorated w/a shaded green & amber interior & decorated on the outside w/a continuous riverside landscape in muted naturalistic earthtones, pierced metal cap stamped "Handel," raised on a bronzed metal slender swelled cylindrical ribbed shaft on a round flattened ribbed foot, 22" h. .............................................. **4,140**

**Table lamp,** 16" d. domical reverse-painted shade decorated w/a small flock of dark blue swallow-like birds flying above tall green grasses w/a dark tan to pale yellow mottled sky in the background, shade signed "Handel 6425 F.C.," on a slender bronzed metal base w/a round foot ........... **5,320**

*Handel Lamp & Paisley-style Shade*

**Table lamp,** 16" d. domical reverse-painted Teroma-style textured glass shade w/a dark tan ground decorated w/a wide border band of colorful paisley-like designs, Model No. 6750, on a slender waisted cast-metal standard w/round foot (ILLUS.)......................................................... **9,900**

**Table lamp,** 16" d. domical shade etched on the exterior w/a pine needles border band against an overall brownish red mosserine finish, raised on a slender ribbed Handel base w/a flaring paneled foot................................................................. **5,488**

**Table lamp,** 16" d. domical shade of Teroma-textured glass reverse-painted wild rose in soft pastel shades of pink, blue, yellow, green as realistic rose blossoms, buds & leafy stems, inscribed on lower edge "Handel 6422," raised on three-socket ribbed base w/cast "Handel"

mark, 21 1/2" h. (some metal patina
wear) .................................................. **6,900**

**Table lamp,** 16" d. domical shade w/an
etched wide border band of pine needles
& a brownish red mosserine finish on the
upper shade, on a slender ribbed
bronzed metal Handel standard w/a flar-
ing ribbed foot..................................... **4,480**

**Table lamp,** 16" d. domical six-panel shade
composed of bent amber slag glass panels within a pierced metal framework w/a
wide band of oak leaves w/applied color
around the scalloped lower rim, raised on
a slender swelled cylindrical bronzed
metal base w/flaring foot, 21" h. (worn,
finial missing, rim repair) ..................... **920**

**Table lamp,** 16" d. reverse-painted shade
w/a domed central section flaring widely
to deep cylindrical sides, decorated
w/large mums in yellow, reddish orange
& a touch of green, the exterior textured
& frosted, raised on a slender squared &
ribbed base, shade signed "Handel
#5698R," overall 24" h. ....................... **5,225**

*Handel Bent-panel Lamp with Filigree*

**Table lamp,** 16" d. six-panel bent-glass
shade, each tapering section of pale yellow slag glass divided by a bronzed metal
band w/lattice border & trimmed around
the scalloped base w/leafy vines painted
green, raised on a signed bronzed metal
Handel base w/a slender shaft above a
domed foot w/leaf-cast rim band, shade
signed "Handel 562" (ILLUS.) ..................... **5,320**

**Table lamp,** 16" l. rectangular reverse-
painted shade w/cut-corners, decorated
w/a unique Aquarium patt., the long flat
sides & end panels painted in autumn
colors w/tropical fish swimming among
sea grasses & seaweed, in shades of
yellow, tan, orange, brown, purple & red,
raised on a slender central shaft flanked
by a pair of upturned candle socket-style
sockets above a domed leaf-cast foot,
two panels w/stress cracks (ILLUS. top
next column) ................................................ **36,400**

*Aquarium Pattern Handel Lamp*

*Handel Lamp with Filigree Landscape*

**Table lamp,** 16" w. nine-panel umbrella-
form shade, each panel w/a large bent
slag glass panel in swirled deep red &
white above a narrow border panel in
green slag, the large panels overlaid w/a
filigreed metal tropical landscape scene
of tall & short palm trees, undulating
loops of metal filigree in the border panels, raised on a slender textured bronzed
metal base w/a round foot, shade signed
on shade ring (ILLUS.)................................. **4,480**

**Table lamp,** 16 1/2" d. reverse-painted
shade w/a blue textured ground trimmed
w/a wide polychrome floral border, raised
on a Chinese style rouleau base incised
w/a band of fretwork above a textured
body w/flaring foot, shade No. 6747,
base & shade signed, 23 1/2" h.
(ILLUS.).......................................................... **7,700**

*Handel Lamp with Chinese-style Base*

minor damage to metal overlay (ILLUS. below) ............................................................ **3,335**

*Overlaid Goldenrod Lamp*

*Handel Lamp with Leaded Shade*

**Table lamp,** 16 1/2" w. paneled domical glass shade composed of small blocks of caramel slag glass w/a patinated metal framework & painted fleur-de-lis border, raised on a slender patinated metal standard w/a raised lapped-leaf design round base on four shaped bracket feet, shade rim tag marked "Handel," 23 1/4" h. (ILLUS.) ...................................................... **2,070**

**Table lamp,** 17" d. domical glass shade w/seven amber slag glass bent panels framed w/metal overlay to depict field flowers painted yellow, raised on three-socket bronzed base w/Teroma-style texture & molded Handel mark, 22" h.,

*Handel Lamp with Filigree Slag Shade*

**Table lamp,** 17" w. paneled domical slag glass shade, ten sunset orange slag glass bent panels above a shaped green slag border, the panels overlaid w/bronzed metal filigree landscapes of leafy trees, the border w/filigree undulating bands, raised on a bronzed metal tree-form standard w/dark patina, needs rewiring, possible glass restoration, 24 1/2" h. (ILLUS.) ........................................ **4,025**

*Handel Lamp with Scenic Shade*

**Table lamp,** 17 1/4" d. domical reverse-painted shade w/'chipped ice' exterior, painted on the interior w/a continuous band of trees silhouetted against a shaded pink sky & pools of blue water, w/blossoming foliage & vines in tones of yellow, orange, black & blue, raised on a bronze base w/a slender central column flanked by three slender scroll supports all resting on a round disk foot, shade signed "Handel 7202 - PAL," wear to base patina, one shade pull missing, early 20th c., 24" h. (ILLUS.)................................................. **6,325**

**Table lamp,** 18" d. conical eight-panel slag glass shade in mottled green, red, orange & yellow overlaid w/a repeating pierced design of tropical trees & water w/slender palm trees, raised on a bronzed metal tapering cylindrical base w/low scroll mounts near the top & raised on a round disk foot w/a notched rim, original patina, unmarked, overall 24" h..... **2,310**

*Fine Handel Landscape Table Lamp*

**Table lamp,** 18" d. domical obverse- and reverse-painted shade, decorated w/"The Road" design featuring an autumn landscape w/a wide path curving between clusters of leafy birch trees in green & rust meadows w/dense trees in the distance under a blue & white cloudy sky, shade signed "Handel 6230," on a bulbous ovoid bronzed-metal "swampy tree trunk" base cast w/a forest scene (ILLUS.)...................................................... **24,640**

**Table lamp,** 18" d. conical reverse-painted shade decorated w/a continuous moonlit landscape w/tall leafy trees & a lake in the foreground w/a forest & hills in the distance under a low full moon & scattered clouds, in shades of dark blue, umber, yellow, orange & tan, shade signed "Handel 7107," on a bronzed metal baluster-form base w/a flared round foot........ **6,160**

**Table lamp,** 18" d. conical reverse-painted shade decorated w/a mound of trees surrounded by choppy water forming waves in the background, shades of green, brown, cream & black, on felt tab-signed Handel urn-form base ................................. **6,440**

*Arts & Crafts Style Handel Lamp*

**Table lamp,** 18" d. conical reverse-painted shade decorated w/an Arts & Crafts style design of long slender blades of grass in shades of green & blackish green against a yellow ground, raised on a slender signed bronzed metal base, shade signed "#5357" (ILLUS.) ............................ **12,320**

**Table lamp,** 18" d. conical reverse-painted shade, decorated w/large leafy trees in the foreground w/dark green foliage & brown trunks, green shrubbery & small trees under the large trees w/a yellow, orange & red sunset sky in the background, shade signed "Handel 6434," large bronzed metal baluster-form ribbed base w/a round scalloped foot also marked...... **14,000**

**Table lamp,** 18" d. conical reverse-painted shade decorated w/stylized floral cartouches in black, green, orange & red against a pumpkin orange ground w/a red border at the top & rim, raised on a slender inverted baluster-form bronzed metal base w/a round, slightly domed foot, shade signed & numbered "7418," base unsigned, 23" h. .................................. **1,760**

*Handel with Tree Landscape Shade*

**Table lamp,** 18" d. conical reverse-painted shaded decorated w/a continuous landscape w/a large leafy tree in the foreground w/meadows & trees against a cloudy sky in the background, in shades of brown, green & yellow, on a baluster-form four-footed basketweave patt. signed Handel base (ILLUS.)...................... **8,400**

**Table lamp,** 18" d. domical acid cut-back "Cameo Peacock" patt. shade, an etched design of a large peacock in red, blue & green perched on a large blossoming tree in shades of brown, green, lavender & yellow against a burnt orange ground, artist-signed on the interior & exterior, signed "Handel 7126 PAL," on a signed bronzed-metal tripod base w/scroll feet on a round stepped foot............................ **25,200**

**Table lamp,** 18" d. domical eight-lobed shade painted on the exterior w/a continuous landscape of slender trees w/delicate green leaves & flying birds, No. 6868, artist-signed, on a bronze metal bulbous ribbed urn-form Handel base w/a rectangular foot,..................................... **8,400**

**Table lamp,** 18" d. domical reverse-painted shade decorated w/a cabin perched on a rocky shoreline at sunset in shades of brown, yellow & purple, partial paper label, raised on a two-socket base in patinated metal w/a pod shape w/ribs &

*Handel Lamp with Cabin Scene*

molded leaves & on four small feet, woven label on base, overall 18 3/4" h. (ILLUS.)....................................................... **2,875**

*Rare Handel Table Lamp*

**Table lamp,** 18" d. domical reverse-painted shade decorated w/a colorful jungle scene in greens, golds, oranges & yellows centered by a pair of large red, blue, green & yellow parrots, raised on a dark bronze shouldered cylindrical base w/an etched shoulder band, 23 1/2" h. (ILLUS.)....................................................... **20,000**

**Table lamp,** 18" d. domical reverse-painted shade decorated w/a continuous sunset landscape w/meadow & clusters of tall trees & shrubs w/mountains in the distance, in shades of brown, green, orange & yellow, on a bronzed metal heavy ovoid base w/a relief-cast band tapering to a domed, stepped round foot, shade signed "Handel 6957," base signed............ **6,160**

**Table lamp,** 18" d. domical reverse-painted shade decorated w/a continuous landscape scene w/clusters of caramel & brown blossoms & buds atop green leaves & stems backed by tall trees w/narrow brown trunks & branches w/yellowish green & dark green leaves, a single large brown bird soars above a distant mountain range in deep violet against a pale blue & yellow sky, signed "7006," on a bronzed metal baluster-form base cast w/tall wide leaves w/curled tips tapering to a round foot, original dark brown & green patina, base impressed "Handel," overall 25 1/2" h. ......................... **6,490**

*Handel with Forest & Birds Shade*

**Table lamp,** 18" d. domical reverse-painted shade decorated w/a continuous landscape of small birds flying among tall slender delicate leafy trees w/small trees in the distance, in shades of green & brown against a golden cream background, raised on a signed bronzed-metal ring-turned Handel base (ILLUS.)........... **7,280**

**Table lamp,** 18" d. domical reverse-painted shade decorated w/a continuous countryside landscape of grassy fields & a stream w/large trees & rail fences in the center ground & woodlands in the background, shade signed "Handel 6754 R," on a slender signed bronzed metal tree trunk base (ILLUS. top on next column) .... **7,840**

**Table lamp,** 18" d. domical reverse-painted shade decorated w/a continuous very detailed landscape scene, pairs of tall realistic leafy trees in the foreground on a grassy hilltop w/clusters of lower trees beyond & water & mountains in the distance, a yellow & brown cloud-streaked sky w/the mountains & water in purple & dark blue & the trees in shades of green, dark & light brown, black & umber, a pathway through the foreground w/small painted figures, raised on a heavy bronze metal ovoid base cast w/a wide raised

*Handel Lamp with Countryside Scene*

band & tapering to a ringed & domed round foot, shade signed "Handel 6823"......................................................... **14,000**

**Table lamp,** 18" d. domical reverse-painted shade, decorated w/a mound of trees surrounded by choppy water forming waves in the background, shades of green, pale yellow, rose red, white & maroon, raised on a bronzed metal slender urn-form standard w/a scroll-embossed rim band & a wide low-domed foot, shade & base signed ............................................... **6,440**

*Handel Lamp with Moonlit Landscape*

**Table lamp,** 18" d. domical reverse-painted shade decorated w/a riverfront landscape w/a split-rail fence & the moon showing through trees, signed "Handel 8025," raised on a heavy bronze metal base w/four slender scrolled legs around a central shaft above a square platform w/small feet, base unsigned, restored, 23" h. (ILLUS.) ............................................. **5,175**

**Table lamp,** 18" d. domical reverse-painted shade decorated w/a silhouetted sunset landscape w/large leafy trees in dark brown against a streaked yellow sky, raised on a tall slender ribbed bronze pedestal swelled at the bottom & resting on a low-footed base ring, shade signed "Handel 6503," overall 24" h. ...................... **4,830**

*Rare Floral-decorated Handel Lamp*

**Table lamp,** 18" d. domical reverse-painted shade decorated w/a wide border of pink & white blossoms against a shaded dark green to cream ground, Model No. 6688, raised on a gilt-metal base w/a squatty urn raised on three slender legs ending in scroll feet, three amber teardrop prisms suspended from urn, all on a lappet-bordered round base (ILLUS.)........................ **18,150**

*Rose & Butterfly Shaded Handel Lamp*

**Table lamp,** 18" d. domical reverse-painted shade decorated w/an overall design of multicolored small roses & butterflies on a pale yellow ground, raised on a slender metal urn-form base w/ribbed, domed foot, shade signed "Handel 7032," base depatinated, 24" h. (ILLUS.) ...................... **8,625**

*Handel Lamp & Overall Floral Shade*

**Table lamp,** 18" d. domical reverse-painted shade decorated w/an overall design of colorful pink, white & red blossoms amid shaded tan & green leafage, Model No. 6688, raised on a bronzed metal base w/a heavy tapering cylindrical standard cast w/fixed S-scroll handles & ending in a ringed disk foot (ILLUS.) ........................ **20,350**

**Table lamp,** 18" d. domical reverse-painted shade decorated w/clusters of mauve & iron-red flower blooms beneath three fall foliaged trees, lavender distant hillside silhouetted against an ivory sky, signed "Handel #7106" & artist initials, raised on an unmarked Handel textured bronze base w/a slender inverted baluster-form standard on domed round foot, overall 24" h. ............................................................ **4,620**

*Handel Daffodil Pattern Shade & Lamp*

**Table lamp,** 18" d. domical reverse-painted shade decorated w/large yellow daffodils & long green leaves & stems against a background w/clusters of black leaves & small reddish orange blossoms divided by thin yellow striping & a pale yellow ground, heavy baluster-form Handel base w/a stepped, round foot, shade signed "Handel P.R. #7122" (ILLUS.) ...... **16,800**

**Table lamp,** 18" d. domical reverse-painted shade in the 'Birds of Paradise' patt., two pairs of long-tailed brightly colored Birds of Paradise perched in brilliant yellowish green blossoming foliage against a black ground, signed at edge "Handel 7026 Palme," mounted on a three-socket Handel gilt-metal base w/a compressed urn raised on three slender legs on a round lappet-bordered base, amber glass teardrop prisms suspended below the urn between the legs, overall 24 1/2" h. ........ **11,500**

*Bird of Paradise Border Handel Lamp*

**Table lamp,** 18" d. domical reverse-painted shade in the 'Birds of Paradise Border' patt., the upper shade w/a bright yellow ground decorated w/alternating black & gold stripes, the border band in black w/colorful clusters of pink blossoms & green leaves w/exotic blue birds, shade signed "Handel 6930," ca. 1919, 23" h. (ILLUS.) ...................................................... **10,800**

*Handel Birds of Paradise Lamp*

**Table lamp,** 18" d. domical reverse-painted shade in the 'Birds of Paradise' patt., decorated w/large long-tailed red & blue exotic birds on gold & black leafy flowering branches against a black ground, signed "Palme," raised on a bronzed metal base w/a squatty urn atop three tall

slender legs w/scrolled feet resting on a lappet-bordered round base (ILLUS.) ...................................................... **14,300**

**Table lamp,** 18" d. domical reverse-painted shade in the 'Birds of Paradise' patt., decorated w/large long-tailed orange, yellow, white & magenta exotic birds on gold & purple leafy flowering branches against a black ground, signed "Handel 7026 - Palme," raised on a bronzed metal base w/a squatty urn atop three tall slender legs w/scrolled feet resting on a lappet-bordered round base, base w/Handel cloth label ...................................................... **23,750**

*Unusual Handel Daffodil Lamp*

**Table lamp,** 18" d. domical reverse-painted shade in the 'Daffodil' patt., decorated w/downward radiating long green daffodil leaves & stems suspending large orange & yellow daffodil flowers against a pale yellow ground, raised on a tall bronzed metal Handel cylindrical base w/raised shoulder band (ILLUS.) ................................ **7,840**

**Table lamp,** 18" d. domical reverse-painted shade in the 'Exotic Bird' patt., large spread-winged colorful exotic birds perched among flowering leafy branches w/dark blue & lavender leaves w/large pink & red blossoms & small yellow blossoms all against a creamy white ground, shade signed "Handel 7125 Bedigie," on a slender paneled bronzed metal signed Handel base (ILLUS. top next page) ........ **17,360**

**Table lamp,** 18" d. domical reverse-painted shade in the 'Exotic Bird' patt., large spread-winged deep reddish orange & purple exotic birds perched among golden flowering leafy branches all against a black ground, shade signed "Handel 7026 Bedigie," on a tall three-legged bronzed metal base w/a short upper urn suspending amber glass teardrops & ending in a round foot w/a lappet rim band .............................................................. **22,400**

*Rare Exotic Bird Handel Table Lamp*

*Handel Floral & Exotic Bird Lamp*

**Table lamp,** 18" d. domical reverse-painted shade in the 'Floral & Exotic Bird' (aka 'Birds of Paradise Border') patt., decorated w/a wide border band of flying dark blue & red exotic birds among clusters of red & pink blossoms & green & yellow leaves all on a black ground, the upper side w/radiating bands of pale yellow separated by narrow black stripes, raised on a gilt-metal slender ring-turned base, shade signed "Handel 6930 Bedigie" (ILLUS.) .......................................... **6,720**

**Table lamp,** 18" d. domical reverse-painted shade in the 'Jungle Bird' patt., decorated w/a pair & a single large colorful macaws perched on jungle branches w/colorful leafy & flowering jungle foliage in the background, on a polychromed metal Handel base w/a vase-form shaft in tan shaded to cream & painted w/delicate white blossoms & green leafy vines, a brown lobed bottom disk above the domed & green-trimmed reeded base band, shade No. 6874 ................................ **21,840**

**Table lamp,** 18" d. domical reverse-painted shade in the 'Oriental Pheasant' patt., large spread-winged exotic bird in blue, green, yellow & white perched on black-leaved swags w/scattered yellow leaves & large blue, white & yellow blossoms all against a dark reddish orange ground, signed "Handel 7021," raised on a slender bronzed-metal ring-turned & leaf-cast standard on a round leaf-cast base ......... **20,160**

**Table lamp,** 18" d. domical reverse-painted shade in the 'Parrot & Floral' patt., molded w/eight vertical lobes & decorated w/a colorful parrot perched on branches amid pink & red rose blossoms & green leaves against a deep turquoise background w/black tree trunks & branches, on a bronzed metal Handel base w/a leaf-cast ring- and knob- pedestal on a round disk foot w/leaf-cast border band, shade No. 7028, artist-signed ..................................... **44,800**

*Superb Handel Rose Blossom Lamp*

**Table lamp,** 18" d. domical reverse-painted shade in the 'Rose Blossom' patt., painted overall w/sprays of pink, white & rosy red blossoms w/green & dark maroon leafage & small butterflies all on a mottled background, on a signed slender ribbed bronzed metal base w/a flaring lobed foot, shade signed "Handel 6688 R" (ILLUS.).................................................. **23,520**

**Table lamp,** 18" d. domical reverse-painted shade in the 'Treasure Island' patt. w/sailing ship & tropical isle in naturalistic colors, raised on a dark cast bronze slender waisted standard w/thick round foot (ILLUS. top next page).............................. **10,000**

**Table lamp,** 18" d. domical reverse-painted shade, 'Love Bird' patt., decorated w/a repeating design of a love bird perched

*Handel 'Treasure Island' Lamp*

among large pink, red & yellow blossom clusters w/reddish leaves against a background of tall slender black leafy trees w/a dark violet-colored background, shade signed "Handel 7127 S.," on a large bronzed metal ribbed urn-form base w/square foot, signed w/felt tab ....... **42,000**

**Table lamp,** 18" d. domical reverse-painted shade, painted on the interior w/a continuous landscape of groups of tall fir trees in a rocky landscape w/other trees in the distance, in shades of dark green, tan, brown & cream, shade signed "Handel 6323," on a signed base w/three slender scrolled legs resting on a stepped round foot ................................................................. **7,280**

*Interior- & Exterior-painted Handel*

**Table lamp,** 18" d. domical reverse-painted shade, painted on the interior w/a continuous landscape w/clusters of delicate trees & shrubbery in greens w/distant trees & shrubs in lavender & pinks against a creamy yellow ground, the trees also painted green on the exterior, shade signed "7117 Handel" & artist-signed, on

a signed base w/three slender scrolled legs on a stepped round foot (ILLUS.) ........ **8,400**

*Handel Lamp with Banded Shade*

**Table lamp,** 18" d. domical reverse-painted shade w/a 'chipped ice' exterior, the interior decorated w/a wide border of repeating flowers, birds & scrolls in shades of brownish green, blue, pink & yellow on a mottled amber ground, raised on a bronze base w/three flattened scroll supports resting on a stepped round base, impressed "Handel Lamps" on top shade rim, felted base w/"Handel Lamps" woven cloth label, base patination loss, early 20th c., 24 1/2" h. (ILLUS.) ...................... **4,888**

*Handel Tapestry Border Shade Lamp*

**Table lamp,** 18" d. domical reverse-painted shade w/a 'chipped ice' exterior, interior decorated w/a floral tapestry border in shades of green, amber, blue & red on a burnt orange ground, signed "Handel Co. S 6750," raised on a three-socket Chinese design patinated bronze wide baluster-form base w/pierced & scrolled disk foot, base unmarked, 24" h. (ILLUS.).......... **6,900**

### Handel Floral Table Lamp

**Table lamp,** 18" d. domical reverse-painted shade w/sand-finished exterior, painted on interior w/two butterflies w/yellow & orange wings hovering amid a field of wild roses in vivid shades of crimson, pink, dusty rose, lavender & white w/yellow centers & green leafage, reserved against a pale green ground, patinated-metal base composed of three long slender scrolls joined at the top & raised on a round, stepped foot, w/finial, shade signed in enamel "Handel 6688," upper ring impressed "Handel Lamps," ca. 1915, 23" h. (ILLUS.) ................... **16,675**

**Table lamp,** 18" d. domical reverse-painted textured shade decorated w/a scene of maroon red & green trees against bluish grey & orange clouds w/sky blue overhead, rim signed "Handel 6937," raised on a three-socket ribbed quatreform bronzed metal standard w/disk foot, overall 22 1/2" h. ......................... **5,465**

**Table lamp,** 18" d. domical shade decorated on the exterior in opal w/overall colorful blossoms in yellow, pink & blue against tall dark brown leaves & stems, No. 6931, raised on a bronze metal base w/a vase-form shaft upon a stepped Oriental-style foot w/curved pierced-scroll design .......................... **8,400**

**Table lamp,** 18" d. domical shade in dark mottled brown painted on the exterior w/an elaborate design of a colorful peacock perched among flowering branches w/golden yellow & blue blossoms & green leaves, early 20th c., 23 1/2" h. (ILLUS. top next column)........................... **31,000**

**Table lamp,** 18" d. domical reverse-painted white-cased shade h.p. on the exterior w/a wide border of delicate repeating foliate designs in the Arts & Crafts style in yellowish amber, inner rim inscribed "Handel 6778 HG," raised on a bronze-fin-

### Choice Handel Peacock Lamp

ished tall base w/a cupped urn atop three tall slender legs w/scroll feet resting on a round foot w/cast lappet border, overall 22" h. ............................................. **4,600**

### Handel Lamp with Poppies on Shade

**Table lamp,** 18" d. mushroom-shaped shade painted w/five large dark orange poppy blossoms atop long scrolled leafy stems w/undulating pod stems all against a shaded bright yellow to pale green ground, on a thin shade ring hung w/a finely beaded skirt, raised on a gilt-metal square standard w/a stepped square foot, shade signed "Handel #2456," 18 3/4" h. (ILLUS.)........................... **920**

**Table lamp,** 18" d. sharply conical leaded glass shade composed of long narrow tapering bands radiating down from the top to a Greek key border band, all in dark green slag glass, raised on a slender reeded standard w/a domed scroll-cast foot ................................................................. **3,360**

**Table lamp,** 18" d. tapering cylindrical open-topped etched & enameled shade, two curved panels decorated w/brilliant orange parrots, two w/brownish amber jungle leafage, signed on lower edge "Handel 7686 Palme," mounted on a slender, ribbed cast-metal Handel base w/rewiring & replaced socket, 28" h. ......... **4,025**

*Handel Lamp with Leaded Shade*

**Table lamp,** 18 1/2" d. conical leaded glass shade w/a wide drop apron, a top geometric border of bluish green glass over radiating panels of light green glass, the drop apron w/a paneled border of diamond-shaped segments in bluish green & opalescent white on a light green ground, raised on a bronzed metal base w/a slender waisted standard & flaring base w/shaped feet, base marked (ILLUS.) ........ **1,725**

*Handel Bent Panel Slag Glass Lamp*

**Table lamp,** 19 1/2" d. domical slag glass shade w/eight bent panels of amber slag glass overlaid w/a linear Art Nouveau metal design & green painted highlights, on a three-socket baluster-form patinated metal base molded w/serpentine decoration over four squared bracket feet, raised marks on shade rim & base, painted decoration possibly retouched, replaced handle, 27" h. (ILLUS.) ................... **4,313**

**Table lamp,** 20" d. domical leaded glass shape w/a lapped petal design in amber & cream slag glass, raised on a slender four-socket patinated copper base flaring to the lapped lily pad base, raised "HANDEL" mark on shade & base, overall 26" h. (wear to patina, crack to one petal) .............................................................. **3,335**

**Table lamp,** 20" d. umbrella-form leaded glass shade w/a domed center & wide rounded shoulder above a wide vertical border w/pointed rim, composed of an overall floral design w/mottled green leaves in the top center w/a shoulder band of mottled yellow & white large blossoms & a border band of large orange blossoms against a green leafy ground, on a bronzed metal tapering & finely ribbed Handel base ........................... **5,600**

**Table lamp,** 20" d. wide conical leaded glass shade w/a drop apron, composed of radiating small squares of green slag glass, raised on a very tall, slender bronzed metal signed Handel base w/a round foot ...................................................... **6,440**

*Handel Rose Filigree Table Lamp*

**Table lamp,** 20" w. domical six-panel shade w/tapering panels of caramel slag glass overlaid w/metal filigree in a design of leafy rose vines highlighted in pale yellow & green paint, on a slender bronzed metal baluster-form signed Handel base, shade signed on ring (ILLUS.) .................... **5,040**

*Handel Geometric Overlay Lamp*

**Table lamp,** 22" d. Geometric Overlay domical leaded glass shade w/radiating bands enclosing graduated green tiles streaked w/yellow & white above a paneled drop border of yellow & white Greek Key design, raised on a slender embossed bronzed standard w/rounded scrolled panel design & low feet (ILLUS.) .. **9,520**

**Table lamp,** 23" d. conical leaded glass shade, the upper section composed of long tapering caramel slag panels enclosed by double narrow bands of striated green & yellow slag continuing down over the flat drop apron to form loops enclosing deep red & maroon stylized tulip blossoms, on a signed Handel tall slender reeded bronzed metal standard w/a knob just above the flat disk foot ................ **4,760**

**Table lamp,** 14 x 20" rectangular pyramidal leaded glass shade w/a Prairie School design w/angled caramel slag top panels within lattice corner bands, a flat base band w/small geometric panels of caramel slag, green & red, on a four-socket bronzed metal pierced double-post base w/a flat rectangular foot, fine original patina, base signed, overall 24" h. ............... **17,600**

**Table lamp,** wide low conical leaded glass shade composed of a lapped arch design frame enclosing striated greenish amber & white slag glass segments, raised on a slender five-socket standard w/swelled base & round disk foot, raised mark on base, patination wear, two panels cracked, ca. 1907, 30" h. (ILLUS. top column) .............................................................. **9,200**

**Wall sconces,** leaded glass, a rounded naturalistic lily-form shape on vine support joining the lily pad form wall mount of bronzed metal, shade composed of overlapping green & white slag glass petals & two green slag glass buds, mount w/rich reddish brown patina, raised

*Simple Slag Glass Handel Lamp*

signature, ca. 1903, one screw missing for shade, 10" h., pr. (ILLUS. of one below) .............................................................. **1,380**

*Handel Lily-form Wall Sconce*

# Pairpoint Lamps

*Well known as a producer of fine Victorian art glass and silver plate wares between 1907 and 1929, the Pairpoint Corporation of New Bedford, Massachusetts also produced a wide range of decorative lamps.*

**Boudoir lamp,** 4" d. "Puffy" domical 'Tivoli' shade in the Dragonfly patt. w/shaded dark green ground, raised on gilt-metal slender hexagonal urn-form pedestal & stepped hexagonal foot ............................. **$9,350**

*Pairpoint "Puffy" Rose Boudoir Lamp*

**Boudoir lamp,** 5" d. "Puffy" bonnet-shaped reverse-painted shade in the Four Color Rose patt., four large rose blossoms in pink, red, yellow & accented white w/dark green leaves around the border, on a slender signed Pairpoint bronzed metal base w/lily pad leaves around the bottom (ILLUS.) ......................................................... **8,960**

**Boudoir lamp,** 5" d. "Puffy" domed & lobed Lilac patt. shade, deep pink & red lilac blossoms w/green foliage & yellow & black butterflies, turquoise edge band, raised on a signed bronze Pairpoint tree trunk base ...................................................... **16,240**

*Puffy Pairpoint Lilac Boudoir Lamp*

**Boudoir lamp,** 5" d. "Puffy" domed & lobed reverse-painted shade in the Lilac patt., each lobe w/a cluster of lilac blossoms in purple, deep rose or pink, some w/a yellow butterfly, against a ground of mottled dark green & yellow leaves, on a Pairpoint tree trunk base (ILLUS.) .................. **24,080**

**Boudoir lamp,** 5" d. "Puffy" pointed domical reverse-painted Pansy patt. shade, the overall large blossoms painted in yellow & red & deep red on a dark green leafy ground, raised on a signed base w/a shade ring supported on a slender baluster-form standard above the domed round foot, rare ............................................ **16,800**

**Boudoir lamp,** 6 5/8" d. "Puffy" domical 'Rose Bonnet' shade, grey ground molded in low-relief w/roses, reverse-painted in red, pink & yellow w/green leaves, raised on a small baluster-form base w/green patina, base impressed "Pairpoint Mfg. Co. - C3025," 10 5/8" h. ........... **11,500**

**Boudoir lamp,** 6 3/4" d. "Puffy" reverse-painted Rose patt. shade w/four rose blossoms painted in pink & yellow on a green ground, raised on a silvered cast metal tree trunk base marked "Pairpoint - B3079" & Pairpoint diamond trademark, ca. 1910, overall 11" h. (two shade support arms missing) ..................... **5,175**

*Pairpoint Boudoir Lamp and Shade*

**Boudoir lamp,** 7 1/2" d. bell-form reverse-painted shade decorated w/a landscape of sheep grazing in a field in shades of purple, green & brown, the cast gilt-metal base in the form of a tree trunk, base molded "Pairpoint - B3079" w/Pairpoint trademark, ca. 1910, overall 14 1/4" h. (ILLUS.) ......................................................... **1,725**

**Boudoir lamp,** 8" d. domical "Puffy" reverse-painted shade in the 'Butterfly and Roses' patt., the wide scalloped border band w/large red & yellow roses & green leaves w/large butterflies above all against a frosted ground decorated w/thin blue bands, raised on a silvered metal slender Pairpoint base cast w/long leaves & w/a matching shade finial, shade signed .................................................. **3,584**

**Boudoir lamp,** 8" d. "Puffy" flat-topped domical reverse-painted shade in the Floral patt., decorated around the lower border w/pairs of large rose blossoms alternating w/five-petal blossoms & leaves, in shades of orangish red, purple & yellow against a frosted white & yellow lattice background, on a slender gilt-metal base w/round, lobed foot ............................. **6,720**

**Boudoir lamp,** 8" d. "Puffy" reverse-painted 'Papillon' shade w/groups of large red, yellow & purple blossoms w/green leaves around the scalloped lower body w/a large colorful butterfly above each group of flowers, raised on a gilt-metal tree trunk base, base signed ............................. **3,360**

*Pairpoint Puffy with Portsmouth Shade*

**Boudoir lamp,** 8" d. pyramidal "Puffy" closed-top shade in the 'Portsmouth' patt., each wide tapering panel reverse-painted w/large blossoms, including pansies, in shades of red, yellow, blue, orange & green on a pale mottled green ground, narrow pale orange border bands between the panels & on the top, raised on a slender flaring gilt-metal standard on an oval dished foot, base signed (ILLUS.) ....................................................... **4,200**

**Boudoir lamp,** 8" w. domical squared & lobed closed-top "Puffy" shade in the 'Butterfly & Roses' patt., pairs of large roses in deep red w/green leaves around the scalloped border w/large yellow & blue butterflies above against a frosted white ground, the closed top centered by a large puffy rose blossom,

*Butterfly & Roses Puffy Pairpoint*

raised on a slender gilt-metal baluster-form standard on a disk foot w/small scroll feet (ILLUS.) ....................................... **8,400**

**Boudoir lamp,** 8" w. domical squared & lobed "Puffy" shade in the 'Butterfly & Roses' patt., pairs of large roses & other blossoms around the scalloped border in shades of deep rose, yellow & blue w/green leaves & large blue or yellow & blue butterflies above all on a black ground, on a signed slender gilt-metal baluster-form standard on a disk foot w/small scroll feet & matching knob shade finial .................................................... **5,600**

*Pairpoint Roses Boudoir Lamp*

**Boudoir lamp,** 8" w. squared domical 'Portsmouth' shade reverse-painted w/large red roses on a pale yellow &

white ground, the design outlined in black & black lines on the exterior, raised on a slender cylindrical bronzed metal standard w/a square foot, shade marked "The Pairpoint Corp'n," base marked "Pairpoint" w/logo, 14" h. (ILLUS.)...................... **2,070**

**Boudoir lamp,** 8 1/2" d. conical reverse-painted shade decorated w/Art Deco stylized large orange roses on green & black leafy stems against a black-streaked ivory ground, raised on a slender nickel-plated bronzed metal slender standard w/a ringed disk foot, base w/impressed mark, shade signed, overall 13 1/2" h. ....... **1,045**

**Boudoir lamp,** 8 1/2" d. reverse-painted 'Exeter' shade decorated w/a continuous landscape of slender leafy trees in shades of green, rust & gold above butterflies & wildflowers, raised on a polished copper slender ringed & knobbed shaft on a heavy stepped foot, base marked, 15 1/2" h. ........................................ **2,035**

**Boudoir lamp,** 9" d. domical six-paneled open-topped shade, each panel w/a mottled slag glass section in swirled shades of yellow, orange, red & lavender resembling a sunset, overlaid w/metal filigree in a tropical landscape of tall & short palm trees, on a signed tree trunk base ............. **2,464**

**Boudoir lamp,** 9" d. "Puffy" reverse-painted 'Papillon' shade, flat-topped domical form w/straight sides molded w/large pairs of rose blossoms & butterflies around the sides in shades of rose, red, green & creamy yellow on a creamy ground, a molded blossom at the center of the closed top, raised on a patinated metal base w/a slender paneled trumpet-form standard on a domed flaring paneled foot, base & shade signed, ca. 1915, 14" h. ................................................ **6,900**

**Boudoir lamp,** 9" d. "Puffy" reverse-painted 'Stratford' flat-topped domical shade decorated in the Dogwood Blossom patt., w/pairs of large lavender & pink roses & green leaves around the rim against a frosted clear ground w/a white lacy lattice design, raised on a patinated metal slender standard cast w/overlapping pointed leaves above the lobed & leaf-cast foot, shade & base signed, overall 14 1/2" h. .... **3,850**

**Boudoir lamp,** 9" d. tapering cylindrical flat-topped reverse-painted "Puffy" shade in the 'Stratford' patt. decorated w/the 'Floral' design, the sides w/pairs of large roses, daisies & other blossoms in deep rose, yellow & blue w/green leaves against a black ground, the flat top in yellow, raised on a slender gilt-metal baluster-form standard on a disk base w/small scroll feet...................................................... **3,920**

**Boudoir lamp,** 9 3/4" d. flaring domical shade in frosted clear painted on the surface w/a continuous band of autumnal leafy trees amid grass w/flowers & butterflies, raised on a slender patinated metal overlapping leaf-cast standard on a round lobed foot, base marked w/raised Pairpoint mark & "C3064," overall 14 1/2" h. ......................................... **546**

**Boudoir lamp,** 10" d. "Puffy" domical shade molded w/large clusters of rose blossoms reverse-painted in red & yellow w/green & blue leaves against a frosted background, on a slender bronze metal shaft on a squared flattened base, shade signed ............................................................ **3,360**

*Pairpoint "Puffy" Rose Bouquet Lamp*

**Boudoir lamp,** 14" d. "Puffy" reverse-painted open-topped shade in the Rose Bouquet patt., decorated w/blossoms in creamy white & pink w/green leaves on a dark green ground, raised on a socket ring support, gilt patinated metal base w/baluster-shaped standard ending in a domed circular base w/raised lily pad & blossom design on floriform feet, base w/impressed Pairpoint mark & "3037," minor shade rim chip, overall 21" h. (ILLUS.)........................................................ **4,025**

**Boudoir lamp,** 8 3/4" d. "Puffy" umbrella-form shade w/flattened top, relief-molded colorful rim bouquets of flowers on a frosted clear ribbed ground highlighted by overall white enamel scrolls, raised brass-colored metal standard on a flattened squared foot w/cut corners marked "Pairpoint," overall 16" h. .......................... **4,180**

**Candle lamps,** each w/a mold-blown "Puffy" shade reverse-painted to depict pansies, in shades of burgundy, yellow, mauve, green, orange & white, stamped company mark, on wooden bases, 7 3/4" h., pr. .................................................. **2,233**

*Pairpoint Candle Lamps*

**Candle lamps,** tall swelled cylindrical shade w/flared rim, 'chipped ice' exterior painted w/a landscape of leafy birch trees on a reverse-painted yellow ground, metal mounts for fitting into the turned mahogany candlestick base w/a domed round foot & slender baluster-turned standard below the tulip-form socket, early 20th c., stress cracks in one shade & metal base of shade, overall 21 1/2" h., pr. (ILLUS.) .................................. **805**

*Pairpoint Mantel & Table Lamps*

**Mantel lamp,** bulbous chimney-form shade enamel-decorated w/stylized green trees against a reddish orange background, mounted on a silvered metal candlestick-form electrolier base w/flared foot, base impressed w/Pairpoint trademark & "E3072," some glass rim chips, silver finish worn, 14" h. (ILLUS. right ) ...................... **230**

**Mantel lamps,** two-arm candelabra-form composed of elaborate silver plated metal fittings joined by controlled bubble ball stems & finials, impressed "Pairpoint" marks under candlecups, 10 1/2" w., 14" h., the pair (silver worn, old wiring) ......... **690**

**Table lamp,** 8" d. "Puffy" reverse-painted Lilac patt. shade, deep purple & deep red clusters of blossoms w/colorful butterflies against a ground of mottled green & yellow leaves, on a gilt-bronze Pairpoint tree trunk base ................................................... **39,200**

*Reverse- & Obverse-Painted Handel*

**Table lamp,** 10" d. domed mushroom-shaped reverse- and obverse-painted shade, decorated on the interior & exterior w/overall large yellow, green & white mottled maple leaves & dark brown branches against a dark brick red ground, raised on a ring above the gilt-metal square tapering standard w/pierced loop reserves near the rectangular foot (ILLUS.) ........................................ **2,240**

*Exceptional Pairpoint Azalea Lamp*

# Early Pre-Kerosene Lighting

## A group of fine cut-overlay fluid-burning lamps, circa 1860-70.

Left to right: A 16¼" h. cut double overlay lamp in cobalt blue cut to white cut to clear with slash, punty and oval designs .................... $9,775

A 16⅛" h. transparent turquoise blue cut to clear lamp with slash, punty and oval designs .................... $4,025

A pair of 11¾" h. cut double overlay lamps in cobalt blue cut to white cut to clear with slash, punty and oval designs, minor imperfections .............. $4,025

A 12½" h. cut double overlay lamp in cranberry cut to white cut to clear with quatrefoil, star and oval designs ...... $2,070

A 10⅝" h. transparent amethyst lamp cut with quatrefoil, oval and punty designs ................... $2,530

A 13½" h. cut double overlay lamp in cranberry cut to white cut to clear with oval and punty designs, imperfections.. $1,955

A 16¼" h. cut overlay lamp in white cut to transparent green with punty and oval designs and gilt trim, minor imperfections .............. $6,900

A 16½" h. cut double overlay lamp in cobalt blue cut to white cut to clear with oval designs, minor imperfections.... $12,650

Courtesy of Skinner, Inc., Bolton, MA.

## A group of colorful early pressed glass fluid-burning lamps, circa 1850-60.

Left to right: A pair of dark turquoise blue pressed Bigler pattern lamps ..... $4,600

A canary Three Printie Block pattern lamp .. $374

A pair of deep amethyst Bigler pattern lamps ................... $4,370

A Waisted Loop pattern canary lamp on a monument-style base.......... $2,990

A cobalt blue faceted design lamp ....... $3,105

Two similar canary Loop pattern lamps..... $805

A blue and clambroth Acanthus Leaf lamp with sand finish.................. $1,150

Courtesy of Skinner, Inc., Bolton, MA.

# Early Pre-Kerosene Lighting

**Fig. 1**

**Fig. 2**

**Fig. 3**

**Fig. 4**

**Fig. 5**

**Fig. 1:** An extremely rare 7" h. whale oil lamp with a deep cobalt blue mold-blown font with sixteen swirled ribs attached with a wine glass-style clear bladed stem to a clear pressed No. R-54 cup plate base. Boston and Sandwich Glass Company, circa 1828-35 . . . . . . . . . . . . . . . . . . . . . $11,000

**Fig. 2:** A deep cobalt blue Petal and Loop pattern candlestick, 7" h. Attributed to the Boston and Sandwich Glass Company, circa 1850. . . . . . . . . . . . . . . . . . . . . . . . $1,760

**Fig. 3:** A 10½" h. bright, light emerald green pressed glass fluid lamp with an octagonal font applied to a shaped octagonal standard and square base. Attributed to the Boston and Sandwich Glass Company, circa 1850-60 . . . . . . . . . $6,600

**Fig. 4:** A 10½" h. pressed glass canary Waisted Loop fluid burning lamp on a pressed hexagonal base. Attributed to the Boston and Sandwich Glass Company, circa 1850. . . . . . . . . . . . . . . . . . . . . . . . . $1,980

**Fig. 5:** A cut overlay 13¾" h. early fluid burning lamp with an amethyst cut to clear font raised on an elaborate gilt brass standard with eight large leaves and a two-step black marble base, New England, circa 1850-60 . . . . . . . . . . . . . . . . . . . . . . . $2,475

# Kerosene Era Lighting

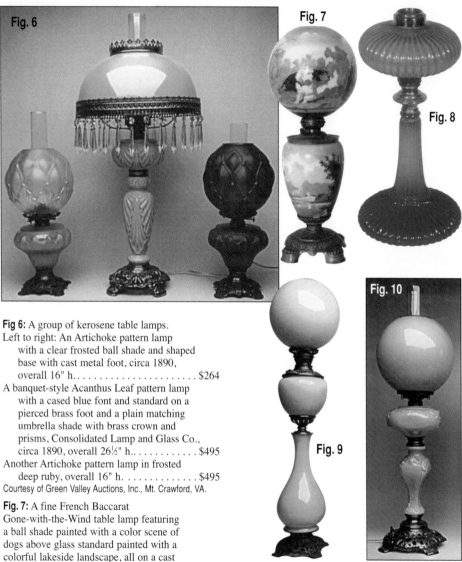

Fig. 6

Fig. 7

Fig. 8

Fig. 10

Fig. 9

**Fig 6:** A group of kerosene table lamps.
Left to right: An Artichoke pattern lamp
with a clear frosted ball shade and shaped
base with cast metal foot, circa 1890,
overall 16" h. . . . . . . . . . . . . . . . . . . . . . $264
A banquet-style Acanthus Leaf pattern lamp
with a cased blue font and standard on a
pierced brass foot and a plain matching
umbrella shade with brass crown and
prisms, Consolidated Lamp and Glass Co.,
circa 1890, overall 26½" h. . . . . . . . . . . $495
Another Artichoke pattern lamp in frosted
deep ruby, overall 16" h. . . . . . . . . . . . . $495
Courtesy of Green Valley Auctions, Inc., Mt. Crawford, VA.

**Fig. 7:** A fine French Baccarat
Gone-with-the-Wind table lamp featuring
a ball shade painted with a color scene of
dogs above glass standard painted with a
colorful lakeside landscape, all on a cast
brass foot, both shade and base signed
"Baccarat," circa 1890, 18" h . . . . . . . . . . $1,848
Courtesy of Fontaine's Auction Gallery, Pittsfield, MA.

**Fig. 8:** An extremely rare powder blue Onion
lamp with a ribbed font and base, complete
with original 12" d. frosted clear floral shade
and double brass burners (shown without
shade and burner), overall 21½" h. . . . . . . $2,090
Courtesy of Collector's Sales and Service,
Pomfret Center, CT.

**Fig. 9:** An impressive Monarch banquet lamp
with a yellow cased font and baluster stem and

a slightly lighter yellow ball shade, with a
brass connector and pierced foot,
Consolidated Lamp and Glass Company,
circa 1890, overall 37½" h. . . . . . . . . . . . . . $770
Courtesy of Green Valley Auctions, Inc., Mt. Crawford, VA.

**Fig. 10:** A cased glass banquet lamp with a
plain pink ball shade, squared pink font
and baluster stem molded with scrolls, a
brass connector and pierced foot,
Consolidated Lamp and Glass Company,
circa 1890, overall 25" h. . . . . . . . . . . . . . . $606
Courtesy of Green Valley Auctions, Inc., Mt. Crawford, VA.

# Kerosene Era Lighting

Fig. 11

Fig. 12

Fig. 13

**Fig. 11:** Various finger and table lamps.
Top row, left to right: Hobbs' Snowflake
  cranberry opalescent finger lamp with
  clear handle and burner and ribbed-edge
  chimney, Hobbs, Brockunier and
  Company, circa 1890, overall 9½" h. . . . . $990
Hobbs' Snowflake blue opalescent finger
  lamp with clear handle, burner and
  ribbed-edge chimney, Hobbs, Brockunier
  and Company, circa 1890, overall 9½" h. . $770
Coin Spot pattern cranberry opalescent
  finger lamp with clear applied and
  crimped handle, with burner, 3½" h. . . . . . $715
Unlisted miniature lamp in milk glass with
  an embossed scroll and floral design on
  base and matching shade, flowers
  decorated in maroon with yellow centers,
  leaves and scrolls in dark green, band of
  light green at bottom of shade and
  below collar of base, overall 7⅞" h. . . . . . $523
Bottom row, left to right: Seaweed pattern
  cranberry opalescent stem lamp with
  an optic font, clear stem and base,
  with burner, 9" h. . . . . . . . . . . . . . . . . $1,430
Eason pattern cranberry opalescent stem
  lamp with a clear stem and base,
  with burner, 9½" h. . . . . . . . . . . . . . . . $385
Hobbs' Snowflake cranberry opalescent stem
  lamp, clear stem and base, original glass
  sleeve with burner, Hobbs, Brockunier
  and Company, circa 1890, 9" h. . . . . . . . $523
Courtesy of Green Valley Auctions, Inc., Mt. Crawford, VA.

**Fig. 12:** Victorian hanging parlor lamp with a
cranberry opalescent Hobnail domed shade
in a brass ring hung with prisms and a brass

crown ring with prisms, a bulbous brass
font flanked by ornate scrolls, circa 1890 . . $3,250
Courtesy of Copake Auctioin, Inc., Copake, NY.

**Fig. 13:** Two Victorian hanging parlor lamps.
Left to right: A blue opaque domed shade
  in a brass ring hung with prisms and a
  brass crown ring with prisms, bulbous
  embossed brass font flanked by ornate
  scrolls, electrified, 13½" d. . . . . . . . . . . . $825
A cranberry Hobnail pattern domed shade
  in a brass ring hung with prisms and a
  brass crown and crown ring, bulbous floral
  medallion embossed brass font with a
  white metal band flanked by ornate
  scrolls, brass smoke bell, shade 13½" d. . . $770
Courtesy of Green Valley Auctions, Inc., Mt. Crawford, VA.

# Fairy Lamps

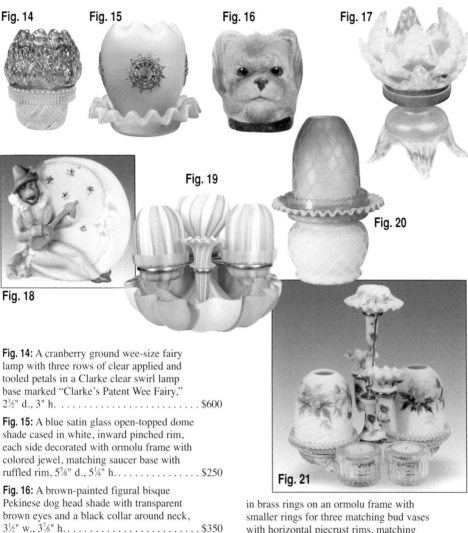

**Fig. 14**  **Fig. 15**  **Fig. 16**  **Fig. 17**

**Fig. 19**

**Fig. 20**

**Fig. 18**

**Fig. 21**

**Fig. 14:** A cranberry ground wee-size fairy lamp with three rows of clear applied and tooled petals in a Clarke clear swirl lamp base marked "Clarke's Patent Wee Fairy," 2½" d., 3" h. . . . . . . . . . . . . . . . . . . . . . . . .$600

**Fig. 15:** A blue satin glass open-topped dome shade cased in white, inward pinched rim, each side decorated with ormolu frame with colored jewel, matching saucer base with ruffled rim, 5⅝" d., 5¼" h. . . . . . . . . . . . . . . $250

**Fig. 16:** A brown-painted figural bisque Pekinese dog head shade with transparent brown eyes and a black collar around neck, 3½" w., 3⅞" h. . . . . . . . . . . . . . . . . . . . . . . . $350

**Fig. 17:** Floral-shaped fairy lamp with light blue ground and rows of applied frosted and iridized petals, matching base shading from light blue to clear with four applied frosted and iridized leaf feet, 5" d., 7" h. . . . . . . . . . . $350

**Fig. 18:** Painted bisque figural pyramid-size fairy lamp shade showing a monkey playing a mandolin on a crescent Man in the Moon with pierced stars. Impressed fleur-de-lis design on unpainted back, 3½" w., 3½" h. . . . . $350

**Fig. 19:** A three-part fairy lamp with three pink, white and narrow opaque striped Cleveland pattern fairy-size shades with embossed ribs with Clarke cups supported

in brass rings on an ormolu frame with smaller rings for three matching bud vases with horizontal piecrust rims, matching upturned bowl base, 10" d., 7¾" h. . . . . . . . $3,500

**Fig. 20:** A fairy lamp with a shaded blue mother-of-pearl satin Diamond Quilted pattern shade in a clear Clarke lamp cup resting on the internal shoulder of a matching bulbous base with a ruffled rim, 5¼" d., 7½" h. . . . . . . $500

**Fig. 21:** A fairy lamp epergne with two satin finished decorated Burmese glass shades and three Burmese satin finished posey vases with a Burmese central column, all with a prunus decoration, includes Clarke candles, candle cups and a Clarke's Patent central post, 9" w., 10" h. . . . . . . . . . . . . . . . . . . . $2,500

All courtesy of the Fairy Lamp Club.

# Fairy Lamps

Fig. 22

Fig. 23

Fig. 24

Fig. 25

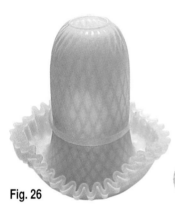
Fig. 26

Fig. 27

Fig. 28

Fig. 29

**Fig. 22:** An embossed rib fairy-size shade in amethyst and white swirls on a smooth-shouldered matching lamp cup base, $3\frac{5}{8}$" d., $4\frac{5}{8}$" h. . . . . . . . . . . . . . . . $250

**Fig. 23:** A red ground fairy-size shade with white mottled or iced surface in a matching smooth-shouldered lamp cup with applied tooled clear feet, $5\frac{1}{4}$" h. . . . . . . . . . . . . . . . $350

**Fig. 24:** A jeweled brass fairy-size domed shade with eight large glass jewels set in individual filigree frames with eight smaller jewels between, on a four-footed brass base with integral candle cup, $3\frac{1}{2}$" d., $4\frac{1}{4}$" h. . $250

**Fig. 25:** A pink ground pyramid-sized dome shade with red peppermint swirl decoration and embossed vertical ribs in a matching lamp cup base, $2\frac{3}{4}$" d., $3\frac{1}{2}$" h. . . . . . . . . . . . $250

**Fig. 26:** A blue mother-of-pearl satin glass Diamond Quilted fairy-size shade in a clear frosted lamp cup with diamond pattern, on a matching squared base with ruffled piecrust rim, $6\frac{1}{4}$" w., $6\frac{1}{4}$" h. . . . . . . . . . . . . . . . . . . . $750

**Fig. 27:** A fairy-size satin-finished Burmese glass shade decorated in the woodbine pattern on a signed Taylor, Tunnicliffe and Co. creamware flower bowl base decorated in flowers, integral Clarke's marked lamp cup, $7\frac{1}{2}$" d., 6" h. . . . . . . . . . $1,000

**Fig. 28:** An embossed frosted dark green figural owl head shade with red-painted eyes in a clear Clarke pyramid lamp cup, 4" d., $4\frac{1}{2}$" h. . . . . . . . . . . . . . . . . . . . . . . . $200

**Fig. 29:** Citron ground Nailsea-type fairy-size shade with white loopings, in a Clarke lamp cup resting on a matching base with upturned ruffled rim, $8\frac{1}{4}$" d., $5\frac{3}{4}$" h. . . . . . . . $500

All courtesy of the Fairy Lamp Club.

# Early Electric Lighting • Handel Lamps

**Fig. 30**

**Fig. 32**

**Fig. 31**

**Fig. 33**

**Fig. 30:** A Handel table lamp with an 18" d. conical reverse-painted shade decorated with a landscape of large leafy trees and meadows below cloudy skies, further painted on the exterior with twisted trees, shade signed "Handel 5889," on a bronzed metal Handel-signed basketweave design base . . . . . . . . . . . . . $8,400

**Fig. 31:** A Handel table lamp with an 18" domical reverse-painted shade decorated in the "Exotic Bird" pattern in dark blue, grey, cream, yellow, red and black, shade signed "Handel 7125 Bedigie," on a bronzed metal Handel-signed slender ribbed base . . . . . . . . . . . . . . . . . . . . . . $17,360

**Fig. 32:** An exceptional Handel table lamp with an 18" domical reverse-painted shade in the "Rose Blossom" pattern in rich shades of deep red, purple, pink and green, signed "Handel 6688 R.," on a slender ribbed bronzed metal Handel-signed base . . . . . . $23,520

**Fig. 33:** A Handel overlay table lamp with a 20" d. domical paneled shade with six panels of caramel slag glass overlaid with intricate metal designs of leaves and vines further highlighted with painted yellow and green trim, shade signed in ring "Handel Pgt. D.," on a slender bronzed metal Handel-signed base. . . . . . . . . . . . . . . . . . . $5,040

All courtesy of Fontaine's Auction Gallery, Pittsfield, MA.

# Early Electric Lighting • Handel Lamps

Fig. 35

Fig. 34

Fig. 38

Fig. 36

Fig. 37

Fig. 39

Fig. 40

**Fig. 34:** A Handel table lamp with a 12" d. mushroom-shaped domed shade decorated with a wide undulating border band in pale yellowish green below a delicate band of scrolling white vine with pink blossoms with jeweled centers, the upper shade in frosted light pink, signed "Handel Co. 2583," on a bronzed metal slender openwork and filigree-cast base.....................$1,288

**Fig. 35:** A Handel overlay table lamp with a 16" d. six-panel domical shade composed of six bent panels of caramel slag glass overlaid with delicate leafy vines and bands of trellis highlighted with painted details, on a slender bronzed metal base signed "Handel 562".....................$5,320

**Fig. 36:** A Handel hanging hall light with a spherical glass shade painted on the exterior with a peacock perched on a flowering branch, signed "Handel 7257 Walter," fitted with a bronzed metal cap and a swag-form pendant drop, 10" d. .........$6,664

**Fig. 37:** A Handel teardrop-shaped night light painted on the exterior of the shade with red stylized parrots perched on clusters of pink and purple blossoms and green leaves against a dark gold ground, signed "F.C. Handel," on an Oriental-style pierced metal base, shade 7" h...........$1,792

**Fig. 38:** A Handel table lamp with an 18" d. conical reverse-painted shade decorated with suspended daffodil blossoms around the rim on long green leafy stems against a pale yellow ground, on a bronzed metal cylindrical Handel-signed base .........$7,840

**Fig. 39:** A Handel table lamp with an 18" d. domical reverse-painted shade in the "Floral and Exotic Bird" pattern, the wide border band with dark rose blossoms and green and yellow leaves with flying blue and red birds against a black background, the upper shade with panels of dark yellow divided by black stripes, signed "Handel 6930 Bedigie," on a slender ring-turned bronzed metal base .................$6,720.

**Fig. 40:** A Handel boudoir lamp with a 7" d. reverse-painted domical shade decorated with a sunset landscape with tall trees and shrubbery, signed "Handel S," on a slender bronzed metal ribbed Handel-signed base .. $3,360

Fig. 41

Fig. 42

Fig. 43

Fig. 44

**Fig. 41:** A "Puffy" Pairpoint boudoir lamp with a 5" d. bonnet-form shade in the Four Color Roses design, painted on the interior with large pink, red, and yellow roses and green leaves accented in white, signed "The Pairpoint Corp.," on a slender bronzed metal Pairpoint-signed lily pad base . . . . . . $8,960

**Fig. 42:** A "Puffy" Pairpoint table lamp with a 14" d. 'Stratford' shade in the Hummingbird and Roses design, painted on the interior with colorful red, blue and yellow blossoms with green leaves against a mottled mauve and black ground, signed "The Pairpoint Corp.," on a slender ribbed bronzed metal Pairpoint-signed base . . . . . . $7,280

**Fig. 43:** A Pairpoint table lamp with an 18" d. 'Exeter' shade reverse-painted in the Exotic Bird pattern with colorful large yellow, orange and blue birds among leafy blue vines with white and pink blossoms and berries against a brown ground, raised on a silvered metal urn-form tripod signed Pairpoint base . . . . . . . . . . . . . . . . . . . . . $5,880

**Fig. 44:** A "Puffy" Pairpoint table lamp with a 14" w. 'Papillon' shade in the Butterfly and Roses design, painted on the interior with colorful red and pink roses and green leaves with yellow and lavender butterflies with a white background streaked with green, on a slender square bronzed metal Pairpoint-signed base . . . . . . . . . . . . . . . $13,440

All courtesy of Fontaine's Auction Gallery, Pittsfield, MA.

# Early Electric Lighting • Pairpoint Lamps

**Fig. 45:** A Pairpoint table lamp with an 18" d. reverse-painted 'Carlisle' shade decorated in the Garden of Allah design with a continuous Egyptian landscape with pyramids, camels, Arabs and palm trees in sunset shades of orange, yellow, blue, green and tan, on a bronzed metal baluster-form Pairpoint-signed base . . . . . . . . . . . . . . . . $4,480

**Fig. 46:** A "Puffy" Pairpoint boudoir lamp with a 5" d. Lilac Tree pattern shade, reverse-painted with deep red and pink lilac clusters and pale orange and green leaves with yellow and purple butterflies, raised on a bronzed metal Pairpoint-signed tree trunk base . . . . . . . $34,160

**Fig. 47:** A Pairpoint table lamp with a 16" d. reverse-painted 'Exeter' shade decorated in the Four Seasons design, large color panels around the sides each representing a different season of the year, each separated by white panels, on a slender urn-form bronzed metal Pairpoint-signed base . . . . . . $4,480

**Fig. 48:** A "Puffy" Pairpoint table lamp with a 16" d. Begonia pattern shade, reverse-painted in bright shades of orange, red, yellow and green, on a bronzed metal Pairpoint-signed tree trunk base . . . . . . . . $67,200

All courtesy of Fontaine's Auction Gallery, Pittsfield, MA.

# Early Electric Lighting • Tiffany Lamps

**Fig. 49**

**Fig. 51**

**Fig. 50**

**Fig. 49:** Tiffany table lamp with a 14" d. bell-shaped shade of gold iridescent and pulled feather design, raised on a slender gilt-bronze base signed "Tiffany Studios - New York 533"..................... $3,920

**Fig. 50:** A very rare Tiffany "Poppy" table lamp with a 16" d. conical leaded glass shade with vibrant orange poppy blossoms and mottled green and blue leaves accented with bronze filigree all against a mottled reddish yellow ground, narrow blue and mottled yellow border bands, raised on a three-arm bronze base with reeded standard and domed base on small tab feet, shade signed "Tiffany Studios - New York - 1461," base signed "Tiffany Studios - New York 362 - 9175" .............. $72,800

**Fig. 51:** A rare Tiffany "Dragonfly" table lamp, a 16" d. conical leaded glass shade with seven dragonflies around the sides with red eyes and wings covered with bronze filigree against a background of caramel slag, raised on a bronze ball-and-claw footed base, shade signed "Tiffany Studios - New York," base signed "Tiffany Studios - New York" .... $44,800

All courtesy of Fontaine's Auction Gallery, Pittsfield, MA.

# Early Electric Lighting • Tiffany Lamps

**Fig. 52**
**Fig. 53**
**Fig. 54**
**Fig. 55**

**Fig. 52:** An outstanding Tiffany "Daffodil" table lamp with a 20" d. conical shade composed of suspended yellowish pink daffodil blossoms on long dark mottled green leafy stems against a background of dark mottled blue, matching border bands, raised on a slender bronze base with dished foot, both shade and base signed . . . . . . . . . . . . . . . . . . . . . . $67,200
Courtesy of Fontaine's Auction Gallery, Pittsfield, MA.

**Fig. 53:** Tiffany "Lily" desk lamp, the bronze leaf-cast base issuing three arched arms ending in electric sockets each fitted with a gold iridescent lily-form shade, shades signed "L.C.T. Favrile" and base signed "Tiffany Studios - New York 320". . $5,040
Courtesy of Fontaine's Auction Gallery, Pittsfield, MA.

**Fig. 54:** A fine Tiffany "Banded Dogwood" table lamp, the 16" d. domical leaded glass shade with a band of white dogwood blossoms and green leaves against a lattice ground of light mottled green glass, raised on an urn-form bronze base with brown-verde patination supported by three slender legs on a round disk foot, shade signed "Tiffany Studios - New York," base signed "Tiffany Studios - New York - 29940" . . . . . . . . . . $26,320
Courtesy of Fontaine's Auction Gallery, Pittsfield, MA.

**Fig. 55:** An unusual Tiffany-Grueby Pottery table lamp with a domical 16" d. leaded glass Tiffany shade in the Acorn pattern with a band of vining yellow acorns against a lattice background of mottled yellowish green glass, raised on a three-arm bronze support fitting into a Grueby Pottery base with tooled and applied wide leaves alternating with thin stems with yellow flower buds, all with an oatmealed matte green glaze, shade signed "Tiffany Studios - New York," base marked with four original paper labels . . . . . . . . . . . . $37,375
Courtesy of Craftsman Auctions, Lambertville, NJ.

# Early Electric Lighting • Miscellaneous Lamps

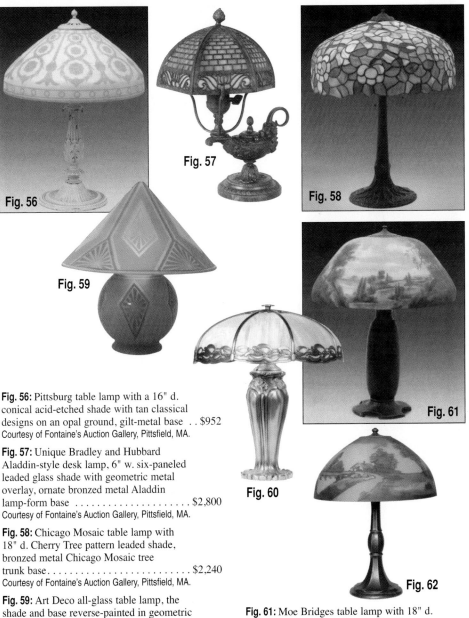

**Fig. 56**

**Fig. 57**

**Fig. 58**

**Fig. 59**

**Fig. 60**

**Fig. 61**

**Fig. 62**

**Fig. 56:** Pittsburg table lamp with a 16" d. conical acid-etched shade with tan classical designs on an opal ground, gilt-metal base . . $952
Courtesy of Fontaine's Auction Gallery, Pittsfield, MA.

**Fig. 57:** Unique Bradley and Hubbard Aladdin-style desk lamp, 6" w. six-paneled leaded glass shade with geometric metal overlay, ornate bronzed metal Aladdin lamp-form base . . . . . . . . . . . . . . . . . . . . . $2,800
Courtesy of Fontaine's Auction Gallery, Pittsfield, MA.

**Fig. 58:** Chicago Mosaic table lamp with 18" d. Cherry Tree pattern leaded shade, bronzed metal Chicago Mosaic tree trunk base . . . . . . . . . . . . . . . . . . . . . . . . . $2,240
Courtesy of Fontaine's Auction Gallery, Pittsfield, MA.

**Fig. 59:** Art Deco all-glass table lamp, the shade and base reverse-painted in geometric designs in deep orange and gold, made in Czechoslovakia, 14" d. shade . . . . . . . . . . . $2,912
Courtesy of Fontaine's Auction Gallery, Pittsfield, MA.

**Fig. 60:** A Bradley and Hubbard table lamp with a 20" d. eight-panel caramel slag shade with a band of cast berries and leaves, gilt bronzed metal base, 23" h. . . . . $1,093
Courtesy of Treadway-Toomey Galleries, Oak Park, IL.

**Fig. 61:** Moe Bridges table lamp with 18" d. reverse-painted shade decorated with a colorful landscape, on a simple bronzed metal base, shade and base signed . . . . . . . $4,480
Courtesy of Fontaine's Auction Gallery, Pittsfield, MA.

**Fig. 62:** A Jefferson reverse-painted table lamp with a 16" d. shade decorated with a colorful landscape. . . . . . . . . . . . . . . . . . . . $805
Courtesy Treadway-Toomey Galleries, Oak Park, IL.

# Early Electric Lighting • Miscellaneous Lamps

**Fig. 63:** Wilkinson table lamp with 19" d. Floral Border leaded glass shade, on a slender bronzed metal base . . . . . . . . . . . . $4,760

**Fig. 64:** Fabulous Duffner and Kimberly lamp with 19" d. leaded glass shade featuring a shell and scroll design, slender ribbed bronzed metal Duffner and Kimberly base . . . . . . . . . . . . . . . . . . . . . $22,400

**Fig. 65:** Suess table lamp with an 18" d. leaded glass shade in caramel slag with a border band of green leaves, slender bronzed-metal base . . . . . . . . . . . . . . . . . $3,640

**Fig. 66:** Riviere table lamp with colorful floral vine 21" d. leaded shade on a slender bronzed metal leaf-cast base . . . . . . . . . . . $7,840

**Fig. 67:** Wilkinson table lamp with 20" d. Water Lily pattern leaded shade, bronzed metal cattail base . . . . . . . . . . . . . . . . . . . $7,840

**Fig. 68:** Fine signed DeVez French cameo glass lamp with pointed ovoid shade cut with a sailboat scene, the matching base with tall cut panels with scenes . . . . . . . . . $5,600

All courtesy of Fontaine's Auction Gallery, Pittsfield, MA.

# Miscellaneous Chandeliers

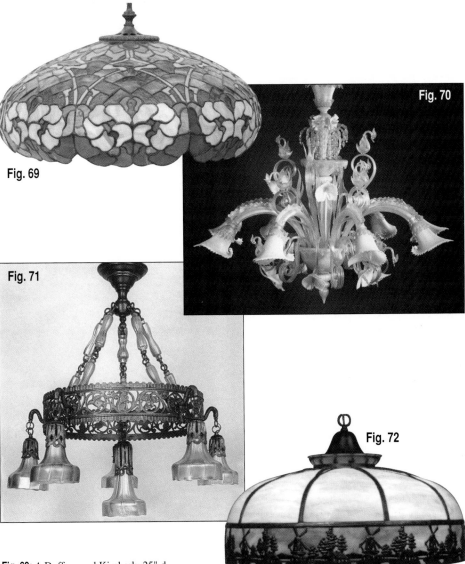

**Fig. 70**

**Fig. 69**

**Fig. 71**

**Fig. 72**

**Fig. 69:** A Duffner and Kimberly 25" d. leaded glass domed chandelier with stylized florals and geometric designs . . . . $14,000
Courtesy of Fontaine's Auction Gallery, Pittsfield, MA.

**Fig. 70:** Fine Venetian blown glass eight-light chandelier in green and white with gold inclusions, 20th century, 48" d., 42" h. . . . . $3,163
Courtesy of William Doyle Galleries, New York, NY.

**Fig. 71:** Rare Oscar Bach gilt-bronze and Steuben glass six-light chandelier, gold iridescent glass sleeves on the hanging chains above the ornate pierced scroll and animal ring suspending signed Steuben gold iridescent shades . . . . . . . . . . . . . . . . . . . $12,880
Courtesy of Fontaine's Auction Gallery, Pittsfield, MA.

**Fig. 72:** A 24" d. ten-panel slag glass domed chandelier with caramel slag panels above a wide skirt band in mottled blue slag overlaid with a metal filigree design of trees and windmills, one panel with a hairline, circa 1920 . . . . . . . . . . . . . . $575
Courtesy of Jackson's International Auctioneers and Appraisers, Cedar Falls, IA.

# Miscellaneous Decorative Chandeliers-Shades

**Fig. 73**

**Fig. 74**

**Fig. 75**

**Fig. 76**

**Fig. 73:** Tiffany 16" d. "Fleur-de-Lis" leaded glass shade with a band of green fleur-de-lis surrounded by small caramel slag segments . . . . . . . . . . . . . . . . . . . . . $10,080
Courtesy of Fontaine's Auction Galleries, Pittsfield, MA.

**Fig. 74:** A Tiffany five-light chandelier with a long ribbed bronze rod issuing five downturned electric sockets each fitted with a signed gold iridescent Favrile glass shade, 16" w., 34" h. . . . . . . . $9,775
Courtesy of Treadway-Toomey Galleries, Oak Park, IL.

**Fig. 75:** Tulip-form gas shade in clear acid-etched glass with a green enameled edge band with small deep pink blossoms and scattered pink blossoms and green leaves trimmed in gold around the sides, circa 1900, 5½" h. . . . . . . . . . . . . . . . . . . . . . $225
Courtesy of Temple's Antiques, Eden Prairie, MN.

**Fig. 76:** "Puffy" Pairpoint 'Pisa' shade with each ribbed panel reverse-painted with roses, leaves and gold scrolls, signed, minor chips, 16" w.. . . . . . . . . . . . $5,175
Courtesy of Treadway-Toomey Galleries, Oak Park, IL.

# BUSINESS REPLY MAIL

FIRST-CLASS MAIL PERMIT NO. 12 IOLA, WI

POSTAGE WILL BE PAID BY ADDRESSEE

**ANTIQUE TRADER**
**CIRCULATION DEPT**
**PO BOX 5016**
**IOLA WI 54945-9939**

**Table lamp,** 10" d. "Puffy" reverse-painted Azalea patt. shade, overall large reddish orange & yellow-streaked blossoms & dark green mottled leaves against a black ground, raised on a gilt-metal base w/the shade ring supported by outswept blossom-cast arms issuing from the top of a pyramidal base on small square feet (ILLUS.) ........................................................ **38,640**

*Pairpoint Puffy Rose Bouquet Lamp*

**Table lamp,** 10" d. "Puffy" reverse-painted Rose Bouquet patt. shade, the pointed domical form molded overall w/large roses in deep red & yellow w/green & yellow leaves against a blackish green ground, raised on an unusual bronze metal base w/a shade ring raised on a center shaft & four incurved supports pierced & cast w/leaves all above a tall pyramidal lower section cast w/large poppy blossoms (ILLUS.) .......................... **20,160**

**Table lamp,** 11 1/2" d. closed mushroom-form domical 'Vienna' reverse-painted shade decorated w/coralene yellow interior w/stylized olive green heart-shaped leaves & red berries, gold outine on exterior, mounted on a ball-trimmed ring support by four arms on a quatreform flaring base molded w/pointed foliate designs, impressed "Pairpoint Mfg. Co. 3052," 20 1/2" h. (ILLUS. lamp, on previous page left, w/mantel lamp) ............................ **2,070**

**Table lamp,** 12" d. bulbous mushroom-shaped reverse-painted 'Venice' shade, decorated w/pointed oval panels of stylized tulip blossoms in deep pink & white alternating w/wide bands of wavy light green & yellow bands & pale white-striped panels w/bands of small yellow ovals enclosing colorful flower clusters, raised on a Pairpoint silvered metal base w/a flattened four-lobed base w/a reeded edge, base & shade signed ........................ **7,840**

*Rare Puffy White Grape Pairpoint*

**Table lamp,** 12" d. domical "Puffy" reverse-painted shade in the 'White Grape' patt., the wide shade decorated w/large clusters of yellowish white grapes w/mottled green, yellow & orange leaves all against a black ground, shade signed, raised on a shade ring w/three curved scroll-cast supports to the signed Pairpoint cylindrical silver-metal standard cast w/large grape clusters above the deep cushion foot w/swirling vines (ILLUS.) ................... **17,920**

**Table lamp,** 12" d. "Puffy" domical 'Papillion' shade w/a rare pale yellow ground, raised on a slender silvered metal shaft w/a round foot ........................................... **12,650**

*Very Rare Apple Tree Pairpoint Puffy*

**Table lamp,** 12" d. "Puffy" reverse-painted Apple Tree patt. closed-top shade, the deep domical form brightly painted w/large red & yellow apples & green leaves alternating w/large pink & yellow apple blossoms w/large colorful butterfles, raised on a bronzed metal tree trunk signed base, shade signed (ILLUS.) ...................................................... **65,520**

*Fine Puffy Rose Bouquet Lamp*

*Fine Apple Tree Puffy Pairpoint Lamp*

**Table lamp,** 12" d. "Puffy" reverse-painted Apple Tree patt. open-topped shade painted w/orangish red, blue & yellow-centered white blossoms against a dark green leafy ground, raised on tree trunk patinated base, rare shade version (ILLUS.) ...................................................... **32,450**

**Table lamp,** 12" d. "Puffy" reverse-painted Azalea patt. shade painted w/white, yellow, peach & red blossoms amid a sea of leafage in various shades of green, yellow & orange, raised on a silver-metal trumpet-form vase w/arched blossom & stem long handles, shade marked "Pat. Applied For," base impressed "Pairpoint Mfg. Co. 8041," overall 19 1/2" h. ............. **17,250**

**Table lamp,** 12" d. "Puffy" reverse-painted Poppy patt. shade raised on silvered metal shade ring over a silver metal base w/a central cylindrical ring-pierced column flanked by three slender reeded & curved ring supports all issuing from the domed round base w/a molded grapevine border band .......................................... **31,350**

**Table lamp,** 12" d. "Puffy" reverse-painted Rose Bouquet patt. closed-top shade decorated w/large red roses against yellow & green leaves on a dark green ground, raised on a bronze metal trumpet-form base w/slender scrolled stem & blossom handles up the sides (ILLUS. top next column) .................................................. **17,600**

*Tulips on Pairpoint Shade with Base*

**Table lamp,** 12" d. reverse-painted 'Venice' shade decorated w/pointed oblong reserves w/large red & yellow tulip blossoms alternating w/wide bands of green & yellow & narrower bands of pink centered by small bands of oval floral reserves, on a signed Pairpoint silvered metal vase w/a slender shaft on a flattened scalloped foot (ILLUS.) ..................... **7,840**

**Table lamp,** 13 1/2" d. "Puffy" flat-topped 'Hummingbird and Roses' shade w/gently flaring cylindrical sides, colorful hummingbirds flutter above a multicolored wreath, a ribbed mottled plum ground, frosty clear crown w/white-painted ribs, raised on a slender ring-, baluster- and knob-turned brass base w/dished round foot marked "Pairpoint #E3032," overall 20" h. .......................................................... **7,590**

**Table lamp,** 14" d. domed straight-sided 'Palm' shade w/a scalloped rim reverse-painted w/a countryside landscape w/tall trees in autumn colors, raised on a cast bronze metal tree trunk Pairpoint base ...... **7,840**

*Extraordinary Puffy Lilac Table Lamp*

**Table lamp,** 14" d. "Puffy" reverse-painted
Lilac patt. shade, large clusters of blossoms painted in dark purple & deep red
w/mottled green & yellow leaves & colorful butterflies, on a bronze Pairpoint tree
trunk base (ILLUS.) .................................. **145,600**

*Pairpoint Lamp with Papillon Shade*

**Table lamp,** 14" d. "Puffy" reverse-painted
'Papillon' shade in the Butterfly & Roses
patt., large clusters of red & pink roses
around the border w/green leaves &
large colorful butterflies against a white &
green-streaked background, on a signed
Pairpoint base w/a slender square shaft
& rectangular dished foot (ILLUS.) ........... **13,440**
**Table lamp,** 14" d. "Puffy" reverse-painted
'Papillon' shade painted on interior w/four
butterflies in shades of orange, yellow,
brown, blue & black amid roses in various shades of pink, rose & crimson,
w/yellow centers & surrounding leafage
in various shades of green & yellow, reserved against a white marbleized
ground w/green veining, exterior height-
ened in gilt, silvered metal handled urn-

form base w/brushed silver finish,
w/finial, ca. 1915, 20 1/2" h. ........................ **9,200**

*"Puffy" Pairpoint Lamp with Irises*

**Table lamp,** 14" d. "Puffy" reverse-painted
'Stratford' patt. shade, decorated w/blos-
soming irises & leaves against a blue &
yellow speckled ground, in shades of yellow, purple, orange, blue & amber,
marked, on a slender silvered-metal
base w/reeded standard on domed leaf-
banded footed base, base marked,
13 7/8" h. (ILLUS.) ........................................ **8,225**

*"Puffy" Pairpoint with Roses Border*

**Table lamp,** 14" d. "Puffy" reverse-painted
'Stratford' patt. shade, decorated
w/molded border of large roses & flying
hummingbirds in shades of deep rose,
purple & yellow on a white linenfold
ground w/thin yellow bands, raised on a
slender patinated metal base w/im-
pressed leaf design on standard &

domed ribbed foot, base impressed
"Pairpoint C 3066," 21" h. (ILLUS.)............. **9,775**

der band & four wide tab feet, shade &
base signed (ILLUS.) ................................. **10,360**

*"Puffy" Stratford Pattern Shade & Lamp*

**Table lamp,** 14" d. "Puffy" reverse-painted
'Stratford' shade, a wide border of large
colorful roses & flying hummingbirds
against a mottled mauve & black background, on a signed Pairpoint base w/a
slender swelled standard on a round
multi-lobed foot (ILLUS.).............................. **7,280**

*Pairpoint Lamp with Palermo Shade*

**Table lamp,** 14" d. reverse-painted 'Palermo' shade, decorated w/wide stripes of
leafy scrolls against a finely striped reddish brown ground alternating w/wide
white stripes decorated w/delicate colorful floral stripes, on a signed worn silver
plated Pairpoint base w/a slender
squared shaft w/a bulbed bottom over
the flaring hexagonal foot (ILLUS.)............. **4,200**

*Pairpoint "Puffy" Gladiola Table Lamp*

**Table lamp,** 14" d. "Puffy" reverse-painted
'Stratford' shade in the Gladiola patt.,
decorated w/large spikes of gladiola flowers in shades of yellow, rose & lavender
on green & blue leafy stems against a
frosted creamy white ground, smaller
blossoms in deep rose, orange & yellow
around the lower border, raised on a gilt-
metal slender reeded standard above a
flaring round base w/an embossed bor-

*Pairpoint Lamp with Tapestry Shade*

**Table lamp,** 14" d. reverse-painted 'Seville'
open-topped shade, decorated w/a
monochromatic green ground w/three
pairs of long-tailed stylized birds amid
scrolling foliage, raised on a bronzed
metal base w/a simple cylindrical shaft &
a square foot cast w/a Greek Key design,
23" h. (ILLUS.) ............................................. **1,840**

*Pairpoint Lamp with Venice Shade*

**Table lamp,** 14 1/2" d. mushroom-shaped reverse-painted 'Venice' shade decorated w/the Rose Tapestry patt., the ribbed rust background w/scrolling leaves & flowers, each panel decorated w/large rose blossoms in shades of pink & green, a central rose medallion at the closed top, on a patinated metal two-socket base w/a squared baluster-form standard w/raised flower & fleur-de-lis designs above the squared domed base, base w/impressed Pairpoint mark & "83058," patina wear, 20" h. (ILLUS.) .............. **6,325**

*Rare "Puffy" Pairpoint Apple Tree Lamp*

**Table lamp,** 15" d. "Puffy" domical Apple Blossom patt. shade, reverse-painted on the large apples in golden yellow & orange w/light green leaves against a dark green ground w/brown branches & flying bees, raised on a patinated metal tree trunk base, shade stamped in gilt "The

Pairpoint Co., Posted July 9, 1906," base w/impressed Pairpoint trademark & "3091," ca. 1907, overall 23" h. (ILLUS.) ..................... **40,250**
**Table lamp,** 15" d. reverse-painted flared 'Exeter' shade w/two urn & griffin motifs spaced by floral reserves, raised on two-socket baluster-form base, impressed "Pairpoint" & numbered, 20 1/4" h. (two small rim chips) ......................... **1,150**

*Pairpoint Lamp with Pastoral Scene*

**Table lamp,** 15" h. reverse-painted domical 'Landsdowne' shade, decorated w/a continuous cottage & countryside landscape, a path & cottage in the foreground w/fields & a red barn in the background, green grass & trees under a blue sky w/white clouds, on a bronzed metal Pairpoint base w/a wide sharply tapering ribbed conical standard on a round foot (ILLUS.) .............. **3,360**
**Table lamp,** 15" d. reverse-painted 'Chesterfield' patt. shade, drum-shaped w/undulating sides, decorated w/a multicolored "Persian Carpet" patt., brick red ground w/green stylized flowers alternating w/white framed yellow & aqua stylized leaves, mounted on a four-arm brass spider support above the squared baluster-form standard & stepped, squared foot w/rounded corners, marked "Pairpoint Mfg. Co. #3088," overall 23" h. .............. **8,800**
**Table lamp,** 15" w. hexagonal reverse-painted 'Directoire' patt. shade, the panels decorated w/an unusual harvest landscape w/harnessed horses & farmer reaping crop, tied bundles of straw standing in a field, farmhouse & barn, fall-foliaged trees painted on exterior & interior silhouetted against amethyst & blue sky & landscape, company gilt stamp mark & patent date, on an ornate tri-arm gilt-metal base on a large controlled-bubble glass ball above the dark marble hexagonal foot, cornucopia finial, overall 26" h. .............. **3,300**

*Pairpoint Lamp w/Devonshire Shade*

**Table lamp,** 15 1/2" d. "Puffy" reverse-painted 'Devonshire' shade decorated w/the Floral Garland patt., grey ground, painted on the interior w/garlands of flowers in various vivid shades of green, pink, yellow, white, purple, burgundy & orange, squared silvered metal baluster-form standard on a squared foot w/incurved edges, base impressed "Pairpoint Mfg. Co. - 3088" w/hallmark, ca. 1915, 21" h. (ILLUS.)............................................ **11,500**

**Table lamp,** 15 3/4" d. tapering drum-shaped reverse-painted 'Seville' shade in textured grey decorated w/a silhouetted tranquil riverscape w/leafing trees, in shades of green, brownish pink & grey, raised on a bronzed metal base w/three angular S-scroll supports w/scroll feet resting on a tripartite foot, greenish brown patina, base impressed "Pairpoint 4084 1/2," 21 1/4" h. ..................................... **5,700**

**Table lamp,** 16" d. domical reverse-painted 'Berkeley' shade, decorated w/a continuous moonlit landscape w/a man in a rowboat approaching building on a tree-lined shore, signed "C. Durand," raised on a dark gold metal figural three-dolphin base impressed "Pairpoint D3076," 21" h. (ILLUS.) .............................................. **4,025**

**Table lamp,** 16" d. domical reverse-painted 'Berkeley' shade, decorated w/a Hawaiian seascape w/birds & distant ships beyond tropical foliage, artist-signed "H. Fisher" & stamped "The Pairpoint Corp'n," raised on a bronzed-metal two-socket base w/bulbous paneled shaft & squared foot w/angled corners, impressed w/Pairpoint trademark, 22" h. ...... **4,600**

*Rare Pairpoint "Puffy" Begonia Lamp*

**Table lamp,** 16" d. "Puffy" reverse-painted Begonia patt. shade, molded overall w/large yellow, red & green begonia leaves on a dark orange ground, raised on a slender bronzed metal Pairpoint tree trunk base (ILLUS.) ................................... **67,200**

*Pairpoint Landscape Table Lamp*

*Butterflies & Apple Blossoms "Puffy"*

**Table lamp,** 16" d. "Puffy" reverse-painted Butterflies & Apple Blossoms patt. on a 'Papillon' shade, Model No. C-3066, decorated w/white, pink & blue blossoms & green leafage w/pale yellow & blue butterflies against a pale yellow ground, on a simple slender silvered metal base (ILLUS.) ...................................................... **16,500**

**Table lamp,** 16" d. "Puffy" reverse-painted flat-topped cylindrical Hummingbird & Roses patt. shade, a frosted white ground w/large yellow, red & white roses & green leaves around the lower border w/a colorful hummingbird above, raised on four arms above the gilt-metal slender square pedestal on a flaring, stepped square leaf-cast foot, shade marked, overall 23 1/4" h. .......................................... **9,775**

**Table lamp,** 16" d. reverse-painted 'Bombay' shade decorated w/a continuous autumn landscape scene w/figures by a lake, raised on a patinated metal tall urnform base w/arched side handles on a disk foot, shade & base marked, overall 22" h. ................................................................ **2,875**

*Pairpoint Lamp with Harbor Scene*

w/foliage & molded "Pairpoint - 49030" w/logo, 22" h. (ILLUS.) .................................. **4,370**

*Oriental Carpet Shade & Lamp*

**Table lamp,** 16" d. reverse-painted 'Chesterfield' lobed drum-form shade, decorated w/an Oriental carpet design in red, green, yellow, white, orange & blue, printed in red "The Pairpoint Corp. - Posted July 9, 1907," the gilt-metal base w/a four-sided baluster-form stem cast & enameled w/foliage on a quatrefoil foot, impressed "Pairpoint Mfg. Co. - B3031" w/logo, shade cracked in half & reglued, wear to base patina, 21 1/4" h. (ILLUS.) ...................................................... **1,610**

**Table lamp,** 16" d. tapering cylindrical reverse-painted 'Lansdowne' open-topped shade, decorated in shades of blue, purple, orange & yellow w/a continuous harbor scene including a rowboat carrying five figures, signed "C. Durand," the gilt-metal base w/a slender central baluster-form shaft surrounded by three slender scroll supports, the tripartite foot cast

*Pairpoint with Grecian Garden Shade*

**Table lamp,** 16" d. tapering cylindrical reverse-painted 'Seville' shade, decorated in shades of yellow, green, rose, brown & blue w/the Greek Garden design, on a patinated metal base w/a squatty urn supported on a central baluster-turned standard flanked by three scroll legs on a tripartite foot, shade unsigned, base signed (ILLUS.) .......................................... **3,900**

**Table lamp,** 16" w. six-sided tapering reverse-painted shade, the flat panels decorated alternatively w/an overall rose design in orange & dark brown on a tan ground or a single small rose blossom & leaf design on a tan ground, narrow yellow border bands, raised on a gilt-metal base w/a slender central handle shaft surrounded by three electric candle sockets all on a triangular onyx plinth set in a conforming metal frame w/small inscrolled feet, base signed .......................... **2,240**

*Pairpoint Lamp with Landscape Shade*

**Table lamp,** 16 1/2" d. domical reverse-painted shade w/a textured exterior surface, decorated w/a continuous landscape of birch trees near water w/boats & mountains in the background, naturalistic colors, raised on a three-socket patinated metal baluster-shaped ribbed knopped base, shade unsigned, base w/impressed Pairpoint mark & "D 3063," minor chips to top rim, 22 1/4" h. (ILLUS.)...................................................... **2,530**

*Pairpoint Lamp with Exeter Shade*

**Table lamp,** 16 1/2" d. reverse-painted 'Exeter' shade decorated w/a pastoral scene of trees & grassy hillside against a shaded blue sky, a decorative yellow band around the shoulder painted w/a repeating windmill design in brown, signed "C. Durand," raised on a gilt-metal urn supported by a double-baluster central column flanked by three scroll supports rest-ing on a tripartite foot, base impressed "Pairpoint - D 3070" & company trademark, gilt wear, early 20th c., 23" h. (ILLUS.)...................................................... **2,990**

**Table lamp,** 17" d. hexagonal tapering "Directoire" shade reverse-painted w/a continuous colorful expansive landscaped ground including a columned waterfront building, iridescent background coloring, paneled borders above & below & marked "The Pairpoint Corp'n" on the border, raised on a candelabrum-style base w/three electric candle sockets on short gilt-metal arms w/pointed drops centered by a knob above a cut glass knop on a gilt-metal tapering pedestal & octagonal dark onyx foot, impressed "Pairpoint Mfg. Co. E3001," 27 1/2" h. ...... **2,645**

**Table lamp,** 17" w. hexagonal reverse-painted 'Directoire' open-topped shade, painted in shades of pale orange, pink, green, blue & brown w/a classical monument in a lakeside landscape between paneled border bands, raised on a gilt-metal & glass Louis XVI-style base w/three electric candle sockets on up-scrolled arms attached to a central column above a large clear controlled-bubble glass ball above the octagonal black foot, ca. 1910, overall 26 3/4" h. (ILLUS. right below)................................................... **7,475**

**Table lamp,** 17" w. reverse-painted glass 'Directoire' shade, painted w/landscapes of towns, forests & castles, in shades of green, brown, purple, grey & pink, alternating w/panels centering a stylized flower in green, purple, white & black reserved against yellow ground dappled w/black, silvered metal base impressed "Pairpoint/D 3084," w/finial, ca. 1915, 24 1/2" h......................................................... **5,462**

*Two Pairpoint Table Lamps*

**Table lamp,** 17" w., tapering open-topped nine-sided reverse-painted shade decorated w/a gold Baroque-style scrolling floral vine design on a green ground between dotted borders, raised on a gilt-metal, glass & marble Louis XVI-style base w/three electric candle sockets on arms above a twisted clear glass column above the round metal & marble foot, ca. 1910, overall 26" h. (ILLUS. left above)..... **1,495**

**Table lamp,** 17 1/2" d. waisted cylindrical dome-topped "Exeter" shade reverse-painted on frosted glass w/a continuous landscape scene w/tall trees in earth-tones, brown, gold & blue, raised on a brass-plated white metal baluster-form base w/an octagonal foot, shade marked "The Pairpoint Corp'n," base marked "Pairpoint," 22 1/2" h. (base plating worn) .................................................. **3,465**

*Pairpoint Garden of Allah Table Lamp*

**Table lamp,** 18" d. reverse-painted 'Carlisle' shade decorated in the Garden of Allah patt., a continuous desert landscape w/Arabs on camels by palm trees & the pyramids in the background against an orange sky, on a ribbed baluster-form bronzed metal Pairpoint base w/a squared foot (ILLUS.).................................. **4,480**

*Pairpoint Exotic Bird Pattern Lamp*

**Table lamp,** 18" d. reverse-painted 'Exeter' shade decorated in the Exotic Bird patt., a long-tailed blue, orange & yellow bird perched among blue leafy vines w/large white blossoms, small yellow blossoms & orange berries on a brown ground, raised on a silver plated base w/a squatty urn raised on a central baluster-turned shaft surrounded by three long slender legs w/scroll feet resting on a tripartite foot, base signed (ILLUS.).................................... **5,888**

*Unique Pairpoint Urn-form Table Lamp*

**Table lamp,** wide urn-form reverse-painted glass body decorated w/an elaborate ribbon & floral garland design in shades of blue, yellow, green, orange, charcoal, rose & eggshell white, the exterior w/gilt highlights, fitted in a gilt-metal round & band frame w/cast griffin heads atop the incurved reeded supports above the square cross-form base, 18" h. (ILLUS.)........................................................ **3,525**

**Table lamp,** 19 3/4" d. domical reverse-painted 'Copley' shade in the Sea Gull patt., a seascape w/birds in shades of dark blue, brown, tan & white, raised on a matching baluster-form glass internally-lit base on a mahogany disk foot, artist-signed & marked, ca. 1915, overall 25 " h. ............................................... **10,925**

**Table lamp,** 19 1/2" d. domical flaring reverse-painted 'Copley' patt. shade, raised on a matching baluster-form glass base, each decorated w/sea gulls above a rough sea, different sailing vessels on each side, in shades of medium blue, purple, green & red, mahogany foot w/the impressed company mark on the metal washer, overall 24" h. .................... **10,450**

*Pairpoint Lamp with Roses on Shade*

**Table lamp,** 20" d. domical reverse-painted 'Berkley' shade, decorated in the upper section w/an overall design of large roses in shades of reds w/green & yellow leaves against a black background, a wide border band w/a yellow band & arched panels enclosing green leaf sprigs on a brown ground, raised on a slender copper-colored baluster-form standard mounted w/leafy swags above the round domed foot, (ILLUS.)................... **6,720**

*Pairpoint Autumn Landscape Lamp*

**Table lamp,** 20" d. domical reverse-painted 'Berkley' shade, decorated w/an autumnal landscape w/large clusters of leafy trees in wide meadows, in shades of dark & light green, orange, yellow, dark & light

grey & blue, on a gilt-metal slender urn-form Pairpoint base w/slender loop shoulder handles & a square notched foot (ILLUS.)................................. **3,640**

**Table lamp,** 20" d. domical reverse-painted 'Copley' shade, decorated w/a scene of two ships & six birds on swirling ocean waves, artist-signed "H. Fisher" on rim, raised on a matching glass baluster-form base w/interior light, stamped "Pairpoint D3000," rewired, new sockets, 24" h. ....... **8,625**

*Pairpoint Lamp with Floral Shade*

**Table lamp,** 22" d. reverse-painted 'Lansdowne' shade decorated w/a colorful band of large blossoms in yellow, pink, blue & orange, dark border bands, raised on a silvered metal base w/a slender central column enclosed by three slender S-scroll columns raised on a banded marble round foot, base marked, 22" h. (ILLUS.)......................................................... **4,600**

## Tiffany Lamps

**Boudoir lamp,** 7" d. sharply conical Favrile glass shade w/knobbed finial, in iridescent white w/stripes of small gold iridescent dots up the sides, raised on a slender signed Tiffany bronze base w/a domed, paneled foot highlighted in each panel w/a band of gold dots, shade signed "L.C.T. Favrile," 14 1/2" h. ............. **$3,080**

**Bridge lamp,** 10" d. domical glass shade w/waisted rim in ivory cased over white decorated w/green pulled feathers reserved against amber, pivoting within a loop ring raised on a tall slender standard w/five slender splayed legs w/pointed pad feet w/a brownish green patina, shade signed "L.C.T.," base impressed "Tiffany Studios - New York - 423," 58" h. ......................................................... **12,650**

**Bridge lamp,** a 10" d. domical glass shade w/waisted rim in ivory cased over white decorated w/green pulled feathers reserved against amber, pivoting within a loop ring raised on a tall slender standard w/five slender splayed legs w/pointed pad feet w/a brownish green patina, shade signed "L.C.T.," base impressed "Tiffany Studios - New York - 423," 4' 10" h............................................................ **12,650**

**Ceiling light,** rectangular, w/hinged leaded glass panel in mottled amber glass centering a gold iridescent turtleback tile surrounded by iridescent cabochon "jewels," the bronze sides w/a pierced design backed by amber glass, 9 x 11", 2 1/4" h. .............................................. **6,325**

*Tiffany October Night Chandelier*

**Chandelier,** "October Night," 27" w. octagonal tapering leaded glass shade w/a design of trelliswork in light green entwined w/vines pendent w/blossoms in shades of blue, rust, yellow, amber & red w/leafage ranging from olive to grass green to emerald green, all reserved against a background of swirled & streaked mauve, white, blue, green, amber & brown glass, bronze hooks & chains w/greenish brown patina, impressed "Tiffany Studios - New York," no electric fittings (ILLUS.) .......................................... **46,000**

**Chandelier,** "Rhododendron," 28" conical open-topped leaded shade w/a border band of large clusters of red & pink blossoms framed by mottled green leaves, on a background of graduated blocks of white to deep red & purple mottled glass, signed ........................................................ **53,200**

*Small Tiffany Desk Lamp*

**Desk lamp,** a mushroom-shaped Favrile glass shade in amber & yellow shading to orange opalescence raised on a shade ring & light socket on a repaired cylindrical stem resting on a domed opalescent & amber iridescent swirled glass foot w/metal liner, metal impressed "Tiffany Studios - New York - TGDCo. - 28N - 27071," overall 11 1/2" h. (ILLUS.) ............. **1,725**

**Desk lamp,** counter-balance style, a 7 3/4" d. deep domical gold & green damascene shade mounted on a bronze base w/high arched arm pivoting w/a large round counter-balance ball above the slender waisted standard on a domed disk foot, shade & base signed, 16" h........ **6,038**

**Desk lamp,** counter-balance type, a 7" d. domed gold Favrile shade w/damascene decoration w/pink & lavender iridescent highlights on a socket at the end of a slender C-form bronze arm adjusting above a ball & socket bronze base w/round foot, shade signed "L.C.T. Favrile," bronze w/original patina & signed "Tiffany Studios - N.Y. - #416"........ **6,050**

**Desk lamp,** Favrile glass & bronze, 7" d. domical iridescent orange glass shade w/iridescent gold scalloped & scrolled decoration, supported by harp-arm bronze base, shade engraved "L.C.T." & base stamped "TIFFANY STUDIOS - NEW YORK - 418," 12" h. ........................... **4,370**

*Tiffany Linenfold Desk Lamp*

**Desk lamp,** "Linenfold," 10" d. domical shade in the Abalone patt., the shade composed of 12 panels of amber linenfold glass between ruffled glass borders, raised on a gilded bronze slender four-sided shaft on an octagonal foot, shade impressed "Tiffany Studios - NY - 1928," base impressed "Tiffany Studios - New York - 604," ca. 1928, 16" h. (ILLUS.)........ **6,900**

*Tiffany Linenfold Desk Lamp*

**Desk lamp,** "Linenfold," 7" d. paneled shade w/each section composed of an amber linenfold panel below a small horizontal matching panel, supported in an arched harp above a slender standard on a domed paneled round base w/small knob feet, shade signed, base signed "Tiffany Studios - New York - 424" (ILLUS.)...................................................... **5,645**

*Two-shade Tiffany Desk Lamp*

**Desk lamp,** patinated bronze base w/oval scalloped foot surmounted by a twisted central stem w/a bud finial flanked by two upcurved arms w/bulbous urn-form electric sockets, reddish green patina, fitted

w/two tulip-form ribbed amber iridescent shades signed "L.C.T. - Favrile," the base signed "Tiffany Studios - New York - 1230," one shade w/chips on fitting rim, shades 5" h., overall 9 1/4" h. (ILLUS.)...... **2,875**

*Turtleback Tile Desk Lamp*

**Desk lamp,** "Turtleback Tile," the domical bronze shade frame w/studded & wire-filigree & inset w/two green-tinted amber opalescent turtleback tiles backed w/mottled opalescent glass diffusion sheets, adjusting above a bronze harp above the domed foot w/ribbed leaves, knobs & small knob feet, base impressed "Tiffany Studios - New York - 28682" w/decorating company monogram, 14 3/8" h. (ILLUS.)...................................... **5,175**

**Floor lamp,** 10" d. domed metal shade w/a glass border w/pierced foliate overlay, suspended in an oblong harp on a tall slender fluted gilt-bronze column supported by three legs resting on recumbent figural rams on a tripartite base, stamped mark, 61" h.................................... **8,625**

**Floor lamp,** 10" d. domical damascene swirled green & gold banded shade suspended from a long S-scroll counter-balance arm above the tall slender knopped bronze standard raised on five tall slender outswept legs w/spearpoint flat feet, shade & base signed................................. **11,200**

**Floor lamp,** 10" d. domical damascene swirled green & gold banded shade suspended from a long S-scroll counter-balance arm above the tall slender knopped bronze pedestal w/a rounded paneled foot, shade signed "5 - L.C.T. - Favrile," base impressed "Tiffany Studios - New York - 677," 56" h. ...................................... **12,650**

**Floor lamp,** 24 1/2" d. domical leaded glass shade w/a perforated serpentine cap, composed of brickwork tiles in mottled shades of amber over a stylized geometric border finished w/a deep drop apron of amber & opalescent, rippled, vertical rectangular glass tiles, six-socket gilt-bronze standard on a cushion-shaped base, shade tag marked "Tiffany Studios - New York - 1616," base impressed "Tiffany Studios - New York - 87," 78" h. (some cracked segments, wear & spotting on bronze) ........................................... **74,000**

**Floor lamp,** bridge-type, a 9 1/2" d. twelve-sided "Linenfold" etched bronze shade No.1936 w/panels of golden amber Favrile glass, mounted upon a swing-socket harp base on tripod legs w/spade feet, shade & base impressed "Tiffany Studios - New York," bronze base numbered "423," overall 4' 7" h. (seven large & four small shade panels cracked) ......... **1,380**

**Floor lamp,** counter-balance type, a 9" w. tapering cylindrical twelve-sided paneled shade in white & amber glass, stamped "Tiffany Studios N.Y. 1963," raised on a tall slender knopped gilt-bronze standard continuing to a spreading circular base, stamped "Tiffany Studios - New York - 619," overall 54" h. ...................................... **5,750**

**Floor lamp,** counter-balance-type, 10 1/8" d. domical iridescent gold glass shade, the gilt-bronze rippled base ascending to a gooseneck arm w/weighted ball supporting shade, shade engraved w/"L.C.T. Favrille [sic]" signature, base stamped "TIFFANY STUDIOS - NEW YORK - 681," 52 1/2" h. ............................... **5,570**

**Floor lamp,** "Curtain Border," 25" d. domical leaded glass shade, the upper section w/radiating blocks of mottled yellow glass above a drop border of small arches above a band of narrow deep mottled amber panels, raised on a tall slender Tiffany ribbed bronze standard w/a wide & deep round footed base cast w/ribbed leaf devices, shade & base signed .......... **72,800**

*Rare Double Poinsettia Floor Lamp*

**Floor lamp,** "Double Poinsettia," a 22 1/2" d. domical leaded glass shade composed of eight trellised panels, each w/three poinsettia blossoms in striated shades of pink, dusty rose, crimson & mauve w/centers in green, amber & white & surrounding leafage in shades of green, mint green & striated bluish green, all set within green, sky blue & amber trelliswork & reserved against a lime green ground, raised on a bronze standard w/applied stringing cast w/lappets, brown patina, w/finial, shade impressed "Tiffany Studios - New York," base impressed "Tiffany Studios - New York - 379," 64" h. (ILLUS. of shade).................. **85,000**

**Floor lamp,** "Geometric," 22" d. domical shade in amber leaded glass, on gilt bronze base, shade impressed "TIFFANY STUDIOS NEW YORK," base stamped "TIFFANY STUDIOS - NEW YORK - 387," 61" h. .................................... **18,400**

*Rare Tiffany Hydrangea Floor Lamp*

**Floor lamp,** "Hydrangea," a 24 1/2" d. high domed leaded glass shade composed of small dark blue, dark green, mottled green & yellow petals at the top above a wide lower border of large mottled yellow, pale blue, dark blue & mottled green petals w/an uneven rim, raised on a tall slender bronze base, shade signed "Tiffany Studios - New York - 1533-21," base marked "Tiffany Studios - New York - 376," replacement metal finial, 78" h. (ILLUS. of shade) .................................... **159,750**

**Floor lamp,** "Lily," twelve-light, Favrile glass & bronze, consisting of gold glass shades supported by twelve intertwined bronze stems on layered lily pad base w/rich greenish brown patina, eight shades engraved "L.C.T. Favrile," the base stamped "TIFFANY STUDIOS - NEW YORK - 685," 56 1/2" h. .................. **29,900**

*Nasturtium Floor Lamp Shade*

**Floor lamp,** "Nasturtium," 22" d. domical shade in a pattern of blossoms in shades of orange, ochre, crimson, russet, amber, pink & white w/leaves in grass green, emerald & lime green mottled w/amber reserved against a light blue striated w/amber & green ground, pierced gilt cap, raised on a tall slender standard w/brownish green patina, shade impressed "Tiffany Studios - New York - 1504-22," base impressed "Tiffany Studios - New York - 319," 5' 1 1/2" h. (ILLUS. of shade)........................................ **46,000**

**Floor lamp,** "Poppy," 20" d. domical leaded glass shade w/red blossoms & green leaves w/pierced overlay, against an amber ground, stamped "Tiffany Studios N.Y. 1531," raised on a gilt-bronze slender knopped standard continuing to a spreading round foot, stamped "Tiffany Studios - New York - 577A," 60" h. ........... **20,700**

*Tiffany Vine Border Floor Lamp*

**Floor lamp,** "Vine Border," 12" d. leaded glass shade composed of bands of mottled yellow tiles flanking a band of mottled yellow leafy vine, on a bronze harp standard floor base w/five tall legs w/pad feet, base stamped "TIFFANY STUDIOS - NEW YORK - 423 H," shade stamped "TIFFANY STUIDOS - NEW YORK" w/an indistinct number, ca. 1910, 4' 10" h. (ILLUS.) ...................................................... **12,925**

*Tiffany Favrile Hall Fixture*

**Hall fixture,** a bronze fixture w/a tight cast coil design above a plain cap supporting a bulbous teardrop-shaped shade in greenish yellow Favrile glass w/a golden amber pulled feather design, shade signed "D 1745," mount depatinated, shade 9" d., overall 52" h. (ILLUS.) ........... **6,900**

*Tiffany Student Lamp & Favrile Shade*

**Student lamp,** a 10" d. domical open-topped Favrile glass shade w/a ribbed design in opal white w/a wavy iridescent gold exterior decoration, fitted on a ring above the long burner supported on an arm extending from an adjustable ball joint also fitted w/a tall cylindrical fuel canister w/applied scrolled wire decoration, all raised on a domed metal base w/applied pebbled texture, shade marked "S2881," base stamped "1539," electrified, small nick on rim of shade, 24 5/8" h. (ILLUS.) ........................................ **9,775**

**Student lamp,** a pair of domical leaded glass shades w/opalescent greenish yellow tapering tile design raised on rings above cylindrical fonts on slender curved arms each adjusting on a slender shaft centering a large cylindrical font, arched cross arm at top, raised on a ringed round base, early 20th c. .......................... **10,450**

*Fine Tiffany Student Lamp*

**Student lamp,** bronze base w/brownish green patina, a squatty bulbous ribbed foot centered by a slender turned standard w/two adjustable arched arms ending in sockets fitted w/9" d. green cased over white glass shades, the exterior w/iridescent amber waves, shades signed "L.C.T." & "L.C.T. Favrile," base impressed "Tiffany Studios - New York - 316," 26 1/4" h. (ILLUS.) ............................ **37,375**

**Student lamp,** the brownish green patinated bronze lamp w/a thick round foot centered by a tall slender standard topped by a ring-looped finial flanked by two down-curved arms suspending 10" d. damascene green & gold iridescent banded domical shades, shades signed "L.C.T.," base impressed "Tiffany Studios - New York - 28600" w/Tiffany Glass and Decorating Company mark, 26" h. (ILLUS. top of next column) ............................ **13,800**

**Table lamp,** 13 3/4" d. domical open-topped shade in green cased over white & decorated w/silvery blue iridescent waves, raised on a bronze three-arm base cast w/lappets above a round marble plinth, shade inscribed "L.C.T.," 19 1/4" h. ........................................ **5,750**

*Two-arm Tiffany Student Lamp*

**Table lamp,** 22 1/2" d. leaded glass globe shade decorated w/mottled green geometric slag glass segments progressively arranged, stamped "Tiffany Studios" on rim, raised on a four-socket bronze standard on domed, stepped, circular base stamped "Tiffany Studios - New York - 532," overall 28 1/2" h. ............................ **19,550**

*Rare Grueby-Tiffany Table Lamp*

**Table lamp,** "Acorn," a 12" d. domical leaded glass shade w/radiating blocks of striated green & yellow glass & a wide band w/a vine w/yellow stylized acorns, raised on a fitting w/cylindrical font inset into a Grueby pottery base w/a cylindrical neck above a squatty bulbous body, the lower body molded w/wide leaves alternating w/thin stems topped by yellow buds, complete w/four original paper labels on the base, shade & base signed, overall 16" h. (ILLUS.)............................................. **37,375**

*Tiffany Acorn Lamp with Urn-form Base*

**Table lamp,** "Acorn," a 16" d. domical leaded glass shade w/a design of radiating orangish amber tiles divided by a wide band of stylized acorns in shades of mottled blue, amber & white, raised on a dark bronze urn-form base raised on four curved supports on a squared foot w/rounded corners, 22 3/4" h. (ILLUS.).... **15,000**

*Acorn Border Tiffany Table Lamp*

**Table lamp,** "Acorn Border," a 16" d. domical leaded glass shade composed of concentric rows of graduated rectangular tiles in heavily mottled deep olive green opalescent glass above a medial band of mottled yellow opalescent glass heart-shaped leaves, w/finial, raised on a large

bronze urn-form font raised on four slender curved legs on quatreform foot w/dark mottled brown patina, shade impressed "Tiffany Studios - New York," insert signed "Tiffany Studios - New York - 161," base unsigned, 22" h. (ILLUS.)......... **6,500**

*Tiffany Apple Blossom Lamp*

**Table lamp,** "Apple Blossom," 12" d. domical leaded glass shade w/a pattern of apple blossoms in pink & white striated glass w/yellow centers, the surrounding leafage in various mottled & striated shades of green, pendent from white & brown branches, all reserved against an opalescent pale blue ground within green borders, the bronze base w/four up-turned support arms on a slender plain standard w/a flaring ribbed round foot, greenish brown patina, shade impressed "Tiffany Studios - New York," base impressed "Tiffany Studios - New York - 11414," 19 3/4" h. (ILLUS.)...................... **34,500**

**Table lamp,** "Apple Blossom," 16" d. domical leaded glass shade composed of overall large mottled pink & white blossoms & green leaves above a narrow dark amber border band, raised on a bronze bulbous amphora-style base w/a low domed top issuing curved shade supports above a bulbous body tapering sharply to a pointed base & held suspended in a slender tripod framework above a wide slightly dished disk foot, brown patina, shade signed, base marked "Tiffany Studios - New York - 29940," 26" h................................................. **29,500**

*Tiffany Apple Blossom Table Lamp*

**Table lamp,** "Apple Blossom," 16" d. domical open-topped leaded glass shade composed of creamy white segments forming the blossoms on metal branches w/dark & light green mottled leaves against lighter mottled green ground, rubbed dark brown bronze base w/a reeded & ringlet-trimmed slender standard above the thick domed base w/scale design raised on four curved feet, shade marked "Tiffany Studios - New York," base impressed "Tiffany Studios - New York - 26878," 21" h. (ILLUS.) ...................................................... **19,550**

*Tiffany Arrowroot Table Lamp*

**Table lamp,** "Arrowroot," 14" d. conical leaded glass shade composed of stylized arrowroot leaves & blossoms in mottled blue & green w/white opalescent blossoms, an upper & lower border of green & white tiles, rare bronze base w/pierced

fern fiddlehead design in various stages of opening on a round foot, shade & base signed (ILLUS.) ........................................... **57,120**

*Very Rare Tiffany Arrowroot Lamp*

**Table lamp,** "Arrowroot," 20 1/2" d. conical leaded glass shade composed of upright arrowroot leaves in shades of grass & lime green striated w/white, the surrounding blossoms in opalescent white w/yellow centers, reserved against a striated blue & white ground w/some pieces infused w/green & pink fractured glass, above a lower brickwork & triangular border in striated green & bluish green glass, raised on a bronze base cast w/upright cattails & lily pads, un-electrified, shade impressed "Tiffany Studios - New York," oil font impressed "Tiffany Studios - New York - 6003," 23 1/2" h. (ILLUS.) ...................................................... **101,500**

*Tiffany Autumn Poppy Table Lamp*

**Table lamp,** "Autumn Poppy," 20" d. domical leaded glass shade composed of large poppy blossoms & buds in shades of crimson red & orange striated, mottled & textured glass, bronze round filigree poppy seed pods scattered among leaves & flowers, raised on a bronze slender reeded Tiffany standard w/a deep rounded foot w/cast ribbed pods raised on scroll feet, based marked "Tiffany Studios Provenance - 363" (ILLUS.) ........................................ **81,200**

### Tiffany Banded Dogwood Table Lamp

**Table lamp,** "Banded Dogwood," 16" d. domical leaded glass shade w/a wide undulating band of large white & yellow blossoms & dark green leaves & brown stems against a background of yellowish green slag blocks, shade signed, raised on three outswept ring supports above the tapering conical standard supported in a banded framework w/the outswept legs w/paw feet on a round disk base, base signed "Tiffany Studios - New York - 29940" (ILLUS.) ........................................ **26,320**

**Table lamp,** "Clematis," an 18" d. wide & sharply tapering conical leaded glass shade composed of large purple, mottled red & dark blue blossoms against a mottled white & mottled green ground, a narrow flat border band of pale yellow mottled blocks, raised on a jeweled bronze base w/a bulbous jeweled knob at the top above a very slender slightly swelled standard on a domed ribbed foot w/flanged rim, shade signed, base marked "Tiffany Studios - New York - 10926," 24 1/2" h. ........................................ **55,375**

**Table lamp,** "Colonial," 16'" d. domical leaded glass shade composed of variegated green slag oval panels, marked "Tiffany Studios, New York," raised on a bronze base w/a slender ovoid font raised on three wishbone legs joining at a pointed domed pedestal on the flattened square foot, base signed "Tiffany - Studios - New York - #444" ........................................ **9,570**

### Tiffany Crocus Lamp

**Table lamp,** "Crocus," 16" d. domical open-topped leaded glass shade w/a repeated pattern of clusters of crocus blossoms in mottled pale yellow & white opalescent, pendent from deep green stems w/leafage in striated green & opalesent white, raised on a slender waisted bronze standard on a domed lightly reeded base w/ball feet, a brownish green patina, shade marked "Tiffany Studios - New York," base impressed "Tiffany Studios - New York - 394 - S197," 23 1/4" h. (ILLUS.) ........................................ **20,700**

**Table lamp,** "Cyclamen," 16" d. domical leaded glass shade w/an overall pattern of cyclamen blossoms & leaves in pale pink & white striated opalescent glass against a ground of striated & textured lavender, the leaves in various shades of green & white striated glass w/some sections in drapery glass, above three rows of brickwork in teal blue, flecked w/lavender, cream & cobalt blue, slender-waisted reeded bronze standard above the domed reeded base on ball feet, deep brown patina, shade unsigned, base impressed "Tiffany Studios - New York - D795," 22 1/4" h. (ILLUS. top next page) ........................................ **27,600**

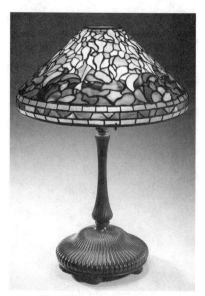

*Fine Tiffany Cyclamen Lamp*

**Table lamp,** "Daffodil," 19 1/2" d. domical open-topped leaded glass shade w/cascades of yellow daffodil blossoms & green leaves issuing from the top & ending in wide border bands of mottled blue, green & yellow blocks, raised on an ornate gilt-bronze base w/a slender tapering standard pierced w/small almond-shaped openings above the lobed round foot w/large pierced leaf-form panels above small penny feet, shade marked "Tiffany Studios - New York - 1919," base impressed "Tiffany Studios - New York - 397," 26" h. ................................................. **75,500**

**Table lamp,** "Daffodil," 20" d. conical leaded glass shade composed of segments representing suspended yellow & orange daffodil blossoms on long green leafy stems against a dark streaky blue ground, the drop border bands in dark blue, yellow & mottled green, shade & base signed .............................................. **67,200**

**Table lamp,** "Daffodil with Dogwood Border," 20" d. domical leaded glass shade set w/daffodils on a mottled green ground, edged w/a band of dogwood blossoms, stamped "Tiffany Studios - New York - 191," raised on a gilt-bronze knobbed & ribbed trumpet-form base, stamped "Tiffany Studios - New York - 868," 28" h. (ILLUS. top next column) ...... **54,625**

**Table lamp,** "Dichroic Dragonfly," 20" d. conical leaded glass shaded w/large overlapping dragonflies in rare blue opalescent mottled & striated glass & green eyes & bodies against a ground of dichroic amber to orangish red narrow panels fitted w/large amber 'jewels,' raised on a gilt 'Four Virtues' bronze Tiffany base, shade signed "Tiffany Studios 1495-6," base signed "Tiffany Studios 557" ............ **56,000**

*Daffodil & Dogwood Lamp*

*Tiffany Dogwood Shade & Lamp Base*

**Table lamp,** "Dogwood," 18" d. domical leaded glass shade, decorated w/a wide band of pink, white, yellow & crimson mottled blossoms w/green striated & mottled leaves against an opalescent & mottled white block background, on a rare gilt-bronze cylindrical base cast w/flowering branches above a ringed & domed matching foot, shade signed, base signed "Tiffany Studios 629" (ILLUS.) ........................................... **44,800**

**Table lamp,** "Dogwood," 18" d. domical leaded glass shade w/an overall design of mottled pink & white blossoms w/green highlights above a border band of matching petal & leaf-form blocks between two narrow bands of mottled green blocks, raised on a brownish green patinated bronze base w/a slender knopped & ribbed standard continuing to a round foot w/radiating raised bands of tight small scrolls ending in small scroll feet, w/pierced shade finial, base marked "Tiffany Studios - New York - 543," 24 1/4" h. ..................................................... **69,758**

*Tiffany Dragonfly Table Lamp*

**Table lamp,** "Dragonfly," 16" d. conical leaded glass shade composed of seven red-eyed large dragonflies against a flame-like caramel slag upper shade & a border of reddish orange rim tiles, the wings covered w/bronze filigree, raised on a signed Tiffany base w/three arm supports above a reeded standard over four outswept ball-and-claw feet, shade & base signed (ILLUS.).............................. **44,800**

**Table lamp,** "Dragonfly," 17" d. conical leaded glass shade composed of seven dragonflies w/outstretched wings in striated shades of green, salmon & white, overlaid in bronze filigree, mottled opalescent white bodies & pale yellow cabochon glass eyes, all reserved against a ground of amber glass striated w/green & white, slender bronze pedestal on a flaring paneled base foot, shade impressed "Tiffany Studios - New York -1468," base impressed "Tiffany Studios - New York - 333," 19 1/2" h. .......................................... **26,450**

**Table lamp,** "Dragonfly," 17" d. wide conical leaded glass shade w/an even bottom edge, composed of a band of large dragonflies below an upper band of yellow & reddish yellow flame-form panels & a double narrow border band of deep reddish & mottled green blocks, on a simple

non-Tiffany patinated metal pedestal base, shade signed, 22 1/4" h. ................. **20,300**

*Dragonfly Table Lamp by Tiffany*

**Table lamp,** "Dragonfly," 20 1/4" d. leaded glass shade composed of a band of large shaded red dragonflies w/filigree overlay on the wings against a mottled green ground w/oval white jewels, shade tag stamped "TIFFANY STUDIOS - NEW YORK," on a simple bronze standard w/a round dished foot, base stamped three times "TIFFANY STUDIOS -NEW YORK - 531," ca. 1910, 27" h. (ILLUS.) .............. **49,350**

**Table lamp,** Favrile glass & bronze, 26 1/4" d. broad & ribbed shallow domed shade w/three radiating bands of pale green shading to white at the scalloped rim, the bronze base cast w/a leaf motif & stamped w/a monogram, tag stamped "TIFFANY STUDIOS - NEW YORK," base stamped "TIFFANY STUDIOS - NEW YORK - 336," 27 1/2" h. .................. **36,650**

**Table lamp,** "Gentian," a 17" d. domical shallow leaded glass shade w/a flaring rim, decorated w/stylized blue flowers & green leaves against a rippled white ground, the border set w/'chipped jewels,' stamped "Tiffany Studios New York 1486," raised on a patinated-bronze knopped standard continuing to a spreading round mushroom base, stamped "Tiffany Studios New York 337," 19" h. .......... **25,300**

**Table lamp,** "Geranium," 16 1/8" d. conical leaded glass shade decorated w/mottled red geranium blossoms above, against a mottled pale blue & green ground, among a profusion of varied colored green leaves below, interspersed w/rippled glass leaves, against a mottled & striated pale pink & green ground, bordered by three bands in mottled pale pink, blue & green, the standard cast w/scrolling tendrils & pods, in rich greenish red patina, tag stamped "TIFFANY STUDIOS - NEW YORK," 23" h. ............... **32,200**

*Tiffany Greek Key Table Lamp*

**Table lamp,** "Greek Key," 16" d. leaded glass shade composed of graduated tiles of mottled yellowish green above a wide border band of Greek Key in mottled yellowish green, the bronze base w/slender scroll-trimmed standard above a knobby cushion base w/curled feet, base stamped w/Tiffany Glass & Decorating Co. monogram & "TIFFANY - STUDIOS - NEW YORK - 28617," ca. 1910, 22 7/8" h. (ILLUS.) ..................................... **18,880**

*Tiffany Harvard Table Lamp*

**Table lamp,** "Harvard," 20" w. tapering octagonal leaded glass shade in green blocks, a red & blue shield in green wreath in alternating panels, stamped "Tiffany Studios - N.Y. - 1914," raised on a slender knopped square bronze standard w/figural relief continuing to a rounded base w/strapwork designs, stamped "Tiffany Studios - New York - 557," 26" h. (ILLUS.) ................................ **11,500**

**Table lamp,** "Heraldic," a 9" w. tapering twelve-paneled leaded glass shade in mottled green glass w/alternating panels depicting shields, stamped "Tiffany Studios N.Y.," the patinated-bronze base w/strapwork designs, stamped "Tiffany Studios - New York - 690," 18" h. ............... **1,380**

*Laburnum Table Lamp*

**Table lamp,** "Laburnum," 21" d. domical leaded glass shade composed of yellow cluster blossoms pendent from brown branches w/green leaves against a sky blue background, tagged "Tiffany Studios - New York - 1539," mounted on a reticulated gilt-bronze adjustable base impressed "Tiffany Studios - New York - 397," 27 3/4" h. (ILLUS.) ........................ **129,000**

**Table lamp,** "Leaf & Berry," a unique pyramidal leaded glass & bronze filigree shade decorated w/a wide border band leaded w/emerald green leaves & yellow & red berries meandering on a deep cobalt blue & purple striated & rippled glass ground, the upper shade w/a swelled pierced filigree band of stylized Queen Anne's Lace blossoms below an upper band of entwined pierced lattice, raised on four arm supports above the large matching urn-form base w/matching bands of floral decoration, shade signed "Tiffany Studios - New York - 783 SX,"

*Unique Tiffany Glass & Bronze Lamp*

base signed "27476 - Tiffany Studios - New York" (ILLUS. ) ................................. **235,200**

*Tiffany Lemonleaf Table Lamp*

**Table lamp,** "Lemonleaf," 18" d. domical leaded glass shade, the top composed of radiating bands of striated white & green slag glass blocks & the wide drop apron composed of similar bands of blocks, a wide central band composed of tightly scrolling leaves in the same colors, shade signed "Tiffany Studios - New York - 1470," on a bulbous baluster-form leaf-cast signed Tiffany bronze base (ILLUS.) ...................................................... **16,800**

**Table lamp,** "Lily," eighteen-light, a rounded full-relief lily pad bronze base centered in a cluster of tall slender stems w/arched

tops ending in petal-form sockets each fitted w/a long lightly ribbed golden iridescent lily-form shade, all shades & base signed ............................................................. **56,000**

**Table lamp,** "Lily," seven-light, seven gold iridescent ribbed long trumpet-form shades mounted on arched or twisted bronze stems issuing from a large lily pad cluster base, shades signed, base marked "Tiffany Studios - New York - 385," 19" h. (one shade replaced w/reproduction, one shade repaired, one stem re-configured) ................................. **12,600**

**Table lamp,** "Lily," seven-light, the long gold iridescent Favrile glass trumpet-form lily shades on a clustered stem bronze doré lily pad base, shades signed "L.C.T. Favrile," base impressed "Tiffany Studios - N.Y. - #385," shades 5" l., overall 22" h. .......................................................... **14,300**

**Table lamp,** "Lily," ten-light, ten long iridescent gold ribbed trumpet-form shades attached to tall upright stems arched at the top & issuing from a large lily pad cluster base, each shade signed & base marked "Tiffany Studios - New York - 381," 20 1/2" h. .................................................... **30,650**

*Tiffany Three-Light Lily Table Lamp*

**Table lamp,** "Lily," three-light, the patinated bronze cushion-form base cast w/a scale-like design below a short knobbed shaft issuing four arching branches, three terminating in petal-form sockets each fitted w/a lightly ribbed golden iridescent lily blossom shade, the fourth arching back to form a high hook, shades & base signed (ILLUS.) ............................... **5,040**

**Table lamp,** "Lily," three-light, the patinated bronze cushion-form base w/petals, lobes & scrolling foliage issuing four upright arched stems, three terminating in foliate mounts w/opalescent striped pale green glass lily-form shades each signed "L.C.T.," base signed "Tiffany Studios - New York - 320," 8 1/2" h. ........................... **4,887**

**Table lamp,** "Lily," twelve-light, a signed bronze lily pad base issuing a cluster of twelve upright slender stems w/arched

*Rare Tiffany Twelve-Light Lily Lamp*

tops ending in sockets each fitted w/a signed trumpet-form gold iridescent Tiffany shade (ILLUS.)...................................... **21,280**

**Table lamp,** "Linenfold," 16" d. ten tapering sides w/panels of linenfold design glass w/narrow border bands at the top & base, on a gilt-bronze base w/a slender stem above a round foot w/molded rim & tab feet, 24" h....................................................... **8,625**

**Table lamp,** "Linenfold," 20 1/4" d. tapering drum-form shade composed of amber sections of linenfold glass bordered by plain textured amber glass, raised on a simple paneled standard w/wide paneled foot w/an acid-etched medium gold patina, w/finial, shade impressed "Tiffany Studios NY Pat Appl'd for 1952," base impressed "Tiffany Studios - New York - 560," 27 1/2" h. ....................................... **20,700**

**Table lamp,** "Linenfold," the 14 1/2" w. twelve-sided slightly tapering shade w/an arrangement of large square amber linenfold panels between smaller amber linenfold borders between amber smooth borders, intaglio finish, shade impressed "TIFFANY STUDIOS - NEW Y0RK - 1950 - PAT. APPLIED FOR," the base impressed "TIFFANY STUDIOS - 442," 24 1/2" h. ...................................................... **5,000**

**Table lamp,** "Linenfold," the 18 1/2" d. wide conical shade composed of stripes of green linenfold glass between metal bands running from a top arched &

pierced gilt-bronze crown to a wider matching border band, raised on a gilt-bronze slender paneled standard w/a round paneled disk foot, shade impressed "Tiffany Studios - New York - 1923," base impressed "Tiffany Studios - New York - 533," 22 1/2" h. .......................... **9,775**

**Table lamp,** "Lotus," 15 1/4" d. bell-shaped shade w/mottled green & white leaves, on ribbed cushion base w/greenish brown patina, tag stamped "TIFFANY STUDIOS - NEW YORK" base stamped "TIFFANY STUDIOS - NEW YORK," 20" h. ........................................................... **20,700**

*Tiffany Nasturtium Table Lamp*

**Table lamp,** "Nasturtium," 22" d. domical leaded glass shade w/overall scattered blossoms in orange, red & pink on a mottled green & translucent pink ground w/brownish stems, apron & border rows of green rectangles mottled w/reddish brown, bronze base w/slender reeded standard above a domed leaf-embossed border & small scroll feet, shade & base signed (ILLUS.)............................................. **72,800**

**Table lamp,** "Nasturtium," 23" d. domical leaded glass shade w/a curved apron, intricately leaded in the design of trailing nasturtium blossoms in red, yellow & orange among foliage in mottled & striated greens, two border rows of bluish green rectangular panels signed w/metal tags, impressed "Tiffany Studios - New York - 1506," supported on a six-socket bronze reeded standard w/an encircling leaf border on the cushion-form footed base, base signed "Tiffany Studios - New York - 5378," few cracked segments, 31 1/2" h. (ILLUS. top next page) ............. **63,000**

*Rare Tiffany Nasturtium Lamp*

*Tiffany Oak Leaf Table Lamp*

**Table lamp,** "Oak Leaf," 18" d. leaded glass shade composed of bands of rectangular mottled green tiles above & below a wide central band of vining brown acorns & green leaves on a mottled green ground, shade tag stamped "TIFFANY STUDIOS - NEW YORK - 1467," base stamped "TIFFANY STUDIOS - NEW YORK 531," ca. 1910, 25" h. (ILLUS.).................. **25,850**

**Table lamp,** "Pansy," 16" d. domical leaded glass shade w/an overall pattern of rectangular tiles in mottled grey & blue opalescent glass streaked w/pale yellow, the pansy border w/blossoms in brilliant shades of deep cobalt blue, striated mauve, mottled yellow & tangerine, the leafage in various shades of green, raised on a three-armed support above a cushion-form base cast w/a raised looping design, further raised on four petal-form feet, greenish brown patina, shade impressed "TIFFANY STUDIOS - NEW YORK," base impressed "TIFFANY STUDIOS - NEW YORK - 6842," overall 41" h. ............................................................. **46,000**

**Table lamp,** "Peacock Feather," a 16" d. high domed leaded glass shade composed of large peacock feather tips w/reddish-orange & mottled blue 'eyes' surrounded by dark blue shaded to green & mottled greenish yellow feathers w/a mottled pale orange & green bottom border, raised on a brownish green bronze base w/a slender waisted standard above a domed, ribbed foot, shade & base signed, 22" h....................................... **64,000**

**Table lamp,** "Peony Border," 24" d. domical leaded glass shade w/radiating golden tiles above the wide border band of mottled red peony blossoms & mottled green leaves, domed pierced bronze cap & raised on a slender bronze tree trunk base w/greenish brown patina, shade marked "Tiffany Studios - New York - 1574," base impressed "Tiffany Studios - New York - 553," 39 1/2" h......................... **90,500**

*Unusual Tiffany Pine Needle Lamp*

**Table lamp,** "Pine Needle," 12" d. domical bent green slag glass shade w/overall pine needle metal filigree, shade signed, raised on a wide bulbous baluster-form signed Tiffany bronze base (ILLUS.)........ **12,320**

**Table lamp,** "Pine Needle," a domical shade in patinated bronze in the pine needle filigree design backed by green striated slag glass, raised on a patinated bronze baluster-form base w/round foot cast overall in low-relief w/pine needles, shade impressed "Tiffany Studios - New York," early 20th c., 21" h. ........................... **6,325**

*Tiffany Pomegranate Table Lamp*

**Table lamp,** "Pomegranate," 18" d. domical leaded glass shade composed of radiating mottled amber & green tile segments & a border of mottled orange & amber pomegranates, metal rim tag reads "Tiffany Studios New York 1457," raised on a three-socket fixture over a slightly swollen slender paneled bronze shaft w/a flaring round foot, dark brown patina, base stamped "Tiffany Studios - New York - 534," minor spotting on base, 22 1/4" h. (ILLUS.) ....................................................... **14,950**

**Table lamp,** "Poppy," 16 1/2" d. conical leaded glass shade w/a design of poppy blossoms in shades of red & orange striated w/white & amber, overlaid w/bronze filigree, leafage in various shades of green, overlaid on the interior w/bronze filigree reserved against a striated amber ground, intaglio finish, shade impressed "Tiffany Studios - New York - 1401," raised on a gilt-bronze base w/a slender standard on a dished round tab-footed bottom, base impressed "Tiffany Studios - New York - 533," 21" h. ........................... **31,050**

*Unusual Tiffany Poppy Table Lamp*

**Table lamp,** "Poppy," 16" d. conical leaded glass shade, undulating band of large reddish orange poppy blossoms, some w/filigree centers & mixed w/striated purple & green poppy buds all against a striated yellow & orange ground w/a lower band of large curved striated green & blue leaves, a border band w/two narrow golden orange bands centered by a striated blue band, shade signed "Tiffany Studios - New York - 1461," raised on a slender reeded bronze standard w/a wide domed & reeded base on tab feet, base signed "Tiffany Studios - New York - 362 - 9175" (ILLUS.)................................ **72,800**

**Table lamp,** "Poppy," 20" d. conical leaded glass shade w/an overall design of poppy blossoms in shades of red & violet opalescent, the centers overlaid w/bronze filigree, the leafage in shades of mottled blue & green & overlaid around the lower border w/bronze filigree, the background in mottled striated blue & white, the apron & upper border in a colorful rippled glass, on a twisted vine bronze base w/wide round swirled foot, base & shade signed...................... **123,200**

**Table lamp,** "Pulled Feather," a 14" d. wide blown bell-shaped shade of gold iridescence w/a gold & white pulled feather design, on Tiffany gold doré slender standard & round dished & footed base (ILLUS. top next page)................................ **3,920**

**Table lamp,** "Spider," 15" d. domical leaded glass shade w/a pattern of radiating panels of green & white mottled glass between raised bronze spider legs, raised on a slender bronze inverted mushroom-cast base w/brownish green patina, w/finial, shade impressed "Tiffany Studios - New York," base impressed "Tiffany Studios - 7000," 17 1/2" h. .................. **23,000**

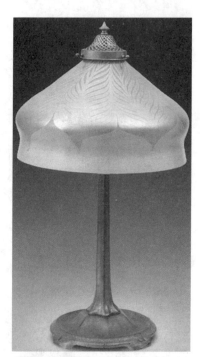

*Tiffany Pulled Feather Shade & Lamp*

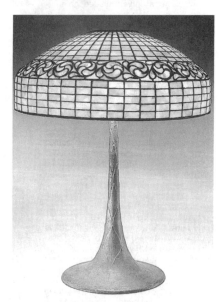

*Tiffany Swirling Leaf Table Lamp*

**Table lamp,** "Swirling Leaf," an 18" d. open-topped domical leaded glass shade composed of radiating small blocks of amber glass w/a shoulder band of mottled green & amber swirling leaves above the wide drop apron composed of amber blocks,

shade marked "Tiffany Studios - New York - 1470," on a slender gilt-bronze standard w/an overlapping pointed leaf design continuing to a widely flaring round foot, base impressed "Tiffany Studios - New York - 1651," 21 3/4" h. (ILLUS.)...................................................... **14,375**

**Table lamp,** "Swirling Lemon Leaf," 18" d. domical leaded glass shade composed of upper & lower sections of small mottled green & yellow tiles flanking a narrow band of swirled yellow & dark green leaves, on a tall bronze base w/a bulbed top above a flaring reeded shaft & wide cushion foot, shade signed & base marked "Tiffany Studios - New York - 28642," 25 1/2" h. ...................................... **18,000**

**Table lamp,** the spherical shade inset w/iridescent green turtle-back tiles, attached to adjustable twin arms, supported on slender bronze standard w/four spade feet, stamped "Tiffany studios - New York - 430," 55" h. ................................................ **11,500**

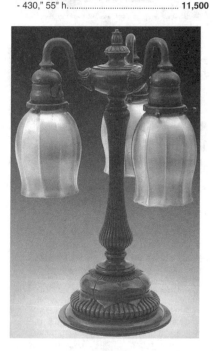

*Tiffany Three-Light Table Lamp*

**Table lamp,** three-light, a signed bronze Tiffany base w/a round, stepped & reeded foot & tall slender reeded standard w/a knobbed top issuing three arched sockets, each suspending a lightly ribbed golden iridescent tulip-shaped shade, two shades signed (ILLUS.)......................... **6,720**

**Table lamp,** "Tulip," 14" d. domical leaded glass shade, composed of an overall design of dark mottled red & violet tulip blossoms on mottled light green & amber stems w/leaves against a mottled dark green & brownish green ground, on a signed Tiffany tree trunk base w/original green patina.................................................. **78,400**

**Table lamp,** "Tulip," 14" d. domical leaded glass shade w/a capped open top, the shade composed of yellow & orangish yellow segments forming tulip blossoms w/dark green leaves & striated lighter blue background segments, raised on a slender dark brown patinated standard w/spaced raised ribs tapering to a round ribbed disk foot on small knob feet, shade marked "Tiffany Studios - New York," base impressed "Tiffany Studios - New York - 431," 21 1/4" h. ........................ **27,600**

**Table lamp,** "Tulip," 16" d. domical leaded glass shade decorated w/red & purple tulips against a green & blue shaded ground, stamped "Tiffany Studios - New York," raised on a slender gilt-bronze base w/a ring of small scrolls at the top & a ruffled spreading foot w/a further band of scrolls, stamped "Tiffany Studios - New York - 584," 21" h. ............................. **48,875**

**Table lamp,** "Tulip," 16" d. domical open-topped leaded glass shade composed of dark golden yellow tulip blossoms & mottled green leaves & stems against a dark blue ground, raised on a slender waisted bronze standard over a domed round base on four ball feet, brownish green patina, shade marked "Tiffany Studios - New York," base impressed "Tiffany Studios - New York - 9954," 22" h. ................. **87,750**

*Tiffany Tulip Pattern Lamp*

**Table lamp,** "Tulip," 16" domical leaded glass shade w/a design of tulip blossoms & leaves in shades of yellow, violet & green, foliage in rippled glass, raised on a heavy bronze urn-form base w/slender strap supports to round foot, shade & base signed (ILLUS.) ................................. **41,440**

**Table lamp,** "Turtleback Tile," 18" d. domical leaded glass shade w/an open

capped top composed of radiating graduated bands of mottled dark & lighter green tiles w/a wide medial band composed of iridescent greenish turtleback tiles, raised on a slender dark blackish brown patinated bronze ribbed standard continuing to the deep leaf-incised cushion base raised on four small curved feet, shade marked "Tiffany Studios - New York - 1432," base impressed "Tiffany Studios - New York - 383," 24" h. ............. **24,150**

*Tiffany Turtleback Tile Border Lamp*

**Table lamp,** "Turtleback Tile Border," 20 1/8" d. leaded glass shade composed of an overall design of graduated mottled yellowish green tiles w/a border band of iridescent green turtleback tiles, shade tag stamped "TIFFANY STUDIOS - NEW YORK," base stamped "TIFFANY STUDIOS - NEW YORK - D806" w/Tiffany Glass & Decorating Monogram, ca. 1910, 25" h. (ILLUS.) ................................. **35,250**

**Table lamp,** "Turtleback Tile," the ovoid shade of triangular section inset w/two domed amber iridescent turtleback tiles & applied w/bosses & wire decoration, pivoting on two curved upright supports continuing to a leaf-cast circular patinated bronze base w/inset amber iridescent glass cabochons, on five ball feet, impressed "Tiffany Studios - New York - 408 - 9948," drilled for wiring, 14 1/2" h. ..... **6,325**

**Table lamp,** "Wisteria," 18 1/4" d. leaded glass shade composed of openwork branches at the top center suspending mottled green leaves above long mottled dark purple blossoms ending in an uneven border, bronze tree trunk base, rounded underside of fitter stamped "7001," top of base stamped "10117 - TIFFANY STUIDOS - NEW YORK - 10117," ca. 1910, 26 3/4" h. (ILLUS. ).................................................... **270,000**

*Rare Tiffany Wisteria Table Lamp*

# Lamps, Miscellaneous

**Alabaster floor lamp,** Neoclassical-style, the tall standard w/leaf-carved & reeded detail, domed shade, Italy, 19th c., 5' 2" h. ............................................................. **$2,875**

*Aladdin Alacite Table Lamps*

**Table lamp,** "Yellow Tulip," 14" d. domical leaded glass shade, a wide continuous band of large, tight yellow tulip blossoms on mottled dark & light green leafy stems against a dark & light brown ground, raised on a slender ribbed bronze standard w/a wide scalloped & reeded round foot, shade signed "Tiffany Studios - New York - 1905," base signed "Tiffany Studios - New York - 337" ............................... **36,400**

**Wall sconces,** "Turtleback Tile," each shade composed of three greenish iridized turtleback tiles resting on a square white marble platform above a glass & metal support arm, pr. (ILLUS. bottom of page) ........................................................... **23,100**

**Aladdin table lamps,** squatty bulbous melon-lobed ivory Alacite glass globe mounted on a cast-metal antiqued gold pierced footed base, tall tapering whip-o-lite fluted shades topped by Alacite scroll finials, ca. 1938, 23" h., pr. (ILLUS.) .............. **288**

**Art Deco table lamp,** figural, a cast metal figure of a standing nude lady leaning against a rectangular metal frame & swag w/a green patina enclosing a frosted glass panel, a stepped plinth on a black marble base, embossed on the side "Fayral," marked on back "Made in France - Ovington New York," patina wear, 1920s, 16 1/2" h. (ILLUS. top next page) .............................................................. **2,300**

*Tiffany Turtleback Tile Sconces*

*French Figural Art Deco Lamp*

**Art Deco table lamp,** figural, a partially draped gilt-metal seated female nude, her outstretched hand resting on her knee holding a petal-form alabaster shade, the figure raised on a rectangular alabaster base, ca. 1930, 5 1/2 x 14", 12 1/4" h. (gilt wear, minor edge chips)........ **460**

*Modern Vandermark Art Glass Lamp*

**Art glass table lamp,** 9" d. high mushroom-shaped shade w/flared rim, in iridescent light blue glass w/iridescent orange & green pulled-feather design, raised on a single-socket three-arm spider support on a vasiform glass base ending in a ruffled foot & decoration matching the shade, shade signed near rim "Vandermark DM - SS 1980," Doug Merit for Vandermark, 22 3/4" h. (ILLUS.)......................... **403**

*Unique Art Nouveau Filigree Lamp*

**Art Nouveau floor lamp,** slag glass & brass filigree, a 21" w. six-sided pyramidal shade w/a deep apron of pointed panels, overall delicate pierced floral & scroll filigree w/caramel slag inserts in the upper shade & reddish slag panels in the apron, raised on a very tall, slender & slightly tapering matching hexagonal standard w/filigree over slag glass & set on a wide matching pyramidal foot, one cracked glass panel in center section, unsigned, early 20th c., 70" h. (ILLUS.) ...................... **3,450**

Art Nouveau table lamp, cameo glass & bronzed metal, a 9 1/2" d. wide domical cameo glass shade in mottled green, white & brown overlaid in dark green & cut w/an overall leafy vine decoration, supported on a ring & bronzed metal tree-form pedestal base w/a model of a large elephant at the base, shade attributed to Muller Freres, overall 15" h. (some base flaws, minor flakes to cameo) .................................................................. **1,045**

Arts & Crafts floor lamp, oak & leaded glass, the four-sided 24 1/2" w. square leaded glass shade composed of curved & oblong glass in red, green, yellow & white, raised on four angled oak arm supports above the original kerosene metal burner fitted atop the tall slightly tapering four-sided base w/an arched opening above three tiered open shelves, the bottom shelf flanked on each side by double oval cut-outs, rounded cut-out feet, original dark finish, paper label of the Shop of the Crafters, Model No. 153, early 20th c., 6' h. .................................................. **4,600**

*Arts & Crafts Student Lamp*

Arts & Crafts student lamp, two patinated metal conical shades w/ruffled rims & four medallions of caramel & white slag glass, raised on arched arms above a cast patinated metal base w/hammered & studded strapwork detail on a pyramidal base, early 20th c., 20" w., 20 3/4" h. (ILLUS.) .......................................................... **1,035**

Arts & Crafts table lamp, a conical hammered copper-framed shade fitted w/wide mica panels raised on a four-arm support above a Japanese mixed-metal double gourd-form spittoon base decorated w/engraved lotus & resting on a round footed carved wood foot, unsigned shade by Dirk Van Erp, ca. 1915, overall 15" h. ................................................................. **1,380**

Arts & Crafts table lamp, cast iron & slag glass, the pyramidal pierced iron frame w/lattice top & base trim, each side lined w/green slag glass, raised on a metal spider frame above the pierced iron square

pedestal base also lined w/green slag glass panels, on a square black glass foot, early 20th c., overall 20" h. ...................... **288**

Arts & Crafts table lamp, hand-hammered copper & mica, the 17" d., conical shade w/a copper framework lined w/four mica panels, raised on a four-socket copper trumpet-form base, by Dirk van Erp, early 20th c., overall 20" h. (some modification to sockets, recent mica & patina) .............. **4,950**

Arts & Crafts table lamp, oak & glass, the wide square oak-framed shade w/four pyramidal panels topped by a low flat gallery pierced w/holes above amber slag glass panels & oak frames above the flat drop apron w/pierced holes over slag glass, raised on a swelled tapering four-sided quarter-sawn oak pedestal w/metal loop handles near the top of each side, set on a square stepped oak foot, original finish, early 20th c., minor glued repair, shade 18 3/4" w., overall 23" h. .................. **1,430**

*Arts & Crafts Wood & Slag Glass Lamp*

Arts & Crafts table lamp, slag glass & oak, a 17 1/2" w. square tapering open-topped shade w/an oak frame, each panel w/slag glass fan & geometric designs in pink, green & red on a striated caramel ground, the scalloped wood apron w/round cut-outs, raised on a pedestal composed of four square columns over a square footed base, early 20th c., a few cracked glass segments, 27" h. (ILLUS.) .......................................................... **978**

Arts & Crafts table lamp, wood & glass, a square oak-framed pyramidal shade fitted w/green slag glass panels around the sides & in the narrow apron, raised on a square oak pedestal pierced for glass panels near the top, resting on a square oak foot, early 20th c., 20 3/4" h. (some repair to frame, one glass panel w/corner damage) ............................................................ **413**

Arts & Crafts table lamp, a low pyramidal upper shade frame in brass & copper enclosing triangular panels of olive green, amber & white & overhanging a vertical pierced metal apron w/pierced overlay designs of landscapes over slag glass in pink, blue & white w/ruby red glass in corner panels, raised on a slender plain square metal pedestal on a square flaring foot, early 20th c., overall 21 1/4" h. ....... **440**

**Arts & Crafts table lamp,** 12" sq. pyramidal slag glass shade, the metal framework w/four panels centered by a small diamond above a narrow flat skirt all over green slag glass panels, raised on four flat angled & pierced support arms joining the tall slightly tapering square wood shaft on a square stepped foot, original black finish on base & shade, early 20th c., 23" h. .................................................. **468**

**Arts & Crafts table lamp,** oak & glass, the 11" square pyramidal oak frame enclosing four green & white slag glass panels, raised on a simple oak base, early 20th c., 24" h. .................................................. **403**

**Arts & Crafts table lamp,** a four-sided domical geometrically-woven wicker shade raised on a four-sided wicker & wrapped post standard on a flaring woven wicker foot, new linen lining inside the shade, unmarked, first quarter 20th c., 20" w., 31" h ...................................... **468**

**Astral-style table lamp,** brass, marble & glass, a small square white marble base supports w/tall slender reeded brass standard below a compressed brass font fitted w/an electric socket & shade ring, a frosted clear ball shade w/a Greek Key design, a "Cornelius, Philad."-style emblem tag, the font hung w/cut glass prisms, second quarter 20th c., 28" h. ......... **220**

*Unusual Austrian Figural Floor Lamp*

**Austrian floor lamp,** figural, jeweled & pierced cold-painted metal, the wide scroll-pierced umbrella-form shade set w/large cabochon jewels above the beaded fringe border, raised on a tall slender urn-form metal standard w/an overall delicate pierced scrolling design & fitted on an octagonal table base in engraved metal set on each side w/rectangular panels of diamond-shaped glass segments, a large cold-painted metal figure of a MIddle Eastern woman seated on the edge of the table, raised on a platform base w/arched aprons, Vienna, Austria, late 19th - early 20th c., overall 55" h. (ILLUS.) .............................................. **6,900**

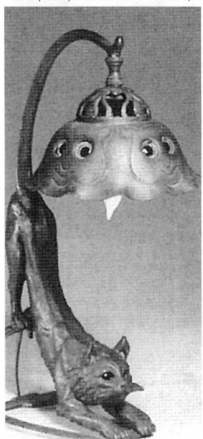

*Unusual Austrian Cat Lamp*

**Austrian table lamp,** figural, a patinated cast bronze base modeled as a stretching cat w/inset glass eyes, the curved tail suspending a bell-form metal shade w/ruffed edges & chased w/four cat faces w/inset green & black glass eyes below a red glass border, signed "TO fecit - mod. Eichberg," reddish brown patina, late 19th - early 20th c., overall 15 1/2" h. (ILLUS.) .............................................................. **3,737**

Benedict table lamp, Arts & Crafts style, hand-hammered copper, a sharply tapering baluster-form base w/incised & raised rings & a domed foot, the top fittings supporting a conical copper-framed 20" d. shade w/large mica panels, fine original patina & mica, early 20th c., overall 32" h. ............................................................. **3,575**

*Best Lamp Company Table Lamp*

Best Lamp Company table lamp, 14" d. domical leaded glass shade composed of repeating panels of geometric blocks above a floral border in shades of pink, green & blue separated by stripes of textured red glass, raised on a patinated metal base w/a twisted vine-form standard on a leafy scroll-cast square foot, raised mark on base "H.A. Best Lamp Co.," Chicago, Illinois, early 20th c., 19 1/2" h. (ILLUS.) ........................................ **1,725**

Bigelow & Kennard floor lamp, 24" d. domical leaded glass shade composed of panels of scale pattern crinkled amber glass divided by tapering panels of dark brown, light brown & amber bands & petals & a scalloped bottom rim composed of brown & mottled tan segments, on a tall bronze slender standard above a wide disk foot w/a lappet border band & a brown patina, ca. 1915, 59" h. (ILLUS. top of next column) .................................... **32,200**

Boch Freres table lamp, a deep round brass base supporting a wide bulbous ovoid pottery vase incised & painted w/an Art Deco design of gazelles in shades of blue & black against a crackled creamy white ground w/blue & green stylized leaves around the top & base, fitted w/a brass collar & electric fittings w/a tall silk shade, ca. 1930s, base 9" h. .................. **920**

Boudoir lamp, 8" d. domical reverse-painted glass shade decorated w/a continu-

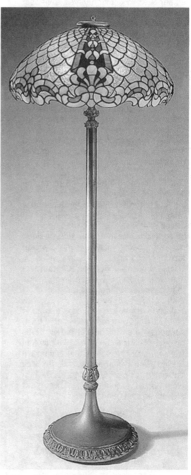

*Fine Bigelow & Kennard Floor Lamp*

ous meadow landscape in crimson & lemon yellow fall trees, artist-signed "D. Lynch," raised on a slender baluster-form bronzed metal base w/blocks & rectangular panels down the stem to the flaring loop-paneled & scalloped round foot, early 20th c., overall 15" h. ........................... **413**

Bradley & Hubbard boudoir lamp, 10 1/2" sq. domical shade w/bent panels of striated green slag glass framed in a dark patinated metal riveted strapwork frame, raised on a single-socket standard w/similar bowed strap over the round domed foot, raised mark on base, early 20th c., overall 18 1/2" h. (ILLUS. top of next page) ...................................................... **1,035**

Bradley & Hubbard desk lamp, a flaring rectangular metal shade frame w/solid ends & front & back rectangular glass panels in narrow ribbed glass reverse-painted w/green, blue & brown stylized Arts & Crafts design bands, raised on forked brass supports joining a knop above the flaring, ringed pedestal base, shade 8 1/2" l., 13" h. ..................................... **460**

*Bradley and Hubbard Boudoir Lamp*

*Bradley & Hubbard Aladdin Lamp*

**Bradley & Hubbard table lamp,** 6" w. six-paneled bent-glass shade w/green slag upper panels under a block design metal filigree above the caramal panel border band w/scrolling tulip-style designs in fili-gree, raised on a gilt-metal Aladdin lamp-

style base w/ornate cast designs & a large stepped, round foot (ILLUS.) ............ **2,800**

**Bradley & Hubbard table lamp,** Arts & Crafts style, the slag glass shade in greens & yellows with a brass frame w/a Greek Key border design, supported by a curving arm to a base w/dual inkwells, cleaned patina, impressed mark, 5 x 9", 14" h. (one inkwell liner missing) ................... **358**

*Bradley and Hubbard Table Lamp*

**Bradley & Hubbard table lamp,** 17 1/4" d. wide domed bent-panel slag glass shade w/green & amber shade & ribbed panels, mounted in a radiating bronze-patinated metal framework w/leafy floral band around the flattened rim, raised on a two-socket tapering & paneled patinated met-al standard w/flared base & raised lappet petal design, early 20th c., minor patina-tion wear, 21 1/2" h. (ILLUS.) ........................ **978**

*Bradley & Hubbard Slag Glass Lamp*

**Bradley & Hubbard table lamp,** 20" d. domical eight-paneled caramel slag shade w/a pierced undulating stylized floral & long leaf design around the bottom rim, raised on a gilt-metal tall ovoid base w/tall pairs of arched leaves forming panels down the sides to the flaring scalloped foot, signed, 23" h. (ILLUS.)............. **1,093**

**Bradley & Hubbard table lamp,** Prairie School-style, 16" sq. pyramidal leaded glass shade w/tapering narrow geometric glass panels in a gilt-metal frame w/pierced overlay, glass in shades of purple, blue & yellow slag, raised on a curved wire spider above the slender square pedestal on a low sloping square foot, early 20th c., 21" h. ............................. **1,380**

**Bronze table lamp,** figural, the standard w/a ringed, trumpet-form shaft resting atop the head of an amusing cast stylized rounded bird w/multiple angular legs on a round disk, modern conical parchment shade, designed by Margo Kempe, ca. 1930, 26 1/2" h. .............................................. **3,162**

**Classique table lamp,** 18" d. domed bell-form reverse-painted shade decorated w/a continuous yellowish brown meadow w/boulder banks, emerald green foliaged trees along a reflective waterway, distant green hills, chartreuse & orange sky, numbered "8271," raised on a bronzed metal hexagonal baluster-form heavy base marked "Classique Lamps" on stem & on cloth label on foot, early 20th c. ........ **1,815**

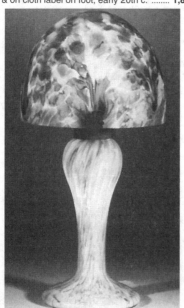

*Czechoslovakian Boudoir Lamp*

**Czechoslovakian boudoir lamp,** blown glass, a high mushroom-form shade in spatter glass in yellow, blue, aqua & green, raised on a matching slender bal-

uster-form base, chased metal three-arm mount, ca. 1930, rim chip, 13 1/4" h. (ILLUS.)................................................................ **460**

*Decorated Czechoslovakian Lamp*

**Czechoslovakian boudoir lamp,** painted glass, a domed shade painted w/a shaded orange to yellow ground decorated w/a primitive country landscape w/windmill & trees in orange, black, green & white, candlestick-form pedestal base w/matching shaded orange to yellow ground & h.p. tree, ca. 1920s, 9" h. (ILLUS.)................................................................ **248**

**Czechoslovakian desk lamp,** a domical oblong glass shade w/a chocolate brown exterior acid-cut to frosted clear w/an overall design of tightly scrolling flowers, leaves & scrolls, the interior rim painted w/a band of orange blossoms framed by brown scrolls bordered w/green, stamped "Bellova Czech," suspended on a bronze arching arm w/electric socket continuing to a tri-lobed foot cast w/acorns & leaves decorated in natural colors above a beaded border band, base marked "Bellova H.C. McFaddin & Co., N.Y.," 8" h. ............................................. **990**

**Czechoslovakian table lamp,** 14" d. sharply pointed conical reverse-painted glass shade, decorated w/an Art Deco design of large diamonds & triangles enclosing radiating designs in yellow &

*Colorful Czech Art Deco Table Lamp*

green against a deep reddish orange ground, the spherical footed base w/matching large diamond reserves against the deep reddish orange ground, signed, ca. 1930 (ILLUS.)............................ **2,912**

**Czechoslovakian table lamp,** domical shade composed of draped rows of clear glass woven beads over a wire basket frame w/cut prisms suspended from the lower edge, raised on a bronzed metal heavy cylindrical standard w/a round embossed disk foot, ca. 1920, 23" h. (ILLUS. below) ................................................. **403**

**Daum Nancy cameo table lamp,** Art Nouveau style, a cameo glass tulip blossom-form shade in yellow overlaid in peach & cut w/petals, mounted on gilt-bronze base in the form of a tall slender curved leafy stem on a fanned scroll-cast foot, shade unsigned, base signed "L. Majorelle - Nancy," France, ca. 1900, overall 20 1/2" h........................................................ **46,000**

*Lamp with Beaded Czech Shade*

**Desk lamp,** a ribbed bell-form gold Aurene iridescent signed Steuben shade mounted on a bronzed-metal gooseneck base w/molded shells on the foot, shade shape No. 2524, shade 4 3/4" l., overall 20" h. .................................................................. **220**

*DeVez French Cameo Banquet Lamp*

**DeVez cameo banquet lamp,** a bulbous ovoid shade tapering to a spearpoint finial in white frosted glass overlaid w/dark blue & acid-etched w/an exotic harbor scene, the tall baluster-form glass base in the same colors etched w/long arched panels w/similar harbor scenes, signed, France, early 20th c., overall 20" h. (ILLUS.)........................................................... **5,600**

*Rare Dirk Van Erp Table Lamp*

**Dirk Van Erp table lamp,** Arts & Crafts style, the wide conical shade composed of tapering mica panels between hammered copper framework, raised on four spider arms above the hammered copper tapering bulbous ovoid base, early 20th c. (ILLUS.) ............................................. **60,500**

*Rare D. & K. Wisteria Floor Lamp*

**Duffner & Kimberly floor lamp,** 27" d. domical bell-shaped leaded glass shade, composed of large wisteria blossom clusters in mottled purple & white on dark green & brown leafy stems against a mottled white & pale greenish yellow ground, the tapering center top w/an ornate gilt-metal scrolling cap, raised on a tall slender bronzed-metal Duffner & Kimberly base w/a lappet-cast band on the round foot (ILLUS. of shade) .............. **67,200**

*Duffner & Kimberly "Owl" Shade Lamp*

**Duffner & Kimberly table lamp,** 14" d. domical leaded glass shade in an Art Nouveau style design w/the scalloped border w/scrolled & curved slag glass segments arranged to resemble a styl-

ized owl face, border in shades of deep purple, white, yellow & light & dark green, the upper shade composed of curved overlapping scallops in white & green striated slag glass, on a bronzed metal Duffner base w/a slender square standard w/small loop handles above the flaring squared foot (ILLUS.) ........................... **7,280**

*Fine Duffner & Kimberly Leaded Lamp*

**Duffner & Kimberly table lamp,** 16" d. domical leaded glass shade, decorated w/an undulating border band of swirled green & yellow slag glass leaves & white berries below the upper shade composed of rounded & oblong pale yellowish green slag segments, raised on a signed Duffner & Kimberly bronzed metal tall slender base w/a round disk foot (ILLUS.) ...................................................... **10,080**

**Duffner & Kimberly table lamp,** 16" d. domical leaded glass shade, the center top w/radiating panels of green slag glass above a wide border band of entwined green & white slag leaves against a mottled dark brown ground, on a bronzed metal slender ovoid standard raised on a tripod base over a round platform foot ...................................................... **5,600**

**Duffner & Kimberly table lamp,** 16" d. domical leaded glass shade w/a scrolled border composed of dark & light green & white slag scrolls w/dark amber fanned shells, the upper body composed of graduated blocks of mottled white & green & white slag glass, raised on a slender bulbed ribbed signed base w/a four-lobed flattened foot ............................... **5,600**

**Duffner & Kimberly table lamp,** 18" d. domical leaded glass shade w/panels of alternating deep brown & caramel slag oblong segments framed by scrolled am-

*Fine Duffner & Kimberly Table Lamp*

ber border bands alternating w/caramel slag & amber stripes, raised on an oblong three-footed bronzed metal base w/round foot (ILLUS.) .................................. **3,920**

**Duffner & Kimberly table lamp,** 19" d. domical leaded glass shade composed of bands & panels of green slag glass, raised on a Duffner slender bronzed metal ribbed standard & domed, lobed foot ..... **3,640**

**Duffner & Kimberly table lamp,** 19" d. domical leaded glass shade w/a large shell & medallion design above an uneven lower border, a bright striated sky blue & multi-hued background w/shells & medallions in vermillon & orange & enclosed w/mottled green leafy scrolls, on a bronze metal Duffner base w/a slender ribbed baluster-form shaft on a round knobbed foot w/greenish verdigris patina .......................................................... **22,400**

*Duffner & Kimberly Geometric Lamp*

**Duffner & Kimberly table lamp,** 19 1/2" d. domical leaded glass shade in geometric green slag glass segments progressively arranged w/tuck-under apron, mounted on a three-socket reeded columnar standard on a stepped round base, crack to one segment, possibly replaced shade cap & finial, early 20th c., 23 1/2" h. (ILLUS.) .......................................................... **2,185**

*Quality Duffner and Kimberly Lamp*

**Duffner & Kimberly table lamp,** 20" d. domical leaded glass shade composed of oblong panels w/golden yellow diamond lattice design framed by brown & amber geometric band & scrolled bands w/large palmettes spaced around the shaped rim, raised on a slender reeded bronze standard continuing into the swirl- and leaf-cast undulating round foot, unsigned, ca. 1910, 24 1/2" h. (ILLUS.) .......................................................... **7,475**

**Duffner & Kimberly table lamp,** 20" d. domical & widely flaring leaded glass shade, a wide border band of Greek Key design in brown against pale green, the upper shade w/graduated white blocks & bands of small pale green diamonds, raised on a slender bronzed metal Duffner & Kimberly base w/a reeded baluster-form standard on a knobbed round foot .................................................................. **6,160**

**Duffner & Kimberly table lamp,** 20" d. mushroom-shaped leaded glass shade, decorated w/large tall leafy clusters in mottled shades of light & dark green alternating w/large spearpoint leaf motifs in similar colors all on a striated light blue to deep purple ground, raised on a Duffner & Kimberly slender reeded shaft w/bottom bulb above a flaring paneled & scalloped foot (ILLUS. top next page) .............. **8,960**

*Duffner & Kimberly Leaf Cluster Lamp*

*Superior D&K Leaded Lamp*

**Duffner & Kimberly table lamp,** 21 1/2" d. domical leaded glass shade in the 'Louis XV' patt., composed of repeating panels of stylized florals separated by raised curved panels in green & amber glass & elaborate gilt-metal overlay, impressed tag "The Duffner & Kimberly Co. New York," raised on a matching slender gilt-bronze base w/cast leafy scrolls & shell-form designs, early 20th c., 28" h. (ILLUS.) .................................................... **26,450**

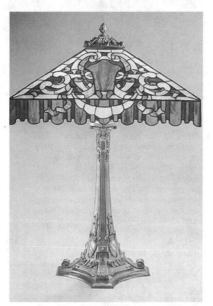

*Rare Duffner & Kimberly Leaded Lamp*

**Duffner & Kimberly table lamp,** 20 1/2" w. square leaded glass shade w/a pattern of cartouches of rose & white striated glass surrounded by scrolling devices in striated shades of amber, brown & white, reserved against a dark blue ground, within pale yellow borders, all above an irregular lower border in striated shades of plum, rose & burgundy, raised on a gilt-bronze base cast w/crests, shade impressed "The Duffner & Kimberly Co. - New York" & "511," ca. 1910, 29" h. (ILLUS.) ...................................................... **21,850**

*Fine Duffner & Kimberly Lamp*

**Duffner & Kimberly table lamp,** 21" d. conical leaded glass shade composed of amber slag background panels centering three repeating intricate heraldic designs of lavender glass superimposed on a crimson red medial band, the lower border in a chevron design w/amber granite & mauve ripple accent colors, raised on a three-socket slender bronzed-metal shaft on a slightly domed scalloped round foot cast w/foliate designs, overall 24" h. (ILLUS.)............................................. **4,600**

**Durand table lamp,** blue iridescent spherical glass base w/brass fittings & base & two-socket electric fittings, unsigned, 19" h. .................................................. **275**

**Emeralite desk lamp,** a flared amber glass shade w/floral-textured surface, reverse-painted w/scrolling twig & floral border, amber glass panel light diffuser set in shade, raised on an adjustable square standard over a domed square patinated metal base, metal manufacturer's tag, H.G. McFaddon and Co., New York, ca. 1916, 8 3/4" l., 12 3/4" h. ............................. **1,380**

**Fenton table lamp,** Victorian-style, the wide domed Burmese shade tapering to a cylindrical open top w/ruffled rim, decorated w/a mountainous landscape, w/a pierced brass shade ring above the electric fittings above the squatty bulbous glass font w/matching decoration, raised on a knopped brass stem above a round base w/four scroll-cast feet, w/glass chimney, signed "Fenton Art Glass Co. Williamstown, W.VA - October 1974 - Hand Painted by Connie Ash 2520," overall 19 1/2" h. (ILLUS. bottom nwxt column)............................................................. **518**

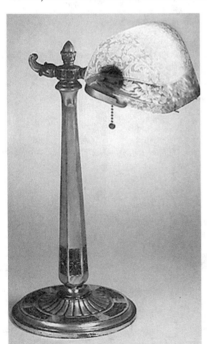

*Emeralite Desk Lamp*

**Emeralite desk lamp,** the long half-round flared glass shade etched w/an overall floral design & a polychrome Arts & Crafts style border, fitted on an adjust-

able silvered-metal arm on a slender tapering paneled standard & disk foot both w/enameled curvilinear paneled designs, w/original tag, 17" h. (ILLUS.)........................ **920**

*Hand-Painted Fenton Table Lamp*

**Floor lamp,** enameled aluminum, a weighted round disk black base centered by a slender cylindrical shaft topped by three adjustable metal arms each fitted w/a long conical aluminum shade each in a different color, yellow, green or orange, ca. 1955, wear, corrosion, 5' 11 1/2" h. ...................................................... **184**

**Floor lamps,** wrought iron, an arrow-shaped finial on a slender shaft w/two sockets above a disk w/wrought scrolls, raised on an angular wrought-iron tripod base, woven striped paneled shade, scattered corrosion, early 20th c., 4' 8" h., pr. (ILLUS. of one below)..................... **805**

*Early Electric Wrought-Iron Floor Lamp*

*Rare Fulper Pottery Table Lamp*

**Fulper Pottery table lamp,** 13 1/2" d. domical pottery shade w/a streaked yellow &
dark brown glaze & inset w/geometric
green & ivory leaded glass pieces, raised
on a tall pottery base w/wide round base
in a fine Cat's Eye flambé glaze, rectangular ink mark, two very short hairlines,
tiny chip on shade, overall 16" h.
(ILLUS.)....................................................... **11,000**

*Rare Grueby & Tiffany Table Lamp*

**Grueby Pottery table lamp,** the wide baluster-form Grueby Pottery base molded
w/large upright leaves & a band of
arched rim handles w/an overall green
glaze, the metal collar & fittings supporting a domical Tiffany Glass "turtleback"
tile shade (ILLUS.).................................... **286,000**

*Scenic Jefferson Table Lamp*

**Jefferson table lamp,** 13" w. hexagonal
flat-topped reverse-painted shade painted w/a continuous stylized landscape
w/large feathery trees in brown & deep
rose in the foreground & lower trees &
water below w/low distant hills in dark
brown all against a cream & yellow sky
w/streaked blue clouds, on a slender
paneled bronzed metal baluster shaft
above a high domed paneled foot
(ILLUS.)......................................................... **1,680**
**Jefferson table lamp,** 16" d. domical re-
verse-painted shade decorated w/a caramel ground w/scattered dark pink wild
rose blossoms w/green leaves above a
two inch wide wine-colored band near
the rim also decorated w/ wild roses,
raised on a bronze-patinated slender baluster-form metal base w/dished & ribbed
foot, signed .................................................. **16,500**

*Jefferson Lamp with Landscape*

**Jefferson table lamp,** 16" d. domical reverse-painted shade decorated w/a stylized landscape scene of a country roadway passing a red-roofed cottage w/green & red trees in the foreground & distance, green grass & orange roadway w/a deep yellow & grey sky, shade signed on the rim, on a slender paneled bronzed metal base w/flaring foot, overall 22" h. (ILLUS.)................................................ **805**

**Jefferson table lamp,** 16" d. scenic domed glass shade w/'pebbled' surface hand-painted on interior w/riverside scene including fence & red-roofed buildings, lower edge numbered "2365," mounted on cast metal two-socket ribbed base inscribed "Jefferson" at lower edge, 21 1/2" h. ...................................................... **1,610**

**Jefferson table lamp,** 18" d. domical reverse-painted shade decorated w/a continuous autumnal landscape w/a winding road passing by a cluster of trees & fall meadows, raised on a slender tall urn-form bronzed metal paneled & ringed pedestal on a flaring dished round foot, original base patina, overall 23" h. .............. **2,420**

*Jefferson Autumn Landscape Lamp*

**Jefferson table lamp,** 18" d. domical reverse-painted shade, decorated w/a continuous autumnal landscape w/a dark blue pond in the foreground framed by rust & brown grass & shrubs w/ tall clusters of trees in shades of dark green, brown, yellow & rust in the distance against a dark blue, yellow & orange clouded sunset sky, shade signed "Jefferson 5612," on the original bronzed metal swelled cylindrical base w/a round, stepped foot (ILLUS.).................................... **4,032**

**Jefferson table lamp,** 18" d. domical reverse-painted shade, painted w/a landscape of a lake & woodland in naturalistic

*Jefferson Lake Landscape Lamp*

tones, two-socket fixture on a tapered five-sided standard w/a flaring foot, dark green patinated metal, shade indistinctly signed "Jefferson Co. WJS," minor shade imperfections, early 20th c., 22 3/4" h. (ILLUS.)............................................................ **2,645**

**Jefferson table lamp,** 21" d. flared domical reverse-painted shade decorated w/a lakeside landscape w/summer trees & distant hills, inscribed on lower edge "1972 Jefferson Co.," raised on an assembled lamp base w/new wiring & sockets, overall 16" h. ........................................... **1,265**

**Jefferson table lamp,** wide domical reverse-painted shade in textured grey glass decorated w/a continuous verdant lakeside landscape in shades of green, brown, blue & white, raised on a gilt-metal slender lobed baluster-form base w/fluted round foot, shade & base signed, ca. 1910, overall 22" h. ................... **2,300**

**Leaded glass table lamp,** 18" d. bell-shaped leaded shade composed of mottled red, pink & yellow overlapping scale-like segments extending down to the deep drop border composed of stylized leaves & fruits in greens, reds, pinks & blues, attributed to Duffner & Kimberly, on a tall slender ribbed bronzed metal standard w/a stepped round foot (ILLUS. top next page)................................ **5,600**

**Leaded glass table lamp,** 22" d. domical shade in a hollyhock design, composed of multicolored segments arranged as blossoming red, orange & yellow hollyhock spikes against a white ground above a curved drop apron of lavender & granite textured golden amber border, raised on a slender baluster-form cast-metal three-socket base w/cast foliate decoration down the stem & around the slightly domed foot, attributed to Wilkinson Co., Brooklyn, New York, early 20th c., overall 30" h. ................................. **6,325**

*Fine Bell-form Leaded Shade on Lamp*

*Unmarked Leaded Glass Lamp*

**Leaded glass table lamp,** a wide domical leaded glass shade in green & white striated tiles w/pink & green flowers above a yellow border w/red, white & green blossoms, raised on a slender patinated metal ribbed standard on a cushion-form base cast w/stylized flower buds on four petal-form feet, greenish brown patina,

cracks & losses to shade, early 20th c., 27" h. (ILLUS.) ............................................... **2,530**

**Leaded glass table lamp,** wide umbrella-shaped domical leaded glass shade w/uneven rim, composed of an overall design of small blossoms & leaves in greens, reds & ambers w/ruby jewels, raised on a slender baluster-form dark brown enameled metal base, 23" h. ............ **550**

**Leaded glass table lamp,** domical hexagonal slag glass shade w/detailed cast white metal filigree over the glass panels forming a landscape of palm trees & church, slag panels in shades of white, caramel, blue & pink, raised on a slender baluster-form bronzed cast-iron base, ca. 1920s, 23 1/2" h. (one panel cracked) ...................... **275**

*Loetz Shades on Desk Lamp*

**Loetz glass desk lamp,** a pair of small domical open-topped glass shades w/raised gold iridescent festoons on a linenfold ground, fitted on a two-socket candlestick-form hammered brass base, adjustable standard w/ball finial & shade supports, wide round foot, Austria, late 19th - early 20th c., 17 1/4" h. (ILLUS.) ..... **1,495**

**Longwy Pottery table lamp,** cylindrical pottery base w/a well for the kerosene font at the top, decorated in an overall polychrome floral enamel design, w/brass fittings & metal base, France, late 19th c., electrified, 12" h. ........................ **121**

**Marble floor lamp,** a deep octagonal red marble base striated w/white supporting a tall red marble columnar standard trimmed w/ormolu swags & leaves & supporting a decorative ormolu urn at the top below the electric fitting w/two sockets, fitted w/a domical silk & lace-trimmed shade, traces of original gilding on metal, early 20th c., overall 69" h. (ILLUS. next page) .............................................................. **1,980**

*McKenny & Waterbury Boudoir Lamp*

metal framed shade, supported by a rectangular black metal base w/raised &
curved armature, w/four applied lion designs, electrified oil canister stamped
"Miller - the Juno Lamp - Made in U.S.A.,"
overall 17 1/4" h. (black over-painting)......... **518**

**Moe Bridges boudoir lamp,** 8" d. domical
reverse-painted shade decorated w/a
continuous landscape featuring large
trees & grass in the foreground w/a silhouetted village & trees in the distance,
done in shades of dark purple against a
deep red sky, on a slender painted metal
urn-form handled base painted black w/a
pointed arch shoulder band in deep yel-
low, 14" h. ....................................................... **460**

**Moe Bridges boudoir lamp,** 8" d. domical
reverse-painted shade decorated w/an
autumnal landscape w/a curving road
passing between two tall trees w/hills in
the distance, on a slender ring-incised
baluster-form bronzed metal pedestal &
flaring ringed foot, marked shade, overall
14" h. ............................................................... **990**

**Moe Bridges table lamp,** 14" d. domical reverse-painted shade, decorated w/a continuous summertime landscape w/a wide
blue river flanked by green meadows &
clusters of green & brown trees w/brown
hills in the distance & a pale blue sky
w/billowing white & grey clouds, on a
slender Moe Bridges Art Nouveau style
bronzed metal base w/a loop-cast scalloped foot, shade signed "Moe Bridges
Co. 177" (ILLUS. top next page) ................. **2,632**

**Moe Bridges table lamp,** 15" d. deep domical reverse-painted shade decorated
w/a lakeside landscape w/trees in naturalistic colors, signed on the rim, raised
on a bronze base w/a swelled cylindrical

*Decorative Marble & Ormolu Lamp*

**McKenny and Waterbury Co. boudoir
lamp,** 8" d. domical reverse-painted
shade decorated w/yellow daffodils & tall
green leaves on an amber ground, raised
on a patinated metal base w/slender
standard on a dished round foot, woven
label on base, early 20th c., 13 3/4" h.
(ILLUS. top next column)............................. **1,150**

**Miller floor lamp,** 21" domical leaded glass
shade w/bent panel shoulder in creamy
caramel textured slag glass over a wide
scalloped slag glass band of light blue &
red stylized blossoms, green heart-
shaped leaves & orange border, raised
on a three-socket slender ringed patinated metal standard on an arched tripod
foot, shade w/metal tag stamped "Miller,"
base also stamped w/name, early
20th c., overall 58 1/2" h. .............................. **1,150**

**Miller table lamp,** Mission-style, four green
slag glass panels set in a black scrolled

*Pretty Moe Bridges Landscape Lamp*

standard above the round undulated foot incised w/a large clover leaf design, marked on the base, shade w/interior rim chip, early 20th c., overall 20 1/2" h. .......... **2,300**

**Moe Bridges table lamp,** 17" d. heavy walled scenic domed glass shade w/'pebbled' surface painted on reverse w/colorful riverside scene of sheep under tall leafy trees, marked "Moe Bridges Milwaukee. San Fran," mounted on two-socket metal vasiform lamp base painted copper color w/green accents, 23" h. (paint chipping).............................. **1,035**

*Moe Bridges Landscape Lamp*

**Moe Bridges table lamp,** 18" d. domical reverse-painted shade, decorated in the foreground w/small steep hillsides w/tall leafy trees & shrubbery flanking a panoramic view of a valley w/a meandering blue river flanked by scattered clusters of tall leafy trees & meadows, a pale blue sky w/pale yellow clouds in the distance, shade signed "Moe Bridges," bronzed metal ovoid base w/flattened cross-form foot also signed (ILLUS.)............................. **4,480**

**Moe Bridges table lamp,** 18" d. domical reverse-painted shade decorated w/a continuous riverside landscape, signed in the lower rim "Moe Bridges Co. 186," mounted on the original gilt-metal base, overall 23" h. (exterior shade stain disappears when lit, sockets replaced, finish seriously worn)............................................. **1,610**

**Mosaic Lamp Company of Chicago table lamp,** 18" d. domical leaded glass shade composed of segments forming nine full-blown pink lotus blossoms amid variegated green leaves around the uneven border & below a wide panel of chartreuse slag glass honeycomb pattern w/a bronzed metal cap, raised on a slender square flaring bronzed-metal base molded w/acanthus leaves, overall 26" h. ......... **2,310**

**Mosaic Lamp Company of Chicago table lamp,** 18" d. domical leaded glass shade, composed of scattered pink rose blossoms & buds & green leaves against an amber ground, uneven border, on a Chicago Mosaic gilt-metal base w/a slender urn-form handled shaft above a ribbed & lobed round foot............................ **3,360**

*Mosaic Lamp Cherry Tree Lamp*

**Mosaic Lamp Company of Chicago table lamp,** 18" domical leaded glass shade in the Cherry Tree patt., composed of clusters of deep pink cherries on brown branches w/green leaves against a mot-

tled greenish yellow ground, raised on a
Chicago Mosaic tree trunk base
(ILLUS.) ........................................................ **2,240**

*Mosaic Lamp Rose Table Lamp*

**Mosaic Lamp Company of Chicago table
lamp,** 18" d. domical leaded glass
shade, comosed of a border band of
large deep rose four-petal blossoms centered in leaf clusters against a caramel
slag ground, the upper side w/bands of
alternating narrow green slag & larger
caramel slag, on a tall slender bronzed
metal baluster-form standard on a round
foot (ILLUS.) ................................................ **3,360**
**Mosaic Lamp Company of Chicago table
lamp,** 18" d. umbrella-form leaded glass
shade, the wide flaring top composed of
a honeycomb design in caramel slag, a
narrow green slag band above the deep
drop border composed of a band of five-
petal pink blossoms & green slag leaves
on a caramel slag ground, raised on a
tree trunk bronzed metal base .................... **2,800**
**Mosaic Lamp Company of Chicago table
lamp,** domical six-paneled shade w/car-
amel slag & blue glass curved panels behind gilt filigree overlay w/an Oriental
landscape in each panel, serpentine rim,
raised on a gilt cast-iron pedestal base
w/ornate detail including rams' heads &
scrolls above the flaring paneled & scalloped foot, base embossed "Mosaic
Shade Pat. Appl. for #69 Chicago," 23" h. ..... **770**
**Muller Freres boudoir lamp,** cameo glass,
the tall pagoda shaped glass shade in
yellow overlaid w/red & deep purple &
cameo cut w/a landscape of tall trees &
grass by a body of orange water, w/a
slender tapering cylindrical matching
glass base on a hammered iron foot,
cameo signature, France, early 20th c.,
overall 15 1/2" h. .......................................... **3,910**

*Muller Freres Art Deco Table Lamp*

**Muller Freres table lamp,** Art Deco style, a
9 1/2" d. rounded, paneled & pointed
etched clear molded shade w/rosette &
geometric skyscraper-influenced designs, on a wrought-iron base w/angular
bars & conical foot, shade signed "Muller
Freres - Luneville," France, ca. 1930,
several minute rim nicks, 19 1/4" h.
(ILLUS.) ........................................................ **1,093**

*Early Electric Newel Post Lamp*

**Newel post lamp,** cast spelter & brass, a round socle base supporting a finely cast figure of a young boy in peasant costume standing & playing a violin, a large plant form rises behind him w/leafy stems issuing four sockets w/large oblong beaded glass light bulb covers, early 20th c., wear, some beads missing, sold w/separate round white onyx base plate, 29" h. (ILLUS.) ............................................................. **825**

*Phoenix Table Lamp with Landscapes*

**Phoenix table lamp,** 18" d. domical reverse-painted shade, decorated w/a crude stylized landscape w/a roadway through fields & a rail fence w/a farmhouse & trees in the distance, in shades of dark brown, medium brown, frosted white, pale yellow & orange, on a tapering cylindrical reverse-painted glass base decorated w/landscape scenes & framed by gilt-metal filigree bands above the egg-and-dart band foot (ILLUS.) .......... **1,176**

**Pittsburgh boudoir lamp,** 7" w. shade w/four flared panels of ribbed & reverse-painted design, metal shade framework & base enamel-painted w/raised Oriental designs, Pittsburgh Lamp, Brass & Glass Co., ca. 1920, 15" h. (worn finish) .................. **230**

**Pittsburgh table lamp,** 12" d. scenic domed yellow glass shade painted on surface w/rough-textured green full-length trees & on iron bronzed foliate base marked "PLB & G Co," for Pittsburgh Lamp, Brass & Glass Co., 18" h. ........ **805**

**Pittsburgh table lamp,** half-round oblong reverse-painted shade decorated w/a riverside landscape in naturalistic tones, supported by a gilt-bronze high curved adjustable arm above the paneled & floral-cast oblong foot, marked on the turn switch, light wear to gilt, 14" h. (ILLUS. top next column) ............................................. **690**

*Pittsburgh Reverse-painted Lamp*

*Acid-etched Pittsburgh Table Lamp*

**Pittsburgh table lamp,** 16" d. domical acid-etched glass shade, decorated w/radiating bands of alternating chain pendants & graduated leafy wreaths in tan against an opal white ground, a narrow border band of small tan circles (ILLUS.) ................. **952**

**Pittsburgh table lamp,** 16" d. domical reverse-painted glass shade marked "Lakes of Killarney" w/a continuous landscape of amethyst & purple mountains along reflective water lined w/evergreens & leafy trees, the exterior painted w/fall-colored leafy trees & small rocky islands, raised on a slender swelled gilt-metal pedestal w/cast acanthus leaf & beaded bands above the scalloped round laurel leaf-cast foot, early 20th c., 23" h. ............ **2,255**

**Pittsburgh table lamp,** 16" d. domical reverse- and obverse-painted shade, decorated w/a continuous summer landscape w/tall leafy trees flanking a stream against a deep orange sky w/small yellow clouds, the trees in dark & light green & yellow, on a patinated metal Pittsburgh base w/a central slender shaft flanked by three C-scroll bottom braces on a tripartite platform foot w/cast border band ......... **2,464**

**Pittsburgh table lamp,** 16" d. domical reverse-painted shade decorated w/a continuous ocean scene of white-capped dark blackish blue waves under a banded deep rose, yellow & blue sunset sky .................................................................... **3,024**

*Pittsburgh Lamp and Seascape Shade*

**Pittsburgh table lamp,** 16" d. domical reverse-painted shade decorated w/a wide seascape w/a cloudy moonlit sky flanked on each side by a shoreline w/tall leafy trees, in dark shades of blue, white, black, brown, maroon & yellow, on a tall slender bronzed metal standard w/a round paneled foot & a pair of small loop handles at the top (ILLUS.) ........................ **3,416**

**Pittsburgh table lamp,** 17" d. domical reverse-painted shade decorated on each side w/a scene of two galleons sailing on stormy seas of teal & blue, cloudy yellow sky, raised on a gilt-metal ribbed gourd-form base tapering to two small loop handles at the top, molded floral pods & leaves around the bottom, early 20th c. .......................................................... **2,200**

**Pittsburgh table lamp,** 17 1/2" d. high domed reverse-painted shade in chartreuse painted w/russet & large maple

*Pittsburgh Lamp with Maple Leaves*

leaves around the sides, raised on a gilt-metal baluster-form lobed base w/a flaring round lobed foot w/red & black enamel highlights, ca. 1915, overall 25" h. (ILLUS.) .......................................................... **2,875**

*Pittsburgh Table Lamp*

**Pittsburgh table lamp,** 17 3/4" d. domical reverse- and obverse-painted shade of frosted & textured glass decorated on the interior w/a continuous mountainous landscape & on the exterior w/painted pine trees, paper label on interior, on a three-socket patinated metal ribbed standard w/a weighted scroll, shield, floral & foliate-decorated base, wear to patina, Model No. 1595, ca. 1920, 27" h. (ILLUS.) .......................................................... **1,955**

*Pittsburgh Lamp & Mosserine Shade*

**Pittsburgh table lamp,** 18" d. domical acid-etched brown Mosserine shade w/long stripes of scroll-tipped spear points radiating down to a border band of oval & rectangular alternating devices, raised on a slender bronzed metal standard w/a domed & paneled foot w/four scrolled projections (ILLUS.)...................................... **3,920**

*Pittsburgh Lamp with Rose Band*

**Pittsburgh table lamp,** 18" d. domical reverse-painted shade, decorated w/a wide border band of large deep pink & yellow rose blossoms & green leaves against a green & white lattice band w/slender

leafy bands radiating down from the top to a narrow leafy band above the roses, frosted white ground, raised on a slender bronzed metal standard w/a flaring ribbed & scalloped foot (ILLUS.)................ **3,640**

**Pittsburgh table lamp,** 18" d. domical reverse-painted shade, decorated w/the "Call of the Wild" landscape scene w/a Native American teepee & campfire amid a cluster of tall trees w/moonlit sky & water at the sides, in dark shades of black, brown, orange & yellow, on a bronzed metal bulbous ovoid ribbed base w/small loop handles at the top ............................... **6,720**

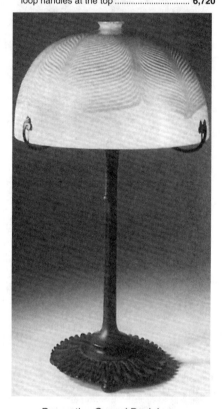

*Decorative Quezel Desk Lamp*

**Quezal desk lamp,** 10 1/2" d. domical shade w/small top opening in opal glass lined w/bright gold iridescence & on the exterior w/a glossy surface w/five broad gold pulled feather designs, signed inside the top rim, mounted on a three-arm spider on an elegant black bronze slender standard w/the round foot composed of overlapping leaf designs, minor nicks to top shade rim, 19" h. (ILLUS.)................ **1,725**

**Quezal desk lamp,** figural, bronze lion reclining on faceted weighted pedestal foot supporting offset curved lamp shaft fitted w/gold, white & green pulled-feather decorated glass shade inscribed "Quezal," 16" l., 13" h. (ILLUS.) ................................... **1,035**

*Quezal Figural Desk Lamp*

**Quezal table lamp,** three long ruffled lily-form shades in reddish gold iridescence each on an upright arched bronze arm extending down into a reeded standard on a wide overlapped tripodal pod base, shades signed, shades 4 3/4" l., overall 14" h. ............................................................. **2,750**

*Quezal Figural Table Lamps*

**Quezal table lamps,** figural cast metal bases, each w/similar Art Nouveau woman on quatreform swirling platform base, mounted w/gold iridescent squared glass shades inscribed "Quezal" at rim, 18 1/2" h., pr. (ILLUS.) ............................... **2,530**

**Rateau table lamp,** patinated bronze w/shade, reeded baluster base stamped "A.A. RATEAU 1392," ca.1921, 23" h. with shade (ILLUS. top next column) ....... **49,350**

**Reverse-painted table lamp,** 19" d. reverse-painted shade composed of six wide tapering ribbed glass panels mounted in a metal framework & painted w/a

*Rateau Table Lamp.*

continuous desert landscape w/palm trees, lakes & mountains, on a tall tapering cylindrical glass paneled base w/matching decoration & mounted in a scrolled & pierced gilt-metal framework on an egg-and-dart embossed foot rim, unsigned, early 20th c., 23" h. (ILLUS. below) ................................................. **990**

*Reverse-Painted Table Lamp*

**Reverse-painted table lamp,** 17 1/2" d. domical reverse-painted shade w/pierced metal cap, decorated w/a repeated scene of a long roadway leading up to a castle on a rocky island among brown & black conifer trees, brownish grey hills reflect in still waters, silhouetted against a peach-colored sky, raised on a slender gilt-metal reeded pedestal on a round foot cast w/pond lilies & pods, early 20th c., overall 24" h. ............................................................. **1,540**

Riviere table lamp, 21" d. domical leaded glass shade composed of segments forming an overall design of leafy morning glory vines w/blossoms in shades of red, pink & blue w/textured green glass leaves all against a pale caramel slag ground, raised on a slender square bronze standard w/four leaves spaced around the round foot, early 20th c. .......... **7,840**

*Slag Glass & Filigree Table Lamp*

Slag glass & filigree table lamp, 10 1/2" d. etched metal & green slag glass lamp, beaded metal framework in grapevine pattern on shade, compatible design on base w/fine greenish bronze patina overall, attributed to Riviere Studios, 21" h. (ILLUS.)...................................... **1,265**

Slag glass table lamp, a high domical shade composed of six bent-glass caramel slag panels divided by metal bands and decorated around the lower border w/florette metal filigree, raised on a bronzed metal waisted & paneled base, early 20th c. ...................................... **840**

Slag glass table lamp, 16 1/2" d. domical open-topped shade composed of six bent panels of striated caramel & white slag glass mounted in a gilt- and enamel floral-decorated framework w/lattice border, raised on a slender tall waisted gilt-metal standard w/ribbing & raised mistletoe design on a round matching foot w/light blue enameled highlights, early 20th c., gilt wear, 21" h. (ILLUS. top next column)................................. **431**

*Lamp with Bent Slag Glass Shade*

*Slag Glass Lamp with Flat Panels*

Slag glass table lamp, 17 1/2" d. eight-paneled shade composed of flat caramel slag glass panels overlaid w/a lattice & urn design patinated metal frame, raised on a two-socket slender reeded & leaf-embossed standard on a round leaf-embossed foot, base marked "EM & Co.," some glass panels replaced, early 20th c., 26" h. (ILLUS.) .................................... **863**

### Ornate Slag & Filigree Table Lamp

**Slag glass table lamp,** 17 1/2" w. paneled pyramidal shape w/striated green & white slag glass panels completely overlaid w/an ornate pierced metal filigree of leaves on trailing vines, beaded & braided trim, raised on a matching tapering paneled standard w/flaring base of matching overlaid slag glass, on four paw feet, four-socket fixture w/wiring for illuminating the base, attributed to Riviere Studios, early 20th c., wear, minor repairs, 26 12" h. (ILLUS.) .............................. **2,300**

### Bent-panel Slag Glass Table Lamp

**Slag glass table lamp,** 18 1/2" d. domical shade composed of six tapering bent panels of mottled blue, green, purple, white & caramel slag glass within a bronze-finished metal frame w/foliate decorated bands, raised on a matching tapering cylindrical glass & metal base w/leaf-tip molded base ring, early 20th c., 22" h. (ILLUS.) .................................................. **805**

### Simple Slag Glass Table Lamp

**Slag glass table lamp,** domical six-panel slag glass shade, each panel in caramel & white slag w/a half-round spiderweb metal filigree along the bottom edge of each panel, raised on a ribbed bronzed metal base w/flaring round foot, ca. 1920, 18 1/2" h. (ILLUS.) ................................ **460**

**Slag glass table lamp,** 19" d. domical caramel slag paneled shade w/floral filigree overlay, supported on a conforming cast-metal base, early 20th c., 24" h. ..................... **880**

**Slag glass table lamp,** 19" d. domical shade composed of six amber slag glass bent panels fitted w/a repainted cast-metal framework, raised on a tapering cylindrical base w/inset amber slag glass panels fitted in the pierced metal framework, early 20th c., 21" h. ............................... **688**

### Slag Glass Lamp with Filigree

**Slag glass table lamp,** 20" w. flattened domical shade composed of six wide tapering caramel slag upper panels & a wide drop apron band of deep red slag glass, delicate stylized floral metal filigree overlay forming bands across the top and around the apron of the shade, raised on a bronzed metal classical-style urn-form base w/a round paneled foot (ILLUS.) .............................................................. **896**

*Filigree-decorated Slag Lamp*

**Slag glass table lamp,** a pyramidal eight-paneled shade w/caramel slag panels in a bronzed metal framework above a conforming vertical border band of matching glass panels faced w/leafy scroll & swag filigree, raised on a slender bronze metal shaft on an embossed stepped, domed foot, early 20th c., 21" h. (ILLUS.) ................. **286**

**Slag glass table lamp,** paneled hexagonal pyramidal shade w/each panel overlaid along the bottom w/cast white metal leafy floral scrolls forming a point in each panel & tapering up to a small flared & pierced crown ring, caramel slag glass panels, raised on a slender bronzed cast-iron base, ca. 1920s, 21 1/2" h. ........................... **336**

*Slag Glass Lamp with Ornate Overlay*

**Slag glass table lamp,** deep domical shade composed of wide bent panels of slag glass overlaid w/an ornate open-work metal overlay w/a landscape of tall trees & woodland meadows, on a slender brass-plated reeded standard above the scalloped & scrolled foot all cast w/leaves & beading, signed "Royal Art Glass Co. - 1912," shade metal w/gold repaint, 24" h. (ILLUS.) .................................... **715**

*Stickley Brothers Lamp*

**Stickley Brothers table lamp,** hammered copper hexagonal base & shade w/an x design over amber glass, good original patina, unsigned, 20" d. x 26" h., one replaced pane, three replaced sockets, very good condition (ILLUS.) ............... **4,250**

*Steuben Desk Lamp*

**Steuben desk lamp,** patinated bronze base w/verdigris finish, the oval domed foot supporting a scrolled upright harp suspending a bell-form gold Aurene glass shade, chip to shade top rim, early 20th c., overall 15 1/4" h. (ILLUS.).............. **1,495**

*Fine Steuben Floor Lamp*

**Steuben floor lamp,** a domical Steuben brown Aurene glass shade w/gold iridescent rim band w/brown stripe suspended from a patinated metal harp above the tall slender standard, early 20th c., 58" h. (ILLUS. of top)............................................ **4,000**

**Stickley table lamp,** 13" d. domical woven wicker shade w/a canework design over a paper lining, on a hammered copper frame support above the wooden base composed of four canted square spindles connected by a cross stretcher on a circular base, fine original finish, unsigned Gustav Stickley, Model No. 611, early 20th c., overall 21" h. (restoration to metalwork) ....................................................... **23,100**

**Stickley table lamp,** 15" w. multi-paneled conical green slag glass shade w/a gently scalloped bottom rim, raised on a hand-hammered copper base w/a cylindrical body & rounded shoulder flanked by large C-scroll strap handles, original patina, impressed Gustav Stickley mark, Model No. 295, 18" h. (minor cracks & glass loss to shade)...................................... **3,080**

**Suess table lamp,** 18" d. domical leaded glass shade with graduated squares of caramel slag glass above a wide border band w/narrow green slag bands flanking a band of stylized green leaves on a caramel ground, on a tall, very slender bronzed metal base....................................... **3,640**

*Fine Seuss Leaded Glass Table Lamp*

**Suess table lamp,** 18" d. conical leaded glass shade w/a flat rim band, composed of radiating panels of caramel & soft green colored glass, the drop apron w/square & triangular red jewels & tile-shaped segments within oblong segments, raised on a slender cylindrical bronze standard w/three sockets on a flattened wide round foot w/an etched wave pattern, early 20th c., minor patina ware, missing shade cap, overall 21 1/2" h. (ILLUS.)...................................... **2,990**

*Suess Lamp with Stylized Flowers*

**Suess table lamp,** 18" d. widely flaring conical leaded glass shade w/a flat drop apron, decorated around the top w/large oblong stylized geometric deep burgundy blossoms w/yellow centers above a swagged vine of dark green leaves & yellow dots all on a background of mottled white & white & green slag, the drop apron w/half-round matching blossoms & leaf sprigs w/green slag swags, raised on a slender bronzed metal standard w/a wide disk foot (ILLUS.) .......................................... **4,480**

**Suess table lamp,** 20" d. domical leaded glass shade, the top w/radiating squares of caramel slag above two narrow green slag border bands flanking a wider band of stylized spearpoint dark green leaves against a pinkish tan slag ground, on a very slender bronzed metal standard w/a wide thin round foot ...................................... **3,640**

*Fine Leaded Glass Suess Lamp*

**Suess table lamp,** 24 1/4" d. wide parasol-shaped leaded glass shade composed of branching striated pink & yellow apple blossoms descending from the top rim on a green ground, raised on a slender bronze three-socket standard w/a wide round disk base etched w/a wave border, Chicago, ca. 1906, spotting on base, 23 1/2" h. (ILLUS.) ...................................... **9,775**

**U.S. Glass Co. table lamp,** figural glass "Parrot" (Cockatoo), red body w/green crest, body on round black base, U.S. Glass Co., ca. 1920s, 13" h. .......................... **345**

**U.S. Glass Company novelty lamp,** the figural glass shade molded as a colorful bouquet of large flowers overflowing a tall waisted black basketweave container resting on a silver plate base w/a decorative chased base band & three ribbed paw feet, electric, small, ca. 1926-35 .......... **660**

**White metal figural lamp,** the base cast as a cylindrical rockwork well w/a scantily clad Art Nouveau maiden seated on the edge holding a water jug w/one hand, the other hand reaching into the tall ornate arching trelliswork of leafy grapevines suspending at the top a glass cluster of grapes enclosing the light fixture, electri-

*Ornate Art Nouveau Figural Lamp*

fied, early 20th c., overall 4' 6" h. (ILLUS.) .......................................................... **3,540**

**Wicker floor lamp,** Arts & Crafts style, a 20" d. deep domical wicker shade w/tightly-woven upper & lower bands & a center loosely woven diamond lattice design, cloth-lined, raised on a slender tall slightly tapering tightly woven standard continuing to a domed foot, natural finish, relined shade, early 20th c., overall 63" h. .............................................................. **1,210**

*Wilkinson & Suess Table Lamp*

**Wilkinson & Suess table lamp,** 19 1/2" d. parasol-shaped leaded glass shade composed of radiating panels of caramel & light green glass segments, drop apron w/square opalescent & red triangular shaped jewels, raised on a slender reeded three-socket standard w/a flaring scroll- and foliate-embossed footed Suess base, early 20th c., some cracked segments, 24" h. (ILLUS.) ........................... **2,070**

*Wilkinson Floral-bordered Table Lamp*

**Wilkinson table lamp,** 19" d. domical leaded glass shade w/the upper shade composed of green & yellow striated slag blocks above the deep border band composed of large stylized blossoms in deep orange, pink & maroon w/green slag leaves, on a tall slender bronzed metal tree trunk-style standard w/four knobs on the round disk foot (ILLUS.) ....................... **4,760**

**Wilkinson table lamp,** 20" d. conical leaded glass shade composed of radiating bands of large & small mottled yellowish amber blocks above a wide border band of nasturtium blossoms in shades of pink, red, green & yellow, serpentine border, on a Wilkinson bronzed metal base w/a slender ribbed shaft above a scroll-cast domed & four-footed base........................... **8,120**

**Wilkinson table lamp,** 20" d. domical bent-panel slag glass shade, composed of eight bent tapering caramel slag glass panels overlaid w/a bronzed metal fish scale filigree above a dark green slag glass border band w/a stylized leafy vine filigree overlay, raised on a bronzed metal tall ringed standard on a round loop-cast foot................................................ **3,360**

**Wilkinson table lamp,** 20" d. domical leaded glass shade w/a design of bands of colorful waterlilies in yellow, white, pink & orange w/green leaves against mottled bluish purple blocks representing water,

*Wilkinson Leaded Water Lily Lamp*

on a bronzed metal standard & footed base cast w/cattails (ILLUS.) ..................... **7,840**

*Wilkinson Lamp with Floral Shade*

**Wilkinson table lamp,** 21" d. conical leaded glass shade w/a bold colorful design of large white, red, pink & yellow blossoms on green leafy stems against a dark brown & white banded background, on original slender baluster-form base w/wide scalloped foot (ILLUS.) ................. **12,320**

**Wilkinson table lamp,** 20" d. scalloped conical leaded glass shade w/yellow-centered pink & peach blossoms & green leaves border amber & green slag segments arranged in ladderwork progression, mount w/locking mechanism on a three-socket metal shaft w/bulbed turnings on a stepped platform base impressed "Wilkinson Co. - Brooklyn, N.Y.," overall 27 1/2" h. ......................................... **3,220**

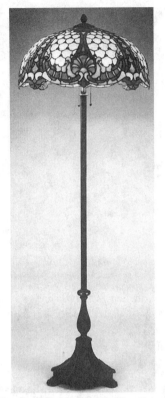

*Quality Williamson & Co. Floor Lamp*

**Williamson & Co. floor lamp,** 22" d. domical leaded glass shade composed of shield-shaped opalescent yellowish white granite segments spaced by green & framed by tannish amber panels centering four green slag shell-form designs at the irregular border, raised on a three-socket bronzed metal slender standard on a flaring paneled base w/three paw feet, early 20th c., overall 62" h. (ILLUS.)........................................................ **13,225**

**Williamson & Co. table lamp,** 20" d. pointed domical leaded glass shade w/amber slag inner panels bordered by a rim design of red tulips among pink & lavender blue spring blossoms on green leafy stems of curved glass, raised on a four-socket integrated gilt-metal shaft w/stylized tulip blossoms above a leafy platform base, base impressed "R. Williamson & Co. - Washington & Jefferson Sts. - Chicago, Ill.," 25" h. (restored cap at top rim) ................................................................ **3,220**

**Williamson floor lamp,** 24" d. domical leaded glass shade, composed of leafy rose branches descending from the top center & ending in large pink, deep red, golden yellow & deep orange blossoms against a background of caramel slag segments, raised on a tall slender reeded & leaf-cast bronze standard above three bent animal legs ending in paws resting on a tripartite foot, overall 70" h. (ILLUS. of shade, below)........................ **30,800**

*Impressive Williamson Floor Lamp*

# CHAPTER 3

# Other Lighting Devices

## Chandeliers

*Rare Gustav Stickley Chandelier*

**Stickley,** four-light, Arts & Crafts style, wrought-iron, glass & wood, four square wrought-iron & amber glass lanterns w/six square cut-outs at top suspended from iron flat crossbar w/original chain & canapes suspended from original wooden cross beam, original patina & finish, amber glass replaced, Gustav Stickley Model No. 670, 24" w., 37" h. (ILLUS.) ...................................................... **$35,200**

*Unique Antler Chandelier*

**Antler,** rustic lodge-style, six-light, a group of entwined large deer antlers w/light sockets inserted at the outer edges, Eu-

rope, late 19th - early 20th c., electrified, 50 1/2" w., 44" h. (ILLUS.) ........................... **2,070**

*Art Deco Glass & Bronze Chandelier*

**Art Deco,** a cast-bronze paneled ceiling mount & lower shade mount cast w/a border of angular designs, the center w/a frosted glass bowl-form shade w/molded stylized flowers & geometric designs, four angled & pointed arms each suspending a conical frosted glass shade w/a molded geometric floral design, ca. 1930, 30" d., overall 26 1/2" h. (ILLUS.) .... **2,300**

**Art Deco,** wrought iron & molded glass, the inverted wide conical pale pink glass shade molded w/a border of roses centering a star, suspended from four candlearms connected at the center to three iron bars applied w/stylized circle & tassel decoration, France, ca. 1925, 48" h. .... **1,265**

**Arts & Crafts,** leaded glass, petal-form shade of radiating bent glass panels of red & amber slag, highlighted by a border of diamond-shaped green glass segments, suspended from patinated metal chains, early 20th c., shade 14" d., pr. .......... **805**

*Arts & Crafts Leaded Glass Chandelier*

**Arts & Crafts,** leaded glass w/six upper angled triangular panels of caramel slag glass above a vertical deep paneled border w/scalloped rim composed of bands & panels of yellow, caramel & green slag glass, some damage, early 20th c., 27" d., 18" h. (ILLUS.) ................................ **1,380**

*Arts & Crafts Three-light Chandelier*

**Arts & Crafts,** three-light, oak & slag glass, a thick triangular ceiling mount suspending three square link wooden chains each ending in a pyramidal wood-framed shade set w/four caramel slag glass panels, wood w/dark brown finish, early 20th c., overall 23 1/2" h. (ILLUS.) ................ **633**

*Unusual Astral Lamp Chandelier*

**Astral lamp chandelier,** tin, brass & glass, the squatty wide tapering conical tin & brass flat-bottomed font issuing four upright scrolled hanging hooks, the top fitted w/an Astral burner & fitted w/an old tulip-form frosted & engraved glass shade w/ruffled top, the font w/traces of

original gilding & paint, stenciled label "Patented Jan 6, 1875," repairs, 5 1/2" h. plus shade (ILLUS.) ...................................... **523**

*Baccarat Crystal Chandelier*

**Baccarat crystal,** eight-light, clear & turquoise cut & molded glass, a central segmented turned standard supporting S-scrolled arms, hung overall w/faceted prisms & chains, unelectrified, late 19th c., 34" h. (ILLUS.) ............................... **4,600**

*Baccarat 25-Light Chandelier*

**Baccarat cut glass,** twenty-five-light, Rococo style ormolu, hung throughout w/pear & lozenge-shaped drops & prisms, the central baluster stem supporting an upper tier of scrolled arms & a lower tier mounted w/obelisks on star-shaped bases, above two tiers of lights, each w/spirally-fluted drip-pan & urn-shaped sconce, w/faceted spheroid terminal, the glass stamped throughout "BACCARAT/DEPOSE," Baccarat, Paris, electrified, ca. 1900, 53" h., 44 1/2" d. (ILLUS.) ....................................................... **18,000**

**Biedermeier,** cut glass, seven-light, the circular corona fitted w/pendent sprays above the tapering body hung w/long ropes of rounded prisms terminating in a circular font w/overhangs, pendent bands of prisms & enclosed by bands of prisms, 19th c., 24" d., 41" h..................... **3,737**

*Blued Steel Chandelier*

**Blued steel,** six-light, Louis XVI-style ormolu, ribbon-tied corona supporting a central stem & quiver of arrows mounted w/Bacchic masks, supporting acanthus-sheathed reeded branches, each mounted w/a bird & terminating in a ram's mask, electrified, in the manner of Pierre Gouthiere, 20th c., 33 1/2" h. (ILLUS.)....... **5,500**

**Bradley & Hubbard,** hand-hammered brass & glass, a wide low domical shade w/a hand-beaten metal frame w/curved straps enclosing six panels of curved caramel slag glass, high domed crown below the heavy brass hanging chain & mounting, attributed to Bradley & Hubbard, early 20th c., 25" d. ............................. **978**

**Brass,** six-light, the six boldly scrolled brass arms hung w/cut glass chains, each arm ending in a gas socket w/an etched glass shade & blue stained-glass decorative sockets & bobêches, American-made, late 19th c., 38" h............................................ **863**

**Brass,** w/five Steuben art glass shades, domed brass ceiling mount terminating w/a hook, chain drop supporting fixture w/raised leaf decorations & five shade mounts & bell-form gold lustre glass

*Brass Chandelier w/Steuben Shades*

shades w/gold hearts & threading & gold Aurene interiors, silver fleur-de-lis acid stamp, Corning, New York, drop 39 1/2", 19" d., chips to some top rims (ILLUS.) ..... **1,265**

*Steuben Glass & Brass Chandelier*

**Brass,** w/six Steuben art glass shades, circular domed ceiling mount w/three chain drops, supporting round domed fixture w/etched curvilinear & floral motifs & extensions suspending six bell-form glass shades w/ruffled rims, creamy white lustre & pulled gold Aurene striations on rims, gold Aurene interiors, shape No. 2282, silver fleur-de-lis acid stamp, drop 23", 20 1/2" d., dents on shade mounts (ILLUS.).......................................................... **6,325**

**Brass,** six-light, a long ring- and knob-turned standard w/ornate S-scrolls attached to the sides above the six down-swept S-scroll candlearms ending in drip pans & tall cylindrical candle cups, a large ball drop at the bottom w/a baluster-turned drop finial, Holland, 18th c., 17" d., 19" h. .............................................. **1,495**

**Bronze,** Art Deco style, a domed metal ribbed ceiling plate suspending a heavy chain composed of alternating ringed alabaster knobs & oblong ribbed metal segments supporting the light fixture modeled as a stylized long-billed & long-tailed bronze bird w/the wide spread wings composed of alabaster panels, inscribed "Albert Cheuret," France, ca. 1925, 24" h. .................................................. **94,000**

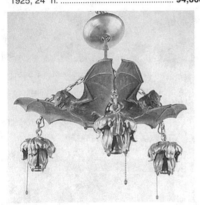

*Unique Bronze Bat Chandelier*

**Bronze,** three-light, figural, composed of three large full-bodied spread-winged bats in a triangular formation suspended from bronze chains & a metal ceiling mount, suspending three brass foliate light fixtures, rich brown patina, early 20th c., 21 1/2" h. (ILLUS.) ......................... **7,188**

*Fine Classical Solar Chandelier*

**Classical style,** brass & cast gilt-metal, four-light, Solar model, the leaf- and grape-cast scalloped corona above a flared reeded standard, enclosed by four leaf scroll chains leading to a circular pan issuing leaf-cast S-scrolled arms sup-

porting tapering fonts w/globular frosted glass & wheel-cut shades, a central leafy base drop, electrified, mid-19th c., 33" w., 36" h. (ILLUS.) ............................... **10,200**

*Cut Glass Chandelier*

**Cut glass,** eighteen-light, Neoclassic style ormolu, w/domed acanthus-cast corona, above a band set w/square lozenges & hung w/drop festoons, above spreading drop chains supporting a similar central band surmounted by anthemion-crested drop-set laurel wreaths, above ten graduated tiers of drops, w/faceted ball terminal, ca. 1900, 70" h. (ILLUS.) ............. **7,500**

*Neoclassic Cut Glass Chandelier*

**Cut glass,** fifteen-light, Neoclassic style ormolu, the scrolled acanthus-cast corona above husk & glass drop chains supporting a band alternately cast w/acanthus-flanked baskets of flowers & flambeaux flanked by adorsed dolphins, above tapering husk-cast straps & further glass drop chains, w/fruit terminal, electrified, ca. 1900, 51 1/2" h. (ILLUS.).... **5,500**

*Ten-light Cut Glass Chandelier*

**Cut glass,** ten-light, the scrolled corona above husk & bead chains, supporting a central foliate-pierced band hung w/ribbon-tied lights & pendant drops, w/further bead chains below, electrified, ca. 1900, 39 1/2" h. (ILLUS.)....................................... **4,500**

*Rococo Cut Glass Chandelier*

**Cut glass,** thirty-six-light, Rococo style ormolu, of cage form, hung throughout w/flowerhead, star & lozenge-shaped drops, ca. 1900, 54" h. (ILLUS.)............... **11,000**

*Ornate Cut Glass Chandelier*

**Cut glass,** twenty-one-light, Neoclassic style ormolu, the acanthus corona above a domed reeded strapwork top hung w/floral swags, above tapering drop & husk pendant chains, terminating in eight down-turned trumpet-shaped lights joined by floral swags, above a guilloché-cast band supporting ten tiers of drops, ca. 1900, 62 1/4" h. (ILLUS.).......... **9,000**

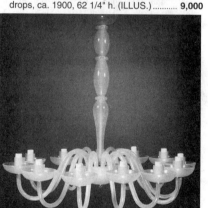

*Czechoslovakian Glass Chandelier*

**Czechoslovakian glass,** twelve-light, a painted metal ceiling mount suspending a baluster- and ring-form long yellowish green glass standard supporting twelve yellowish green glass arms each fitted w/a shallow cupped bobêche & candle-form socket, ca. 1930, 28 1/2" d., 23" h. (ILLUS.)............................................................. **748**

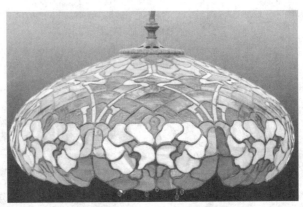

*Stylized Flowers on D&K Chandelier*

*Daum Nancy Chandelier*

**Daum Nancy-signed,** Art Deco style, the metal standard w/three flaring pale amber glass cups above the spreading circular frosted shade, shade signed "Daum Nancy France," ca. 1930s, 24" d., 18" h. (ILLUS.) ......................................................... **1,265**

**Duffner & Kimberly-signed,** 25" d. domical leaded glass shade, composed of pairs of large stylized striated white, pink & tan blossoms around the scalloped lower border against a dark brown & tan slag ground w/delicate undulating stems in pale yellow (ILLUS. top of page) .............. **14,000**

**Duffner & Kimberly-signed,** 26" d. bell-form wide leaded glass shade, the shoulder & wide rounded apron decorated w/pairs of pale yellow & brown cornucopias w/the large ones in the border pouring forth large bouquets of large pink, pale lavender & deep rose blossoms & dark green leaves, the upper shade composed of striated green slag glass blocks ............................................................. **14,000**

**Duffner & Kimberly-signed,** 28" d. wide conical leaded glass shade composed of a wide interlocking ovals design in caramel panels above a three-band drop rim w/two glass slag bands flanking an orangish slag inner band (ILLUS. bottom of this page) ....................................................... **5,600**

**Duffner & Kimberly-signed,** 28" d. widely flaring conical leaded glass shade, Trumpet Vine patt., decorated w/a wide band of large stylized deep red & green blossoms & large swirled green, blue & white slag glass leaves, bands of green slag glass blocks above & below the flower band ......................................................... **14,560**

**Dutch Baroque-style,** brass, eight-light, a wrought-iron chain suspending a ring-turned slender standard, the medial collar issuing eight spurred scrolling candle-

*Duffner & Kimberly Signed Chandelier*

arms centering star designs & terminating in drip pans & cylindrical candle sockets, a large ball-shaped lower drop w/a pendent finial, late 19th - early 20th c., 24" d., 18" h. ........................................... **1,035**

**Empire-style,** gilt- and patinated bronze, twelve-light, a large round central patinated bronze disk w/a conical top & a slightly round bottom centered by a pineapple drop, the edge band mounted w/four large figural spread-winged gilt-bronze swans each supporting three candle sockets, suspended from four chains composed of metal disks, rods & classical masks hung from the upper small round support ring w/gilt acanthus finials, Europe, 19th c., 36" h. ...................... **7,200**

**George III-style,** giltwood & cut glass, six-light, the leafage-carved standard supporting scrolling candlearms, all hung w/strings of glass beads, drops & pendants, 19th c., 33" d., 43" h. ...................... **4,887**

*Handel Bent Glass Slag Chandelier*

the long pointed leaf-form green slag panels w/pointed tips, the leaf tips alternating w/white slag diamonds (ILLUS.)...................................................... **2,632**

*Jasper Ware Three-Light Chandelier*

**Jasper Ware & brass,** three-light, a brass tall pointed leaf-cast crown & connector above an ovoid blue jasper ware bulb w/applied white relief classical figures & leaf & scroll devices above a long ring-turned brass connector issuing three long S-scroll leaf-cast arms each ending in a socket above the dished matching jasper ware lower bowl w/a wide rolled rim & a brass knob drop, unmarked Wedgwood, England, late 19th c., overall 19 1/4" h. (ILLUS.)...................................... **1,093**

**Lalique,** "Champs Elysées" patt., a large ball-shaped shade in frosted clear glass molded in high-relief w/overall acanthus-style leaves, suspended in a brass mount w/arched & pierced fruit-design crest suspended from three chains, model introduced in 1926, unsigned, 16" d. (ILLUS. top next page)................................ **5,175**

**Lalique glass,** "Bandes de Roses," wide & deep bowl-form in frosted grey, molded w/four narrow graduated bands of stylized rose blossoms in blocks alternating w/wide plain bands, introduced in 1924, original brown patina, molded name, 20 1/2" d...................................................... **28,750**

*Gilt Metal & Cut Glass Chandelier*

**Gilt metal & cut glass,** twenty-four-light, Italian Baroque style, lace work, hung throughout w/beaded drops & flower-heads, w/beaded corona above latticed cage-form upper section, the central upright supporting an upper tier of eight beaded branches & a lower tier of sixteen, each w/circular drip-pan & cylindrical sconce, terminating in a spheroid finial, electrified, ca. 1880, 51" h., 43" d. (ILLUS.)...................................................... **19,000**

**Gilt-metal,** Louis XV-style, twelve-light, a tapering & tiered gilt-metal cage w/scrolled candlearms hung overall w/grape-form glass pendants & prisms, hollow glass ball base drop, 19th c., 44" h.................................................................. **4,600**

**Handel-signed,** 24" d. domical bent-panel shade w/a flaring open crown top w/green slag pointed segments above

*Lalique Champs Elysées Chandelier*

*Lalique Molded Glass Chandelier*

**Lalique-signed,** molded glass, "Fougeres," Rene Lalique, designed in 1924, 33" h., 31 1/2" d. (ILLUS. bottom previous column)................................................................. **17,625**

*Lalique Opalescent Glass Plafonnier*

**Lalique-signed,** opalescent glass plafonnier, "Deux Sirenes," molded "R. LALIQUE," Rene Lalique, designed in 1921, 15 1/2" d. (ILLUS.)..................................... **14,100**

**Leaded glass,** 22 1/2" d. conical leaded glass shade w/a wide flat drop apron, the top section w/hexagonal segments in striated green & caramel slag, the deep apron w/an irregular border decorated w/eight large red & orange striated glass stylized flowers on a curvilinear green & caramel slag ground, three-light fixture, unsigned, a few cracked segments, early 20th c., 11" h. (ILLUS. below)........................ **460**

*Unsigned Leaded Glass Chandelier*

*Leaded Glass Chandelier*

**Leaded glass,** Greek Key shade, domed shade composed of radiating geometric segments of striated caramel & white glass, lower cobalt blue glass Greek Key pattern border, early 20th c., America, shade 11 3/4" h., 24 1/2" d., hardware not original (ILLUS.) ........................................ **173**

*Louis XV-style Chandelier*

**Louis XV-style,** gilded brass & porcelain, eight-light, the central standard composed of a rolled brass cap above a conical brass cap on a squatty spherical porcelain ball w/dark blue bands flanking a wide band transfer-printed in color w/flowers & figures in 18th c. dress, joined w/a brass connector to a tapering ovoid long porcelain section w/matching decoration & flanked by scrolled handles, all above the bottom brass & porcelain base drop issuing eight leaf-cast S-scroll candlearms ending in cupped electric candle-style sockets, early 20th c., 28" h. (ILLUS.) ............................................................. **990**

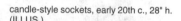

*Louis XV-style Chandelier with Putto*

**Louis XV-style,** nine-light, gilt-bronze, a scroll-cast ceiling plate suspending a long central rod flanked by three long scrolled supports each issuing three short scrolled arms ending in light sockets, a figure of a putto at the center above leafy swags, early 20th c., 36" h. (ILLUS.) .......................................................... **10,800**

*Louis XV-style Chandelier with Prisms*

**Louis XV-style,** six-light, gilt-metal & cut glass, the pierced baluster-form central standard issuing a corona & six scrolling arms w/candle sockets & bobêches, densely hung w/shaped cut prisms & a pendant glass drop, drilled for electricity but unwired, late 19th c., Europe, 38" h. (ILLUS.) .......................................................... **2,520**

**Louis XV-style,** gilt-bronze, 18-light, of scrolling leafage basket-form, supporting six arms, each cresting in three foliate bobêches & urn-form candle sockets, Europe, 19th c., 35" d., 40" h. ................... **4,312**

*Louis XVI Gilt-Bronze Chandelier*

**Louis XVI,** gilt-bronze, twelve-light, the leaf-tip-cast central standard supporting foliate-scrolled candle branches, the upper section fitted w/a gilt-bronze & marble urn within a tri-form cage hung w/tasseled drapery, France, 18th c., 56" h., overall 86" h. (ILLUS.) ................................ **18,400**

*Louis XVI-style 15-light Chandelier*

**Louis XVI-style,** fifteen-light, gilt-bronze & glass, the top section w/five C-scrolled glass-trimmed arms supporting five long glass-trimmed arms, each arm ending w/one upturned socket & one exterior downturned socket w/beaded trim, a lower metal basket-form framework densely trimmed w/prisms & enclosing five additional sockets, a scroll-decorated base w/a pineapple drop, Europe, early 20th c., 54" h. (ILLUS.) ................................. **5,100**

**Louis XVI-style,** six-light, ormolu & blued steel, the ribbon-tied corona supporting a central stem & quiver of arrows mounted w/Bacchic masks, supporting acanthus-sheathed reeded branches, each mounted w/a bird & terminating in a ram's mask, in the manner of Pierre Gouthière, France, 20th c., 33 1/2" h. ............................ **6,463**

*Napoleon III Bronze Chandelier*

**Napoleon III,** twelve-light, gilt- and patinated bronze, a central circular tier supporting S-scrolled candlearms modeled w/anthemion & foliage, suspended from flattened oval link chains, France, mid-19th c., 28" d. (ILLUS.) .............................. **4,600**

*Neoclassical-style Chandelier*

**Neoclassical-style,** eight-light, bronze, the trumpet-form fluted central standard topped by flat leaves, flaring outward to the eight fluted cornucopia-shaped candlearms w/squat ovoid fluted nozzles, the standard ending in a similar ovoid form, finishing in an inverted pineapple finial, electrified, late 19th c., 28" w., 28" h. (ILLUS.) ........................................................ **3,450**

**Neoclassical-style,** eighteen-light, ormolu & cut glass, w/a domed acanthus-case corona, above a band set w/square lozenges & hung w/drop festoons, above spreading drop chains supporting a similar central band surmounted by anthemion-crested drop-set laurel wreaths, above ten graduated tiers of drops, w/faceted ball terminal, Europe, ca. 1900, 70" h. ................................... **8,813**

**Neoclassical-style,** fifteen-light, ormolu & cut glass, the scrolled acanthus-cast corona above husk & glass drop chains supporting a band alternately cast w/acanthus-flanked baskets of flowers & flambeaux flanked by adorsed dolphins, above tapering husk-cast straps & further glass drop chains, w/fruit terminal, electrified, Europe, ca. 1900, 51 1/2" h. ............ **6,463**

**Neoclassical-style,** five-light, gilt-bronze, a tall trumpet-form central standard w/cast leaf detail above a broad disk issuing five wide upswept & tapering arms ending in leaf-trimmed sockets & w/a cast tassel, the panel-cast lower surface w/a central floral drop, possibly by E. F. Caldwell & Co., New York, New York, early 20th c., 23" h. (ILLUS. top next column) ................. **2,400**

*Five-arm Neoclassical Chandelier*

**Neoclassical-style,** gilt-bronze & cut glass, 18-light, the corona w/etched branches suspending a bead link above a circular tier supporting scrolling candlearms cresting in sockets, all hung w/faceted cut glass drops & pendants, Russia, early 19th c. ................................................... **21,850**

*French Rococo-style Ormolu*

**Ormolu,** thirty-three-light, French Rococo style, the pierced corona hung w/fruit & floral pendants, above a central palm trunk upright flanked by scrolled acanthus volutes, supporting an upper tier mounted by three music-making putti & w/three lights, above a lower tier of six acanthus branches each supporting five naturalistically-cast lights, w/acanthus &

fruit terminal, ca. 1880, 46" h.
(ILLUS.) ...................................................... **32,000**

*European Tin & Wood Chandelier*

**Painted tin & turned wood,** eight-light, a
slender baluster- and ring-turned upper
post w/a serrated tin cap ring above a
thick round central disk issuing eight S-
scroll-trimmed candlearms, a long ring-
turned drop pendant at the bottom, probably northern Europe, first half 19th c.,
very minor losses, minor paint loss,
31" h. (ILLUS.)................................................ **1,495**

*Patinated Bronze Chandelier*

**Patinated bronze,** eight-light, French ormolu, the scrolled acanthus corona
above a pierced barrel upright mounted
w/a pair of satyrs supporting flambeaux &
grotesque beast branches, w/a further
pair of dragon branches each terminating
in two lights, the lower section cast w/a
coiled dragon, w/cut & frosted glass
shades, possibly by Ferdinand Barbedi-
enne, Paris, ca. 1880, 43 1/2" h.
(ILLUS.)...................................................... **18,000**

**Pewter,** six-light, the central baluster- and
knob-turned standard suspending a large
round ball w/acorn drop finial, the top of
the ball issuing six long S-scroll arms
ending in candle sockets w/drip trays, Europe, probably 19th c., 24" d. (several
arms sagging from metal fatigue) ................... **550**

**Queen Anne-style,** brass, six-light, a slender ring- & urn-turned top section suspended from a heavy hanging ring, a
large spherical ball base suspending a
small ring, six S-scroll long arms issuing
from the top section & ending in wide-
dished drip pans centered by tall tapering
cylindrical candle sockets, 18th c.,
27 1/2" d., 21" h. plus hanging chain
(chain not old)................................................ **3,080**

**Quezal-signed,** five-light, bronze & glass, a
heavy metal baluster-turned drop shaft
supporting a large inverted-dome disk
suspending five long conical sockets each
fitted w/a signed trumpet-form Quezal
shade w/a ruffled rim, each exterior in iridized white w/a gold band, each shade
5" d. .............................................................. **2,240**

*Quezel Bowl-form Chandelier*

**Quezel-signed,** a large 13 3/4" d. bowl-form
glass shade in iridescent ivory decorated
w/radiating iridescent gold & green leaf
decorations, supported on a brass ring
suspended from three ball chains & a
two-socket fixture, shade signed, overall
21 1/2" h. (ILLUS.)...................................... **6,325**

**Quezel-signed,** six-light, Arts & Crafts style,
a large brown patinated metal central disk
w/curled inward rim panels suspended
from straight brackets connected to a
central hooked hanger, the disk suspending six brackets w/leaf-form sockets each
fitted w/a ribbed golden iridescent tulip-
form signed Quezel glass shade, 19" w.,
overall 37" h. (ILLUS. top of page) ............. **9,487**

*Metal Chandelier with Quezel Shades*

**Rococo-style,** cast brass, six-light, long triple leafy scrolled drop arms above a central inverted dome issuing six arms ending in sockets, each ornately cast w/acanthus leaves w/further pendent trumpet-form blossoms & leaves, cast-in label "Made in Spain," mid-20th c., 24" d., 20" h. (braised repairs on two flowers)..................................... **330**

*Rococo-style Ornate Chandelier*

**Rococo-style,** gilt-bronze, amber & clear glass, eight-light, of cage form w/C-scroll metal bands around the top suspending large teardrop prisms above a central ring centering long slender scroll bands w/large teardrop prisms & ending in eight candle sockets, the central shaft composed of several clear bulbs of glass w/facet-cutting, Europe, 19th c., 44" h. (ILLUS.) ......................................................... **2,300**

**Rococo-style,** gilt-metal & cut glass, eight-light, the flowering urn-form standard within a basket-form frame supporting scrolling candlearms, all hung w/rows of glass beads & pendants, Europe, 19th c., 25" d., 31" h. ................................................. **3,450**

*Silvered Bronze & Alabaster Chandelier*

**Silvered bronze,** w/alabaster panels, inscribed "Albert Cheuret," ca. 1925, 23" h., approx. 19" w. (ILLUS.)............................. **22,325**

*Paneled Slag Glass Chandelier*

**Slag glass,** domical form w/ten curved caramel slag panels set in a frame above a wide blue slag flat apron band overlaid w/an embossed metal filigree design of windmills alternating w/clumps of trees & cottages, ca. 1920, one panel w/hairline, hanging cap & chain, 24" d. (ILLUS.) ............ **575**
**Steuben-signed,** six-light, designed by Oscar Bach, a gilt-bronze framework w/a domed ceiling cap suspending five chains composed of metal rings alternating w/long gold iridescent glass waisted tubes, four outer chains suspending a wide pierced metal ring cast w/round scrolls enclosing different designs including birds, squirrels & flowers, the ring mounted w/five downcurved short arms each suspending a bell-shaped ribbed iridescent gold Steuben shade, a central chain suspending a sixth matching shade, each shade 6 x 6" (ILLUS. top next page)..................................................... **12,800**

### Unique Steuben Glass Chandelier

**Tiffany-signed,** "Black-eyed Susan," a 29" d. sharply tapering open-topped leaded glass shade composed of large swirled pale yellow & shaded dark gold & brown blossoms above dark green, mottled green & pale yellow leaves & stems, dark amber narrow border band w/a finely beaded metal edging, suspended from long chains.................................................. **64,000**

### Tiffany Daffodil Chandelier

**Tiffany-signed,** "Daffodil," a wide leaded glass inverted dome shape, composed of two amber-brown border bands, clusters of mottled yellow daffodils & bluish green spiked leaves on an amber fractured glass ground, closed center w/leaded symmetical circle, the interior fitted w/four hooks, circlet & hooks later added by Tiffany Studios, metal rim tags impressed "Tiffany Studios - New York - 144...," all suspended from a patinated metal ceiling mount w/four chains, shade 16" d., drop 21" (ILLUS.) ........................... **32,200**

### Fine Tiffany "Moorish" Chandelier

**Tiffany-signed,** bronze & glass "Moorish" style, an arched bronze ceiling mount supports elaborate twisted wire double ring suspending bronze beading, decorative balls & six sockets w/gold iridescent ribbed bell-form Favrile glass shades w/a large triple-bulbed matching central shade, marked "L.C. Tiffany Favrile" at rim, adjustable, 30" h. (ILLUS.) ................. **18,400**

### Tiffany Five-light Chandelier

**Tiffany-signed,** five-light, a bronze domed ceiling plate suspending a long slender reeded shaft to a large ball issuing five downturned arms each ending in a socket w/a ribbed tulip-shaped gold iridescent signed shade, 16" w., 34" h. (ILLUS.) ........ **9,775**

**Tin,** six-light, a round flat band fitted w/six candle cups w/drip trays suspended from three chains of linked metal rods joined to a small top disk, 19th c., 26" h. (wear)... **1,725**

*Ornate Victorian Cast-iron Chandelier*

**Victorian,** cast iron, four-light, a tall central bar shaft flanked by four long tapering scroll-pierced flanges tapering down to upturned flat arms ending in pierced cup sockets for supporting clear pressed-glass kerosene lamp fonts, complete w/fonts, burners & chimneys, ca. 1875-85 (ILLUS.) ..................................................... **1,100**

*Venetian Art Glass Chandelier*

**Venetian art glass,** the trumpet & baluster-shaped shaft w/thirty-two branching floral & leaf glass armatures in white, yellow, transparent green & clear, one branch missing, minor loss to glass, Italy, mid-20th c., 29" h. (ILLUS.) .................................... **863**

*Williamson & Co. Chandelier*

**Williamson & Co.,** three bell-form leaded glass shades w/opalescent white granite ovals surrounded by tannish amber segments centering green slag shell-form designs at the border, suspended from curved arms joining a central bronzed metal leaf-cast & scroll-trimmed cup suspended from a long cylindrical shaft, adjustable, R. Williamson & Co., Chicago, early 20th c., shades 5" d. (ILLUS.)........... **2,875**

**Wood & tin,** twelve-light, country-style, a slender central ring- and rod-turned shaft issuing twelve slender iron wire arched & upturned arms each supporting a tiny candle cup w/crimped edges, 20th c., 24" h. ................................................................. **550**

**Wrought iron,** eight-light, a central shaft w/hook at each end w/eight curved arms

*Unique Venetian Glass Chandelier*

**Venetian glass,** eight-light, in green & white glass w/gold inclusions, the knopped central standard surrounded by delicate leaves & scrolls set w/applied swans, the long down-turned lily-form socket arms w/applied clear sawtooth edging, early 20th c., 48" d., 42" h. (ILLUS.).................... **3,163**

which extend to form candle sockets, American, early 19th c., 23" d., drop 25" .............................................................. **2,875**

**Wrought iron,** six-light, a wide central ring w/six incurved scrolled iron drops & six S-scroll iron bar arms around the top each ending in a candle socket, three shaped short iron bars for the three hanging chains, blacksmith-made, probably 19th c., 22 1/2" d., overall 38" h. ............................ **770**

# Lanterns

**Barn candle lantern,** punched tin & glass, a pierced pyramidal cap w/large ring strap handle above a tin framework enclosing panes of glass, one side a door & each side fitted w/wire guards, candle socket inside, 19th c., 11 1/2" h. plus handle (some resoldering on wire guards) .......................................................... **$110**

**Barn candle lantern,** wood & glass, an upright mortised wood framework w/corner posts, four glass panels, tin top & wire bail handle, 10" h. (one pane cracked) ........ **275**

**Barn candle lantern,** wood & glass, an upright mortised wood framework w/corner posts mortised through top & base & held w/pegs, tin candle socket & lined air hole in top, wire hinges, latch & handle, 9 3/4" h. plus handle (minor edge damage & burned hole in top) .............................. **523**

**Barn lantern,** oak or ash & pine w/glass, the upright pegged wooden framework enclosing glass sides & door, original dark finish, wire bail handle & wrought-iron hardware, early, 14 1/2" h. ............................ **578**

**Barn lantern,** pierced tin & blown glass, a metal frame w/the top pierced w/a star & diamond design, the base separates from the removable oil font, mid-19th c., 14 3/4" h. (very minor dents)....................... **1,955**

*Primitive Wood & Glass Barn Lantern*

**Barn lantern,** pine & glass, an upright dark-stained pine frame, enclosed glass sides

& door, chamfered corners on frame, wire bail handle, copper deflector at top, various nails including some wire, crack in door glass, splits in frame, late, 14" h. (ILLUS.)............................................................ **248**

*Painted Tin & Glass Barn Lantern*

**Barn lantern,** tin & glass, triangular, two glass panels, one hinged, in a painted tin frame w/angled top & arched heat vent w/a wire bail handle w/wooden grip, hanging loops on the back, interior fitted w/a glass kerosene lamp & chimney, painted brown w/black trim, mid-19th c., no reflector, one hanging loop missing, corrosion & paint wear, 19" h. (ILLUS.) ........ **345**

**Barn lantern,** painted pine & glass, a pine frame w/old greenish paint enclosing a wooden door & three panes of glass, reputtied glazer's bevel w/brownish red paint, 14 1/2" h. ............................................. **303**

**Bicycle lantern,** kerosene-type, nickel-plated brass w/red & green jewels, marked "Jim Dandy," made by The Plume & Atwood Mfg. Co., patent-dated 1896 .............. **154**

**Bicycle lantern,** miniature, painted tin, a cylindrical dark brown japanned tin case w/a pointed vented top & wire loops at the back, fitted on the front w/revolving red & green interior lenses, late 19th - early 20th c., 4 3/4" h. .................................... **165**

**Bicycle lantern,** carbide-type, brass w/worn nickel plate, large round clear front lens on square form w/covered top vent opening, marked "Lucas, Silver King, Birmingham," England, late 19th - early 20th c., 5" h. ............................................. **94**

**Candle lantern,** painted pine, cherry & glass, the upright rectangular dovetailed frame w/chamfered & pierced top & wrought-iron handle above four scratch-beaded sides w/diamond glazed & pierced panels, one panel forming a hinged door opening to a candle socket & pierced tin reflector, original bluish green paint, New England, early 19th c. ............. **25,300**

Candle lantern, pierced tin Paul Revere-type, cylindrical w/hinged doors & conical top w/ring strap handle, pierced designs w/the initials "N.A." in the door, 13 1/2" h. plus handle (some battering & repair) .......... **303**

*Two Old Candle Lanterns*

Candle lantern, punched tin Paul Revere-style, cylindrical w/curved hinged door & conical top w/vent holes & a ring strap handle, pierced overall w/a star & diamond design & the punched inscription "P.O. More, Bellfontaine,O.," rusted finish, 13 1/4" h. plus handle (ILLUS. right) ..................................................... **633**

*Paul Revere-type Tin Lantern*

Candle lantern, punched-tin Paul Revere-style, cylindrical w/a pierced design of circles & quarter arcs, a hinged door on the side, a tall conical cap w/pierced design & vent holes, large strap ring handle at top, 19th c. (ILLUS.).................................... **110**

Candle lantern, punched-tin Paul Revere-style, cylindrical w/a pierced design circles & rays on the hinged door, overall piercing around the sides, a tall conical cap w/pierced design & vent holes, large strap ring handle at top, 19th c. (light pitting overall, a small hole)................. **275**

Candle lantern, sheet copper, Arts & Crafts style, an upright square form w/one side forming a hinged door, each side pierced through w/banded designs w/three starbursts in vertical allignment, each centered by a colored glass jewel, a low pointed four-sided top, original dark patina, Bradley & Hubbard, early 20th c., stamped mark, 7" sq., 12" h........................... **385**

Candle lantern, tin & glass, a small cylindrical tin font base supporting a large round clear blown glass globe w/a cylindrical cap & conical pierced top w/ring strap handle, traces of old dark japanning w/light rust, 10" h. plus handle (candle socket replaces font)...................................... **385**

Candle lantern, tin & glass, a pyramidal tin cap pierced w/a star & rayed arch design below the large ring strap handle, tin frame & base enclosing glass sides w/one forming the door opening to a candle socket, marked "Parker's Patent 1859, Proctor'sville, Vt.," 7 1/2" h. plus handle................................................................. **358**

*Early Patented Candle Lantern*

Candle lantern, tin & glass, a tin framework w/glass sides & door w/wire protectors, pyramidal top pierced w/stars & circles, large strap ring handle, stamped mark "Parker's Patent - 1855 - Proctersville, VT," mid-19th c., 15 3/4" h. (ILLUS.)............. **523**

Candle lantern, tin & glass, hexagonal, tall upright form w/six vertical glass panels each w/vertical wire guards & two forming the door, tall crimped conical vented cap w/ring handle, single candle socket inside, New England, early 19th c., 15 1/2" h. (minor corrosion, electrified) ........ **805**

**Candle lantern,** tin & glass, upright rectangular form w/tin frame w/four glass sides, one forming sliding door, pyramidal top w/a punched design & large ring handle, wire loop side protectors, 12 1/2" h. plus ring handle (one old glass panel) .................. **165**

**Candle lantern,** tin & glass, upright square dark tin framework w/four glass sides, one forming a hinged door w/cross-form wire guard, flat top w/cylindrical capped vent cover w/shaped wire swing bail handle, old glass, some soldered repair, 13 1/2" h. plus handle (ILLUS. on previous page left w/Paul Revere-style) ............... **358**

**Candle lantern,** tin, hanging-type, eight-sided tapered glass globe w/a tin font, base & top, mushroom top w/ring handle, top & base w/star & diamond-shaped piercings, 10" h. plus ring handle (brass burner appears to be old replacement) ......... **330**

**Candle lantern,** tin, hanging-type, three glass panels w/a tin sliding back panel, mushroom top w/ring handle, 19th c., 14 1/2" h. (corrosion, one broken glass panel) ................................................................. **115**

**Candle lantern,** tin, upright square form w/the sides composed of vertical tin strips originally enclosing three panes of glass, square tin base & top w/pierced conical cap & large ring handle, 19th c. (glass missing) ...................................... **165**

**Candle lantern,** tin w/glass sides, domed top w/two vents, punched leaf & star designs & ornate pierced top, double fluted candle sockets w/snuffer (now attached to base), one side panel opens, yellow repaint w/red striping, 4 3/4 x 9 1/8", 15 3/4" h. (minor wear to paint) ..................... **358**

**Candle lantern,** tin w/three glass sides w/wire guards, pointed top w/punched star design & ring handle, back marked "Parker's Patent, Boston, 1853," 11" h. plus ring handle ..................................... **385**

**Candle lantern,** wood & glass, a primitive wooden framework w/corner posts through the top, wire bail handle & strap heat shield across the top, glass sides & a glazed door opening to a candle socket, 19th c., 9 1/2" h. ................................. **413**

**Candle lantern,** wood & glass, the upright hard- and softwood square frame w/four panes of reputtied glass, one side a hinged door, top vent hole & wire bail handle, traces of red, 14" h. (age cracks & worm holes) ...................................... **193**

**Candle lantern,** tin & glass, a semi-circular tin frame w/a flat glass front & tin back door, a pyramidal top w/punched circle designs, small loop handle, cylindrical tin candle socket, 19th c., 12 1/4" h. plus handle (light rust) ............................ **380**

**Candle lantern,** tin & glass, triangular form w/two glass sides w/wire guards, conical pierced cap w/ring handle, 19th c., 12 1/2" h. plus handle ..................... **358**

*Bronze & Glass Ceiling Lantern*

**Ceiling lanterns,** patinated bronze & engraved glass, cylindrical-form, surmounted by crown of five foliate scroll supports w/a mark terminal above a curved clear glass pane engraved w/central star within a stylized floral border, vertical supports cast w/pendant husks, golden brown patina, 28 1/2" h., pr. (ILLUS. of one) ................................................................. **3,162**

**Floor lantern,** Gothic Revival, enameled green metal, hexagonal, w/openwork panels of Gothic arches & foliage, flared feet, 20th c., 34" h. .......................................... **374**

**Fluid lantern,** blown glass & tin, a short cylindrical tin font w/brass collar below the squatty onion-form clear glass globe topped by a cylindrical top w/pointed cap & large ring handle, the top w/star & diamond pierced designs, old pitted finish, mid-19th c., 10" h. plus handle ...................... **440**

**Fluid lantern,** tin & glass, a short cylindrical tin font supporting a cobalt blue blown glass ovoid globe topped by a cylindrical cap w/pierced design air vents & wire bail handle, 19th c., 10 1/2" h. (small chips on top edge of cap, brass burner replaced) ....... **578**

**Footman's lantern,** wood & glass, a rectangular wood-framed box-form w/a lift-top w/arched bail handle, three sides w/glass pane w/wire guards, back w/punched tin plate, frame painted dark green w/h.p. red border designs & porcelain buttons, top w/yellow stenciled label "H.B. Ost... Manufacturer, Angola, N.Y....," inside of top w/floral felt panel, hook damaged, minor wear, 19th c., 5 1/4 x 7 3/4", 6 1/4" h. plus handle (ILLUS. top next page) ...................................... **220**

*Early Footman's Lantern*

**Hall lantern,** Arts & Crafts style, slag glass, a slightly tapering upright square form w/a wide four-sided tapering top w/electric fitting, the sides composed of narrow & slightly wider stripes of varied caramel slag glass, the sides of the top w/light caramel slag panels, fitted in a metal framework w/worn patina, early 20th c., 8" w., 13" h.......................................................... **880**

*Tiffany Turtleback Tile Lantern*

**Hall lantern,** bronze & glass, a squared Arts & Crafts bronze frame set w/four amber iridescent turtleback tiles in the sides & leaded panels in the base, scroll hooks at top corners & hanging bars & chain, L.C.Tiffany, early 20th c. (ILLUS.)............. **20,900**

*Louis XV-style Hall Lantern*

**Hall lantern,** gilt-bronze, four-light, Louis XV-style, a rounded cylindrical gilt-bronze frame enclosing three clear glass curved panels, the frame decorated w/a top foliate-scrolled band & hung w/floral festoons topped by four tall arched & leaf-scrolled supports, a pierced metal gallery band around the bottom, France, 19th c., 34" h. (ILLUS.) ................................. **8,625**

*Fine Glass & Brass Hall Lantern*

**Hall lantern,** glass & pressed gilt brass, hexagonal form w/each glass panel wheel-cut & acid-etched w/alternating Gothic arches & large diamond & dot designs, an ornate stamped crown crest band w/six leafy scroll hanging hooks, a round stamped base cap w/drop finial, very minor chips, missing smoke bell, mid-19th c., 15 1/4" h. (ILLUS.) .................. **2,530**

*Arts & Crafts Hall Lantern*

**Hall lantern,** oak & glass, Arts & Crafts style, a carved oak four-sided frame w/peaked top, set w/panels of leaded amber slag glass within arched windows, suspended by a heavy iron link chain, early 20th c., panels loose, some glass cracked, nick in wood, 20" w., 30" h. (ILLUS.) ......................................................... **1,265**

*William IV-style Hall Lantern*

**Hall lantern,** William IV-style, gilt-bronze & glass, hexagonal w/each arched clear glass panel cut w/a central starburst, the ornate reeded framework w/scroll-cast arched panel tops & base scrolls at each corner, six upper scroll arms join at the top of the central reeded shaft, England, 19th c., 18" w., 30" h. (ILLUS.) .................. **2,875**

**Hall lanterns,** brass, four-light, Georgian-style, round w/glazed panels between the brass uprights, one panel a hinged door, the upper rim w/beaded swags suspended from ribbons, undulating braces from the top rim to the center shaft which drops down into the center & curves up to end in candle sockets, England, 12 1/2" d., 14 3/4" h., pr. (electrified) ......... **4,025**

**Hanging lantern,** ormolu, Louis XVI-style, squared metal framework w/gently tapering sides w/glass panels, four angled small brackets & a ball drop at the base, the upper corners of the frame decorated w/bold acanthus scrolls, stepped slender S-scroll brackets from the top corners to the ball at the top of the center shaft topped by a plume cluster finial, 20 1/2" w., 4' 6" h. (electrified) .................... **6,900**

*Early Signed Kerosene Lantern*

**Kerosene lantern,** brass & glass, a tall clear cylindrical glass globe topped by a pierced cylindrical brass cap w/pierced air holes & a domed top w/a swing strap handle, the base w/a short cylindrical font & burner on a round foot, bottom labeled "N.E. Glass Co. Patented Oct. 24, 1854," split in foot, top dented, 16 1/2" h. plus handle (ILLUS.) .............................................. **330**

**Kerosene lantern,** bull's-eye style, japanned tin & glass, cylindrical w/sliding door at the back opposite the clear thick glass convex hinged front lens, tiered pointed & ruffled vented top, double wire handles & belt clip, late 19th - early 20th c., 7 1/2" h. (wear) .......................................... **248**

**Kerosene lantern,** tin, brass & glass, a round slightly domed foot centered by a short cylindrical font w/air holes around the top & fitted w/a brass double spout burner, clear glass pear-shaped globe within wire cage, cylindrical cap w/pierced air holes & a wire bail handle, removed base marked "Pat. Sep. 14. 78," late 19th c., 9 1/2" h. (some resoldering)........................................... **83**

*Rare Early Nautical Lantern*

**Nautical lantern,** tin & glass, a clear glass hexagonal fixed globe in the Beaded Double Bull's-eye patt. fitted w/a cylindrical pierced tin top w/conical cap & ring strap handle, a pierced short cylindrical font base, mid-19th c., corrosion, restoration, 12" h. (ILLUS.) ..................................... **2,300**

**Signal lantern,** tin & glass, a short cylindrical base w/font & tall pierced cylindrical top w/conical cap & large loop handle, fitted w/a blown cranberry glass globe engraved "C.R.R., first half 19th c., 12 1/2" h. plus handle (replaced brass font w/burner) ............................................. **1,100**

**Skater's lantern,** brass, tin & glass, a domed & ringed font base supporting a round burner fitted w/an emerald green glass baluster-form globe, pierced domed cap w/a wire bail handle, 7" h............ **468**

**Skater's lantern,** tin & glass, a cobalt blue glass pear-shaped globe fitted w/a pierced tin domed cap w/wire bail handle, on a tin burner ring on a domed tin font base, late 19th - early 20th c., 6 3/4" h. ........ **275**

**Skater's lantern,** tin & glass, a domed font base supporting a round burner fitted w/a clear pressed glass globe, pierced domed cap w/a wire bail handle, "Perko Wonder Junior," 6 7/8" h. plus handle............ **72**

*Tin & Glass Skater's Lanterns*

**Skater's lantern,** tin & glass, a pierced domed tin cap w/bail handle & tin font base support a light green globe, 6 5/8" h. (ILLUS. center)................................. **275**

**Skater's lantern,** tin & glass, a pierced domed tin cap w/bail handle & tin font base support a cornflower blue glass globe, 7 1/8" h. (ILLUS. right, with other colored globes below)..................................... **303**

**Skater's lantern,** tin & glass, a pierced domed tin cap w/bail handle & tin font base support an aqua globe, 6 1/4" h. (ILLUS. right)..................................... **303**

**Skater's lantern,** tin & glass, a pierced domed tin cap w/bail handle & tin font base support an electric blue glass globe, tin w/black & gold designs, 7" h. (ILLUS. left) ..................................... **330**

*Skater's Lanterns with Colored Globes*

**Skater's lantern,** tin & glass, a pierced domed tin cap w/bail handle & tin font base support an emerald green glass globe, 6 1/2" h. (ILLUS. left)........................... **440**

**Skater's lantern,** tin & glass, a pierced domed tin cap w/bail handle & tin font base support an amethyst glass globe, 7" h. (ILLUS. center with other colored globes)............................................................. 523

**Skater's lantern,** tin & glass, a ringed & domed tin font base w/side handle & ring support for the clear pressed glass tapering shade w/a domed pierced cap & swing wire bail handle, 7" h. ........................... 83

**Skater's lantern,** tin & glass, pierced domed cap & domed font base, wire bail handle, peacock green glass globe, traces of red paint on tin, 7 3/8" h. (bail handle replaced)..................................................... 358

**Skater's lantern,** brass & glass, tapering round brass font base & domed, pierced brass cap w/wire bail handle, clear glass globe marked "Perko Wonder Junior," polished, early 20th c., 6 3/4" h. (small split in brass cap) ......................................... 160

**Skater's lantern,** tin & glass, round base w/burner & round pierced domed vented top w/wire bail handle, clear glass globe, marked "Dietz Sport," 7 3/4" h. ..................... 193

**Traveler's lantern,** tole & glass, square scalloped frame, collapsible w/mica panels, brown japanning w/yellow stenciling & label "Minor's Patent, Jan 24th 1865," 5 1/8" h. (minor wear)..................................... 385

**Wall lanterns,** embossed copper & slag glass, Arts & Crafts style, tall square designed w/a pagoda-form metal top, the side panels composed of cut & embossed metal scenes of New York City enclosing striated opalescent glass panels in shades of green, red & white, suspended from a scrolling bracket & small chains, unsigned, ca. 1915, 9 1/2" h., pr. .................................................................. 1,804

*Brass Whale Oil Lantern*

**Whale oil lantern,** brass, a squared metal font base below the upright square framework enclosing four beveled clear glass panels, one forming a hinged door, a domed metal top w/mushroom-form vent cap, wire bail handle w/turned wood grip, fitted w/unusual whale oil burner, damage & splits to vent cap, 9 1/4" h. plus handle (ILLUS.) ....................................... 110

*Beehive Pattern Whale Oil Lantern*

**Whale oil lantern,** glass & tin, a clear mold-blown Beehive patt. glass globe fitted w/a pierced cylindrical top w/conical cap & ring strap handle, pierced cylindrical font base w/flared round foot, mid-19th c., paint loss, minor corrosion, 12 1/2" h. (ILLUS.)......................................................... 1,035

**Whale oil lantern,** tin & glass, a round tin base w/flared foot supporting the clear blown glass pear-shaped globe, cylindrical cap w/conical top w/pierced designs & large ring handle, removable font w/whale oil burner, worn original brown japanning, probably New England Glass Co., first half 19th c., 11" h. plus handle ....... 358

**Whale oil lantern,** tin & glass, a short cylindrical tin font w/flattened flaring foot supporting a single wick burner enclosed by a clear blown glass squatty onion-form globe within a wire guard, the cylindrical cap pierced w/vent holes below the conical top w/strap ring handle, 19th c., 9" h. plus handle (some resoldering)..................... 385

**Whale oil lantern,** glass & tin, a cylindrical pierced tin top w/a conical cap & wide hanging ring, a clear blown ball globe above a low pierced cylindrical tin base, worn black paint, rust on base, no font or burner, 8 1/2" h. plus ring handle .................. 182

**Whale oil lantern,** glass & tin, the cylindrical top w/pierced star & diamond designs below the conical cap & wire loop handle, paneled glass tapering sides above a removable tin font w/whale oil burner, probably by the New England Glass Co., traces of black paint, 11" h. plus handle (wire handle a replacement, short glass crack under tin, base dented & damaged) ............. 154

**Whale oil lantern,** tin & glass, a pierced cylindrical top w/a conical cap & wide ring handle above the ovoid blown cobalt blue globe above a short pierced cylindrical base w/a flared & slightly domed foot, worn brown japanning, removable whale oil font, probably New England Glass Co., 11 1/2" h. plus handle (font chips resoldered) ......................................................... 495

# Shades

*Lime Green Optic Ribbed Shade*

**Art glass,** flora-form, lime green optic ribbed form w/widely flaring ruffled rim, enameled w/large pink & white stylized blossoms & aqua & white leaves on thin white branches, 6 1/4" d., 5 1/2" h. (ILLUS.) ....................................................... $145

**Art glass,** long tapered ruffled bell-form w/intricate gold & green Zipper patt. gold iridescent interior, attributed to Fostoria, 8" h. ................................................................ 288

*Acid-etched & Enameled Shade*

**Art glass,** tulip-shaped w/flaring ruffled rim, a frosted acid cut-back overall design w/the smooth areas painted as deep maroon & yellow blossoms on gold-trimmed leaves & stems, dark green border band, 7" d., 5 1/2" h. (ILLUS.) .................................... 225

**Art glass,** wide squatty bulbous form w/closed pointed top, dark creamy wide ribs alternating w/pale yellow translucent panels, unmarked, probably Fry, 8" d., pr. ...................................................................... 605

**Art glass,** slender hexagonal bell-form, mottled & streaked iridescent green & amber glass, 5 3/4" h., set of 4 (chips) ........ 198

**Ball shade,** spherical pink cased glass, decorated w/a large gilt rampant lion & fleur-de-lis designs, possibly Consolidated Lamp & Glass Company, ca. 1900, 8" h. ....... 440

**Bigelow, Kennard-signed,** 21 3/4" d. domical leaded glass shade in a rose design, irregular border, overall trailing yellow & amber rippled glass roses w/striated green leaves on a blue slag ground, embossed metal rim tag "Bigelow Kennard Boston," early 20th c. (ILLUS. at bottom of page) ...................................................... 14,950

*Fine Bigelow, Kennard Shade*

*Rare Bigelow, Kennard Leaded Shade*

**Bigelow, Kennard-signed,** domical leaded glass shade composed of rose blossoms in reddish orange undulating glass segments, rippled green leaves within a striated green & red ground, irregular border, two metal rim tags, one impressed "Bigelow Studios," the other "Bigelow, Kennard & Co., Boston," early 20th c., some cracked segments, 21 1/2" d., 9 1/4" h. (ILLUS. on previous page) ........ **20,700**

**Bigelow, Kennard-signed,** leaded glass, a broad parasol form composed of thirty-two bluish green tapering rectangular narrow panels in the Prairie School manner, tagged at the rim "Bigelow Kennard Boston," early 20th c., 24 1/2" d., 5 1/4" h. (small split in metal rim) ............... **1,610**

**Bigelow, Kennard-signed,** large conical leaded glass shade w/white opalescent brickwork segments above & below a border belt of repeating reddish amber ripple glass pine cones & shaded green needles w/yellow border glass, rim tag signed "Bigelow Kennard Boston Studios," four border glass segments broken out, early 20th c., 22" d., 9 1/2" h. ............. **2,760**

**Bohemian,** blown trumpet-form w/a gold iridescent papillon surface w/green & red raised spots & vertical stripes, attributed to Loetz, 6" h. ................................................. **431**

*Decorated Cranberry Glass Shade*

**Cranberry glass,** flora-form, optic-ribbed w/a widely flaring ruffled rim, decorated around the middle w/a gold & white painted swag & tassel band, 7" d., 5 1/2" h. (ILLUS.) ................................................ **195**

*Ornate Pink Cased Hall Lamp Shade*

**Hall lamp shade,** large ovoid form w/a wide flared top rim, cased glass in light pink shading down to dark pink, a molded blown design of overall scales w/a band of acanthus leaves around the top & scrolls & medallions around the bottom, 4 1/4 x 6", 11" h. (ILLUS.) ............................... **165**

**Handel,** leaded glass, domical top above a wide straight skirt, composed of segments forming pink & amber flowers on green leafy vines against a ground of green & white striated tiles, unsigned, ca. 1905, 24" d. ................................................... **8,625**

**Handel-signed,** 20" d. umbrella-form nine-paneled shade w/bent slag glass panels in striated tones of rose & yellow above a border band of green slag glass, the upper panels w/a patinated overlay of tropical trees, the border band w/undulated overlay design, scalloped rim, joints reinforced, early 20th c. (ILLUS. below) .......... **7,475**

*Handel Bent Panel Slag Glass Shade*

*Handel Leaded Glass Shade*

*Large Leaded Glass Handel Shade*

**Handel-signed,** 23" w. squared domical leaded glass shade, shaped edges, decorated around the rim & corners w/clusters of yellow, white, amber & pink blossoms w/green leaves, the sides w/brown trellis reserved against a teal blue ground, molded "Handel," ca. 1910 (ILLUS.) ....................................... **12,650**

**Handel-signed,** domed acid-etched form in shaded amber, decorated w/bursting fireworks, signed in enamel "HANDEL 5658," ca. 1910, 14" d.................................. **1,035**

**Handel-signed,** domical leaded glass shade composed of red flowers on a green ground, irregular border, 24" d. ........ **5,750**

**Handel-signed,** ball-form shade w/iridescent orange interior, the exterior h.p. w/a scenic landscape w/two birds in flight, rim signed "Handel 7004," base hole drilled, some rim chips under edge, 3 1/8" d., 6" h. ............................................. **1,495**

**Handel-signed,** 22 1/2" d. domical leaded glass shade composed of caramel & white striated glass tiles & a border of pale pink & pale green stylized flowers, ca. 1910 (ILLUS. at top of page) ..................................................... **1,150**

**Handel-signed,** massive octagonal conical leaded glass shade composed of leaded amber slag & tan panels geometrically arranged w/greenish amber rippled ladderwork, the flat drop apron decorated by bronzed metal scenic tree framework h.p.

to enhance the forest design, "Handel" tag impressed on the side, replaced electrical mounts, 27 1/2" w. ............................. **1,840**

*Cranberry Hobnail Hanging Shade*

**Hanging parlor lamp shade,** high domed form w/an open top, mold-blown cranberry Hobnail patt.,10" d. base, 4 1/2" h. (ILLUS.)............................................................. **440**

**Leaded glass,** 18" d. domical shade w/oblong panels of rectangular amber slag glass enclosed by four bands flaring at the rim to form pairs of tulips in shades of amber & pink w/green & amber slag trim, irregular bottom rim, metal cap w/hanging ring & ceiling escutcheon, early 20th c. ............................................................. **385**

*Large Leaded Glass Shade*

**Leaded glass,** 21 1/2" d. domical shade composed of blocks of mottled butterscotch & creamy slag glass w/a border of butterscotch Xs, early 20th c. (ILLUS.) ...... **1,150**

*High-quality Large Leaded Shade*

**Leaded glass,** 22 1/2" d. domical leaded glass w/a brown slag ground & colored floral border band in rose & yellow, early 20th c. ............ **880**

**Leaded glass,** wide domical open-topped shade composed of oblong panels of graduated creamy yellow glass segments between scrolls in mottled shades of blues, greens & browns w/large green & yellow shell designs acround the scalloped lower border, possibly by Duffner & Kimberly, 24" d. (ILLUS. above) ................ **6,720**

**Leaded glass,** 16" d. domical shade composed of rose pink slag glass blocks w/a lower band of vining green acorn-shaped leaves, attributed to Bigelow & Kennard, areas of restoration, early 20th c. ............. **1,150**

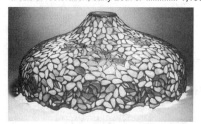

*Fine Leaded Glass Shade*

**Leaded glass,** wide parasol-shaped open-topped shade w/dropped apron & undulating rim, composed of a background of cascading mosaic segments in shades of pale mauve, pink & dichronic glass, interspersed w/rose blossoms, rose blossom & bud border executed in striated reds & pinks, some w/green & orange undertones, green border segments, w/metal mounts, needs rewiring, some cracked segments, early 20th c., 22" d. (ILLUS.).... **1,725**

**Leaded glass,** wide domical shade composed of a radiating pattern of light turquoise blue slag glass above a wide intricately leaded drop apron of turquoise blue & amber fleur-de-lis & foliate designs on a deep maroon & navy blue striated ground, attributed to Duffner and Kimberly, early 20th c., few cracked segments, 22 1/2" d. (ILLUS. at bottom of page).............. **9,775**

**Leaded glass,** conical form composed of glass sections forming floral garlands on a striated amber slag ground w/a blue & green border w/pink jeweled flowers, early 20th c., 23" d. ......................................... **1,035**

**Leaded glass,** 24 1/2" d. domical shade w/a wide floral border of glass arranged as tulips in green & clouds of pink, the upper portion formed by graduating small

*Leaded Shade with Ornate Border*

blocks of mottled amber & white, irregular edge border, metal ring at top opening, early 20th c. ............................................. **825**

**Leaded glass,** narrow-topped umbrella-shaped shade w/dropped apron, composed of four bright red starburst blossom designs w/yellow disks on green stems, all arranged on green slag background segments, matching design on the apron, opening 3" d., 17 1/2" d. (some restoration to inside leading) ............. **633**

**Lotton-signed,** slender cylindrical form w/ruffled flaring rim, gold w/pink & platinum iridescent highlights, Charles Lotton, signed & dated "1975," 4 1/2" h., set of 3 ..................................................................... **176**

**Lustre Art-signed,** bell-form, amber lustre glass w/five pulled white feathers on an iridescent gold ground, ca. 1920, each signed "Lustre Art," 2 1/2" d., 5" h., pr. .......... **403**

**Lustre Art-signed,** elongated blossom-form w/angled shoulder, sixteen lighted molded ribs, plain opal exterior, iridescent gold interior, rims marked "Lustre Art," 2 1/4" d., 5 1/4" h., set of 3 ................... **230**

**Mother-of-pearl satin,** ribbed tulip-form w/flaring ruffled & crimped rim, shaded yellow satin exterior, white interior, 8" d., 5" h. .................................................................. **295**

**Opalescent glass,** heavenly blue shaded to white opalescent in a swirled design, deeply crimped & ruffled rim, peg lamp-type, 5 1/2" d., 4 1/4" h., pr. ............................ **245**

**Pairpoint,** miniature "Puffy" type, tapering form w/open top, molded & painted w/pansies in purple, red, yellow & brown w/green leaves, against an aqua ground, apparently unmarked, some paint loss, ca. 1920, 5 1/4" d., pr. (ILLUS. below) .......................................................... **2,990**

**Pairpoint,** candle lamp-type, flared shape w/'chipped ice' finish, exterior enamel-decorated w/leafy birch trees over an interior painted yellow ground, metal mounts, early 20th c., 9" h., pr. (stress cracks to one mount) ..................................... **403**

**Pairpoint candleshades,** flared colorless glass chimney shades w/'chipped ice' surface & scenic decoration, mounted to gilt metal inserts for sconces or candlesticks, stamped "patented July 19, 1901 The Pairpoint Corp" inside, 9" h. ................... **575**

*Puffy Pairpoint Pisa Shade*

**Pairpoint-signed,** 16" w. "Puffy" paneled 'Pisa' shade, reverse-painted in the panels w/an overall design of deep red & pink rose blossoms & green leaves trimmed w/a gold scrolling border, the low domed closed top w/a rayed band design, black border bands, minor chips, signed (ILLUS.) ...................................................... **5,175**

*Pink Opalescent Decorated Shade*

**Pink opalescent,** tulip-form blown shade in Inverted Thumbprint patt. w/crimped & ruffled rim & long collar, enameled w/gold & silver leaves & blue & white blossoms, late 19th c., 4 7/8" d., 5" h. (ILLUS.) ............. **165**

**Quezal-signed,** a wide ruffled bottom opening & wide squatty bulbous rim tapering sharply to a ringed fitted neck, creamy white exterior w/gold pulled-feather decoration, gold iridescent interior, signed, 5" h., pr. ................................................................. **605**

*Miniature Puffy Pairpoint Shades*

*Signed Quezal Shade*

**Quezal-signed,** elongated tulip-form ribbed shade in overall gold iridescence, incised signature, 6" h. (ILLUS.) ................................. **286**

**Quezal-signed,** swelled long blossom-form w/flaring scalloped rim, gold & green pulled feather decoration on an iridescent gold ground, white interior ..................... **138**

*Quezal Bell-form Shade*

**Quezal-signed,** tall ribbed bell-form w/overall gold iridescence w/magenta highlights, 5 1/4" h., pr. (ILLUS. of one) .............. **275**

**Quezal-signed,** trumpet-form, gold iridescent ground w/pulled feather design outlined in green, pr. ....................,........................ **440**

*Quezal Tulip-shaped Shades*

**Quezal-signed,** wide tulip-shaped shade w/gently flared & ruffled rim, sixteen lightly molded ribs, overall gold iridescence, signed on base flange, 5 1/4" h., pr. (ILLUS.) .............................................................. **330**

**Quezal-signed,** ribbed morning glory shape, iridescent white exterior w/a golden rick-rack band, iridescent gold interior, 5" h. ...................................................................... **248**

**Quezal-signed,** elongated tulip-form, the exterior w/five green pulled feathers on a white ground, the interior w/gold iridescence, signed on rims, 2 1/4" d., 5" h., set of 3 ................................................................ **460**

**Quezal-signed,** bulbous baluster-form w/a flaring slightly ruffled rim, wide stripes of iridescent gold in a scale-like pattern alternating w/thin opal white stripes, iridescent gold interior, 5 1/4" h., pr. ..................... **550**

**Quezal-signed,** tall trumpet-form w/flattened flaring & scalloped rim, applied random gold threading over iridescent gold & green heart leaf design, gold iridescent interior, 5 1/2" h., pr...................... **550**

**Quezal-signed,** bell-form w/a paneled Calcite white exterior & a gold iridescent interior, signed, 5 3/4" h.................................. **121**

**Quezal-signed,** bulbous mushroom cap shape in cased opal to amber w/four large pulled & hooked feathers in lime green around the exterior against fine gold iridescence, signed incised curved rim, smoothed rim chip, 12 1/2" d., 5 3/4" h. ................................................. **1,380**

**Quezal-signed,** ribbed w/flared rims, golden iridescence, pr., 6" h................................. **660**

**Quezal-signed,** elongated ovoid form w/a flat rim, slightly ribbed sides, overall gold iridescence, 6 1/8" h. (pinpoint flakes on bottom edge) ..................................................... **165**

**Quezal-signed,** trumpet-form, gold pulled feather design & green outlined in white, 6 1/4" h.................................................................. **165**

**Quezel-signed,** a hipped opal flaring form w/green & gold leaves on white w/gold threading & a gold iridescent interior, signed on inner rim, 5 1/4" h., set of 5 (minimal thread damage) .............................. **748**

**Quezel-signed,** a swelled cylindrical form w/an upright crimped rim, the exterior w/green & gold pulled-feather design on a creamy white ground, gold iridescent interior, incised signature, 5" h. (small flake on fitter rim)........................................ **138**

**Quezel-signed,** ten-ribbed bell-form w/flared rim, signed on top edge, 4 1/2" h., set of 3............................................ **518**

*Lovely Satin Glass Shade*

**Satin glass,** squatty bulbous tulip-form w/widely flaring ruffled rim, deep rose mother-of-pearl Diamond Quilted patt., white lining, 5 1/4" d., 3 1/2" h. (ILLUS.) ....... **250**
**Steuben-signed,** Intarsia pattern w/Aurene border, brown ................................................ **675**
**Steuben-signed,** ribbed tulip-form in overall gold iridescent Aurene, signed, 5" h., pr. (rim rubs & pinpoints) ............................. **330**
**Steuben-signed,** tapering cylindrical form w/the rim opening band narrower than the body, Ivrene w/slight iridescence & acid-etched w/a medallion & swag design, 3 1/2" d., 4 1/2" h. ................................... **86**

*Rare Green Aurene Steuben Shades*

**Steuben-signed,** globe-type, a bulbous ovoid form w/pointed tip, white Aurene ground decorated w/gold iridescent random loopings & heart-shaped leaves, 6 1/2" h. (ILLUS. below) ................................. **500**
**Steuben-signed,** tall trumpet flower-form w/ten lightly molded ribs, overall gold Aurene iridescence, marked on the rims, 6 1/2" h., set of 4 ............................................. **748**

*Rare Steuben Brown Aurene Shade*

**Steuben-signed,** bell-shaped w/flattened drop rim, the main exterior body in brown Aurene w/random gold iridescent looping, the rim in creamy white Aurene w/random gold looping & leaf-like designs, 5 1/2" h. (ILLUS.) ................................. **1,000**
**Steuben-signed,** ribbed trumpet-form, overall gold Aurene iridescence, 5 1/2" h., pr. ...................................................... **440**
**Steuben-signed,** waisted tulip-shaped w/stepped shoulder, dark green Aurene body w/a silver & amber iridescent flared base band trimmed w/green & white zigzag bands, 5 1/2" h., pr. (ILLUS. top next column) ......................................................... **3,000**

*Steuben Globe Shade*

**Tiffany,** high domical blown shade w/eight pinched ruffles, yellow-tinted opalescent w/a damascene gold iridescent wavy exterior decoration, 10" d. .............................. **3,737**

*Tiffany Crocus Pattern Shade*

*Tiffany Leaded Glass Acorn Shade*

**Tiffany,** "Crocus," 16" d. domical open-topped leaded glass shade composed of large pendent crocus blossoms in orangish amber & green against a striated dark green ground, amber tile border, unsigned (ILLUS. bottom of previous page)............................................................ **10,350**

**Tiffany-signed,** "Acorn" patt., 14" d. domical leaded glass shade composed of mottled green segments w/a band of mottled amber & green acorns, stamped rim tag, early 20th c., 5 3/4" h. (ILLUS. above)................................................ **7,475**

*Tiffany Acorn Pattern Shade*

**Tiffany-signed,** "Acorn," 14" d. domical open-topped leaded glass shade com-posed of radiating tile segments & a center band of acorn-shaped segments in mottled shades of pale green, grey, dark green & amber, rim impressed "Tiffany Studios - New York - 1420 - 21," some cracked segments, early 20th c. (ILLUS.)............................................................ **5,463**

**Tiffany-signed,** conical w/ruffled rim, overall gold iridescence w/green pulled & coiled decoration, stretch iridescence at lower rim, signed "L.C.T.," 7" d., pr. (small chips to top rims)................................ **1,495**

**Tiffany-signed,** "Fleur-de-Lys," 15 5/8" d. domical leaded glass shade w/a design of radiating mottled green glass tiles w/a band of mottled greenish amber fleur-de-lis, rim impressed "Tiffany Studios New York 1437-5," 6 1/2" h. (out of round, cracked segments)........................................ **6,038**

**Tiffany-signed,** "Fleur-de-Lys," 16" d. domical leaded glass shade composed of graduated blocks of caramel slag glass above a wide band of dark green fleur-de-lis devices above a lower border w/bands of caramel slag (ILLUS. below)............................................ **10,080**

*Tiffany Fleur-de-Lys Pattern Shade*

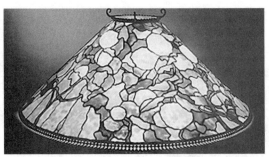

*Rare Tiffany Hydrangea Shade*

**Tiffany-signed,** "Hydrangea," 28 1/2" d. conical leaded glass shade w/numerous white mottled blossoms among variegated leaves in shades of green & blue, some in rippled & textured glass on a ground of pale sage green, green-patinated bronze beaded borders at upper & lower rims, rim tag "Tiffany Studios New York," 11" h. (ILLUS.)................................ **68,500**

*Tiffany-signed Favrile Shade*

**Tiffany-signed,** oblong bullet-form, iridescent gold cased over white & decorated w/a pulled green feather design, signed, w/replacement bronze hardware, 7" d., 11 1/4" h. (ILLUS.)...................................... **8,400**

**Tiffany-signed,** high domed open-topped ten-ribbed form w/a white exterior decorated overall w/green swirls highlighted w/trailing gold iridescent ribbons, white interior, rim signed "L.C.T. Favrile," 7" d. (rim chips, wear on iridescence) ................ **3,738**

**Tiffany-signed,** "Swirling Leaf," 18" d. domical lead glass shade w/an arrangement of radiating graduated rectangular glass tiles in mottled green centered by a medial band of swirling lemon leaves in mottled yellow & white reserved against a mottled green, bronze framework w/a brownish green patina, impressed "TIFFANY STUDIOS - NEW YORK".................. **6,037**

**Tiffany-signed,** "Crimson Bouquet," 28" d. wide cone-shaped leaded glass shade designed as a bouquet of radiant red, pink & creamy white unfolding buds & full-blown blossoms w/mottled yellowish orange centers, the leaves in striated greens, some w/pink, grey & blue undertones, the background colors (some in confetti glass) include grey, blue, violet & green, the border segments in rippled mossy green, beaded bronze edge at top & bottom, three bronze hooks at top, metal tag impressed "Tiffany Studios - New York" (some cracked segments)...... **71,800**

**Tifffany-signed,** "Linenfold," 19 1/4" w. twelve-sided conical shade w/amber glass panels bordered by rectangular matching drapery glass, bronze frame impressed "Tiffany Studios New York pat. Applied for 1927," chips & cracks to border panels, 7 1/4" h. (ILLUS. below)..... **8,625**

*Tiffany Linenfold Shade*

**Verre Moiré,** shaded blue w/panels of white swags, flaring deeply ruffled & crimped rim, peg lamp-type, 5 1/2" d., 4 1/8" h., pr. ...................................................................... **265**

*Wedgwood China Lithophane Shade*

**Wedgwood-signed,** bone china lithophane-type, a wide shallow dished form, pale yellow ground w/intaglio design of Dancing Hours design surrounding a central ring of radiating acanthus leaf & bellflower design, 20th c., printed mark, 13 7/8" d. (ILLUS.)........................................ **1,265**

**Williamson-signed,** 24" d. wide bell-shaped leaded glass shade, the open center top w/a band of oval caramel slag segments over a metal ring, the top of the shade in caramel slag segments arranged in a honeycomb design above the wide curved apron decorated w/large rose blossoms in deep purple & deep rose w/alternating matching bud blusters & smaller scattered blossoms all on a background of green slag leaves (ILLUS. below) ............................................. **3,920**

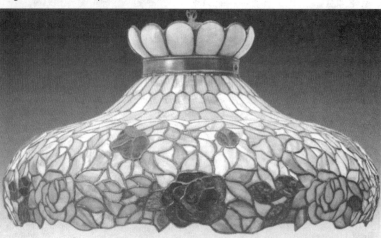

*Williamson Lead Glass Chandelier*

# CHAPTER 4
# LIGHTING GALLERY
# Electric Lamps & Lighting

## Handel Lamps

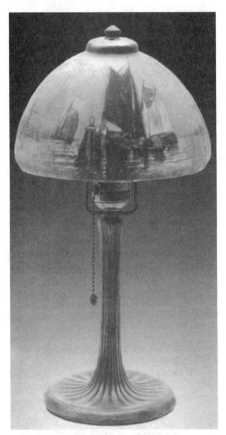

*Handel Harbor Scene Boudoir Lamp*

*Handel 'Tea Rose' Boudoir Lamp*

**Boudoir lamp,** 7" d. domical reverse-painted shade, decorated w/a Venetian harbor scene in sunset colors of orange, yellow, brown & blue, on a slender reeded bronzed metal Handel base (ILLUS.)...................... **$3,640**

**Boudoir lamp,** 7" d. domical reverse-painted shade, decorated in the 'Tea Rose' patt., yellow roses among dark green leaves against a pale green ground, on a slender lobed bronzed metal Handel base (ILLUS.) .............. **3,080**

**Boudoir lamp,** 7" d. conical reverse-painted shade, decorated in the 'Treasure Island' patt., in shades of dark blue & white, shade No. 6558, on a slender ribbed bronzed metal Handel base (ILLUS. top next page).... **3,640**

*'Treasure Island' Boudoir Lamp*

*Handel Boudoir with Flower Baskets*

**Boudoir lamp,** 8" d. domical reverse-painted shade, molded & scalloped & painted w/a pale yellow ground & a colorful basket of flowers above a tan & brown scrolled painted border, on a Handel bronzed metal slender base w/a basketweave design (ILLUS.) .......................... **4,480**

**Boudoir lamp,** 8" d. domical reverse-painted shade, molded & scalloped & painted w/yellow flowers, green foliage & blue & white cloudy sky, raised on a Handel bronzed metal stylized tree trunk base (ILLUS.) ........... **3,080**

*Handel Boudoir with Molded Shade*

*Handel Desk Lamp with Slag Shade*

*Forest Scene Shade on Boudoir Lamp*

**Boudoir lamp,** 8" d. domical & ribbed reverse-painted shade w/square, scalloped rim, decorated w/a continuous woodland scene in shades of brown, green, orange & yellow, artist-signed, shade No. 6468, on a

*Handel with Oval Shade & Base*

bronzed metal Handel ovoid base molded w/a dense forest design (ILLUS.)......................... **3,640**

**Boudoir lamp,** 10" l. oval domical reverse-painted shade, decorated w/a sunset scene of tall trees around a small lake in shades of green, brown, orange & yellow, on an original bronzed metal oval Handel base (ILLUS.) ....... **4,480**

*Handel Wild Roses Desk Lamp*

**Desk lamp,** tapering four-sided slag glass shade in mottled orange & mauve overlaid w/a metal filigree design of palm trees, attached to a socket suspended from an arched arm on the square bronzed metal Handel base, hairline cracks (ILLUS. on previous page).......................... **2,240**

**Desk lamp,** 8" l. half-round reverse-painted shade, decorated w/an overall design of white & pink wild roses w/pink & green foliage against a yellowish orange ground, raised between uprights over the paneled bronzed metal Handel base w/round foot, shade No. 7076 (ILLUS.) ................................... **3,360**

**Floor lamp,** 5" w. four-sided caramel slag tapering shade, decorated w/a diamond lattice overlay & a narrow green slag border w/further overlay, suspended in a large harp above the tall slender bronzed metal Handel base (ILLUS.) .............. **2,520**

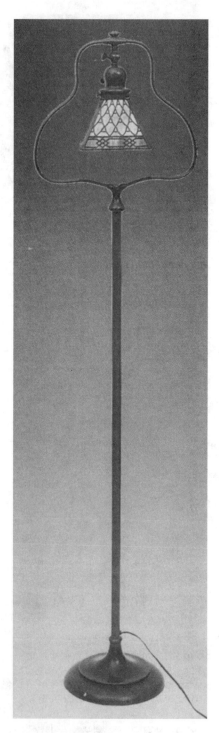

*Handel Floor Lamp with Small Shade*

*Handel Floor Lamp & Flower Shade*

**Floor lamp,** 6" w. six-sided caramel slag shade w/intricate metal overlay & painted along the lower apron to show red roses & green leaves, lower border w/intricate interior filigree also, raised on an arched arm on a tall slender bronzed metal standard w/pointed finial & tripod base (ILLUS.)............................ **3,416**

**Floor lamp,** 10" d. domical reverse-painted shade, decorated w/a border of stylized dark yellow flowers & green leaves against a pale yellow ground, suspended from an arched harp atop the bronzed metal Handel tall base (ILLUS. of part).......... **5,824**

**Floor lamp,** 10" d. domical reverse-painted shade in the 'Jungle Bird' patt., a pair of large dark red & blue parrots on slender leafy branches against a creamy shaded yellow ground, suspended in a harp on a tall slender rare Handel base w/round wooden shelf, artist-signed shade No. 6853 (ILLUS. of part top next page)............. **12,320**

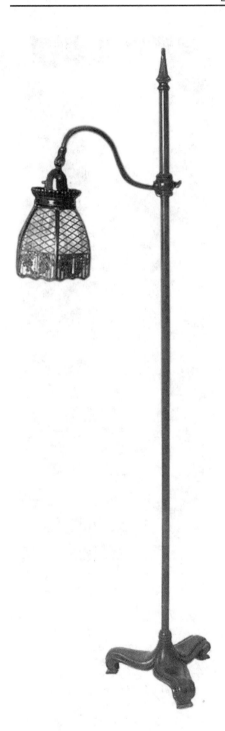

*Tall Slender Handel Floor Lamp*

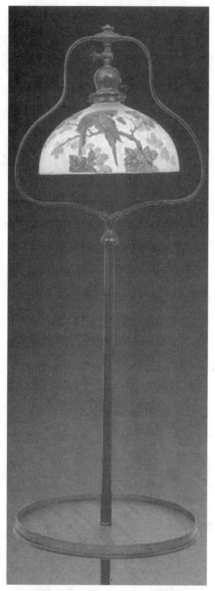

*Rare Handel Jungle Bird Floor Lamp*

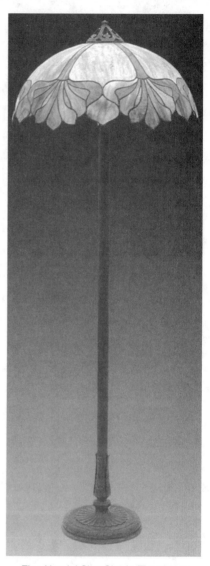

*Fine Handel Slag Shade Floor Lamp*

**Floor lamp,** 24" d. domical leaded glass shade, composed of upper panels of caramel slag divided by dark green slag stems continuing to large fanned leaf clusters around the border, on a tall bronzed metal Handel base (ILLUS. top next column) ....... **10,080**

**Floor lamp,** 25" w. eight-sided slag glass shade, green & white mottled slag glass arranged in tapering rectangular blocks above the flat drop apron w/panels of mottled reddish, purple & green slag overlaid w/pierced metal filigree designs of villages & dense forest, raised on a tall Handel bronzed

*Rare Handel Floor Lamp & Shade*

*Parrot-decorated Handel Hall Light*

metal base w/a slender reeded standard on a rounded, stepped base mounted w/three figural seated griffins, 65" h. (ILLUS.) ................................. **25,200**

**Hall light,** 10" d. spherical shade w/chipped ice finish, the exterior painted w/a large realistic dark blue parrot perched on slender vines w/orange, green & brown leaves against a rosy orange ground, original bronzed metal cap & base tassel (ILLUS.) ....... **3,920**

*Handel 'Birds in Flight' Hall Light*

*Handel Piano Lamp & Leaded Shade*

**Hall light,** 10" d. spherical shade w/chipped ice finish, the exterior painted w/the 'Birds in Flight' patt., tall slender leafy trees & small flying birds in shades of brown, dark green, umber against a dark tan iridescent ground, original bronzed metal cap & base tassel (ILLUS bottom previous page.) ................. **4,200**

**Piano lamp,** long half-round frosted shade w/a 'chipped ice' finish, reverse-painted w/a dark forest scene in shades of brown & yellow, signed "6577 Handel Co. - S.," on a high curved adjustable bronzed metal arm & oblong Handel base, 8" h. (ILLUS.) ................................... **2,468**

**Piano lamp,** conical leaded glass shade w/flat drop apron, in a geometric design of mottled green slag blocks & small pink slag bands, suspended on a long gently arched bronzed metal arm & round base (ILLUS.) ................................... **1,960**

**Table lamp,** conical paneled leaded glass shade composed of radiating bars of mottled green & white slag glass above a double border band w/oblong slag panels divided by tiny pink slag dia-

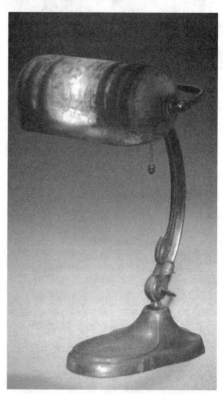

*Handel Piano Lamp & Painted Shade*

monds, on a ribbed bronzed metal urn-form Handel base w/square foot (ILLUS. top next page) ........................................ **5,600**

*Fine Leaded Slag Glass Handel Lamp*

*Handel Lamp & 'Chipped Ice' Shade*

*Small Handel Rose Border Lamp*

**Table lamp,** 12" d. frosted 'chipped ice' glass shade, the flattened top divided by metal bands into panels above the paneled drop apron

w/metal swag overlay, on original bronzed metal Handel base
(ILLUS.) ...................................... **784**

*Handel Lamp with Mosserine Shade*

*Handel with Stylized Landscape Shade*

*Handel Daffodil Overlay Slag Lamp*

**Table lamp,** 12" w. squared four-panel slag shade, light yellowish caramel panels overlaid around the bottom edge w/a wide metal filigree band of roses & leaves trimmed in red & green, on a slender squared bronzed metal Handel base (ILLUS. previous page) ............ **1,960**

**Table lamp,** 14" d. domical Mosserine shade, decorated on the exterior w/an Arts & Crafts style design of clusters of green & dark brown grape leaves on slender brown vines against a pale yellow ground, artist-signed, shade No. 6584, on a bronzed metal leaf-cast Handel base (ILLUS.) ........ **4,144**

**Table lamp,** 14" d. domical shade in white painted on the exterior w/a 'chipped ice' finish, basketweave & loop design along the bottom edge, raised on a slender bronzed metal Handel base, shade signed "Brown Handel 5636," 23" h. ........................ **1,998**

**Table lamp,** 15" d. domical reverse-painted shade, decorated w/a stylized landscape of trees & bushes in shades of dark green & reddish brown on a hillside against a pale sunset sky, slender bronzed metal Handel base w/round knobbed foot (ILLUS.) .................................... **3,920**

*Handel Floral Border Leaded Lamp*

*Handel Lamp with Berry Vine Shade*

*Handel Slag with Leaf Filigree Border*

**Table lamp,** 16" d. domical six-panel slag glass shade, pale yellow slag panels overlaid around the bottom rim w/a border of stylized daffodils painted yellow w/green leaves, on a slender bronzed metal Handel base (ILLUS. previous page) ...................................... **3,360**

**Table lamp,** 16" d. conical leaded glass shade, composed of radiated stripes of mottled light green, mauve, purple & yellow slag above a drop apron composed of large stylized blossoms & leaves in caramel slag & dark green, on a slender bronzed metal Handel base (ILLUS.) ........................... **3,080**

**Table lamp,** 16" d. umbrella-form molded & reverse-painted shade, decorated around the drop border w/a wide band of red berries on stems w/mottled red, green & yellow leaves all against a pale yellowish orange ground, on a slender bronzed metal Handel base w/a square foot, shade No. 6735 (ILLUS.) ................... **5,600**

**Table lamp,** 17" d. bell-shaped double bent slag glass shade, pale yellowish caramel slag w/the drop border panels overlaid w/leafy metal filigree trimmed in green, on a slender squared bronzed metal Handel base (ILLUS.) ........................... **5,040**

*Handel Lamp with Wild Rose Shade*

*Handel Filigree & Slag Glass Lamp*

**Table lamp,** 18" d. domical reverse-painted shade, a finely painted floral design w/a wide band of large pink & red wild roses against dark & light green foliage w/an upper background in shaded yellow & tan, on a rare bronzed metal ovoid Handel base cast w/wide upright leaves above a pierced Chi-

*Fine Handel 'Daffodil' Table Lamp*

*Handel Trees & Sunset Lamp*

nese-style cushion foot, artist-signed shade, shade No. 6524 (ILLUS. top previous page).................................... **23,520**

**Table lamp,** 18" w. domical six-panel slag glass shade, each large upper panel in mottled mauve, pink, white, green & blue glass overlaid w/dividing borders of metal filigree showing tall trees, a narrow undulating border band in green slag overlaid w/a filigree pine needle design, on a tall slender ribbed bronzed metal Handel base w/a flaring foot (ILLUS. bottom previous page) ............................. **8,120**

**Table lamp,** 18" d. domical reverse-painted shade, decorated in the 'Daffodil' patt., pairs of large yellow daffodils on yellowish green leafy stems backed by small red blossoms & black & green shrubs alternating w/a pale green ground, shade No. 7112, on a slender bronzed metal Handel base (ILLUS.)......... **22,960**

**Table lamp,** 18" d. domical reverse-painted shade, decorated w/a large clump of trees in the foreground & distant hills be-

*Rare Handel Slag & Filigree Lamp*

hind, in sunset colors of red, dark orange, brown, green & yellow, artist-signed, shade No. 6957, on a slender bronzed metal Handel base w/a round dished foot (ILLUS.) ................. **4,480**

**Table lamp,** 18" d. conical six-panel slag glass shade in border streaked red & yellow overlaid w/ornate filigree designs of

*Very Rare Handel Peacock Lamp*

tropical trees in the foreground
& others in the distance, raised
on a bronze metal Handel tree
trunk base (ILLUS. previous
page)..................................... **10,640**

**Table lamp,** 18" d. domical reverse-painted shade, decorated
in the 'Peacock' patt., acid-
etched w/the peacock bird &
painted on the exterior w/gold &
color-accented plumage amid
dark red & blue blossoms &
green leaves on a brown branch
against a dark orange ground,
on a tall slender bronzed metal
Handel tripod base, shade
signed "Bedigie - 7126"
(ILLUS.) ................................ **56,000**

**Table lamp,** 18" d. domical six-
panel curved slag glass shade
in streaked creamy yellow overlaid w/borders of roses & leaves
highlighted in red & green........ **5,040**

**Table lamp,** 18" d. domical six-
panel slag glass shade, pale
streaky yellow panels w/a wide
drop border overlaid w/large
leaves highlighted in green, on a

*Handel Slag Overlaid Leaves Lamp*

*Handel Sunset Landscape Lamp*

bronzed metal tree trunk Handel
base (ILLUS.) .......................... **5,600**

**Table lamp,** 18" d. domical reverse-painted shade, decorated
w/a landscape of tall trees &
shrubs beyond a large lake in
the foreground, in shades of orange, red, yellow, brown &
green, artist-signed, shade No.
7104, on a slender bronzed
metal Handel base (ILLUS.
above) ..................................... **6,160**

*Handel 'Oriental Pagoda' Lamp*

*Handel Lamp with Forest Landscape*

*Handel 'Venetian Harbor' Lamp*

**Table lamp,** 18" d. domical reverse-painted shade, decorated in the 'Oriental Pagoda' patt., a tall pagoda in the distance above a dense woodland, in shades of dark green, orange, brown, yellow & pale blue, on a slender reeded bronzed metal Handel base (ILLUS.) ............. **7,840**

**Table lamp,** 18" d. domical reverse-painted shade, decorated in the 'Venetian Harbor' patt., sailing ships in a harbor in moonlight in deep shades of orange, yellow, tan, brown & gold, on a bronzed metal Handel bulbous urn-form base, shade signed "Broggi - 6757" (ILLUS.) ..................................... **8,400**

**Table lamp,** 18" d. domical reverse-painted shade, painted on the interior & exterior w/a continuous dense forest landscape in shades of dark orange, yellow & browns w/water in the foreground, on a bronzed metal footed baluster-form Handel base, shade No. 6209 (ILLUS.) ..................................... **8,960**

**Table lamp,** 18" d. domical reverse-painted shade, decorated in the 'Treasure Island' patt., in shades of dark grey, light grey & yellow, artist-signed, shade No. 6391, on a slender bronzed metal Handel base flaring at the bottom (ILLUS. bottom next page) ..................................... **10,640**

**Table lamp,** 18" d. domical reverse-painted shade, decorat-

*Handel with Autumn Landscape*

*Rare Handel 'Treasure Island' Lamp*

ed w/a finely painted autumn landscape w/sparse woodland,

on a slender Handel tree trunk bronzed metal base, shade artist-signed & numbered 6754 (ILLUS. above) ........................ **7,840**

**Table lamp,** 18" d. domical reverse-painted shade, decorated in the 'Maple Leaf' patt., in shades of green, brown & gold on a shaded golden yellow ground, raised on a slender bronzed metal Handel base, shade signed "Palme" (ILLUS. top next page) ........................ **12,320**

**Table lamp,** 18" d. domical reverse-painted shade, painted on the interior & exterior w/a woodland road scene w/a three-dimensional effect, on a slender lobed bronzed metal Handel base, shade signed "Handel 6230 J.B." (ILLUS. bottom next page) ................................................... **26,320**

*Fine Maple Leaf Pattern Handel Lamp*

*Outstanding Handel Landscape Lamp*

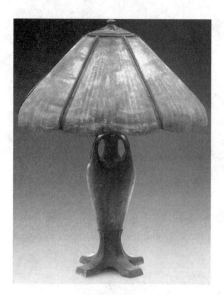

*Handel Lamp with Paneled Shade*

*Handel Lamp with Seashore Scene*

*Handel Table Lamp with Birds*

**Table lamp,** 18" d. domical reverse-painted shade, com-
posed of six ribbed panels decorated w/a continuous
woodland landscape, on an
ovoid bronzed metal Handel
base w/top loop handles &
squared feet, shade signed
"Handel 6640" (ILLUS.)............ **6,440**

**Table lamp,** 18" d. domical reverse-painted shade in the
'Birds of Paradise' patt., two
pair of colorful birds amid flowering branches against a dark
turquoise blue ground, on a
bronzed metal Handel base w/a
paneled vase-form standard on
a rounded raised & pierced foot,
shade signed "Handel 7036"
(ILLUS. bottom previous col-
umn)....................................... **18,480**

**Table lamp,** 18" d. domical reverse-painted shade, decorated
w/a continuous seashore landscape w/clusters of trees, sail-
boats & sea gulls, on a slender
bronzed metal Handel base
(ILLUS.).................................... **7,840**

**Table lamp,** 18" d. domical reverse-painted shade, decorated
w/a border of deep red flowers
below a landscape w/slender
trees & distant hills, on a
bronzed metal Handel Oriental-
style base, shade artist-signed
& w/number 7196.................... **6,160**

**Table lamp,** 18" d. domical reverse-painted shade in the 'Jungle Bird' patt., a pair of dark red,

*Fine Handel Jungle Bird Table Lamp*

*Handel Slag Shade & Feather Filigree*

*Handel Artist-signed Landscape*

blue & yellow macaws among pale tan foliage & large rose-colored blossoms against a black ground, artist-signed, No. 7023, on a slender bronzed

metal bamboo-form Handel base (ILLUS.).......................... **10,640**

**Table lamp,** 18" d. domical reverse-painted shade, decorated w/a sunset landscape of tall green trees beyond a lake, background shades of orange, yellow & brown, on a bronzed metal Handel leafy tree trunk base, shade signed "Palme" (ILLUS.)..................................... **6,440**

**Table lamp,** 18" w. nine-paneled slag glass shade w/curved yellow panels above a drop apron of red slag panels, overlaid overall w/a delicate stylized feather filigree design (ILLUS.)..................................... **7,280**

**Table lamp,** 18" d. domical reverse-painted shade, decorated w/an overall colorful design of shaded pink & pink & white roses & green leafage against a mottled pink, purple, green, light blue & yellow ground w/small butterflies above, on a bronzed metal Handel tripod base w/round foot, shade No. 6688 (ILLUS. next page)................ **24,080**

*Fine Handel Roses Table Lamp*

*Tropical Overlay Handel Slag Lamp*

*Handel Slag Lamp with Tree Border*

*Fine Handel Overlay Lamp*

**Table lamp,** 20" d. domical eight-panel slag glass shade, the upper tapering panels in streaky green & yellow slag overlaid w/a geometric filigree above a drop border w/streaked mauve & purple slag overlaid w/a metal filigree design of palm trees, on a bronzed metal tapering ovoid Handel base w/four blocked feet (ILLUS.)............................. **5,600**

**Table lamp,** 20" d. domical six-panel slag glass shade, each panel of boldly striped red, orange, mauve & white slag overlaid w/tall palms & tropical foliage, on a bronzed metal Handel base (ILLUS. above right)........ **8,960**

*Rare Handel Slag on Poppy Base*

**Table lamp,** 20" w. nine-sided green slag glass shade w/curved upper panels & a drop apron, ornately overlaid overall in a bronzed metal filigree design of leafy branches, on a rare Handel tree trunk base, shade signed in ring, base impressed "Handel 5839" (ILLUS. bottom right previous page) .................. **7,840**

**Table lamp,** 24" d. domical six-panel slag glass shade, wide streaky mauve, white & yellow glass panels w/a band of small green evergreens along the lower edge & overlaid w/tall slender filigree trees trimmed w/brown & green, the narrow border band in streaked yellow, green & pink overlaid w/a pine needle design, on a rare bulbous bronzed metal Handel 'poppy' patt. base (ILLUS.) .... **13,440**

**Table lamp,** 24" d. umbrella-form six-panel slag glass shade w/ornate metal filigree overlay in the 'Sunset Palm' patt., each upper panel in dark red streaked w/white above a narrow drop border w/streaked green & brown slag panels overlaid w/repeating looped whiplash

*Rare 'Sunset Palm' Handel Lamp*

*Handel Lamp & Leaded Glass Shade*

overlay, on a bronzed metal Handel base w/four strap ribs dividing the flaring sides & w/a cast whiplash base band (ILLUS.) .................................. **11,750**

**Table lamp,** 24" d. conical leaded glass shade composed of pink blossoms & green leaves & a light green background, on a signed bronzed metal Handel base w/a round pierced cushion base on curled tab feet, shade signed (ILLUS.) ....................... **6,720**

# Pairpoint Lamps

*Rare Lilac Puffy Boudoir Lamp*

*Pairpoint Puffy Rose Tree Lamp*

**Boudoir lamp,** 5" d. "Puffy" domed & lobed reverse-painted Lilac patt. shade, each lobe w/a cluster of lilac blossoms in purple, deep rose or pink, some w/a yellow butterfly, against a ground of mottled dark green, orange & yellow leaves, on a Pairpoint tree trunk base (ILLUS.) .............................. **$34,160**

**Boudoir lamp,** 8" d. "Puffy" reverse-painted Rose Tree patt. shade, molded around the border w/large pink & yellow roses & blue leaves w/a yellow butterfly above against a frosted ground w/thin bands of blue, on a slender bronzed metal urn-form Pairpoint base w/notched foot (ILLUS.) ........................... **4,480**

*Fine Rose Tree Shade on Tree Base*

**Boudoir lamp,** 8" d. "Puffy" reverse-painted Rose Tree patt.

shade, decorated around the border w/large clusters of pink roses below a background of dark & light green leafage & a large brown, yellow & blue butterfly, on a gilt-metal Pairpoint tree trunk base, 17 5/8" h. (ILLUS. previous page).......... **38,775**

**Boudoir lamp,** 8" d. "Puffy" reverse-painted Tulip patt. shade, molded around the border w/large deep red & dark orange & yellow blossoms against a ground of shaded green leaves, on a slender bronzed Pairpoint base w/knobbed standard above the serpentine square foot, 13 3/4" h. (ILLUS.) ......... **17,625**

*Rare Pairpoint Puffy Tulip Lamp*

*Puffy Pairpoint with Torino Shade*

*Group of Pairpoint Candle Lamps*

*Handel Vienna Shade with Leaves*

*Pairpoint Puffy Lotus Pattern Lamp*

**Candle lamps,** each w/an 8" d. "Puffy" open-topped shade in various reverse-painted floral designs including pansies, lilacs & roses, each on a turned wooden base, set of 8 (ILLUS. bottom previous page) ........... **15,680**

**Table lamp,** 9" "Puffy" reverse-painted 'Torino' shade, molded on the squared sides w/large blossoms in orange & red w/green leaves & red buds against a hammered frosted ground, raised on a slender gilt-metal squared neoclassical Pairpoint base (ILLUS. top right previous page) ........................ **9,520**

**Table lamp,** 10" d. domical reverse-painted 'Vienna' shade, decorated on the interior & exterior w/large yellow, green, & white leaves on brown stems against a rust red ground, raised on a square tapering gilt-metal Pairpoint base w/pierced panels on each side (ILLUS.) .............. **3,192**

**Table lamp,** 10" d. "Puffy" reverse-painted Lotus patt. shade, low domed form w/large molded pink & white blossoms among mottled dark green & yellow leafage, on a shade ring above the slender round swelled bronzed metal Pairpoint base w/slender open bands down the side above the disk foot on small scrolled feet (ILLUS.) .................................... **11,760**

**Table lamp,** 10" d. "Puffy reverse-painted Rose patt. shade, molded w/large yellow roses & green leaves, raised on a bronzed metal Pairpoint Art Nouveau base w/a square ornate scroll-pierced standard above a pyramidal foot engraved w/further scrolls (ILLUS. top left next page) ..................................... **17,920**

**Table lamp,** 14" d. "Puffy" reverse-painted Orange Tree patt. shade, large molded oranges against a dark green ground & mottled greenish yel-

low leaves, on a bronzed metal
Pairpoint tree trunk base
(ILLUS. at right) ..................... **60,480**

*Very Rare Yellow Rose Puffy Pairpoint*        *Extremely Rare Orange Tree Pairpoint*

*Pairpoint Puffy with Papillon Shade*

*Pairpoint Lamp with Malta Shade*

*Pairpoint with Venetian Harbor Shade*

**Table lamp,** 14" d. "Puffy" reverse-painted 'Papillon' shade, decorated w/large red & pink roses w/green leaves & a large yellow, red & blue butterfly against a frosted ground, raised on a slender bronzed metal lappet-cast Pairpoint base w/round lobed foot (ILLUS. bottom previous page)..................................**7,840**

**Table lamp,** 14" d. reverse-painted ribbed 'Malta' patt. shade, decorated w/a continuous sunset landscape w/a man in a rowboat beside a lakeshore w/another figure near a large group of trees, in shades of yellow, orange, black, tan & grey, on gilt metal bulbous baluster-form Pairpoint base ILLUS.)..............**4,480**

**Table lamp,** 14 3/4" d. domical reverse-painted 'Carlisle' shade, decorated w/a Venetian Harbor scene in naturalistic colors, artist-signed, on a tall bronzed metal Pairpoint urn-form handled base, few chips on shade,

*Pairpoint Lamp with Murano Shade*

wear to base, 21" h. (ILLUS. above right)..................**2,645**

**Table lamp,** 15" d. umbrella-form reverse-painted 'Murano' shade, decorated w/a garland of pink roses & green leaves around the shoulder below alternating pan-

*Chesterfield 'Garden of Allah' Shade*

els w/thin yellow stripes all against a clear frosted ground w/a basketweave design around the border raised on a slender bronzed metal Pairpoint base (ILLUS. previous page).............. **3,920**

**Table lamp,** 16" d. domical reverse-painted 'Berkeley' shade, decorated w/a continuous moonlit landscape w/a man in a rowboat beyond a tree-lined shore, signed "H. Fisher," raised on a bronzed metal Pairpoint base w/a slender urn-form standard above four scrolled & outswept arched legs (ILLUS. bottom next column)....................... **4,200**

**Table lamp,** 16" d. "Puffy" reversed-painted 'Chesterfield' shade, decorated in the Garden of Allah patt., a continuous desert landscape scene w/a grouping of Arabs & camels, in shades of brown, orange, yellow, black & green, on a slender silvered metal Pairpoint

base flaring to a square foot (ILLUS. of shade above)........**13,440**

**Table lamp,** 16" d. reverse-painted ribbed 'Livorno' shade, the flat flaring ribbed sides decorated on the interior w/a yellow

*Handel Lamp with Berkely Shade*

*Pairpoint Lamp with Livorno Shade*

*Unique Painted Pairpoint Lamp*

*Pairpoint Lamp & Lansdowne Shade*

ground decorated w/scrolls & w/large round white reserves & white base & top bands, raised on a slender bronzed metal Pairpoint base w/disk foot (ILLUS.) .................................... **2,744**

**Table lamp,** 18" d. domical re-verse-painted    'Lansdowne'

shade, decorated w/a continu-ous landscape w/cows in a meadow framed w/pale green trees, brown shrubs & distant hills beyond in pink & lavender under a pale yellow & blue sky, on a silvered tripod Pairpoint base, 22" h. (ILLUS.)............... **2,300**

**Table lamp,** 18" d. domical re-verse-painted shade, decorated w/an    elaborate    landscape w/large windmills, cows & peo-ple near a tree-lined waterway, on a baluster-form obverse-painted matching glass base w/a round wooden foot, artist-signed "Durand," 25" h. (ILLUS. above right)................ **7,475**

# Tiffany Lamps

**Candle lamp,** 4" d. ribbed bell-form gold iridescent Favrile shade w/ruffled top opening

*Flora-form Tiffany Candle Lamp*

*Tiffany Favrile Glass Candle Lamp*

raised above a tulip-form pierced bronze socket w/green glass insert attached w/a shaped arm extending from a slender stem topped by a thumb grip & curving down to a wide diamond-form foot, shade & base signed, overall 11" h. (ILLUS.) .................. **$4,760**

**Candle lamp,** the gold iridescent Favrile glass base w/a swirled tapering form & cupped rim supporting a candle-form socket w/a lined & pierced sterling silver shade hung w/a bead fringe (ILLUS.) .................................... **1,232**

**Desk lamp,** bulbed Favrile glass shade w/five pulled green & gold feathers on a pale gold lustre ground suspended in a wide harp above the domed & fluted foot, base w/dark gold pebbled finish, shade & base signed, 13" h. (ILLUS.) ........................ **5,750**

*Tiffany Desk Lamp with Favrile Shade*

*Tiffany Favrile Glass Desk Lamp*

*Fine Tiffany Desk Lamp*

**Desk lamp,** tall conical iridescent striped green glass shade trimmed w/gold dots, raised above a matching base w/a slender swelled shaft on a domed foot, shade finial decorated w/small applied prunts, signed, 13 1/4" h. (ILLUS.) ...... **3,290**

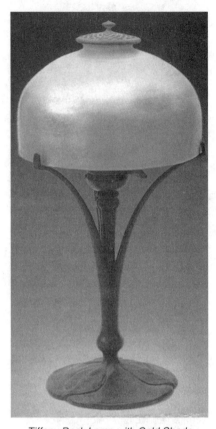

*Tiffany Desk Lamp with Gold Shade*

**Desk lamp,** 7" d. domical molded rib shade decorated on the exterior w/a green & silver iridescent swirled design, suspended in a harp above the slender bronze Tiffany base w/a dished & paneled foot (ILLUS.) ......... **10,640**

**Desk lamp,** 7" d. domical shade in gold iridescence, raised on a bronze Tiffany base w/three curved support arms & a central shaft w/a socket, leaf-cast round foot, shade cracked (ILLUS.)................................... **1,008**

**Desk lamp,** 7" d. mushroom-shaped Favrile glass shade w/pulled green feather designs outlined in gold on an ivory ground, raised on three upturned supports on the telescoping bronze standard w/four

*Tiffany Desk Lamp with Favrile Shade*

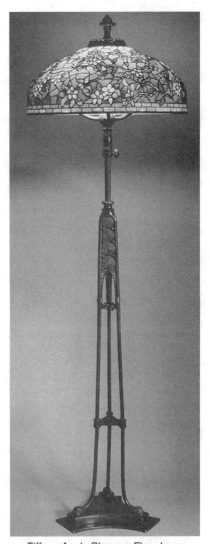

*Tiffany Apple Blossom Floor Lamp*

slender legs resting on a round disk foot, shade & base signed, overall 21 1/2" h. (ILLUS.) .................................. **4,313**

**Floor lamp,** "Apple Blossom," 22 1/2" d. domical leaded glass shade, depicting blossoming apple branches w/pink & white blossoms on dark green leafy branches on a pale green shaded to apple green ground, two border bands of yellow & light green, raised on a tall slender bronze tripod base w/coiled wiretwist & beaded decoration, shade marked "Tiffany Studios -

New York - 1512-7," base also signed, cracked segments, loss to one segment, 71 1/2" h. (ILLUS.).................................. **63,000**

**Floor lamp,** counter-balance type, a 10" d. domical shade in opal glass cased w/amber iridescent w/a pulled gold design, supported on an arched counter-balance above the tall slender bronze Tiffany base w/six tall flared legs w/spade feet, 55 1/2" h. (ILLUS. left next page) ........................... **8,625**

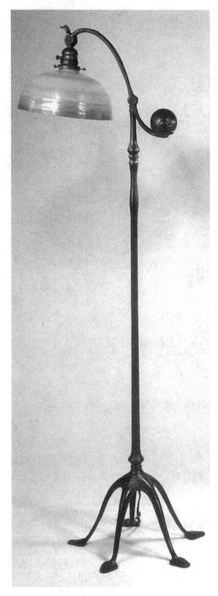

*Amber Tiffany Shade on Floor Lamp*

**Floor lamp,** tall cylindrical shade composed of large vertical prisms within a framework w/stepped cap, raised on a tall slender bronze standard above six tall arched legs ending in pad feet, base signed "Tiffany Studios - New York - 429," overall 46" h. (ILLUS. right) ............. **5,040**

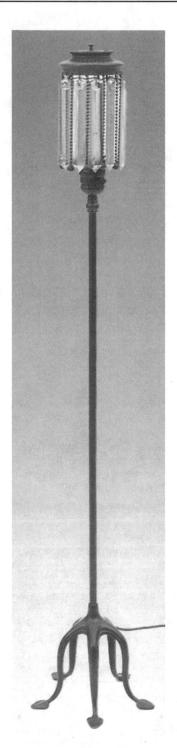

*Tiffany Floor Lamp with Prism Shade*

*Rare Tiffany Double Student Lamp*

*Unusual Tiffany Mantel Lamp*

**Mantel lamp,** a tall gold iridescent ribbed shade tapering to a flaring open top, raised on shade supports above a bronze Tiffany urn-form base w/kerosene font inset, raised on four curved & reeded legs above the quatrefoil foot, shade & base signed, base 7" h. (ILLUS.) .................... **6,440**

**Student lamp,** double-style, a matching pair of 10" d. domical leaded glass shades in a mottled green & yellow in a geometric design, raised on frames & cylinders on support arms extending from a high double framework centered by the cylindrical font, on a domed round foot, shades signed & base

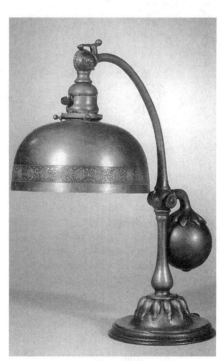

*All-metal Tiffany Table Lamp*

signed "Tiffany Studios - New York - 20708" (ILLUS.) ............ **13,440**

**Table lamp,** counter-balance style, domical metal shade w/an incised geometric border design

*Metal Tiffany Lamp with Shade in Harp*

*Unusual Tiffany Table Lamp & Shades*

suspended on a high curved arm & counter weight above a slender standard w/a petaled domed center on the round foot, pebbled surface, signed, 17 1/4" h. (ILLUS. previous page) .............. **5,750**

**Table lamp,** domical metal shade w/incised geometric border band suspended in the harp of a gilt bronze Tiffany base w/slender standard & fluted & domed foot, base impressed "Tiffany Studios - New York - 424," some finish wear, 17 1/2" h. (ILLUS.) ...................................... **4,025**

**Table lamp,** the bronze Tiffany base w/four entwined tendril arms supporting three downturned & one central upright sockets each w/a Favrile glass flaring diamond quilted design shade w/five pulled feathers on a

*Tiffany Favrile & Gilt Bronze Lamp*

blue iridescent ground, shades signed, overall 28 3/4" h. (ILLUS. above right)................. **14,950**

*Tiffany Chinese Design Lamp & Base*

*Tiffany Shade on a Pottery Base*

*Geometric Tiffany Table Lamp*

**Table lamp,** 8 1/4" d. domical Favrile glass shade decorated w/a gold iridescent damascene design, suspending in the harp of a telescoping gilt bronze standard w/a ribbed petalled & trumpet-form design & upturned edges, chips to shade rim hidden by fitter, 23" h. (ILLUS bottom right previous page.) .......... **4,025**

**Table lamp,** 10" w. eight-sided gilt-metal filigree shade in the Chinese design overlaid on amber slag panels, raised on a gilt-bronze Tiffany base w/a flaring squared shaft foot also engraved w/stylized Chinese designs, shade signed "Tiffany Studios - New York - 535" (ILLUS.) ...................................... **7,840**

**Table lamp,** 16" d. domical leaded glass shade, a geometric design w/radiating caramel slag segments w/a border of striated green square segments, on a metal fitting set into a large pottery base w/flaring sides flanked by open angular handles above the wide squatty bottom, pottery w/a dark green drip over mottled glossy maroon glaze, unmarked base, minor wear, 17 1/2" h. (ILLUS.) ...................... **7,475**

**Table lamp,** 16" d. domical leaded glass shade, composed of large radiating mottled green tiles above a border band of

*Tiffany Shade on Pittsburgh Base*

*Tiffany Lamp with Geometric Shade*

*Tiffany Acorn on Pierced Bronze Base*

small tiles, raised on a bronze Tiffany base w/a slender standard on a dished foot (ILLUS. bottom right previous page) ..... **7,840**

**Table lamp,** 16" d. domical leaded glass shade, unusual geometric design w/horizontal bands of lozenge-shaped pale amber & white segments among arched segments in mottled soft green & white, trimmed w/round white opalescent jewels, a lozenge, X-design & brick border band, on a bronzed metal Pittsburgh Bronze bulbous owl base, few cracked segments, loose sockets, 22 1/2" h. (ILLUS.)..................... **14,950**

**Table lamp,** 20" d. conical leaded glass shade, composed of an overall design of radiating mottled green & white tiles, on a bronze Tiffany base w/a tall slender standard & cushion foot cast w/wide leaves & raised on scroll feet (ILLUS. above right)............... **15,120**

**Table lamp,** "Acorn," 14" d. domical leaded glass shade, radiating bands of mottled green framing a band of mottled yellow, white & green acorns on a vine, raised on a bronze standard resembling thin branches

*Tiffany Golden Acorn Table Lamp*

*Tiffany Acorn Shade Kerosene Lamp*

w/berries, overall 24 1/2" h. (ILLUS. previous page) .......... **24,150**

**Table lamp,** "Acorn," 16" d. domical leaded glass shade, mottled light green & yellow tiles above a band of golden yellow acorns on a mottled yellow & green ground above a border of golden yellow tiles, raised on a bronze Tiffany base w/a tall slender standard on a knobby cushion base w/scroll feet (ILLUS. top) ........ **14,560**

*Tiffany Acorn on Unusual Base*

**Table lamp,** "Acorn," 16" d. domical leaded glass shade, a dark mottled green tile ground w/a wide band of amber acorns on an undulating vine, raised on shade supports above the urn-form bronze base w/kerosene font insert raised on four strap legs above the quatrefoil foot (ILLUS. bottom previous column) .......... **15,000**

**Table lamp,** "Acorn," 16" d. domical leaded glass shade, dark mottled green & yellow tile ground w/a wide band of mottled pale yellow acorns on vines, raised on a large bronze ovoid Tiffany base insert w/groups of oblong turtleback glass tiles, shade signed "Tiffany Studios - New York - 1435-172," base signed "Tiffany Studios - New York" (ILLUS. above) ................ **16,576**

**Table lamp,** "Banded Rose," 16" d. domical leaded glass shade, bands of dark green tiles above a wide border band of mottled red & white rose blossoms & light green & yellow leaves, raised on a tall bronze Tiffany base w/an ovoid stan-

*Rare Banded Rose Tiffany Lamp*

*Fine Tiffany Dogwood Table Lamp*

*Tiffany with Suspended Daffodil Shade*

dard supported between three uprights over the square foot (ILLUS.).................................... **35,280**

**Table lamp,** "Daffodil," 20" d. conical leaded glass shade, a design of pale mottled yellow daffodil blossoms & long mottled green leaves suspended from

the upper rim above a mottled white & pale green ground, on a bronze signed Tiffany base w/a slender shaft cast w/small scrolls above the dimpled cushion foot on scroll feet (ILLUS.)...................................... **42,560**

**Table lamp,** "Dogwood," 16" d. domical leaded glass shade, overall mottled white & pink blossoms & mottled green leaves against a 'fractured glass' ground, raised on a bronze Tiffany base w/a slender rounded standard above the domed & lightly ribbed base on ball feet, shade signed "Tiffany Studios - New York" base signed "Tiffany Studios - New York - 9944" (ILLUS.) .............. **36,400**

**Table lamp,** "Dragonfly," 20" d. leaded glass shade composed of a band of large caramel dragonflies w/filigree overlay on the pale green & cream wings against a mottled greenish blue & red ground, on a slender bronze

*Extraordinary Tiffany Dragonfly Lamp*

*Tiffany Linenfold Table Lamp*

standard on a wide cushion foot w/green glass blown from behind in the pierced teardrop openings, on scroll feet, shade & base signed (ILLUS.) ......................... **78,400**

**Table lamp,** "Linenfold," 15" d. ten-panel shade composed of ribbed amber panels below narrow border bands, w/original shade cap, on a slender bronze Tiffany base, shade signed "Tif-

*Tiffany Nautilus Table Lamp*

fany Studios - New York - 1947," base signed "Tiffany Studios - New York - 534 (ILLUS.)........................................ **8,960**

**Table lamp,** "Nautilus," a leaded shade modeled as a large nautilus shell & composed of segments of opal white shading to deep green, supported in a bronze standard w/a deep cushion base cast w/petals, 13 1/2" h.(ILLUS.) ......................... **10,925**

**Table lamp,** "Pansy," 16" d. domical leaded glass shade, large central band of blossoms in mottled red, blue, orange, purple, white & yellow w/mottled & striated green leaves against a radiating ground of mottled green segments, raised on a bronze Tiffany base w/an ovoid standard on supports above the square foot, shade signed "Tiffany Studios - New York - 1448," base signed "Tiffany Studios - New York - 444," some

*Tiffany Pansy Table Lamp*

*Tiffany Tulip Lamp with Wide Border*

*Tiffany Poinsettia Table Lamp*

cracked segments, minor corrosion, 22 1/2" h. (ILLUS.).......... **29,900**

**Table lamp,** "Poinsettia," 17 3/4" d. domical leaded glass shade, composed of radiating mottled green geometric segments above a wide band of poinsettia flowers & foliage in striated pink, green, yellow, blue & purple & two border bands of green & amber, tagged "Tiffany Studios-New York - 1558," on a bronze Tiffany base w/a slender geometric standard & round foot, impressed marks & number 528, a few cracked segments, 25 1/2" h. (ILLUS.) .................... **37,950**

**Table lamp,** "Tulip," 22" d. domical leaded glass shade, composed of a dense top design of mottled red & white tulips & mottled pale green leaves above a wide mottled green & gold leaf & band border, raised on a bronze Tiffany base w/a slender reeded standard above a leaf-cast cushion base on scroll feet (ILLUS. above) ..... **106,400**

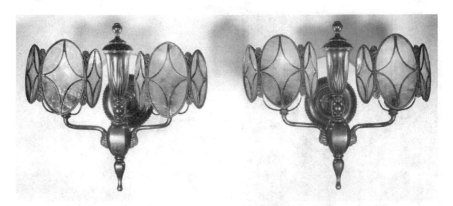

*Rare Tiffany Wall Sconces*

**Wall sconces,** classical bronze wall mounts w/two upturned arms ending in a shield shade, each shade comprised of three parts w/mottled amber & green glass, 16" w., 15 1/4" h., pr. (ILLUS. above) ......................... **17,250**

# Lamps, Miscellaneous

**Art Deco torchere,** brushed metal, a disc-shaped gilt-metal foot & slender shaft terminating w/a tiny crown & supporting six straight branches each w/horn-shaped arms & conical orange shades, attributed to Gio Ponti, for Fontana Arte, Italy, ca. 1938, 82 1/4" h. (ILLUS. at right) ...... **$9,400**

**Art Deco torchere,** gilt-metal & glass, a round gilt-metal foot supporting a tall slender cylindrical vellum-veneered shaft terminating in two thick concentric glass rings, supporting an inverted gilt-metal inverted bell-form shade, Jean Perzel, France, ca. 1930, shade 18" d., overall 71 1/2" h. (ILLUS. left next page) ................ **5,875**

**Art Deco wall sconces,** glass & metal, a fanned & ribbed frosted clear shade on a V-form silvered metal wall mount, France, ca. 1928, minor edge nicks, 5

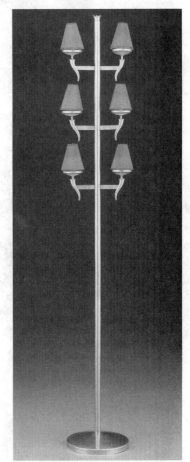

*Art Deco Brushed Metal Torchere*

1/2" w., 12" h., set of 4 (ILLUS. of one next page) ...................... **1,150**

*Two Art Deco Glass & Metal Sconces*

**Art Deco wall sconces,** glass &
metal, a cascading green glass
mount supporting a hemispheri-
cal white-finished metal shade
w/a flat-sided lunette-shaped
glass reflector, Fontana Arte,
ca. 1930, 11 2/3 x 16 3/3",
22 1/4" h., pr. (ILLUS. top next
page) ......................................... **3,525**

**Art glass & metal table lamp,**
bulbous        mushroom-shaped
glass    shade    in    iridescent
shades of amber & gold, raised
on an ornate patinated metal tripod base w/leaf clusters, reeded flat legs & a tripartite foot,
possibly Loetz, Austria, early
20th c., overall 16 1/2" h.
(ILLUS. next page) .................... **1,553**

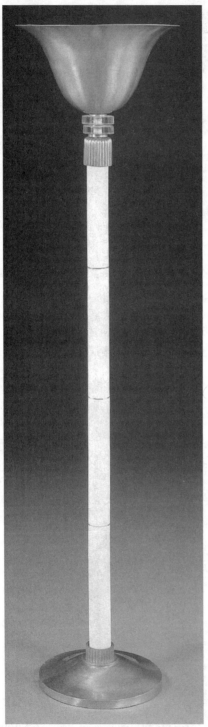

*Art Deco Metal & Glass Torchere*

*Art Deco Glass & Metal Sconces*

*Art Glass Shade on Tall Metal Base*

*Green Jade Glass & Ormolu Lamp*

*Rare & Lovely Art Glass Torchere*

*Bradley & Hubbard Overlay Lamp*

**Art glass & ormolu table lamp,** the base composed of an acid-etched jade green glass vase w/a tall trumpet neck & bulbous footed base acid-etched w/large leaves, resting on an ornate ormolu base w/a leaf-cast band above four paw feet resting on a quadripartite foot, ormolu collar & reeding stem for the light fixture topped w/a pierced Oriental-style alabaster glass finial, glass attributed to Steuben, base impressed "957," ca. 1920s, overall 23 3/4" h. (ILLUS. of base on previous page) ............................ **1,380**

**Art glass torchere,** a large bell-form inverted glass shade in amber w/an overall heavily crackled silver iridescent surface finish, resting in slender gilt-metal leaf supports atop a tall slender standard w/a round bead-trimmed base on small scroll feet, early 20th c., shade 9" d., 8" h., overall 67" h. (ILLUS.) ...................................... **22,400**

**Bradley & Hubbard table lamp,** 20" d. paneled slag glass shade, each mottled green slag panel centered by a large orange medallion & overlaid w/intricate leaf-form overlay, raised on a bronzed metal tree trunk base (ILLUS.) ............................. **2,800**

**Bronze & glass table lamp,** cast in the form of a lizard set w/gold, ruby red, emerald green & orange glass, the tall upturned tail suspending a domed pierced metal shade set w/lozenge-shaped pearly white glass 'jewels,' Austria, ca. 1910, 20 1/4" h. (ILLUS. top next page) ........... **16,450**

*Rare Austrian Lizard Lamp*

*Classique Lamp with Landscape*

**Classique table lamp,** 18" d. conical reverse-painted shade, decorated w/a stylized landscape of dark green trees & shrubs beside a brown path w/a blue lake to the side under a blue sky, on

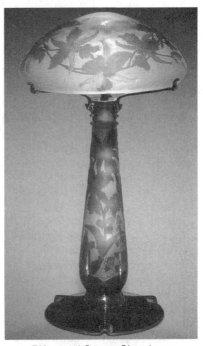

*D'Argental Cameo Glass Lamp*

a bronzed metal paneled base (ILLUS.)......................................... **2,240**

*Duffner & Kimberly with Simple Design*

**D'Argental cameo glass lamp,**
11" d. domical cameo glass
shade w/a salmon colored
ground overlaid in olive green &
etched w/orchids, ferns & foliage, raised on a slender
swelled cylindrical matching
base w/a flattened round foot,
signed, overall 22" h. (ILLUS.
on previous page) ..................... **3,995**

**Duffner & Kimberly table lamp,**
19" d. domical leaded glass
shade, composed of bands of
mottled green & brown glass
segments below two bands of
pointed segments at the top,
raised on a bronzed metal Duffner base w/slender reeded
standard & round foot (ILLUS.
above left) ................................... **4,200**

**Duffner & Kimberly table lamp,**
20" d. bell-shaped leaded glass
shade, upper panels of irregular
mottled pink segments divided
by pale green bands above a
wide band of large stylized dark
pink flowers & dark green leaves
against an orange ground, three
thin border bands in mottled pale
green & orange, on a bronzed
metal base w/open bowed up-

*Fine Duffner & Kimberly Floral Lamp*

*All-green Duffner & Kimberly Lamp*

rights joined at the scalloped
leaf-cast foot (ILLUS.).............. **10,640**

**Duffner & Kimberly table lamp,**
22" d. leaded glass shade, the
wide flat & sloped top composed of mottled white & dark
green panels & stripes composed of matching small segments, a deep drop apron
w/matching block segments &
dark green leaf-like clusters &
border scrolls, raised on a
bronze Duffner base w/a slen-

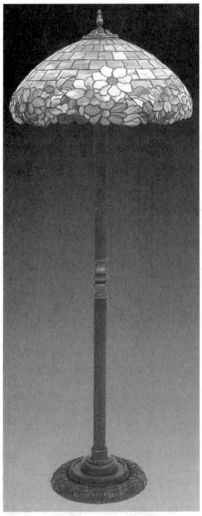

*Exceptional D&K Floor Lamp*

der reeded standard on a square stepped foot (ILLUS. bottom right previous page) ..... **6,720**

**Duffner & Kimberly floor lamp,** 26" d. domical leaded glass shade, large mottled green & white tiles above a wide border of large blossoms in mottled white, light orange, dark orange & green w/mottled dark green & blue leaves, on a tall bronzed metal reeded standard over a round leaf-cast base (ILLUS.) ...................... **39,760**

*Durand Art Glass Table Lamp*

**Duffner & Kimberly floor lamp,** 27" d. domical leaded glass shade, a background of crackled amber fish scale segments divided by panels of abstract brown & amber geometric segments above the amber scrolls around the rim, raised on a bronzed metal reeded standard on a reeded dished base on small knob feet (ILLUS. left next page) ........................... **23,520**

**Durand Art Glass table lamp,** a baluster-form Durand glass vessel in iridescent blue glass decorated w/overall random threading, mounted on a paneled gilt-metal base & electric fittings at the neck, minor breaks in threading, ca. 1925, glass 12" h., overall 27 1/2" h. (ILLUS. above) ........................... **633**

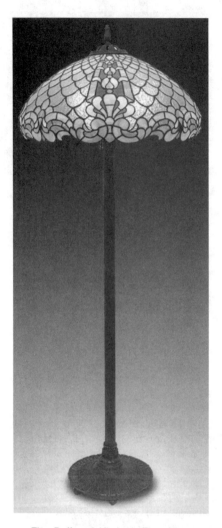

*Fine Duffner & Kimberly Floor Lamp*

**Edgar Brandt & Daum table lamp,** the ornate Brandt iron base in the form of a flowering bush w/roots at the round foot below the twisted opening stem shaft below the full-relief cast leaves & blossoms top supporting a domical Daum art glass shade reverse-painted w/blackberries & foliage, France, early 20th c., 21" h. (ILLUS.) ............ **14,950**

**Gorham table lamp,** 16" d. domical leaded glass shade, wide

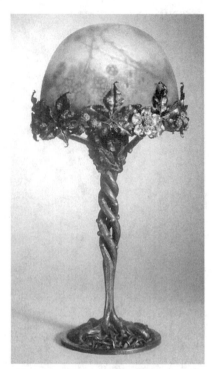

*Rare Brandt & Daum Table Lamp*

*Gorham Lamp with Banded Design*

sections of large graduated amber slag segments divided by four mottled purple scroll bands

*Gorham Floral Shade on Square Base*

*Rare Gorham Leaded Table Lamp*

centered by a green & white herringbone band terminating w/a large stylized red & white blossom, raised on a slender bronzed metal base w/a scroll-cast squared foot (ILLUS. on previous page)............................ **7,280**

**Gorham table lamp,** 18" d. domical leaded glass shade, the background composed of graduated blocks of caramel slag w/stylized pink & red blossoms above the green scallop band border, raised on a large silver metal base w/tapering square shaft cast w/lions above a stepped square foot (ILLUS. above) ...................................... **1,680**

*Jefferson Scenic Table Lamp*

*Jefferson Boudoir Lamp*

**Gorham table lamp,** 19" w. conical paneled leaded glass
shade, the upper panels
w/graduated green slag segments framed w/mottled amber
& green borders, the flat drop
apron w/a dark blue Greek key
design against mottled green
w/each panel featuring a ring
enclosing a monogram or a flor-
ette design, raised on a slender
bronzed metal standard w/a
scroll-cast squared foot (ILLUS.
bottom previous page) .......... **11,200**

**Jefferson boudoir lamp,** 7" d.
domical reverse-painted shade
decorated w/a sunset landscape w/a large tree in the foreground, in shades of orange,
yellow, green, brown & blue, on
a bronzed metal base w/a
squared standard & squared
paneled foot (ILLUS.) ................ **1,680**

*Leaded Lamp with White Flower Rim*

**Jefferson table lamp,** 18" d.
domical reverse-painted shade,
decorated w/a continuous landscape w/tall slender trees in the
foreground w/water in the background, shades of brown, tan,
green, blue & yellow, on a large
ovoid dark painted glass base
w/a round foot (ILLUS.) ............. **3,920**

*Leaded Lamp with Jeweled Band*

*Flower-bordered Leaded Table Lamp*

**Leaded glass table lamp,** 16" d. domical leaded glass shade, the flaring drop & upper section of the deep drop apron composed of graduated square caramel slag segments above a wide border of large stylized white flowers w/slender green leaves, on a slender bronzed metal base, possibly Duffner & Kimberly (ILLUS. bottom right previous page) .......................... **1,960**

**Leaded glass table lamp,** 16" d. domical leaded glass shade, overall graduated amber slag tiles w/a band of square white opalescent 'jewels' set near the border, on a slender bronzed metal base w/dished foot (ILLUS. above)........................... **2,800**

*Leaded Lamp with Large Flowers*

*Great Orange Tree Leaded Lamp*

**Leaded glass table lamp,** 18" d. umbrella-form leaded glass shade, the upper section w/large radiating mottled green & white slag segments above the wide border w/large stylized pink blossoms & dark green leaves, on a bronzed metal handled cylindrical base w/round foot (ILLUS. bottom previous page) .............. **1,904**

**Leaded glass table lamp,** 18" d. domical leaded glass shade, the upper section paneled w/mottled pale green & white slag above a wide border band w/large stylized pink blossoms & dark green leaves, on a bronzed metal base w/a slender standard & scroll-cast foot (ILLUS. above)........................... **1,456**

*Modernist Style Wall Sconces*

**Leaded glass table lamp,** 20" d. domical leaded glass shade, mottled yellowish green honeycomb design ground w/a wide border of large oranges & green leaves, raised on a solid bronze base cast w/overlapping leaves, attributed to Suess (ILLUS. bottom previous page) .............. **16,800**

**Modernist wall sconces,** painted & gilt-metal, lozenge-shaped back in white & black w/gilt-metal reflectors, designed by Gio Ponti for Arredoluce, w/paper label reading "Made in Italy - Arredoluce Monza," ca. 1950s, 13 7/8 x 27 3/4", pr. (ILLUS.) ... **4,113**

**Moe Bridges table lamp,** 16" d. domical reverse-painted shade, decorated w/a detailed sunset landscape w/large groups of leafy trees & green meadows beside a blue lake beneath a blue & pale yellow sky, on a slender bronzed metal Pittsburgh base w/scalloped foot (ILLUS. next column) ................ **1,960**

*Moe Bridges Landscape Shade*

**Moe Bridges table lamp,** 18" d. domical reverse-painted shade, decorated w/a lakeside sunset scene w/geese in flight, in shades of dark orange, yellow,

*Fine Moe Bridges Lamp with Geese*

*Moe Bridges "Greek Ruins" Lamp*

white, black & brown, on a bronzed metal ovoid handled base w/round foot (ILLUS. above) .......................................... **7,840**

*Mosaic Lamp with Cherries Design*

*Mosaic Lamp Floral Leaded Lamp*

**Moe Bridges table lamp,** 18" d. domical reverse-painted shade, decorated in the "Greek Ruins" patt., classical pillared ruins in grey & brown in a mountainous landscape in brown, green, yellow & blue, on a tall waisted bronzed metal base w/a cracked dark green patina (ILLUS. bottom previous page).................... **3,360**

**Mosaic Lamp Company of Chicago table lamp,** 16" d. domical leaded glass shade, overall design of large deep red cherries & mottled green leaves against a mottled amber ground, raised on a simple bronzed metal base w/round foot (ILLUS. above).................. **3,360**

*Mosaic Lamp with Florals & Ribbons*

*Mosaic Lamp Floral & Leaf Lamp*

**Mosaic Lamp Company of Chicago table lamp,** 19" d. domical leaded glass shade, composed of large stylized pink blossoms scattered on dark brown branches among green leaves against a mottled amber & green ground, on a bronzed metal tree trunk base (ILLUS. bottom previous page) ............ **2,184**

**Mosaic Lamp Company of Chicago table lamp,** 24" d. bell-shaped leaded glass shade, random white tile ground decorated w/large dark red bows connected to clusters of dark pink blossoms & green leaves & alternating w/angled bands of golden tiles connecting single large pink rose blossoms & green leaves, on a bronzed metal tree trunk base (ILLUS. above)................. **5,040**

*Table Lamp with Unique Mesh Shade*

**Mosaic Lamp Company of Chicago table lamp,** 24" d. conical leaded glass shade, a detailed background of dark green leafy vines among mottled pale green & yellow segments above groups of pink & dark red blossoms around the border, raised on a bronzed metal tree trunk base (ILLUS. bottom previous page) .............. **4,480**

**Mutual Sunset & Bradley & Hubbard table lamp,** 17 3/4" w. nine-paneled shade of metal screen mesh painted & coralene-decorated w/scallops & flourishes in each panel, tagged "Mutual Sunset Lamp Co.," on a slender bronzed metal Bradley & Hubbard base w/garland decoration on the round foot, minor wear to decoration, wear to metal, ca. 1920. 22 1/4" h. (ILLUS.) ......................................... **633**

**Pittsburgh table lamp,** 15" d. low domical shade acid-etched from light brown to white w/neoclas-

*Pretty Acid-etched Pittsburgh Lamp*

sical leaves & a scroll border, on a matching glass base w/similar designs on a round white glass foot (ILLUS. above) ......................................... **1,736**

*Pittsburgh Lamp with Swan Scene*

*Pittsburgh Lamp with Daffodil Shade*

**Pittsburgh table lamp,** 16" d. domical reverse-painted shade, decorated in the Swan design, white swans swimming on a dark pool surrounded by very dark green & black trees, on a reeded bronzed metal base w/round foot (ILLUS. above) .... **3,024**

*Fine Pittsburgh Indian Design Lamp*

*Pittsburgh Lakeside Sunset Lamp*

**Pittsburgh table lamp,** 16" d. domical reverse-painted shade, decorated w/large clusters of yellow & white daffodils & green leaves against a shaded rose ground, raised on a bronze Pittsburgh 'owl' style base (ILLUS. bottom previous page) .......................................... **2,800**

**Pittsburgh table lamp,** 18" d. domical reverse-painted shade, decorated w/a scene of a Native

*Pittsburgh Lamp with Scenic Shade*

*Pittsburgh "Call of the Wild" Table Lamp*

American drinking from a rocky brook, in shades of cream, tan, dark brown & black, raised on a glass standard decorated w/bands of Indian designs & lit from the interior, on a round metal foot (ILLUS. top previous page) .......................................... **6,160**

**Pittsburgh table lamp,** 18" d. domical reverse-painted shade, decorated w/a lakeside sunset scene w/bushes & a large tree in the foreground in shades of light & dark brown, the lake in shades of blue, white & yellow w/the sun setting over distant hills in yellow, brown & rust under a pale yellow & orange sky, on a bulbous ribbed bronze Pittsburgh base w/a ruffled round foot (ILLUS. bottom previous page) ..... **2,800**

**Pittsburgh table lamp,** 18" d. domical reverse-painted shade, decorated w/a sunset landscape scene w/a lakeshore w/large trees in the foreground & the sun setting over distant mountains, in shades of yellow, rust, black & brown, on gilt-bronze Pittsburgh 'owl' style base (ILLUS. top left) ............... **3,024**

*Unusual Mushroom-shaped Lamp*

**Pittsburgh table lamp,** 18" d. domical reverse-painted shade, decorated in the "Call of the Wild" patt., moonlit lake scene w/a teepee on the shore, on a bulbous bronzed metal Pittsburgh 'owl' style base (ILLUS. top right) ....................... **4,480**

**Reverse-painted table lamp,** 14" d. large bulbous mushroom-shaped reverse-painted shade decorated w/a bold Moorish-style design highlighted w/clus-

*Lamp with Windmill & Water Scene*

*Simple Landscape on Shade & Base*

ters of pink & green roses, textured ground, stamped "Patented April 29th, 1913," set in a brass & metal mount w/small side handles, chips to base of shade not visible, possibly by Pairpoint, 14" h. (ILLUS. bottom right previous page) .............. **690**

**Reverse-painted table lamp,** 18" d. domical reverse-painted shade, decorated w/a fairly crude landscape w/trees, windmill & a village beside blue water w/a sailboat, yellow setting sun under blue sky (ILLUS. above) ......................................... **1,344**

*Woodland Scene on Painted Shade*

*Unique Decorated Shade & Base*

**Reverse-painted table lamp,** 18" d. domical reverse-painted shade, crudely painted w/a landscape featuring a pathway leading to red & white buildings & a large windmill, water at the sides, in shades of dark blue, green, brown, yellow & black, on a matching tapering cylindrical glass base lighted from the inside & framed by pierced metal bands on a round foot w/an egg-and-dart border (ILLUS. bottom previous page)............................. **896**

**Reverse-painted table lamp,** 18" d. domical reverse-painted shade, decorated w/a landscape of a pathway among large trees & shrubs in shades of grey, black, green, rust & gold, on a bronzed metal base w/a slender standard & round leaf-cast foot (ILLUS. above) ......................................... **1,064**

*Rare Slag & Filigree Figural Lamp*

**Reverse-painted table lamp,** 21" d. eight-panel reverse-painted shade, the panels decorated w/a continuous landscape scene w/small lakes alternating w/fields & scattered trees, in shades of yellow, rose, green, brown & white, raised on a matching tapering lighted cylindrical base w/four glass reverse-painted panels w/similar scenes (ILLUS. bottom previous page) .............. **3,360**

**Slag glass table lamp,** 17" domical eight-panel slag glass shade, each upper panel in mottled green & pink & overlaid w/an ornate fish scale filigree, narrow border panels in deep red w/geometric filigree overlay, raised on a figural bronzed metal base showing a seated mermaid holding a shell aloft to support the shade (ILLUS.) .................................... **16,240**

*Slag Glass Shade on Pottery Base*

*Wilkinson Lamp with Stylized Florals*

**Slag glass table lamp,** 25 1/2" d. parasol-form slag glass shade, composed of radiating segments of caramel slag w/sunburst & geometric borders in salmon & orange glass, raised on a later pottery base w/a cylindrical base, two applied scrolled shoulder handles, rust & brown drip glaze over a matte yellow-glazed ground, overall 29 1/2" h. (ILLUS. above) ......... **3,450**

*Wilkinson Floral Border Table Lamp*

**Wilkinson table lamp,** 18" d. domical leaded glass shade, graduated amber slag tiles above a wide border w/a repeating stylized floral design in red, white & green, on a bronzed metal Wilkinson base w/a tall slender reeded standard & a dished ribbed foot (ILLUS. bottom previous page).................... **7,840**

**Wilkinson table lamp,** 19" d. domical leaded glass shade, graduated mottled green & yellow tiles above a wide border band of large stylized blossoms in pink, blue, orange, yellow & green, raised on a bronzed metal Wilkinson base w/a slender standard round cast foot (ILLUS.)...................................... **6,720**

# Other Lighting Devices

## Chandeliers

**Art Deco chandelier,** a widely flaring conical glass shade molded w/bold Art Deco stylized

*Chandelier of Swans & Glass Shades*

*Degue Glass Chandelier*

florals in a pale blue, suspended on gilt-metal hangers, ca. 1930 (ILLUS. top next page)............. **$1,400**

**Art glass,** five-light, wide shallow ribbed inverted bowl-form shades in pink iridescent glass w/dark reddish amber threading, fitted on sockets atop the heads of gilt-metal figural swan arms projecting from a black-painted central shaft w/ribbed drop, all suspended from a single chain, overall 30" h. (ILLUS. top right)............................................. **1,232**

**Degue-signed,** 13 5/8" inverted bowl-form shade in frosted clear glass w/a geometric Art Deco

*Art Deco Floral Glass Chandelier*

*Handel Reverse-painted Chandelier*

molded design, suspended on four cords connecting to a ceiling plate, ca. 1930 (ILLUS. previous page) ..................................... **575**

**Handel-signed,** 18" d. domical reverse-painted inverted shade, decorated w/the 'Road' design, a continuous autumn landscape w/clusters of slender leafy trees in dark brown, green, white & black & dark rust & brown shrubs below a mottled dark & light yellow sky, shade No. 6230, origi-

nal metal fittings (ILLUS. above ) ......................................... **8,960**

**Handel-signed,** 24" w. eight-sided caramel slag shade, each upper panel composed of graduated blocks & bars of caramel slag w/the flat drop border outlined in caramel w/mottled green & purple slag panels overlaid w/metal filigree landscape of trees, several cracks (ILLUS. top of next page) ............................................ **5,040**

*Handel Slag Glass Chandelier*

*Lalique-signed Chandelier*

**Lalique-signed,** 15 1/2" d., composed of multiple molded glass panels w/an elaborate fern design under an original brown stain, signed in block letters, supported by bronzed metal

*Unusual Egg-shaped Chandelier*

arms & a ceiling cap that may not be original, missing pieces at bottom center, few minor chips, 30" h. (ILLUS.)................. **1,840**

*Simple Slag Chandelier with Flowers*

*Ornate Leaded Floral Chandelier*

**Leaded glass,** 17" l. egg-shaped shade divided into panels composed of chuncks of pearly white leaded glass, top ring w/large incurved hooks connecting to hanging chains, overall 21" h. (ILLUS. bottom right previous page)................. **5,600**

**Leaded glass,** 22 1/2" d. leaded glass shade, a conical top above a wide drop apron, overall green & amber slag segments w/the wide apron highlighted by eight red & orange striated stylized large blossoms, unsigned, few cracked segments, 11" h. (ILLUS. top of page) ..................... **460**

*Bell-shaded Leaded Chandelier*

*Fine Poppy Design Chandelier*

**Leaded glass,** 24" d. umbrella-form shade w/a scalloped top open crown composed of caramel slag segments, the top of the shade w/mottled white & caramel honeycomb segments above a very wide band of stylized blossoms & large roses in pinks, dark blues & dark red among dark & light green leaves (ILLUS. bottom previous page) .......................................... **7,280**

**Leaded glass,** 24" d. bell-shaped leaded glass shade, the background of white streaked w/tan glass tiles decorated overall w/undulating dark green vines w/deep red & pink blossoms around the bottom edge (ILLUS. above) ........................... **2,520**

**Leaded glass,** 28" d. conical leaded glass shade, the upper background of caramel slag rectangular segments above

*Geometric Leaded Glass Chandelier*

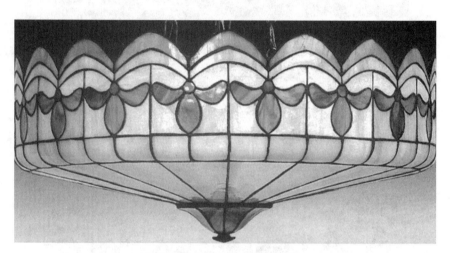

*Inverted Leaded Glass Chandelier*

the wide border band of dark red & purple stylized poppy blossoms & buds w/dark green leaves, attributed to Duffner & Kimberly (ILLUS. bottom previous page)............................................ **13,440**

**Leaded glass,** 29" d. domical leaded glass shade, a flared top crown of pinkish white segments above the shade w/a background of graduated pinkish white blocks w/small scattered red diamonds above the zigzag geometric border in orangish red, red & green segments (ILLUS. above top) ....................................... **952**

**Leaded glass,** inverted umbrella-form leaded glass shade composed of radiating panels & bands of caramel slag glass w/a border of large red fleur-de-lis & light & dark brown slag swag border bands (ILLUS. above)...... **784**

**Quezel-signed** five-light, a gilt-bronze baluster-form center post above a wide disk issuing five upturned arms each suspending a socket fitted w/a waisted trumpet-form Quezel

*Chandelier with Quezal Shades*

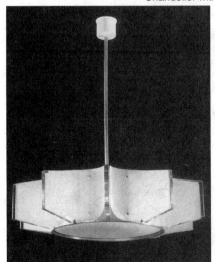

*Unusual Modernist Chandelier*

*Italian Glass & Brass Chandelier*

glass shade in white iridescence w/scattered green leaves & trimmed w/gold random threading (ILLUS. above) ......... **3,080**

**Modernist,** ten-light, metal-mounted frosted & clear glass, a star-shaped design w/the circular metal frame enclosing ten frosted glass flattened panels, Fontana Arte, Italy, ca. 1950, 31

1/4" d., overall 34 1/2" h. (ILLUS. bottom left) ................... **2,350**

**Modernist,** 24-light, glass & brass, the tall flame tip-shaped shades in peach and green tinted glass on alternating short & tall brass electric candle sockets joined to a central ring sus-

*Pairpoint 'Albemarl' Chandelier*

*Unique Slag Glass Chandelier*

pended from three slender bars, w/matching wall sconces, Fontana Arte, Italy, ca. 1950, chandelier 23" w., 39 1/2" h., the set (ILLUS. of chandelier on previous page)............................ **4,465**

**Pairpoint-signed,** 12" w. "Puffy" square reversed-painted 'Al-bermarl' shade, green ground decorated w/white wavy lines & blossoms above the wide border of bold red & pink roses & green leaves w/a yellow, brown & blue butterfly, original Pairpoint hanger (ILLUS. above top)................................... **6,720**

*Chandelier with Steuben Shades*

**Slag glass,** 20" d. bell-form slag glass shade composed of long caramel slag panels below an arched leaf-cast cap & w/a wide flat cast iridescent metal drop border w/a repeating design of quatrefoils & leaftips, one glass panel damaged (ILLUS. bottom previous page) ............................ **1,008**

**Steuben-signed,** five-light, a cast brass frame w/a central reeded urn above a wide round disk tapering to a pointed drop & issuing five upturned arms each suspending a socket fitted w/a bell-shaped Steuben glass shade in a gold iridescent surface w/random gold threading, gold iridescent interiors, chips to some shade top rims, 19" w., overall 39 1/2" h. (ILLUS. above) .......... **1,265**

# Shades

**Prairie-style leaded shade,** 21" w. six-panel domical leaded shade w/a wide drop apron, the top panels composed of graduated bars of dark brown, pink, yellow & blue mottled slag glass topped by a large turned metal finial, each panel of the drop apron w/a rectangular Prairie-style design center w/a herringbone block, made in Illinois, from the Giannini & Hilgart studios of Chicago (ILLUS. top next page) .......................................... **3,360**

**Leaded glass shade,** 12" bell-shaped shade, the upper ground composed of dark mottled green, yellow & brown segments above arches of large pink blossoms & green leaves above the wide drop apron w/rows of milky white slag glass, attributed to Duffner & Kimberly (ILLUS. bottom next page) .......................................... **1,512**

*Rare Prairie-style Leaded Shade*

*Leaded Shade with Flower Arches*

# GLOSSARY OF SELECT LAMP & LIGHTING TERMS

**Angle lamp -** A style of kerosene lamp produced by the Angle Lamp Company. Most popular from the 1890s through the 1920s, it featured a stamped metal central font with one or two short angled arms terminating in a burner enclosed by a clear ball shade supporting a milk glass chimney-style shade.

**Argand lamp -** A new type of oil-burning lamp invented around 1782 by Aimé Argand in Geneva, Switzerland. This lamp featured a glass tube up through the font that supplied air to the tubular burner and was topped by a tubular glass shade. It was a very expensive form of lighting but produced a much brighter light than candles could.

**Astral lamp -** This is an early variation of the Argand lamp that featured a shallow fuel font that reduced the amount of shadow cast by the burner.

**Betty lamp -** A name for a very early form of crude oil burning lamp. Usually made of wrought iron, it was formed as a flat-bottomed dish with a spout at the front edge and an upright hanging handle at the back. It was made either open or as a closed dish with just the spout open. Filled with a crude burning fuel, such as lard, the wick was simply laid with one end in the fuel and the other end hanging out of the spout where it could be lit. This was a crude and not very efficient light source but cheaper than hand-made candles. Beware of 20th century reproductions.
Also see "crusie lamp."

**Boudoir lamp -** The general term for a small decorative lamp, usually from the early electric era, which was meant to sit on the dressing table of a lady's boudoir.

**Bridge lamp -** A style of floor lamp especially popular in the 1920s and 1930s where a single decorative metal arm extended from the top of the lamp standard and ended in an electric socket, which could be covered by a glass, cloth or waxed paper shade.

**Burner -** The part of the lamp that fitted into the top of the fuel reservoir and held the wick away from the fuel source. In kerosene lamps the height of the wick in the burner could be controlled using a simple turn knob projecting from the burner.

**Camphene -** A very volatile burning fluid used in the 1840s and 1850s. It was a mixture of turpentine and alcohol and could explode easily. A special burner was designed for it that had long "rabbit ear" forked tubes that kept the wicks as far as possible from the fuel font. It was less expensive to use than whale oil but was discontinued as soon as kerosene became widely available.

**"Chipped ice" -** A term used to describe the rough exterior finish found on many early glass electric lamp shades. Many of the shades were painted on the exterior with landscapes, florals or birds.

**Cold painted -** A term used to describe painted decoration applied to the unheated surface of a metal lamp or statue.

**Crown -** A narrow decorative pierced metal band designed to sit around the top opening of the decorative domed glass shades used on many late Victorian kerosene hanging lamps.

**Crusie lamp -** A close cousin of the betty lamp, it also burned crude grease or lard. The crusie was shaped very much like the betty lamp but usually featured two dishes fixed one just above the other.

**Flint glass -** A term describing early blown and pressed glass that included lead oxide in the glass mixture. This ingredient produced a very clear, heavy glass which, when gently tapped, would usually resonate with a bell-tone ring. This type of glass was first developed in England in the 17th century when burnt ground flint was added to the glass mixture. By the 18th century flint was replaced by lead oxide, but the old name stuck.

**Font -** The fuel reservoir on early lighting devices. A burner, which supported the cloth wick, was placed at the top opening of the font.

**Gone-with-the-Wind lamp -** A popular form of late Victorian kerosene table lamp. It usually featured a ball-shaped glass shade enclosing the burner and chimney and a ball-shaped or other form of glass base, usually raised on cast-metal feet. The shade and font were usually decorated with a matching design. The name originated with collectors after the release of the movie "Gone With The Wind" because such a lamp, although totally inaccurate for the Civil War era, was used in one famous scene.

**Harp -** In early electric lamps this refers to an arched metal loop at the top of the lamp that suspended a shade above the base.

**"Linenfold" -** A term used for a specific type of decorative glass shade, especially a type produced by Tiffany. A translucent glass panel was impressed with an overall design of fine ribbing meant to emulate the look of delicate folded linen. The panels were then assembled to form the sides of the shade.

**Lithophane -** A thin flat, usually rectangular sheet of bisque porcelain that was impressed before firing with a finely detailed landscape or portrait scene. The delicate molding in the finished piece produced a lovely shadowy scene when held up to bright light. Most were produced in Germany in the last half of the 19th century and some were set in metal frames and used as lamp shades.

**Nailsea-style -** Nailsea was an early English glassmaking center but twentieth century glass collectors used the term to describe any glass composed of one color looped throughout during production with white or contrasting bands of glass. The technique was used for simple utilitarian forms such as rolling pins, flasks and witch balls and was later commonly used in more artistic glass such as the shades of fairy lamps.

**Organ lamp -** A term used to describe a late Victorian kerosene floor lamp. The tall slender metal lamp standard, often supported on scrolled legs, was topped by a metal kerosene font fitted with a decorative glass ball-shaped shade. It stems from its usual use beside a pump organ or upright piano.

**Ormolu -** A French term for gilt-metal, usually brass or bronze. Eighteenth and early nineteenth century French furniture usually featured decorative mounts of this material and it continued to be used on decorative pieces, including lamps, into the 20th century.

**Patinated -** A term used to describe a metalware given an artificial surface finish or "patina." Usually a base metal such as spelter or copper was treated with various substances to produce the aged look of old bronze. The finish was especially popular on late nineteenth and early twentieth century statuary and lamp bases.

**Peg lamp -** A type of lamp that consists of only a rounded glass font with an integral 'peg' at the center bottom that would let it sit in the socket of a candlestick. Early examples were made in the first quarter of the nineteenth century, but by the late Victorian era they were usually made of highly decorative colored glass fitted with kerosene burners.

**Pricket-type candelstick -** An early form of metal candlestick that featured a slender sharp spike at the center of the disk at the top. This spike kept the candle in place. By the 18th century smaller candles led to the use of a socket cup to hold the candle.

**"Puffy" -** The term used to describe ornately mold-blown shades produced by the Pairpoint Corporation for its fine early electric lamps. The molded designs usually featured various types of flowers and butterflies, which were decorated on the interior with bright colors.

**Reverse-painted -** The term used to describe early electric lamp shades that had decorative scenes hand-painted on the interior of the shade. Landscapes, floral designs and birds were the most popular themes used, and the finest examples are usually associated with Handel and Pairpoint lamps. Shades or glass decorated on the exterior are referred to as obverse-painted.

**Sinumbra lamp -** A variation of the early Argand lamp. It featured a shallow fuel font with a ring supporting the frosted glass shade. It was developed in the 1850s and could burn a less refined fuel than whale oil. The name roughly translates to "without shadow," since it was designed to reduce the shadows caused by the fuel font.

**Slag glass -** A form of glass commonly used as panels in early electric lamp shades. It is glass combining a white glass swirled throughout with a contrasting color, usually a caramel tan or green although other colors were also used. The thin glass panels were often bent while hot and then fitted into a metal framework. The lamp shade panels were then quite often overlaid with delicate metal filigree designs.

**Student lamp -** A style of kerosene desk lamp popular in the late nineteenth and early twentieth century. Usually made of brass, it generally consisted of a round metal foot centered by a tall slender metal shaft supporting an adjustable crossbar with a cylindrical metal fuel font to one side and an arm supporting the burner, shade ring and pyramidal glass shade on the opposite side. Double student lamps feature a pair of arms opposite each other with the large fuel font supported in the center.

**Teroma glass -** A form of art glass developed by the Handel Company early in the twentieth century. Most often used to produce vases, it consists of a frosted crystal glass with a 'chipped ice' exterior finish, sometimes also given a satin finish. The exterior was then hand-painted with a delicate colorful forest landscape, sometimes including some birds. A similar style of decoration was used in producing some Handel-made lamp shades.

**"Turtleback" tile -** A glass tile produced by Tiffany Studios. Generally ovoid in form with a slightly domed top with a dimpled surface, they resembled the shells of turtles. Produced in dark transparent glass with an iridized surface, Tiffany sometimes inset them into a shade framework for his lamps.

**"Verre moiré" -** A French term that translates roughly to "watered glass." In fabric, the term moiré silk is used to describe "watered silk," which features a wave-like design. In glass the term is used to refer to the wave-like loopings of color typical of Nailsea-style glass. In particular this term is used to describe a decorative style of late Victorian fairy lamp.

**Whale oil -** An early lamp fuel derived from the oil of the sperm whale. It was used in the late eighteenth through the first half of the nineteenth century. It was cleaner burning and less volatile than other lamp fuels of the era and produced a brighter light. However, it was costly and not widely available to many working class households.

# SELECT BIBLIOGRAPHY FOR LAMPS & LIGHTING

## Nineteenth Century Lamps & Lighting:

Bacot, H. Parrott. *Nineteenth Century Lighting - Candle-powered Devices: 1783-1883*. West Chester, Pennsylvania: Schiffer Publishing, Ltd., 1987.

Cooke, Lawrence C., ed. *Lighting in America - From Colonial Rushlights to Victorian Chandeliers, New and Expanded Edition* (from The Magazine Antiques). Pittstown, New Jersey: The Main Street Press, 1984.

Courter, J.W. *Aladdin Collectors Manual & Price Guide #20 - Kerosene Mantle Lamps*. Kevil, Kentucky: self-published, 2000.

_____. *Aladdin – The Magic Name in Lamps, Revised Edition*. Kevil, Kentucky: self-published, 1997.

_____. *Aladdin Electric Lamps, Third Printing*. Kevil, Kentucky: self-published,
.

_____. *Aladdin Electric Lamps Collectors Manual & Price Guide #4*. Kevil, Kentucky: self-published, 2002.

_____. *Angle Lamp Collectors Manual & Price Guide*. Kevil, Kentucky: self-published.

Miller, Richard C. and John F. Solverson. *Student Lamps of the Victorian Era*. Marietta, Ohio: Antique Publications, 1992.

Myers, Denys Peter. *Gaslighting in America - A Pictorial Survey, 1815-1910*. New York, New York: Dover Publications, Inc., 1978.

Thuro, Catherine M.V. *Oil Lamps - The Kerosene Era in North America*. Radnor, Pennsylvania: Wallace- Homestead Book Company, 1976, 1992.

_____. *Oil Lamps II - Glass Kerosene Lamps*. Toronto, Ontario, Canada: Thorncliffe House, Inc.; Paducah, Kentucky: Collector Books; Des Moines, Iowa: Wallace-Homestead Book Company, 1983.

_____. *Oil Lamps 3 - Victorian Kerosene Lighting, 1860-1900*. Toronto, Ontario, Canada: Thorncliffe House, Inc.; Paducah, Kentucky: Collector Books, 1994, 2001.

## Early 20th Century Electric Lighting:

*Better Electric Lamps of the 20's and 30's with prices - Including color catalogs of Moe Bridges, Pittsburgh, Lightolier and others*. Gas City, Indiana: L-W Book Sales, 1997.

Black, James Edward, ed. *Electric Lighting of the 20's-30's - Volume 1*. Gas City, Indiana: L-W Book Sales, 6th Printing, 2001.

_____. *Electric Lighting of the 20's-30's - Volume 2*. Gas City, Indiana: L-W Book Sales, 1990.

DeFalco, Robert and Carole Goldman Hibel and John Hibel. *Handel Lamps, Painted Shades & Glassware*. Staten Island, New York: H & D Press, Inc., 1986.

Grant, Joanne C. *The Painted Lamps of Handel*. Cornwall, New York: self-published, 1978.

Hibel, Carole Goldman and John Hibel and John Fontaine. *The Handel Lamps Book*. Pittsfield, Massachusetts: Fontaine Publishers, 1999.

Koch, Robert. *Louis C. Tiffany's Glass - Bronzes - Lamps - A Complete Collector's Guide*. New York, New York: Crown Publishers, Inc., 1971.

Malakoff, Edward and Sheila. *Pairpoint Lamps*. West Chester, Pennsylvania: Schiffer Publishing, Inc., 1990.

Neustadt, Dr. Egon. *The Lamps of Tiffany*. New York, New York: The Fairfield Press, 1970.

Pratt, JoAnn W. *Moe Bridges Lamps & Lighting Fixtures*. Winston-Salem, North Carolina: Hunter Publishing Co., 1981.

St. Aubin, Jr., Louis O. *Pairpoint Lamps, A Collectors Guide*. New Bedford, Massachusetts: self-published, 1974.

## Other Lighting Devices:

### Lanterns:

*Collectible Lanterns - A Price Guide*. Gas City, Indiana: L-W Book Sales, 1998.

Pearson, Dennis A. *Classic Lanterns with Value Guide*. Atglen, Pennsylvania: Schiffer Publishing, Ltd., 1998.

Wood, Neil S. *Collectible Dietz Lanterns - Original 1917 Catalog with Current Prices*. Gas City, Indiana: L-W Book Sales, 1977.

### Miniature Lamps:

McDonald, Ann Gilbert. *The Evolution of the Night Lamp*. Des Moines, Iowa: Wallace-Homestead Book Company, 1979.

Smith, Frank R. and Ruth E. *Miniature Lamps*. New York, New York: Thomas Nelson & Sons, 1968.

Smith, Ruth E. *Miniature Lamps - II*. Exton, Pennsylvania: Schiffer Publishing, Ltd., 1982.

Solverson, John F. *Those Fascinating Little Lamps*. Marietta, Ohio: Antique Publications, 1988.

### Shades - Art Glass:

Roberts, Darrah L. *Art Glass Shades - Quezal - Steuben - Tiffany*. Des Moines, Iowa: Wallace-Homestead Book Company, 1968, 1975.

Roberts, Darrah L. *Collecting Art Nouveau Shades*. Des Moines, Iowa: Wallace-Homestead Book Company, 1972.

# APPENDIX

## Specialty Lamps & Lighting Clubs

**Aladdin Knights (The)**
J.W. Courter
3935 Kelley Road
Kevil, KY 42053-9431
Ph: (270) 488-2116
Fax: (270) 488-2055
e-mail: brtknight@aol.com
Web site: www.aladdinknights.org

**Fairy Lamp Club & Newsletter**
Jim Sapp
7422 Haystack Road
Alexandria, VA 22310-3308
Ph: (703) 971-3229
Fax: (508) 448-8917
e-mail: sapp@erols.com
Web site: www.fairylampclub.com

**Historical Lighting Society of Canada**
Alan Goulding
P.O. Box 561, Postal Station R
Toronto, Ontario, Canada M4G 4E1
Ph: (416) 724-0703 or (905) 824-4117
e-mail: goulding@idirect.com
Web site: www.historical-lighting.on.ca

**Incandescent Lamp Collectors Assoc. (The)**
c/o Museum of Lighting
Hugh F. Hick, Curator
717 Washington Pl.
Baltimore, MD 21201-5235
Ph: (410) 752-8586

**International Coleman Collector Club**
Ron Bowers
2282 W. Caley Ave.
Littleton, CO 80120
Ph: (303) 794-2415
e-mail: ron@colemancollectors.com
Web site: www.colemancollectors.com/

**International Guild of Lamp Researchers**
Fil Graff, Sec.
10111 Lincoln Way West
Saint Thomas, PA 17252-9513
Ph: (717) 369-3577
Fax: (717) 369-5546
e-mail: fgraff@epix.net
Web site: www.dapllc.com/lampguild/

**Rushlight Club, Inc. (The)**
Dan Mattusch
260 Maryland Ave. NE
Washington, D.C. 20002
Fax: (561) 760-8018
e-mail: info@rushlight.org
Web site: www.rushlight.org/

**Night Light Miniature Lamp Club**
Bob Culver
38619 Wakefield Court
Northville, MI 48167-9060
Ph: (248) 473-8575
e-mail: rculver107@aol.com